9/6
OS '17

Tabitha Morgan read English at Cambridge and has spent the last decade reporting on Cyprus and the Eastern Mediterranean for the BBC. Before moving to Cyprus she worked as a BBC radio producer, making features and historical documentaries for BBC Radio 4 and the World Service. She is married to the writer and journalist Gerald Butt.

Sweet and Bitter Island

A History of the British in Cyprus

Tabitha Morgan

To Johnny - Boy,
have Again!

Much love
Tabitha
X X
7.7.10

I.B. TAURIS

LONDON · NEW YORK

Published in 2010 by I.B.Tauris & Co Ltd
6 Salem Road, London W2 4BU
175 Fifth Avenue, New York NY 10010
www.ibtauris.com

Distributed in the United States of America and in Canada Exclusively by Palgrave Macmillan,
175 Fifth Avenue, New York NY 10010

ISBN: 978 1 84885 329 4

A full CIP record for this book is available from the British Library
A full CIP record is available from the Library of Congress

Library of Congress Catalog card: available

Printed and bound in India by Replika Press Pvt. Ltd.

To My Husband

Contents

Preface

This book aims to tell the story of the British in Cyprus in an accessible manner which will be entertaining and informative for the average reader. It makes no claims to be an academic history. I have drawn unashamedly on existing scholarship and have sought to fill in gaps in the published history of the island from archival sources. While the narrative covers the period of the British occupation of Cyprus, 1878–1960, it does not intend to provide a definitive account of this period, but rather to provide a flavour of the colony seen through British eyes.

It would not be appropriate for me to attempt to tell the story of the generations of Cypriots who lived under British rule. My narrative therefore concerns itself exclusively with the British experience of Cyprus, telling the story entirely from the perspective of the colonisers rather than those they were governing.

In attempting to do so I have drawn heavily on oral testimony, and personal archival material in an attempt to capture something of the mood of the time.

Cyprus did not technically become a British colony until 1926 and uncertainty over its sovereignty during the first five decades of the British occupation was a major obstacle to its development. I have nevertheless referred to it as a colony and to its British administrators as colonists from the outset, since it enables the reader to see the island more clearly in the context of Britain's other imperial territories.

The senior administrative official in charge of the Secretariat in Nicosia was, at various times, referred to as the 'colonial secretary' and the 'chief secretary'. To avoid confusion with the cabinet post of Secretary of State for the Colonies, I have used the term 'chief secretary'.

Because of different conventions of transliteration over the years proper names occasionally appear spelt slightly differently, but not so differently as to be unrecognizable. I hope the purists will forgive this.

Acknowledgements

This book would not have been possible without the help, encouragement and co-operation of many people. I owe a huge debt to Ruth Keshishian who first persuaded me to try and tell the story of the British in Cyprus. She subsequently supplied me with a huge range of books and journals, put me in touch with several interviewees and was constantly enthusiastic about the project.

My thanks too go to those people who lived in Cyprus during the British occupation and who extended friendship and took the time to share their memories and experiences. Penelope Tremayne and Tony Willis even provided me with accommodation when I travelled to interview them, while Eirwen Harbottle, George Lanitis, Jean Meikle and Donald Waterer and their families generously provided lunch or sometimes dinner. In addition Mark Chapman and Paul Griffin gave me access to unique manuscript material. Thanks are also due to: Beryl Arnold, Betty Benson, Jim Beveridge, Diana Bridger, Glafcos Clerides, Rauf Denktash, Suha Faiz, Clare and Will Harrap, Jenny Hayward, Berin Lewis, Sandra Oakey, Matthew Parris, Akis Petris, Gordon Pirie, Gus Prattley, Elsie Slonim, Peter Twelvetrees and Brenda Waterer. I am especially grateful to Jane d'Arcy for her great encouragement and generosity. This book would not have been possible without her help.

As someone who is not a trained historian I was grateful for the support I received from those whose knowledge of Cypriot history will always be far greater than mine. In particular I would like to thank Robert Holland and Rita Severis who both made helpful and constructive comments on my first draft. Also Hubert Faustmann, Diana Markides and Andrekos Varnava, who all generously lent me material and offered advice. I owe particular thanks to Tim Reardon for his detailed reading of my chapters on the Second World War and his willingness to share the fruits of his extensive research.

Tom and Jo Fitzalan Howard introduced me to ex-servicemen living in Cyprus and put me on the trail of a range of useful material. Laura Craig Gray read closely early drafts of the first two chapters and made helpful recommendations. My mother Jenny Morgan made detailed suggestions for changes to the first draft and my brother Owen provided a useful chronology of events of the First World War.

In Oxford, both Lucy McCann of the Bodleian Library of Commonwealth and African Studies at Rhodes House and Debbie Usher of the Middle East Centre Archive at St Antony's College gave invaluable help in accessing material relating to Cyprus and made my time there a pleasure.

In Cyprus, Maria Economidou at the Cyprus Museum library was invariably welcoming and friendly and even provided cups of tea. Stuart Haggart, the headmaster of the English School, gave me access to school facilities, while Helen Leonidou went out of her way to enable me to use the material contained in Newham's trunk. Ricardo Lopez of the film department at the Cyprus Press and Information Office (PIO) took the time to arrange a private screening of the Laurie Lee film *Cyprus Is an Island*. Koulla Hatzouli helped me find my way through the Cyprus State Archive, while Maria Oikonomou in the library of the Agriculture Department enabled me to access copies of the *Cyprus Journal*. Yiannos Miltiadou of the PIO's photographic department helped me to find relevant photographs, as did Loukia Hadjigavriel and Nicos Pampoulos of the Leventium Museum and friendly officials at Cyprus Forestry Department. Lellos Demetriades, Michael Savvides and Christos Zenonos helped me to clarify the location of various buildings in the old city of Nicosia. I am grateful to them for the effort they exerted on my behalf.

Finally, I would like to thank Liz Friend-Smith at I.B.Tauris for her support.

British Rulers of Cyprus

High Commissioners

22 Jul 1878–23 Jun 1879	Sir Garnet Joseph Wolseley	
		(b. 1833–d. 1913)
23 Jun 1879–9 Mar 1886	Sir Robert Biddulph	
		(b. 1835–d. 1918)
09 Mar 1886–5 Apr 1892	Sir Henry Ernest Gascoyne Bulwer	
		(b. 1836–d. 1914)
05 Apr 1892–23 Apr 1898	Sir Walter Joseph Sendall	
		(b. 1832–d. 1904)
23 Apr 1898–17 Oct 1904	Sir William Frederick Haynes Smith	
		(b. 1839–d. 1928)
17 Oct 1904–12 Oct 1911	Sir Charles Anthony King-Harman	
		(b. 1851–d. 1939)
12 Oct 1911–8 Jan 1915	Hamilton John Goold-Adams	
		(b. 1858–d. 1920)
08 Jan 1915–31 Dec 1918	Sir John Eugene Clauson	
		(b. 1866–d. 1918)
31 Dec 1918–10 Mar 1925	Sir Malcolm Stevenson	
		(b. 1878–d. 1927)

Governors

10 Mar 1925–30 Nov 1926	Sir Malcolm Stevenson	
		(b. 1878–d. 1927)
30 Nov 1926–29 Oct 1932	Sir Ronald Storrs	
		(b. 1881–d. 1955)
29 Oct 1932–8 Nov 1933	Sir Reginald Edward Stubbs	
		(b. 1876–d. 1947)

08 Nov 1933–4 Jul 1939 Sir Herbert Richmond Palmer
(b. 1877–d. 1958)

04 Jul 1939–3 Oct 1941 William Denis Battershill
(b. 1896–d. 1959)

03 Oct 1941–24 Oct 1946 Charles Campbell Woolley
(b. 1893–d. 1981)

24 Oct 1946–4 Aug 1949 Reginald Thomas Herbert Fletcher, Baron Winster
(b. 1885–d. 1961)

04 Aug 1949–1953 Sir Andrew Barkworth Wright
(b. 1895–d. 1971)

1954–25 Sep 1955 Sir Robert Perceval Armitage
(b. 1906–d. 1990)

25 Sep 1955–3 Dec 1957 Sir John Harding
(b. 1896–d. 1989)

03 Dec 1957–16 Aug 1960 Sir Hugh Mackintosh Foot
(b. 1907–d. 1990)

Abbreviations

The following abbreviations have been used in the notes:

RHO   Bodleian Library of Commonwealth and African Studies at Rhodes House, Oxford

IWM   Imperial War Museum, London

MECA   Middle East Centre Archive, St Antony's College Oxford

NA   The National Archives of the United Kingdom, Kew

SA1   State Archive of the Republic of Cyprus, Nicosia

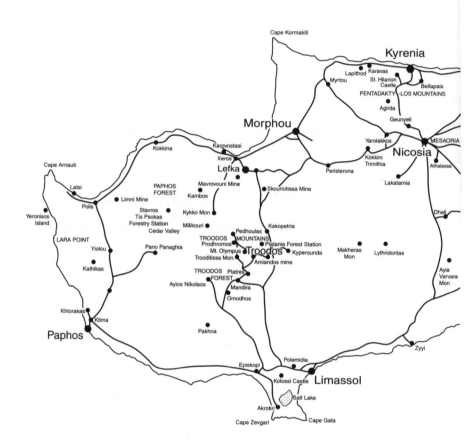

Cyprus 1960 – Principal

10   5   0   10   20
Miles

Cape Kormakiti

Kyrenia

Lapithod Karavas
Myrtou   St. Hilarion
              Castle   Bellapais
PENTADAKTY -LOS MOUNTAINS

Agirda

Geunyeli

Morphou

Yarolakkos   MESAORIA
Kokkina   Karovostasi
Xeros   Kokkini   Nicosia
Cape Arnauti   Lefka   Trimithia   Athalassa
                        Peristerona
Latsi   PAPHOS   Mavrovouni Mine   Lakatamia
          FOREST   Kambos   Skouriotissa Mine
Polis   Limni Mine
Yeronisos   Dhali
Island   Stavros   Kykko Mon
          Tis Psokas
LARA POINT   Forestry Station   Milikouri   Kakopetria
          Cedar Valley
          Pedhoulas
          TROODOS MOUNTAINS
Yiolou   Pano Panaghia   Prodhromos   Platania Forest Station
          Mt. Olympus Troodos Kyperounda   Makheras   Lythridontas
          Trooditissa Mon.   Mon
Kathikas   Amiandos mine
                                          Ayia
          TROODOS Platres   Varvara
          FOREST   Mon
          Ayios Nikolaos   Mandira
                  Omodhos
Khlorakas
      Ktima   Pakhna
Paphos   Zyyi

                  Polemidia
          Episkopi
                  Kolossi Castle Limassol
                  Salt Lake
          Akrotiri
Cape Zevgari   Cape Gata

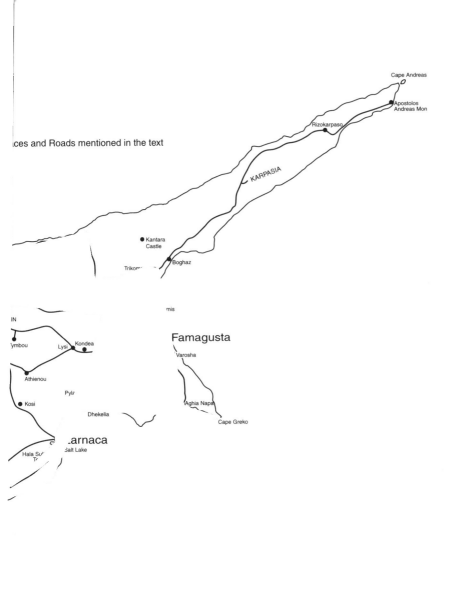

ces and Roads mentioned in the text

Cape Andreas

Apostolos
Andreas Mon

Rizokarpaso

KARPASIA

Kantara
Castle

Trikom Boghaz

mis

Famagusta

Varosha

IN

ymbou   Lysi Kondea

Athienou

Pyla

Kosi

Dhekelia

Aghia Napa

Cape Greko

Larnaca

Hala Su   Salt Lake
Tr

1

Where Are the Forests?
1878–82

A large family from Birmingham is preparing for a long day at Larnaca public beach, pale limbs indicate that the holiday is just beginning. Two men drag sun loungers across the sand and rearrange blue and white umbrellas in a semi-circle around a sleeping child in a pushchair. The child's grandmother pins a white cloth around the edge of its buggy to provide shade. A woman in a pink bikini unpacks bottles of sun cream, placing them in a line in the sand. Behind her, in between *Sea Front Fish and Chips* and the *Multi Mahal Indian Restaurant*, *The Irish Pub* offers all-day English breakfast and the chance to see Blackburn playing Wigan on wide-screen television.

The grandmother gazes out to sea in the general direction of Lebanon as pink bikini woman begins to rub sun cream into her back. As she does so, she explains, 'we're very close to Sicily here. In fact, on a fine day you can actually see Sicily.' 'Really?' the grandmother replies, 'You'd think they'd be speaking Italian then.'

The British have often felt confused about Cyprus, although perhaps not as confused as this. But uncertainty about the territory, in particular about who their colonial subjects were, provided a leitmotif throughout the British occupation of the island. At the same time the colonists found many aspects of their new territory, particularly its geography and its archaeological and linguistic connections with ancient Greece, reassuringly familiar, in some cases even an extension of home. The tension generated by these conflicting impulses, by the urge simultaneously to find and recognise an idealised, Utopian 'Britishness' in Cyprus, while exoticising and Orientalising the island, came to define much of the character of British rule in Cyprus.

The holidaymakers from Birmingham have set up their beach camp a few metres from the point beneath Larnaca's squat seventeenth-century Ottoman fort where the men of the 42nd Royal Highland Regiment (the Black Watch) waded through the shallow waters of Larnaca Bay to come ashore on a sweltering hot Sunday in July 1878.

Engravings of the landing printed in the *Illustrated London News* a fortnight later show an orderly process in which various boats, some rowed, some powered by steam, land men and supplies on a series of specially constructed wooden piers, each one identified by a numbered sign. But the newspaper pictures bore little relation to the chaotic scenes that actually unfolded.

Preparations for the occupation of Cyprus had been made hastily with limited knowledge of the island and the men who waded ashore in temperatures of up to 40 degrees centigrade, dressed in standard issue red woollen tunics and thick 'English pattern trousers',[1] came poorly prepared for the Cypriot climate. They brought with them a consignment of warming pans and several large iron coal boxes which were soon abandoned on the beach.[2] Ships bringing provisions were delayed, leaving the men without food on the night of their arrival, while senior officers were expected to 'forage for themselves, and had nothing for dinner that night but eggs and champagne, as even water was not to be procured'.[3]

Sir Garnet Wolseley, the highly regarded career soldier who had been charged with establishing a British presence on the island, was appalled at the inadequacy of the preparations and wrote irritably in his diary that the disembarkation had been 'very unsatisfactory'. His frustration grew when he discovered 90 mule carts brought from Malta scattered in pieces on the shore, alongside the discarded coal bins. The carts were useless because the quartermaster had forgotten to arrange for the 'link pins', vital for their assembly, to be packed in the same consignment. Wolseley concluded that the man was 'incapable', resolving never 'to start again any expedition unless I am allowed to select my own Commissionary [*sic*] General'.[4]

By the time he arrived in Cyprus, Garnet Wolseley had already distinguished himself in Burma, China and Canada. Dutiful and courageous, he embodied many of the values which the Victorians believed lay behind Britain's imperial greatness and by the end of his life was held in such high esteem that he was buried next to the Duke of Wellington in Westminster Abbey. Wolseley had doubts about the occupation of Cyprus, writing in his journal before he left Britain, 'I have thought it over for many an hour…anxious to find out good reasons for the move, and yet never able thoroughly to satisfy myself of the wisdom of the measure…the annexation of Cyprus is a half-and-half measure that will certainly entail great outlay upon us to secure us – what? For the life of me I cannot tell.'[5] Misgivings about the political and strategic merits of Britain's latest territorial acquisition began to be voiced in both Cyprus and London almost as soon as Wolseley came ashore and continued to be heard, intermittently, throughout the British occupation of the island.

Britain had acquired Cyprus in secret, in the course of a larger manoeuvre in the 'great game' of competing for stakes in the crumbling Ottoman Empire. It was a game played out in the final decades of the nineteenth century between the most powerful nations in Europe; Russia, Austria, Britain, France and Germany. For Benjamin Disraeli, Britain's Conservative prime minister, the principal reason for occupying Cyprus was to defend the empire against what he believed were Russian designs on India. This could only be achieved, the prime minister argued, by a clear commitment to support the sultanate of Abdul Hamid II against Russian expansionism.

Disraeli's opportunity arose in the aftermath of Russia's invasion of the Ottoman Empire in April 1877 when the Sultan was forced to accept humiliating terms that virtually dismembered his territory, dividing it up into a number of Christian Slav states. Russia was granted the Black Sea port of Batoum and the frontier fortresses of Kars and Ardahan. Other European nations, alarmed at this disruption to the balance of power on the continent, pressed for the terms of the treaty to be revised.

It was against this background, just nine days before the start of the Berlin Congress which was intended to re-negotiate Russia's bilateral treaty with the Ottoman Porte, that on 4 June 1878 a secret 'Convention of Defensive Alliance', subsequently referred to as the Cyprus Convention, was signed in Istanbul. The convention stipulated that Britain would provide military support to the ailing Ottoman Empire and that 'any further encroachments by Russia upon Turkish territory in Asia will be prevented by force of arms'. In return Britain required vague assurances from the Porte that the rights of Ottoman Christians would be respected, and, more importantly for Disraeli, it demanded the right to occupy and administer Cyprus as a military base. Although the island would retain Ottoman sovereignty, a semi-permanent British military presence there would enable Britain to come rapidly to the defence of Turkish interests. If at any future date Russia surrendered the Ottoman territories it had recently occupied, 'the proposed agreements will cease to operate' and Britain would leave the island.[6] This conditionality was to inhibit the development of the island until Britain finally annexed the territory in 1926.

The British delegates to Berlin, including the prime minister and Lord Salisbury, the foreign secretary, announced that the deal had secured 'peace with honour'. Equally importantly for British imperial interests, Cyprus, 'the key to Western Asia', as Disraeli described it, would play a vital strategic role in maintaining the security of India. His delegation returned home to lavish, highly choreographed celebrations.

Others in government were less convinced that this neglected backwater, part of the sleepy Ottoman Empire for 300 years, was a worthwhile addition to Britain's imperial portfolio. One cabinet minister confided in Wolseley on the eve of his departure for Cyprus that he 'hated the whole arrangement.'[7]

On 28 July 1878, after the chaotic disembarkation Wolseley and the men of the Black Watch made their way to an area which the British later came to know as *Chiflik Pasha*[8], close to a stream near the Larnaca salt lake, around three miles outside the town. Etchings of the camp published in the *Illustrated London News* depict a raised area of flat land with an aqueduct in the background.

During the march the force suffered its first casualty. Sergeant Samuel McGaw, who had won the Victoria Cross fighting alongside Wolseley in the Ashanti Wars in Ghana, succumbed to 'heat apoplexy' and was buried at the camp beneath a wooden cross. Sickness was to be a recurrent problem during the summer of 1878, when at any one time a quarter of Wolseley's troops were incapacitated through sunstroke or malaria.

Although the area around *Chiflik Pasha* had obvious strategic advantages – a clear view of the surrounding countryside and a valuable source of fresh water – it offered little protection from the fierce summer sun. One of the officers there, Andrew Scott-Stevenson, was joined on the island two months later by his outspoken wife Esme, who subsequently wrote a popular account of her life on the island, *Our Home in Cyprus*. Although Esme Scott-Stevenson went to great lengths to portray herself as a retiring wife who hesitated to publish her memoirs, she pulled no punches in her criticism of the poor facilities provided for the soldiers. 'For miles around there was not a tree or a shrub of the height of a foot, and the blazing sun penetrated through the thin canvas of the single bell tents, as if mocking the puny efforts of men to protect themselves from its fierceness. The soldiers might just as well have had no covering at all, for these wretched tents are only fit for sham fights in England, or for the volunteers at Wimbledon ... Thus, on the very hour of their arrival, their constitutions must have received a shock which rendered them unable later to cope with the fever, the result entirely, in my mind, of solar exposure.'[9]

Poor planning and ignorance of local conditions continued to hamper the progress of the newly arrived British contingent. When, at last, the baggage train left the camp for the 26-mile march to Nicosia, the absence of link-pins for the mule carts meant that provisions had to be transported by 'camels and in native carts'.[10] Wolseley and his party followed the next day but somehow managed to leave Larnaca by the wrong road and 'wandered about in a helpless state at first for some time until we found the made road with its accompanying telegraph poles'.[11]

Morale declined further as the men marched through the arid landscape, noticing the chalky treeless hills and the absence of running water. 'Where are the forests we thought Cyprus was covered with?' Wolseley pondered in his journal, before concluding that 'like everything else that made this country a splendid one in ancient times, the forests have disappeared under the influence, the blighting influence, of the Turk'.[12] The concept of a degraded landscape, its decline attributed to both native apathy and Ottoman greed, recurs frequently in colonial writing on Cyprus. Opponents of Disraeli's expansionism used the image to reinforce their arguments that the colony was of little intrinsic worth and would only be a drain on British taxes. Conversely, supporters of a British presence in Cyprus, like Horatio Kitchener, who drafted the first comprehensive land survey of the island, maintained that, as a civilising nation, Britain had a moral obligation to restore Cyprus to its former prosperity. Kitchener argued that there were 'many places in the island … just waiting for the hand of the capitalist to change them from barren wastes to their former fruitfulness'.[13]

Esme Scott-Stevenson, was to travel the same route as the 42nd Highlanders with her husband two months later. Her journey was made particularly arduous by her insistence on carrying her pet dog. 'It was very alarming on our route, to meet the half-wild dogs which would fly savagely at us from every corner we passed,' she wrote. 'Sometimes they would spring almost as high as my saddle; and as this naturally caused my horse to plunge about, I had great difficulty in holding my own little dog which I had in my arms. My husband's hunting crop was the only thing that kept them at a distance.'

Captain Scott-Stevenson, a thick-set man who sported a flamboyant handlebar moustache and displayed his wife's name tattooed on his right arm, was used to getting his own way; and he adopted a similar approach with the residents of Nicosia. Soon after entering the walled city the couple decided that the washing facilities at their hotel, the grandly named Army and Navy, were not up to scratch. Scott-Stevenson requisitioned the hotel's bread-making utensils, triumphantly carrying off a large wooden trough, 'despite of [sic] a frantic resistance',[14] for his wife to use as a bath.

Later that evening the Scott-Stevensons dined with Wolseley at his camp outside the city walls, sitting at tables decorated with 'passion flowers and jessamine [sic]'[15] By setting up camp outside the Mediaeval walled capital, Wolseley adopted the conventional British practice of establishing a physical distance between the colonisers and the natives. His temporary headquarters were on raised ground near the monastery of Ayios Prokopios, which was linked with the influential Greek Orthodox monastery of Kykko, high in the Troodos Mountains. Wolseley's initial hopes that the men would quickly be able to abandon their flimsy bell tents in favour of wooden huts soon faded after the wrong sort of hut was despatched from Britain. 'They are of the pattern I said were very bad when I asked for huts and asked specially not to have them,' he wrote in his journal, adding with a note of resignation: 'I suppose the fact is that they had

a stock [on] their hands...and they wouldn't go to the expense of buying others...they will afford but a very poor protection from hot or cold weather.'[16]

The well-being of Wolseley's troops and the question of whether Cyprus
would be a healthy environment for foreigners, attractive to those private
investors who might bring capital to the island, was discussed at length in the
British press. An article in the London *Contemporary Review* of August 1878
advocated that potential British settlers should 'establish themselves within a
few hours' ride of Larnaca until the administration has been thoroughly established' but warned 'it is doubtful whether English children can be safely reared
on the island'.[17]

The first British merchants took little notice of such words of caution. Having
followed the regiment to Cyprus, they lost no time in setting up shop. Some five
weeks after the troops disembarked at Larnaca, the colony's newly established
English language newspaper recorded with approval that, 'although Cyprus has
enjoyed little more than a month of English protection, a wonderful change has
already taken place. At the port of Larnaca, restaurants, inns, ship-chandlers, and
stores of every description have sprung up like magic. There has been a perfect
race, as to which should open first.'[18] Proof of this transformation was provided in
the subsequent advertisement for Messrs Henry S. King and Co., whose choice of
commodities included 'Swedish timber, ironmongery of every description, beer,
gin, whisky, champagne, Ballthal Apollinaris and tonic waters. Cigars, gun powder, portable water closets. Camp furniture of every description, articles of all
kinds in electro-plate, Milners fire and thief-proof safes, galvanized iron buckets,
tar brushes, melting pots, bales and ladles. Roofing felt, American stoves, paraffin
oil, lanterns, glass crockery and towels, bedspreads etc.'[19]

Despite Wolseley's reservations and those of certain members of the cabinet in London, newspaper accounts of the time convey a feeling of exuber-
ance about the commercial potential of the new colony – a sense that anything
might be possible. Numerous money-making schemes, many highly imprac-
tical, were investigated with enthusiasm. During the early years of British
rule in Cyprus, as Wolseley's temporary military government was gradually superseded by a more permanent civilian one headed by a high commissioner, the colonists applied themselves vigorously to putting down economic
and cultural roots. One suggestion involved opening the island's abandoned
Phoenecian copper mines, using 'trained miners, probably from Cornwall',
who would enable the work to be carried out 'with all the vigour that money
can produce'.[20] The colonists were more serious about the development of the
island's wine industry and hoped it might one day rival those of France or
Germany.[21]

Subsequent administrations put considerable effort into the development of
viticulture, planting over a million vines in 'four villages alone in the district

of Limassol'.[22] The *National Review* assured its British readership that there was 'a margin for profit and for improvement of some hundreds [*sic*] per cent'.[23] In an effort to create a market for Cyprus wines, Wolseley's successor, High Commissioner Sir Robert Biddulph met with the leading citizens of Larnaca to impress upon them the commercial opportunities of the Bordeaux wine exhibition. As a result, no fewer than 63 different Cyprus wines were submitted to the exhibition of 1882, nine of which were awarded medals.

The significance attributed to the wine-growing villages and their future role in the island's prosperity prompted the administration to invest in the latest modern technology. Just three years after Wolseley set foot in Cyprus the village of Mandria in the foothills of the Troodos Mountains could boast of its own telephone connection to the port of Limassol. The telephone – which had been invented only five years earlier – was, the *Cyprus Herald* suggested, 'excellent practice for people who spoke indistinctly, or desired to improve their elocution'.[24]

The first serious threat to this vision of unexplored commercial potential appeared less than a year after the colonists' arrival. In the spring of 1879 swarms of locusts were observed converging on the harvest and devouring crops as they stood, leaving behind only 'a few brown stalks issuing from what appears to be a fallow field'.[25] Colonel Falk Warren, the administration's chief secretary, recorded riding through 'an army of locusts'[26] that extended for seven miles around the village of Peristerona on his way to Mount Troodos.

At a loss to know what to do, the administration initially continued the existing Ottoman practice of purchasing and destroying the locust eggs (in 1881 2,000 tons of eggs were collected and burned at a cost to the colonial budget of £9,000),[27] while attempting to encourage natural predators such as storks, blue cranes and 'bee flies'.

Eventually the administration adopted a technique that had been developed some years earlier by Richard Mattei, an Italian landowner and agricultural pioneer. A descendent of one of the Italian families who had settled on the island before the Ottoman conquest, Mattei owned two 'model farms'[28] and a town house in Larnaca on the seafront.

Mattei's 'screen and pit' method involved trapping juvenile locusts in the spring, before their wings grew. As the insects crawled along the ground, long canvas screens three feet high and topped with a wide band of oilcloth were planted 'athwart the line of march' and a series of pits six feet long and three feet deep, dug at right angles to the screens. Unable to crawl over the slippery oil cloth the insects slid down the screens and 'hopped along until they fell into one of the pits' where, as the *Cyprus Handbook* of 1913 explained, with a surge of sentiment, 'the poor locusts are buried alive'.[29]

The technique was adopted island-wide and the government imposed a 'locust tax' to finance its implementation. Nearly 2,000 people were employed in the campaign of 1880, and 'no less than 315 miles of screens ... almost enough to encircle the whole coast line of the island',[30] were erected. Mattei was subsequently awarded a pension by the Legislative Council in recognition of his services and decorated with the Order of St Michael and St George. By 1894, regular locust infestations were a thing of the past, although when the locust eradication programme was at its height visitors to Cyprus occasionally complained of 'dreadful exhalations'[31] created by the decomposing insects.

The island's commercial potential as a tourist destination was recognised relatively early on in the British occupation. In 1878, the weekly newspaper *Cyprus* noted that 'a London Firm of Tourist Agents contemplate arranging for an excursion to this island, during the Autumn; and we are confident that when English visitors have once become acquainted with this place, it will soon be largely patronised by those on their way to and from Syria. There are spots in the mountain portion of this Island quite equal to any part of Switzerland.'[32] Two energetic early colonists appear to have taken the paper at its word. Barely a month after the appearance of this report the inhabitants of the village of Kosi, on the road from Larnaca to Nicosia, witnessed the opening of 'Hardman's', a hotel and stables run from a bell tent, also known – in a laboured Victorian pun – as the 'Dewdrop Inn'. Here, Esme Scott-Stevenson was at last able to obtain 'an excellent cup of tea, or, if preferred, a brandy and soda'.[33]

This explosion of commercial speculation was accompanied by a widely held belief that the British presence in Cyprus, after centuries of Ottoman rule, would be not only civilising but also redemptive. Cyprus and her inhabitants would be restored to their 'past prosperity that has been destroyed by the Moslems'.[34] Through the benign influence of Britain, 'the most tolerant government in the world',[35] the island would be transformed into 'a model of good government, an oasis in the surrounding desert of unenlightened administrations'.[36] The more ruthless manifestations of capitalism would – accordingly – be moderated, as long as Britain fulfilled its moral obligations to the new colony to 'raise her out of the depths of moral degradation and material bankruptcy into which an unenlightened foreign domination has plunged her'.[37]

This happy synthesis of material and ethical considerations was only part of the picture. The Orientalist Reginald Stuart Poole went so far as to claim that by governing Cyprus Britain could bring about its own moral regeneration. In a complicated and convoluted analogy he likened Imperial Britain to Republican Rome, and Ottoman Turkey to Carthage, asking, 'How many internecine wars did Rome prevent, how often did she stay the invader, how often did she restore the shattered administration of Eastern kings, when Carthage was content to govern territories as mere sources of revenue? It was not till Rome imitated her fallen rival that her decline began.'[38] In other words, the extension of enlightened government to a degraded colony such as Cyprus would, in turn, ensure the maintenance of a robust moral integrity at the imperial centre.

The first tangible manifestation of imperial rule appeared with the construction of Government House in December 1878. A standard issue, flat-pack structure, shipped out from Britain, it was intended for use as any colonial building – in any colony. The normally stoical Wolseley complained that the finished product consisted of 'a large wooden house with by no means well-fitting doors and windows, lofty rooms and heaps of windows, no stoves or fireplaces'. The building was located two miles away from the Mediaeval walled city and 'perched on a rocky hill where it enjoys every blast of wind'.[39] By the time Wolseley's much loved wife Louisa (or Loo, as he called her) joined him at Christmas 1878, the house was even less inviting, for strong winds had smashed many of the windows. But, dutiful as ever, he resolved that '[we] must make up our minds to "bivouac" in a half finished and almost totally unfurnished house for some time to come'.[40]

Loo had chosen wallpapers and soft furnishings for Government House from the range produced by Morris and Company, reassuring her husband in letters from England that she had 'bought with regard to economy'.[41] In many ways Louisa Wolseley – an army officer's wife who came from an old moneyed family – epitomised the practical good sense expected of a colonial wife of her class. But her choice of William Morris wallpaper for Government House was also significant.

The Arts and Crafts movement that underpinned the Morris wallpaper company centred on a rejection of the mechanistic, impersonal forces of industrial capitalism in favour of a traditional, organic – and largely fictionalised – vision of a pre-industrial past. It was a vision that, when exported into a colonial context, encouraged the idealisation of indigenous societies which were seen as a natural part of 'an authentic world of ordered, harmonious, time-hallowed social relations... that had to be cherished, preserved and nurtured overseas as a more wholesome version of [British] society'.[42] The philosophy that went with the Morris wallpapers lent itself to the creation of an Arcadian fantasy of the colonies as the location of idyllic pre-industrial societies. When that philosophy was applied to Cyprus, where the colonists were surrounded by what they believed to be traces of a 'lost', specifically classical, civilisation, it acquired a particularly seductive dimension, one that profoundly influenced British understanding of 'Cypriotness' and who the island's inhabitants really were.

At about the same time as Wolseley and his wife moved into their unwelcoming new home, the first high commissioner recorded in his diary that a new government engineer had arrived in Cyprus. Wolseley hoped his presence might 'lead to something in the way of Public Works for this much neglected island'.[43]

The engineer, Samuel Brown, was to be responsible for the development of the territory's infrastructure during the first 10 years of colonial administration. He supervised the construction of a network of arterial roads, the restoration of an irrigation system on the central plain, and the building of iron piers at Larnaca and Limassol. The tentative idealism he expressed on arrival in Cyprus contrasts with the more hyperbolic descriptions of Britain's function on the island that appeared in the British press. 'Is it impossible', Brown asked, 'under just laws and equal rights, to induce a people of mixed race and creed to live peaceably and happily together, to remove by education much of their ignorance and resulting prejudice; to develop material resources, revive agriculture, reclothe the bare hills with forest, create commerce, and thus provide for the maintenance of a largely increased population?'[44] Samuel Brown earnestly wished that it could be – and that the results would be beneficial for the entire region.

The just and equal administration that Brown hoped to be a part of did not acquire dedicated premises in Cyprus until 1882, when the Secretariat – the administrative hub of the colony – moved into new offices outside the city walls. The low-key building, originally intended as a police barracks, formed three sides of a square, with a sloping tiled roof and a wooden balcony running along the first floor.[45] The new offices may have been modest, but the *Cyprus Herald* recorded the move with relish. 'During the past week, carts filled with tables, chairs, blue-books [annual government reports filed by every colony throughout the empire] and other official *impedimenta* have been constantly discharging their loads at the new buildings. A refreshment-room has been opened by Hadji Yango Solomides for the purpose of providing luncheon for the various officials. The Nicosia ladies are understood not to approve of this plan, but the gentlemen are looking forward to occasional games of lawn-tennis (for which purpose two courts are being made) in the intervals of business, and seem to bear the prospect of remaining all day at the offices with great equanimity.'

Two weeks before the great move was carried out, the 'bachelors of Nicosia' appropriated the new building for a St Patrick's Day ball. The *Cyprus Herald* recorded that, despite the bare walls, the hosts 'overcame all difficulties, and with the aid of carpets, curtains and rugs converted the first of the rooms, which open one into the other so as to form a complete suite, into a handsome and comfortable drawing-room'. Furniture and flags were provided by the ladies of Nicosia, the band of the Royal Sussex Regiment played 'the latest and prettiest dance music', and the guests 'danced with great energy ... up to a late hour and then left with regret'.[46] The bachelors may have begun their evening with *The Cyprus Gallop*, a dance tune specially composed to celebrate the occasion of the British occupation.

In between polka-ing its way through the new government buildings the administration also found time to cut a new roadway across the Mediaeval walls of the city, between the Venetian bastions of Tripoli and D'Avila, to allow government officials easier access to the new Secretariat building. Until then, the boundary between the city and the surrounding countryside was absolute, with entry to the walled city obtained only by passing through one of three enormous gates which were often obstructed by animals and merchants. Today, the road through the walls forms part of Eleftheria Square, not much of a focal point but still the nearest thing to a civic centre in the southern part of the divided city.

Accounts of the colony's first years are full of enthusiasm and activity, but the cast of characters was small. The same names that appeared on the guest list for the St Patrick's Day Ball, for example, also appear in accounts of road building and wine promotion, or in newspaper reports of tennis tournaments and amateur theatricals. Samuel Brown, the idealistic government engineer, appears to have thrown himself with particular gusto into every initiative, making a memorable appearance which 'fairly brought the house down',[47] in a charity performance of 'a well known *commedietta*' in aid of the Cyprus Leper Farm.

Despite the early colonists' enthusiasm for hi-jinks on stage, both their public and private writings reveal a degree of self-consciousness and anxiety about how their behaviour – as representatives of the greatest empire in the world – would be perceived by their new subjects. This concern was most clearly voiced during ceremonial occasions, when the public face of government was on display. When the band of the Royal Sussex Regiment gave a concert in Rosslyn Square in Limassol in January 1882, the correspondent of the *Cyprus Herald* was appalled to see that the majority of the audience did not remove their hats during the national anthem. 'Among the natives doubtless, this is to be attributed rather to ignorance of the national custom, than to any feeling of disloyalty; and if all the Englishmen present showed the example, we believe the natives would quickly follow: unfortunately we saw several Englishmen who ought to have set a good example, taking no more notice of the grand old hymn than if the Band had been playing *Pop Goes the Weasel*.[48]

The comparatively understated ritual of standing to attention during the national anthem, observed – or perhaps occasionally ignored – in parks and before bandstands on Sunday afternoons throughout Victorian Britain, acquired far greater significance when it was acted out within the imperial territories themselves. Articles such as this one, suggest that many colonists saw themselves as ambassadors for Britain's imperial project, believing that it was through their own exemplary behaviour as individuals, that the islanders would be convinced of the empire's intrinsically moral and civilising nature and, by implication, of the desirability of being a part of it.

Thus when Wolseley telegraphed London to insist that women and children should not join his party until adequate accommodation could be provided for them, he was not only concerned about risks to their health but also feared that 'if English women were to be crammed into such unsuitable tents for the purpose as ours are, it would lower the Cypriots' opinion of us as a nation'.[49]

In the same spirit, in June 1883, Captain Scott-Stevenson, who was by then commissioner of the port of Kyrenia on the island's northern coast, arranged for the re-interment of the remains of Sergeant McGaw, the officer from his regiment who had died on the march to *Chiflik Pasha* in August 1878. Scott-Stevenson had previously purchased a small plot of land for use as a cemetery, 'shaded by olives and carob trees'. McGaw's re-burial in Kyrenia was completed with full regimental honours, his coffin covered with a Union flag and transported on the shoulders of six Turkish military policeman or *zaptiehs* while Scott-Stevenson, dressed in the full ceremonial uniform of the 'Black Watch' followed behind. Esme Scott-Stevenson subsequently wrote approvingly that the burial and the establishment of the cemetery 'had a good effect in showing the Cypriotes [*sic*] that the English not only could be just to the living, but respected and cared for the remains of their dead'.[50]

Sport also had a role to play in the civilising mission and it was particularly hoped that the manly outdoor activities of the Nicosia Hunt might inspire and uplift the native character. In November 1881, the first meet of the season took place under the supervision of Major Luttman-Johnson at 'the fourth milestone on the Larnaca Road', to the satisfaction of the *Cyprus Herald*'s equestrian correspondent, Man-on-the-Cob.

But his enthusiasm was short-lived. Man-on-the-Cob soon realised that the sport had done little to enhance relations between the colonisers and their subjects in the way that other organised sports – particularly cricket – were believed to have done in other colonies: 'The native equestrians are not well represented,' he lamented, adding 'perhaps if they knew the dates and places of the meets, and were aware how glad the members of the Hunt would be to see them taking part in so exhilarating a form of sport, there would be a larger attendance.' It is more likely that the 'native equestrians', doubting the sanity of the new arrivals as they tally-hooed their way across the Messaoria plain, wisely decided to give them a wide berth. But the Man-on-the-Cob's cheery paternalism ignored the complex social hierarchies at work whenever the hunt set out. A subsequent report in the *Cyprus Herald* described attempts by a solitary Cypriot rider to participate in the Limassol hunt. The paper noted that the field was 'varied by the presence of a native mounted on a mule the pack saddle of which was made soft by the addition of many indescribable garments ... [the mule] had a tendency to deposit on the ground the said garments and the rider much to the amusement of the field, but not at all to the discomfiture of the rider who appeared to be quite used to it'.[51] Although the sport of riding to hounds could be an inclusive one, capable of accommodating aristocratic colonial subjects (in the case of India, for example) as well as the British lower classes, both groups were expected to conform to the appropriate social code which reflected their relative status. The subversive Limassol donkey rider, perched on top of his customised saddle and unable to control his mount, clearly did not.

But with or without the participation of the locals, hunting, with its symbolic overtones of mastering the landscape, also allowed the early colonists to penetrate the heart of their new territory and uncover its secrets. R. Hamilton Lang was the British consul in Cyprus for five years under Ottoman rule and wrote extensively about the island in the immediate aftermath of colonisation, when demand for information about the new acquisition was at its height. His description of riding to hounds across the Messaoria plain allowed for an instructive digression into Cypriot geology after he came across what appeared to be a large bed of oyster shells. He described them as 'jolly big oysters, such as are eaten in England, not the puny ones offered us in Constantinople – and in the moments of surprise we feel inclined to ask what costermonger has been throwing out his shells here? Getting down, we pick up some of the finest specimens, thoroughly petrified, and look round to discover the sea which left these disconsolate oysters high and dry'.[52] The flat central part of Cyprus that lies between the Troodos and Pentadaktylos mountain ranges was once covered by a pre-historic sea. The 'disconsolate oysters' discarded by Hamilton Lang's careless costermonger were the fossils of crustacea that had lived there 3 million years before.

If the prospect of their new colonial masters galumphing across the landscape after foxes or performing amateur theatricals dressed as women still did not convince Cypriots of the benefits of belonging to the British Empire, the new arrivals could always conjure up the shining example of imperial India. Writing in the *Contemporary Review* in August 1878, Reginald Stuart Poole justified British rule in Cyprus on the grounds that having – by unspecified means – observed the benevolence of British administration in India, Cypriots had concluded that they too wished to be members of the imperial family. 'Profoundly dissatisfied with the rule of Constantinople and Cairo, the subjects desire a system, which shall be at once strong, just, and tolerant. It is not difficult to understand why the native Christian, even when he is of the ambitious and intelligent Greek race, should be not unwilling that the difficult task of government should be given to safe hands … It is the spectacle of India that has convinced him … the natives of India are perfectly aware that they are the subjects of the fairest and most tolerant government in the world.'[53]

Poole acknowledged that, unlike other colonies, the majority of the population of Cyprus was already Christian, members of the Greek Orthodox Church, and, moreover, part of 'the Greek race' which ranked higher in the racial hierarchy than darker-skinned inhabitants of tropical climates.[54] This clearly posed a problem, since, as the article implied, 'the ambitious and intelligent' Cypriots were likely to require rather more convincing than was usual of the benefits of British rule. In an attempt to do so, the writer felt obliged to expand his terms of reference beyond the shores of Cyprus itself to include Britain's most successful example of colonial government – India.

Although welcoming the fact that the majority of Cypriots were Christian, the early colonists were disconcerted by the presence of the Orthodox Church in Cyprus, believing Eastern Christianity to be alien and incompatible with the muscular Protestantism of empire. For its part the Orthodox Church was suspicious of the new rulers who withdrew the privileged status it had enjoyed under the Ottomans and suspended its right to collect taxes. During Ottoman rule the church had been the guardian of Hellenic ethnic and cultural identity on the island and as such exerted enormous influence over the Orthodox population. Throughout the colonial period it continued to nurture Greek nationalist aspirations and to press for union with the motherland (enosis in Greek), a role which frequently brought it into conflict with the British administration.

Not only did the colonists have misgivings about the nature of the Christianity they encountered in Cyprus, the fact that it was not possible to convert the 'natives' and bring about religious salvation undermined one of the ideological cornerstones of British imperialism. Elsewhere in the empire, commercial and personal ambition was often sanctioned, and to some degree tempered, by the understanding that British imperialism brought spiritual enlightenment in its wake. Unable to offer religious redemption, the British in Cyprus were at a loss to find a moral imperative for their imperial mission. Instead, the colonists developed vague notions of a romantic arcadia, a historically imprecise golden age of antiquity that was submerged beneath centuries of Oriental indolence, with 'few traces left of its ancient splendour'.[55] If 'native' salvation could not be effected by religious conversion, it could be achieved perhaps by re-acquainting the Cypriot subjects with this highly romanticised version of their classical heritage. Much of the energy that might, elsewhere, have focussed on mission schools or hospitals was instead directed towards the establishment of a national museum of antiquities – a place that would inspire Cypriots by encouraging them to contemplate their (classical) past.

In May 1882, excavations began at Salamis, financed by the British Museum under the supervision of Claude Cobham, the energetic district commissioner for Larnaca, who was also a keen antiquarian. In the same month a series of letters to the Cyprus Herald stressed the advantages of setting up a museum in Nicosia, an institution that would 'exercise so great an influence upon the education of the native mind and preserve the relics of the past grandeur and importance of the Island'.[56] Cypriots, ignorant for so long about their origins and history, were to be re-introduced to the 'past grandeur' of their forgotten civilisation through the benevolent intercession of the colonial power. The following month an 'influential deputation', chaired by the high commissioner, with Horatio Kitchener as secretary, was set up for the purpose.

But the prevailing uncertainty that many colonists still felt about their relationship with their new subjects, coupled with the necessity for exemplary public and social behaviour, inevitably had an impact on the structure of colonial society itself. It contributed in part to a sense of social insecurity periodically expressed by members of the colonial administration throughout the British occupation of the island. For the newly arrived colonists, busily defining themselves as an imperial class through the process of governing, it became particularly important to reiterate and reconfirm the boundaries of social acceptability. The process of defining their relationship with their new Cypriot subjects inevitably involved shoring up their own social hierarchy. A visitor to the island in the early 1880s complained to the *Cyprus Herald* that British residents declined to mix with other foreigners, a reluctance which caused 'relations of the different parties to be somewhat "cold" '.[57]

There are signs that social tensions within the colonial hierarchy had begun to emerge remarkably quickly. Just weeks after the colonists arrived, at a time when Wolseley was expending enormous effort organising his staff and attempting to secure basic facilities for his troops, problems that would have entirely occupied the attention of other men, he was already expressing concerns about the delineation of class distinctions within the tiny British community, and in particular the prospect of women arriving on the island.

Esme Scott-Stevenson had been the first middle-class British woman to encroach on the masculine world of the colonial adventurers. Wolseley, who considered Scott-Stevenson to be 'a very foolish creature' with 'a grating and unpleasant voice', alluded in his journal to her role in a scandal that had taken place the year before in Malta, adding that in Cyprus she would 'have an entire Regiment to flirt with and to admire her, so I presume that will compensate her any amount of discomfort'.[58]

The mysterious scandal in Malta appears to have so damaged Esme Scott-Stevenson's reputation that on arrival in Cyprus she was socially ostracised, and some officers of the regiment refused to call on her. Wolseley chronicled her exclusion from polite society with malicious pleasure. He wrote in his diary: 'The Colonel told the husband he had not called because if his wife came over, she would not call. They all look upon her as a disgrace in the Regt. so they will have nothing to say to her.'[59] Subsequent regiments posted to the new territory did not, however, share the same qualms as the 42nd Royal Highlanders, taking both lunch and tea with the Scott-Stevensons.

Wolseley's unease over the presence of Esme Scott-Stevenson was echoed when another female visitor arrived, this time in the rather grander form of Lady Anne Brassey. The wife of an unashamedly nouveau-riche liberal MP, whose father had made a fortune building railways across the colonies of Canada and India, Anne Brassey and her husband spent 20 days in Cyprus during a voyage on their luxury yacht *Sunbeam*. Wolseley was invited to lunch on board where, seated in the yacht's dining room, with its walls crammed full of Landseer-style oil paintings, its upright piano and revolving globe, he confessed to enjoying 'the first really delicious meal I have had since I left England'. Predictably he was less complimentary about Lady Brassey's taste, particularly her conspicuous display of wealth, condemning the interior of the *Sunbeam* as resembling 'a flash sitting room owned by a lady of loose morals in St John's Wood. Such taste! Oh how melancholy to see riches at the disposal of a woman without really, any taste at all.'[60] The encounter represented a clash between new money – wealth which was itself the result of recent colonial expansion – and the imperial establishment, one in which Wolseley 'found Annie Brassey badly wanting in every respect'.[61]

Much of Wolseley's irritability may have derived from his frustrations at the limitations of his life in the new colony. He was – in the mind of the British public – one of the great military heroes of the age, a man who was far happier performing deeds of 'imperial masculinity'[62] and dedicating himself to fighting the Ashanti than establishing the administrative foundations of the new colony. He wrote in his diary at the end of 1878: 'Where I shall be this day twelve months is hard to say. I hope not here, if these wars in Afghanistan and Zululand become serious.'[63] Five months later his hopes were realised when he was recalled from the island to fight against the Zulus. Gradually the regiments, too, were deployed elsewhere and the military officials who had acted as the island's first colonial administrators began to be replaced by civil servants. While the pioneering spirit which characterised the early years of the British occupation remained for some years more, much of the glamour associated in the public imagination with Wolseley and his small band of 'brilliant and distinguished staff'[64] disappeared with him. Despite this, he laid the foundations for the structure of British administration on the island which remained largely intact until independence in 1960. Nowhere were the changes initiated by Wolseley more visible than at the point of his arrival on the island – Larnaca.

When Wolseley's great bête noire Esme Scott-Stevenson returned to Larnaca one year after her arrival in Cyprus, she was delighted to find 'a really most comfortable hotel – called the "Army and Navy" – clean and bright, and as unlike its abominable namesake at Nicosia. The management is liberal, the *cuisine* excellent, infinitely superior to many so-called first-class hotels in England. Travellers arriving in Cyprus need no longer be afraid of having to "rough it."' The hotel, situated in newly named 'Wolseley Street', reassured homesick travellers with the promise of English servants and 'two of Thurston's best billiard tables', specially imported from England.[65]

Other noticeable changes in the town, overseen by the civil commissioner of Larnaca, Colonel White, involved improvements to the local medical and sanitary facilities. During his brief term in office White had supervised the construction of nine public lavatories, a hospital, a slaughter house and underground drains – with the consequent eradication of flies – while ordering the compulsory whitewashing of shop interiors and the removal of the packs of stray dogs that had made the Scott-Stevensons' first journey to Nicosia so difficult. The commissioner, whose enthusiasm for urban cleanliness was so great that he adopted the unconventional and highly illegal practice of imposing his own localised system of taxation in order to pay for it, also placed 'a fine large clock'[66] above the door of his office, in an effort to encourage punctuality. Esme Scott-Stevenson took particular pleasure in her visit to the colonel's garden which contained 'a wonderful nursery of every description of eucalyptus-trees'.[67] White and Wolseley had been working together to 'discover the sort of tree that is most suited to Cyprus'[68] and several acres in the grounds of the new Government House had already been planted with eucalyptus seeds, imported from Australia. Although the connection between malaria and mosquitoes had not yet been established, it was known that swampy ground was unhealthy and the 'abominable marsh' near the church of St Lazarus in the centre of Larnaca was considered to be 'one of the principal causes of fever during the summer season'.[69] The introduction of fast-growing eucalyptus was one method of draining low-lying marshy areas and thereby reducing the malarial threat. The presence of copses of mature eucalyptus in Cyprus today – often close to riverbeds – is usually evidence of attempts by the British administration to eradicate disease.

Larnaca's transition from a chaotic improvised landing station to a stable commercial centre also gained the approval of the *Cyprus Herald*, which commented that the town was now the site of 'peaceful and sober progress as compared with the feverish and unusual activity of a military occupation'.[70] But despite her delight at the facilities offered by the new Army and Navy Hotel, Esme Scott-Stevenson confessed to having mixed feelings about the urban improvements. While the experience of *being* in Larnaca was more hygienic, with fewer health hazards and unpleasant smells, *observing* it was no longer so interesting. 'Larnaca has become now almost Europeanized', she wrote, 'and has lost much of its picturesqueness; the streets are being paved, and the drains that formerly ran in the centre of every byway are closed over. Shops full of European goods have taken the place of the old bazaars; and one sees more people in English than Greek costume.'[71]

If Larnaca was no longer exotic enough to excite the sensibilities of the traveller in search of the Orient, its development as an efficient commercial port made it attractive to the small band of British businessmen and traders who hoped that the new colony would provide lucrative markets. On 14 November 1882, Sir Robert Biddulph, Wolseley's successor as high commissioner, officially opened the town's new iron pier in a flurry of flags, bunting and triumphal arches. Biddulph and a party of 10 other dignitaries solemnly set off in a life-boat from one of the original wooden jetties, only to disembark moments later on the new iron pier in order to be received with a salute.[72]

But despite the fanfare and congratulations from local businessmen, Biddulph's speech was surprisingly subdued. He expressed regret that although three quarters of the island's imports arrived through Larnaca, the shallowness of the bay had made it impossible to extend the pier 'to such a depth of water as would have enabled large vessels to have come alongside'.[73] The cost involved in reaching a depth suitable for large vessels to dock would have been prohibitive. As was to be the case so often in the colony's lifetime, restrictions on budget meant that the finished product, completed after much compromise and cost-cutting, no longer fulfilled its original intended function. Larnaca had its new pier, but the unmistakable disappointment expressed in Biddulph's speech suggests it would not be the gateway to prosperity that many had hoped for.

This extemporising approach became a feature of the British presence on the island and resulted from a combination of factors. Politically, Cyprus, unlike any other colony, was an anomaly. Its occupants, unlike other colonial subjects, were Christians with what the colonists perceived to be echoes of classical Greek in their speech, echoes which resonated in the picturesque ruins of the landscape. At the same time the colonists located the island very firmly in the Middle East rather than Europe and derived particular pleasure from its exoticism. At the level of policy, doubts over the island's changing strategic value led to confusion and an absence of long-term planning, while development programmes were hampered – or abandoned entirely – because of financial constraints. Despite the enthusiasm and energy of the first British arrivals on the island, the foundations of colonial rule were far from firm.

2

The Whitest of White Elephants
1882–90

The usual silence in the gardens of St Paul's Anglican Cathedral in Nicosia is broken by barks and by cries of childish excitement. The annual Nicosia Dog Show, held in support of the city's animal shelter, has begun. Trays of flapjacks and urns of hot water are carried into the sunshine by capable women in floral aprons, who sidestep the vicar's Great Dane. A small girl, clutching a leash, is dragged backwards into a plumbago bush by a terrier. It is a very British occasion. Similar events have been taking place here for generations. St Paul's is the only building in Cyprus that has been used continuously by the British community on the island since the nineteenth century.

Despite its grand designation, St Paul's Cathedral is a modest building, a single-vaulted nave having neither a bell tower nor a spire. Inside, the plain white walls contrast starkly with the elaborately decorated interiors of Greek Orthodox churches elsewhere in the city. For the colonists, weekly services here not only responded to personal spiritual needs but also served to reaffirm a common religious identity and with it a sense of cultural superiority.

The foundation stone of the building was laid at lunchtime on a sunny March day in 1893 by Lady Sendall, the wife of the high commissioner, to the sound of 'tasteful and refreshing' hymn singing from the newly formed church choir. But while 'a great many of the fashionable world of Nicosia were present', it was noted with regret that there was 'a scarcity of the men folk'.[1]

Perhaps the indifference of the hard-pressed civil servants, shuffling papers in the nearby Secretariat building, was understandable. The ceremony marked the colonist's third attempt to establish an Anglican church on the island. The previous building, established on neighbouring St George's Hill, had been carefully demolished four years earlier after it began, inexplicably, to subside.[2] For those few officials who had arrived with Wolseley at Larnaca beach and had chosen to remain on the island during the decades that followed, both the demolished church and its successor of 1893 represented the collapse of British colonial ambitions for Cyprus. The first British colonists had originally nurtured far more ambitious plans. They hoped to lease and restore the ancient church of St Nicholas of the English, an imposing Gothic structure with elaborate carved archways, next to Nicosia's grand mosque. Negotiations began with the Turkish religious trust that owned the building but had to be abandoned when British government interest in the new colony suddenly began to wane. Just two years after the British occupation began, Disraeli's departure from office and the election of Gladstone's liberal party meant that Cyprus's value as a strategic asset in the defence of India was called into question. The sense of enthusiasm and infinite potential that accompanied the earliest arrivals rapidly disappeared, replaced by the cautiousness and frugality that was to characterise British rule on the island until independence. In 1894, Falk Warren, the colony's disconsolate chief secretary, explained the failure of the church restoration project in *The Times*: 'Political power changed hands at home: Cyprus fell into disfavour: enthusiasm cooled: no-one seemed to know whether England meant to retain or surrender the island: contributions [to the church fund] accordingly ceased.'[3]

William Gladstone was resolutely opposed to Disraeli's policy of infinite imperial expansion. Not only did he object to the practice of 'land grabbing' on moral grounds, he also argued that the demands imposed by the endless extension of British frontiers would soon become impossible to meet.[4] In opposition Gladstone had vigorously denounced the secret agreement under which Cyprus was acquired as 'an insane convention'[5] and contemplated handing the island over to Greece.

The uncertainty that immediately followed this change of government at home proved disastrous for the new colony. The terms of the Cyprus Convention, under which Britain acquired the right to administer the island, meant that it could be handed back to the Ottoman Sultan at any time if Russia ceased to pose a military threat to the Ottoman Empire. One outspoken war correspondent complained that 'far from being the proud owners of a new acquisition, we are mere tenants'.[6] The prospect that Britain might suddenly be required to vacate the island inhibited the development of a long-term strategy for the colony's development and contributed to the provisionality, the sense of 'muddling through', which characterised the administration over the decades that followed.

From the outset, British rule in Cyprus was hampered by the issue of sovereignty. Within weeks of Wolseley's arrival in 1878, his efforts to introduce legislative changes on the island were frustrated 'over the question of whether Cyprus is Turkish or English territory',[7] leading him to conclude that 'at the root of all our troubles here lies the burning question of who is King of Cyprus? Under what flag do we sail?'[8]

Four years later the atmosphere of uncertainty remained, discouraging investment and stifling commercial initiatives. Travellers on the road from Larnaca to Nicosia were disappointed to find that they could no longer obtain a refreshing brandy and soda at the celebrated Dewdrop Inn, since the premises were now 'closed and deserted'.[9]

Months after assuming office Gladstone reluctantly concluded that although he still hoped 'before the close of my long life, to see the population of that Hellenic island placed by friendly arrangement in organic union with their brethren of the kingdom [of Greece] and of Crete',[10] it would nevertheless be politically unwise for Britain to abandon Cyprus. The deciding factor behind this change of direction was his fear that any attempt either to revoke the Cyprus Convention of 1878 or to change its terms might alienate the Ottoman Porte.

In making this decision, based on political expediency, Gladstone established a pattern which continued throughout the colony's existence. British policy towards Cyprus was always provisional, determined principally by external political factors and shifting regional alliances. More importantly, his actions reflected the vague, unspoken belief that although the island had no *clear* advantages, it might be of use in the event of some future unspecified military crisis and should not, therefore, be abandoned. This acknowledgement that 'the island was of only potential or negative rather than actual and positive value' contributed to an attitude of ambivalence about Cyprus, one that persisted throughout the lifetime of the colony and contributed to the failure of successive governments to develop 'a consistent, constructive British policy'.[11]

Doubts over Disraeli's claim, that Cyprus was strategically vital for the protection of India, began to be voiced in the British press almost as soon as Wolseley's troops arrived on the island. The decision, four years later, in 1882, during preparations to invade Egypt, to muster the British fleet at Crete, rather than the Cypriot port of Fagmagusta, served to underline the new colony's apparent failings. Famagusta, it transpired, was too shallow to accommodate large ships. Many in government endorsed the opinions of Liberal MP Charles Dilke that Cyprus had become 'the whitest of white elephants', and the description of the colony stuck.

The issue of whether Cyprus was indeed a valuable acquisition was finally settled in 1882, during 40 minutes of artillery fire at the Battle of Tel al-Kabir, when British forces routed a small Egyptian army less than one-third their size, thereby gaining a secure base in Egypt. From then on control of the Suez Canal meant that British interests in India could be safeguarded far more effectively from Port Said and Alexandria than from Famagusta. Ironically the man whose brilliant campaign in Egypt consigned Cyprus to strategic insignificance and the lower rungs of the colonial hierarchy was Sir Garnet Wolseley.

None of the arguments over military tactics and imperial defence would have assumed such significance had it not been for the exacting terms of the Cyprus Convention. Other British colonies which had no obvious strategic advantage were still considered to be valuable additions to the empire and their status was never questioned. But in this respect as in so many others, Cyprus was unlike any other colony. The Cyprus Convention of 1878 consigned the new territory to penury even before British troops came ashore and was to make it a continual drain on the British Treasury. When Britain took over Cyprus, it also shouldered an annual debt of approximately £6 million in today's prices. The agreement struck with the Ottoman Porte stipulated that every year the sultan was to receive whatever remained from the colony's revenue after the sums necessary for its administration had been deducted. Undesirable though it was for the island's profits to be siphoned off elsewhere, the arrangement might possibly have been sustainable. The catch came in the demand that the figure paid, known as the Tribute, should be calculated *only once* and should be based on previous *Ottoman* expenditure on the infrastructure of the island. Ottoman policy in Cyprus, as in all its territories, had been to impose severe taxes on the inhabitants and to spend as little as possible on development. The average cost of Ottoman administration in Cyprus over the five years preceding the British occupation was calculated at around £30,000, while the island's income was about £130,000. After various other sums had been deducted the annual figure payable to the Porte was fixed, with what Governor Ronald Storrs (who ruled the island in the late 1920s) was later to describe as the 'scrupulous exactitude characteristic of faked accounts',[12] at £92,799, 11s 3d. By contrast in 1879, a year after the British occupation, the costs incurred by the new administration ran at £117,455, while revenue remained around £148,360.

The authorities both in London and Nicosia soon realised that it would be impossible both to pay the Tribute and to develop Cyprus. To add insult to injury the money raised never even reached the sultan's exchequer. Instead it was used to pay the interest on an old Ottoman loan of 1855, on which the Porte had defaulted and which had been underwritten by British and French specu-lators. This iniquitous arrangement and the financial constraints it imposed frustrated successive colonial administrators and was to be a major source of resentment amongst Cypriots until its abolition in 1927.

The obligation to pay the Tribute meant that construction projects – such as Larnaca pier, or the long-awaited Nicosia-to-Famagusta railway – were con-stantly scaled down to comply with tight budgets. Other plans, such as those for the development of a deep-water harbour at Famagusta, or a mountain rail-way connecting the villages of the Troodos region, were abandoned altogether.

Heavy port dues, fixed by the government in an attempt to raise revenues, discouraged ships from calling at the island and inhibited the development of trade. The constant need to economise meant that 14 years after the British arrived in Cyprus, the island's roads remained largely undeveloped, 'practically only fit for summer traffic', according to the indignant correspondent of the *Times of Cyprus* who complained that even then 'they must be negotiated with some 12 inches of dust'.[13] At one stage, desperate to cut back on expenditure, the government in London even proposed abolishing the subsidised mail ships that served the colony via Alexandria and provided its only regular means of communication with the rest of the world.[14]

The contrast between the optimism of the new arrivals, who hoped to establish a model administration that would become the pride of the Levant, and the cynicism expressed 16 years later is striking. In 1894 the English language daily the *Times of Cyprus* commented that the Tribute left 'absolutely nothing for improvement in the Island, everything is swallowed by the English and French locusts ... the island is so parsimoniously farmed as to ultimately end in its utter ruin'.[15] In the event, Cyprus managed to pay the Tribute in full just three times between 1879 and 1902. As a result, the British government had to allocate an annual grant-in-aid to make good the difference. Throughout its lifetime, the colony would be a drain on treasury resources.

Cypriot historian George Georghallides, in a study published in 1985, described Britain's acceptance of such crippling financial obligations as 'an inexcusable failure of common sense'.[16] In fact, it was a monumental blunder, an oversight so huge it suggests that those who negotiated the deal considered it only a temporary expedient and never expected Britain to retain long-term possession of Cyprus. Whatever the original intentions, the Tribute was to have a lasting impact on the colony's development, up to the time of Cypriot independence in 1960, long after the payment itself had been abolished.

The necessity to constantly cut costs and reduce overheads affected the morale of colonial civil servants, and within the colonial office the island quickly acquired the reputation of being a poor relation. More importantly, it had a serious impact on the calibre of staff sent out to administer the colony. The salaries of colonial office staff varied significantly from one territory to another, and since each colony was expected to be financially self-sufficient, costs were borne locally. For Cyprus, the long-term implications of this policy – when combined with the demands of the Tribute – were crippling. It meant that the island was never able to afford top-quality officials, who, naturally, chose postings elsewhere with better terms and prospects. Technical and scientific appointments, in particular, often remained vacant for several years because Cyprus could not afford to pay the salaries such posts commanded in other imperial territories. In 1894, after the colony had been without a government doctor for several months, the *Times of Cyprus* noted that 'the pay for an English practitioner is very small, and it is a difficult matter to get a good man to come to a place like Cyprus'.[17]

Just over 30 years later a cabinet memo of 1927 summed up the position bluntly: 'We have never provided it [Cyprus] with technical officers of the best calibre as the cheese-paring policy which has had to be adopted has long ceased to attract the best men.'[18] The 'cheese-paring policy' did not deter those men of independent means who sought a quiet life, bookish classicists such as Claude Cobham, one of the early district commissioners for Larnaca, who spent his evenings translating Farsi texts into Arabic and Greek. But the long-term effects on Anglo-Cypriot relations were profound.

The consequences of the administration's modest wages bill were exacerbated by continual uncertainty over the island's future and whether it was to remain a part of the British Empire. A newspaper announcement in 1894 that 'the British garrison will be withdrawn'[19] the following year added to the climate of unease, fuelling rumours amongst the Cypriot population that the colonists were about to leave en masse.

Anxiety across Cyprus over the impending troop withdrawal reached such a pitch that some months later, following requests from the high commissioner, the secretary of state for the colonies was obliged to issue a public statement in London that the imminent withdrawal of so many soldiers did not 'foreshadow the abandonment of the Island by this country'. His statement, which appeared in Greek, Turkish and English newspapers, assured readers that the departure of the troops was instead a testimony to his government's confidence that 'there is no section of the population which is disposed either to attack any other section of it or to resist the civil power...[and to] the good sense and generally law-abiding character of the Cypriot people'.[20]

Nonetheless the loss of up to 1,000 British troops and the business they brought with them was a severe financial setback, particularly to Limassol, the closest town to the Polemidia garrison. From the start of the British occupation, revenue from the regiments stationed on the island had helped to compensate for the demands of the Tribute. News of the soldiers' departure, during a year when global grain prices had plummeted, drastically reducing the value of the island's exports, was yet another blow to the fragile Cypriot economy.

The year 1894 was the colony's worst thus far under British rule. In November, following three weeks of constant rains, a third of Limassol was destroyed in a flash flood. Unknown numbers were killed and hundreds were left destitute and homeless, their livestock washed away. Flood defences for Limassol had been proposed 14 years earlier, in the aftermath of a less devastating inundation, and it was pointed out that 'had sufficient money been allowed by the Government... to carry out the necessary alterations required the Town of Limassol would not have suffered as much as it has done to-day'.[21]

The poor state of the island's roads, yet another consequence of the Tribute, meant that relief supplies were delayed in reaching the scene of the disaster. Even in good weather it could take up to 10 days to travel overland from Nicosia to Limassol, a mere 60 miles. In an attempt to reach the flooded town faster, James Cunningham, the director of the Public Works Department (PWD), and Dr Heidenstam, the long-awaited government doctor, prepared to sail to Limassol by steam ship from Larnaca.

Like most imperial administrators, particularly those working in such a small and under-funded territory, Cunningham found that his professional responsibilities at the PWD were broad and varied. His departure from Nicosia was delayed by the need to 'superintend the construction and erection of a scaffold (on the model of that in use at Newgate, with some mechanical improvements of his own) for the execution of two murderers, side by side'. After assuring himself that the 'mechanical improvements' had worked satisfactorily, he 'energetically without delay mounted mule back'[22] and headed off towards the waiting ship at Larnaca. Dealing with natural disasters, travelling on impassable roads, even arranging public hangings, were all part of daily life for the Britons governing Cyprus in the early years of the occupation. They were challenges that many would have relished, conforming to popular perceptions of what a bracing life in the colonial civil service involved.

Less well documented in public accounts of colonial life was the demoralising daily routine of administering a forgotten territory with insufficient funds on meagre salaries. For many of these underpaid civil servants, often in remote towns with only a few other British families within riding distance, life in Cyprus was only made bearable by the annual expedition to Troodos.

It was usual practice throughout the empire for the British government to decamp to a cooler hill station during the summer months. In Cyprus, anxieties about the health of the troops and their susceptibility to disease made the establishment of healthier summer quarters a matter of urgency. The uninhabited summit of Mount Troodos, 6,000 feet above sea level and covered in pines, was selected for the purpose. By the summer of 1879, the Royal Engineers, along with an unrecorded number of Cypriot men, women and children who laboured alongside them, had constructed a 22-mile road connecting Limassol to Troodos, linking up with the economically valuable wine regions that lay between.[23] Five men from the regiment who died during the second summer of the British occupation were buried in the austere military cemetery on the mountain. This remote spot, managed today by the Commonwealth War Graves Commission, is some distance outside Troodos village and, like the rest of the mountain range, is submerged in snow for several months every year. Every June, throughout the British occupation, the start of the summer season was marked by the regiments of the Polemidia garrison marching up the

British troops playing polo on Mount Troodos, in the 1880s.

[*Reproduced by kind consent of Mrs Demetriou, of the Lanitium Gymnasium, Limassol. © The Lanitium Gymnasium, Limassol.*]

mountain road on their way to Troodos. Since the military were responsible for maintaining the water supply to the government camp, they and their families were always the first to arrive and the last to leave.

The process of moving civilian officials, their wives, children and domestic staff, not to mention all the government paraphernalia – the stationery, typewriters and files – was a laborious one. As many as 20 camels were needed to carry the files and office furniture of the Nicosia Secretariat to the summer hill station. Some domestic servants also travelled by camel, but the British themselves and their administrative staff generally chose to hire mules, or occasionally horses, from an animal trainer, or *keradji*. Not only did these animals provide a more comfortable seat than a camel, they were also specifically trained to walk with a gliding motion, moving fore and hind legs together, so that goods or people could be carried over uneven mountain roads without being shaken.[24] Heads of departments were allowed 10 mules to transport them, their families and private effects for the summer, while clerks and translators had to make do with five apiece.[25]

The arrival of motor transport inevitably made the journey faster, but even in the 1930s progress was slow. The cavalcade of vehicles required to transport Governor William Battershill, his household and his extensive menagerie up to the summer hill station could hardly have travelled at great speed. First the groom rode the family horses up from Nicosia, a journey that took up to three days. He was followed by a fleet of buses in which rode the governor's domestic staff, their wives, children, parents and in-laws. After them came a lorry containing his excellency's donkey, his wife's pet cow and his children's flock of chickens. The last two cars contained the governor himself and his wife and children, plus their three pet cats, their governess and the family dog.

On arrival, the summer visitors were confronted by clusters of cream-coloured bell tents dotted amongst the pines, linked by rocky pathways marked out with lines of painted white stones. Improvised wooden signs distinguished the tent allocated to the Roman Catholic Church from that of the post office, and if first-timers found the accommodation a little basic, they soon realised this was part of its charm. It was literally a camp, where everything, from government business to dinner parties, took place under canvas. Etchings from the *Illustrated London News* of 1879 show a photographer's studio tent, the canopied headquarters of His Excellency Major General Robert Biddulph, and a canvas theatre erected between the trunks of two trees where a group of soldiers, including several dressed, to general hilarity, in unconvincing drag, strike 'attitudes' on the stage.[26]

The first permanent structure to be built on Mount Troodos was the high commissioner's summer residence. A grey stone building that resembled 'a rather gorgeous Scottish shooting lodge',[27] it was known as 'Government Cottage'. Even this had a romantic twist, and its occupants delighted in telling visitors that the poet Arthur Rimbaud had supervised its construction. Until recently a typewritten notice there read, 'This house was built by the poet Rimbaud the friend of Verlaine in 1885. Since when it has been largely re-built by the Public Works Department.'

Officials of the Secretariat were housed in tents on a slope some 500 feet below. Here, accommodation was allocated according to rank. While senior government officials could expect a suite of large interconnected bell tents with wooden floors, including reception and dining areas in which to entertain guests, government clerks had to share a basic ridge tent with their colleagues. By 1921 all this had changed and even junior office workers could boast of stone-built summer quarters, which included private bedrooms, a mess and a shared recreation room.[28] Visitors to the island, or those not included in the government allocation, stayed at one of the commercially run hotel camps.

Summer accommodation in Troodos remained largely under canvas until the Second World War – possibly through choice. It gave the camp an other-worldly air, unlike other imperial hill stations, such as Shimla, where everything was 'so English and un-picturesque … one would fancy oneself at Margate'.[29] Part of the attraction the hill station held for the colonists was its emptiness. Until the British arrived, there was no Troodos village, no indigenous community that had to be improved, pacified or negotiated with. The rocky outcrop was an empty slate on which they could inscribe a self-contained colonial experience and enact a shared fantasy of how Cyprus ought to be. Government could be carried out at arm's length, almost as an abstract exercise, without the uncomfortable compromises often required down on the plains, and free of contact with those educated urban Cypriots whose demands could complicate the business of effective colonial administration.

If the colonists' hopes for their new subjects were to be frequently disappointed, their expectations of the landscape were at least in part realised. At Troodos, files could be consulted while sitting amongst the trees in 'magnificent air, all scented with pine', briefings were carried out undisturbed by 'any noise, except for a few birds', while all official papers and communications 'were carried to and fro by mounted police orderlies who lent a slightly mediaeval air to the place'.[30] Several decades later, in 1932, *The Times* noted that 'even such an august person as a Colonial Secretary[31] may be found transacting high political business at his desk in shorts and a tennis-shirt, while nymphs may be discovered wandering the valleys in bathing costume'.[32]

In a lecture on the colony given to the Royal Geographical Society in November 1889, Sir Robert Biddulph, a former governor, invited his audience to accompany him on an imaginative journey through Cyprus and to 'listen to the shepherds piping to their flocks; to follow the mountain tracks, where amidst the murmuring of the streams, by the side of a hazel copse, or under a shady old walnut tree, you might listen to the cawing of the crows and imagine yourself in England'. Biddulph presented the Cypriot scenery not as an exoticised Oriental landscape, but as an Arcadian classical one, with a note of reassuring Anglo-Saxon familiarity thrown in. Warming to his theme, he commended the advantages of being 'in a country so near to civilisation, and yet where news from the outside world arrives only once a fortnight, and where there are no railways! Such is the place to refresh the mind wearied with daily papers, telegrams, sensational news, and advertisements, with the postman coming ten times a day with letters which you don't want to get.'[33]

For Biddulph, the island's unique attraction derived from the fact that it was comfortingly near to 'civilisation' while at the same time it allowed for a retreat from the technological developments of the modern world and the demands they brought with them. Paradoxically, his professional position as governor involved strenuous efforts to introduce the very technological 'progress' that he privately longed to escape from. By the time he left Cyprus in 1886, the colony produced several daily newspapers in English, Turkish and Greek, there was at least one telephone link on the island, and the Secretariat had begun discussions on the development of a Cyprus railway. Biddulph's depiction of the island as an oasis of tranquillity owed far more to an idealised notion of the Golden Age than to an accurate description of the life of a civil servant in the Cyprus Secretariat in the late nineteenth century. In much the same way, his description of the colony's proximity to 'civilisation' was not based on its actual geographical distance from either London or Paris, both places considered to be synonymous with the civilised world at the time. In practice, the colonists' journey from London to Nicosia involved changing ships at Port Said or Alexandria, and connecting with one of the notoriously erratic ferryboats of the Fouadh line for the final leg of the journey to Famagusta. As a result, the travelling time separating Cyprus from 'civilisation' was considerably greater than that from Egypt or Syria. Biddulph's vision, therefore, was hopelessly at odds with the logistics of international travel. It derived instead from a vague and persistent idea that vestigial traces of the classical roots of European civilisation still lingered on the island itself.

This highly romanticised vision of Cyprus exerted a powerful hold over the collective imagination of the British colonists and could be expressed most freely through their relationship with the Troodos summer camp. Accounts of life on the mountain frequently allude to the privileged life of Olympian deities, elevated above the cares of daily life on the plains below. The *Illustrated London News* described the summer camp as situated on 'the ancient Olympus',[34] conflating Mount Olympus and the mythical home of the Classical Greek Gods.

At times, descriptions of life at the hill station suggest nothing less than paradise, a pre-lapsarian Eden, where the British could enjoy 'the new and delightful experience'[35] of eating cherries and peaches direct from the trees, the governor's private secretary could join the general officer in command in building trout pools in mountain streams,[36] while his excellency's wife could be left in peace to milk her pet cow.[37]

This idyllic tableau was completed for many families by the arrival of their children from boarding school in Britain. Unlike the majority of imperial postings, a station in Cyprus enabled colonial officials to see their children at least once a year. Extra boats were laid on at the beginning and end of the school holidays, and for a return fare of £25 in 1924, British children were able to enjoy 'a splendid holiday upon Troodos, all picnics and ponies and bathing in waterfalls'.[38] Jane d'Arcy, daughter of Governor William Battershill, remembers 'loading up the donkey with provisions and spending the entire day walking in the mountain or playing in the streams'.[39]

The purity of the hill station was carefully protected. The select group of Cypriot traders and shopkeepers awarded contacts to supply the British with provisions during the summer season had to rent their premises from the government. Unlicensed private trade was prohibited and only the administration was allowed to build. The small number of British settlers in Cyprus involved in commerce and trade spent their summers at the more lively hill stations of Platres and Prodomos lower down the mountain, which were popularised by wealthy Levantine Greeks, who brought with them a touch of glamour and sophistication.

Even today there is a strange transient feeling about Troodos, as if the utilitarian stone cottages – still allocated (according to seniority) to government civil servants for their two-week holiday in August – were part of a film set, which might disappear by the next morning. No one lives in the village, and the traders in the central square, the coffee shop owners, the man offering horse rides through the forest and the stall-holders selling leather belts and Cyprus honey, all disappear after dark.

Whatever the novelty of out-door tea parties and life under canvas, the principal function of the Troodos encampment was that of the official summer seat of the British administration. The summer camp provided the colonists with an opportunity to carry out village inspections in the surrounding area. This contrived and uneasy ritual – practised throughout the empire – was generally popular with colonial administrators in Cyprus, who believed it gave them the chance to meet 'real Cypriots', to understand them and – as many of them sincerely hoped – to respond to their demands. Each visit followed roughly the

A tea party on Mount Troodos. Anton Bertram, one of the colony's senior judges, is seated fourth from the left, wearing a bow tie, 1903.

[*Reproduced courtesy of The Bodleian Library, University of Oxford.*]

same pattern. The governor or district commissioner and his entourage would arrive at a designated village where they would be received by the *mukhtar* (the headman or mayor) and a number of hand-picked local dignitaries. The visitors would generally be escorted to the village coffee shop where they would make polite conversation through an interpreter over Cypriot coffee and preserved fruit. Highly drilled schoolchildren might be produced to sing the British national anthem and proclaim their loyalty to the crown, after which the *mukhtar* would submit his requests for a new road, a regular mail service or a better irrigation system. The government party would then shake hands, promise to consider the request and leave. This was colonial government at its most benevolent and paternalistic, outdoors, 'doing good' to a respectful and compliant population. The budgetary constraints that would inevitably lead to a red line through so many of the submissions were temporarily forgotten.

For the ebullient Harry Luke, assistant government secretary in 1911–12 (author of a memorable account of how to cook and eat a camel's hump), the annual visits to the mountain villages resembled a luxury scouting expedition. 'Each morning the camp would go ahead to our destination for the night, while we took with us our picnic luncheon of sandwiches and fruit. When we arrived at our camping-places in the late afternoon, there was the camp ready for us. Hot hip-baths in our bedroom tents and a hot dinner in preparation,

Anton Bertram, at work on Mount Troodos, 1904.

[*Reproduced courtesy of The Bodleian Library, University of Oxford.*]

to be consumed in the more elaborate tent that did service as our dining and sitting-room.'[40]

For those British civil servants isolated at more distant parts of the island, such as the three colonial administrators and their families based at the remote outpost of Paphos, the annual trip to Troodos provided a longed-for opportunity to rejoin polite society and to meet other members of the colonial community. The picnics, band concerts, parties and amateur theatricals contained faint echoes of the social gatherings of the London season, as provincial families converged on the summer hill station to exchange news of the latest overseas postings, negotiate professional alliances and, occasionally, arrange good marriages. The colonial marriage market in a territory the size of Cyprus was minuscule. Nevertheless, the island still received periodic visits from members of what was known pejoratively as 'the fishing fleet'. The 'fleet' consisted of young single women of the upper-middle classes who had been unable to make a suitable marriage at home and were despatched to relatives and friends in the imperial territories where it was hoped they might have more success. One (married, female) writer helpfully suggested that young unmarried women visiting Cyprus might avoid potential social embarrassment by explaining they had 'really come to look at the scenery'.[41]

While the annual pilgrimage to Troodos fulfilled many functions, it was primarily a regenerative experience, the enactment of a fantasy of what colonial life could be like, which also gave meaning to the colonists' own role in the great imperial project. For district administrators in the provinces, who might receive a visitor from Nicosia only every three months, the gradual dispersal of the camp at the end of the summer could be a melancholy occasion and have 'quite a depressing effect'.[42]

The idiosyncratic image of empire which the Troodos encampment perpetuated was one that sustained and replenished generations of colonial administrators during the remaining nine months of the year, as they confronted the constant lack of funds, their own low salaries and a people, unlike other imperial subjects, whom they never entirely understood.

3

A High Degree of Mental Culture
1900

Twenty teenage boys are noisily convincing their parents and friends that 'There Is Nothing Like a Dame'. As they stomp downstage a cardboard palm tree concealing the orchestra shimmies.

There is loud applause as the song draws to a close. Pupils at the back of the hall stamp their feet. This could be any school musical, at any school or village hall in Britain, but here the audience is chatting together in Greek.

The Nicosia English School production of *South Pacific* is being performed by Greek Cypriot students in a vaulted assembly hall where angular stone lions carved above the outer doors provide a daily reminder of the school's colonial roots. Outside, the towered entrances and cloistered inner quadrangle echo the standard design of countless British public schools.[1] The sand-coloured building stands on an elevated site close to the spot once occupied by Garnet Wolseley's draughty Government House.[2] Directly opposite the main entrance is a monument to Michaelis Karaolis, executed by the colonial administration in 1956, a few years after he left the English School, for his part in the armed EOKA struggle against the British for union with Greece.

It is surprising that such a potent symbol of colonialism should have survived the violence and anti-British feeling of the 1950s with its name and so many of its founding principles intact. The school's continued existence appears even more intriguing given the antagonism it provoked early on in its lifetime from the self-styled guardian of Hellenism – the Orthodox Church. The English School provides an interesting prism through which to view the colonial era. Many of the contradictions it has struggled to reconcile throughout its history have reflected in miniature the deep-seated confusion which underpinned British education policy in Cyprus. This confusion extended beyond the classroom to include the cultural assumptions that the British made about their Cypriot subjects, about their role as colonists and even in some cases about their own children. One consequence of this was that the island's classrooms became, at different stages during British rule, the focus of fierce ideological battles over the colony's ethnic and cultural identity and, by extension, its political future.

Today the English School is an elite fee-paying establishment. Classes are in English, as they have been since the school's foundation in 1900. Pupils follow a British curriculum and 95 per cent of them go on to university in the United Kingdom. The head teacher has always been British, usually an Oxbridge graduate, nowadays answerable to a Cypriot board of governors. Major issues of school policy are decided in the boardroom. In a far corner of the room, placed behind the polished boardroom table, is a modest tin trunk with the words 'Newham Larnaca' stencilled on its front. Brown and flaking with rust now, it was used in 1900 to transport the private library of a young idealistic curate from a small Kent village, Frank Darvall Newham. He arrived on the island to teach English to future government clerks and officials, remaining there for the rest of his life and founding one of the few British institutions in the colony that genuinely attempted to realise the lofty Victorian vision of a 'civilising empire'.

Once English became the official language of government in Cyprus, virtually all public interaction with Cypriots themselves – the business of administering justice, implementing legislation and receiving petitions – required the efforts of large numbers of translators fluent in English, Greek and Turkish. For ambitious young Cypriot men looking for jobs within the colonial administration fluency in English was a prerequisite. Only then could they be eligible for 'many of the posts now occupied by English men, or by foreigners'.[3] Canon Newham was largely responsible for ensuring that several generations of young men, many from poor or disadvantaged backgrounds, were at least equipped with the skills necessary to engage with the colonists in their own language.

At the bottom of Newham's rusty book box, is the school's first register. The binding has disintegrated and the brittle, brown-edged pages flake off in the hand. But the detailed records of the school's first pupils, written out in the founder's careful copperplate, give insight into his vision for the new institution.

The first two pupils to register at the new school in September 1900 were Jules Vitalis and his brother Tancred, the sons of a government clerk, listed as 'Roman Catholic French Smyrnites'. Their classmates, boys with equally poetic names – Arthur Mavrogordato, Maurice Constantinidi and Alfred Griffin – were all sons of mixed Anglo-Greek marriages, along with 'Syrian Smyrnites' such as Edwin Prince, Thales Cababe and Josef Carletti, whose mother was Armenian and whose father, an Italian doctor, practised in Larnaca.

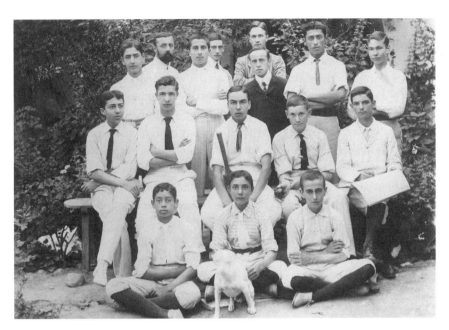

The English School Cricket Team, 1903. Canon Newham, back row, second from left.
[*Reproduced courtesy of The English School, Nicosia.*]

As late as the 1930s, a decade after the Eastern Mediterranean had been divided up into modern nation states, English School pupils still reflected the enormous racial and cultural diversity that had once characterised the Ottoman Levant. The children's ethnic origins are listed in the school register in detail, along with their fathers' remarkably varied occupations. In its early years, the school intake appeared to cut across economic as well as ethnic distinctions. The solemn faces staring out from posed school photographs belonged to the sons of Lebanese merchants; Greek Cypriot tinsmiths, doctors and shoemakers; Turkish Cypriot judges and labourers; Armenian clerks and translators; English police chiefs and Maltese hoteliers.

This social and ethnic mixture appears to have been deliberately encouraged and played an important part in defining the early character of the school. At prize-day in 1908 Newham recorded his satisfaction that 'the different nationalities cause no friction', citing his school's original motto, the distinctly un-Victorian maxim 'Respect Each Other's Feelings'.[4]

Pencilled notes next to the names of certain students not only provide details of their subsequent careers but also testify to the freedom of movement many pupils took for granted, as they moved effortlessly between the overlapping British and Ottoman Empires. While the majority of English School graduates fulfilled government expectations and took up posts in the colony's administration, others went on to public schools in England, to Robert College in Istanbul or the American College in Beirut. Newham's trunk also contains photographs sent back from old boys who worked for Greek banks in Cairo and Alexandria, for Armenian art dealers in Beirut, or as interpreters in foreign consulates in Aleppo or Smyrna (modern day Izmir, on the west coast of Turkey).

But the school was more than just a language crammer. Newham also strove to foster the ideals of the Victorian public school amongst the Greek-speaking Levantine boys in his care. Classics were taught to inculcate a sense of honour and public service, while boys who smoked or 'repeated bad words from the coffee shop'[5] were marked down. Pupils were encouraged to take part in competitive sports, activities intended to foster a sense of team spirit and fair play,[6] as well as in public speaking competitions, in drama and music contests. The curriculum reflected nineteenth-century ideas of what constituted a liberal education, ideas which were themselves based largely on a highly selective reading of Ancient Greek history. To that extent the English School presented a Levantine but predominantly Greek-speaking community with an Anglicised, specifically imperial, vision of the educational practices of Ancient Greece. The same system, believed capable of equipping the aristocratic youth of both fourth century BC Athens and nineteenth-century industrialised Britain to play a leading part in society, had been exported to Britain's only Greek-speaking colony. In keeping with this ethos the guest speaker at the school's 1908 prize-giving reminded the boys that schools like theirs instilled 'a love of freedom [and] the duties and rights of citizenship'.[7] But the mainly Greek-speaking audience listening to his words were not fully enfranchised citizens, they were imperial subjects.

Newham's trunk contains tantalisingly little information about the man himself; but it is known that he graduated in theology from Cambridge at the comparatively late age of 32. He is remembered as a stocky, gregarious man with a drooping walrus moustache, who regularly appeared at the English Club in the early evening ready to stand a round of sundowners. There, he would 'jolly along with all the boys and then say, "Come on now lads, I've stood you a drink, how about coming to church next Sunday?" He was such a delightful, charming person, he usually got his way.'[8]

But if relatively little is known about Newham himself the activities of his school were chronicled at length in the island's newspapers. The short-lived paper *The Anglo-Cypriot* provided particularly enthusiastic coverage and reported one appropriately uplifting prize-day speech by the island's retired high commissioner, Sir Robert Biddulph. While in office Biddulph had been a strong advocate of English language education in all the colony's schools. He endorsed the English School wholeheartedly, not only because of its language policy but also because of the values and traditions it embodied. Biddulph reminded his audience that the importance of education lay not just in winning

Canon Newham, with the school dog, Skibboo, 1915.
*[Canon Newham, the founder of The English School. The English School Cricket Team, 1903.
Reproduced courtesy of the English School, Nicosia.]*

prizes but 'in being able to bear in a patient spirit the disappointment of failure
and to feel pleasure in the success of others'.[9]

For Biddulph and his successors events at the English School became regular fixtures in the diary of public engagements, a reflection of the high status the
school enjoyed. As long as it continued to be the principal source of English-
speaking Cypriot civil servants it would be essential to the smooth running of
the colonial administration. Cyprus differed from other colonies in that education in Cypriot schools was never conducted through the medium of English, a
policy which severely restricted the pool from which more junior-level clerical
staff could potentially be drawn.

The debate over which language to use in the island's schools reflected the
widely differing ideological perspectives from which the colonists viewed their
subjects, and the impact of British education policy in Cyprus has been extensively researched in several comprehensive studies.[10] Less well documented is
the extent to which the colonists' ambivalence about how and what their Cypriot
subjects should be taught resulted from the peculiarities of their own educational
and cultural backgrounds, in particular the disproportionate emphasis placed
on the study of Classics at British public schools and universities. Most British
colonial officials arrived armed with experience gained from administering
other crown possessions. But Cyprus, they discovered, was a case apart. The

way individuals responded to these challenges, particularly when they involved questions about *who* the Cypriots were and what they should be educated *for*, had a direct and significant impact on Anglo-Cypriot relations. It is tempting to speculate that had these issues been resolved differently the course of Cypriot history in the nineteenth and twentieth centuries might have been changed.

For Orientalists, such as Samuel White Baker, who visited the island in 1879, 'one of the most urgent necessities [was] the instruction of the people in English', if corruption was to be eradicated and the 'natives' rescued from the venal practices of dishonest Ottoman officials. Until English was more widely understood, Baker believed, 'it is not to be expected that any close affinity can exist between the governing class and the governed'. Once the locals had acquired adequate mastery of English, Baker claimed they would at last 'feel themselves a portion of our empire'.[11]

This view was endorsed by Sir Robert Biddulph during his time as high commissioner [1879–1886]. In a despatch to London in 1880, he maintained that 'by teaching [the Cypriots] English we open to them the door to every species of modern learning and advancement, for we shall thus give them the means of access to every branch of human knowledge'.[12] For Biddulph and Baker the acquisition of English was a practical necessity, if Cypriots were to function effectively as loyal subjects of an English-speaking empire.

But crucially for Cyprus, Biddulph's plans to follow standard colonial practice and establish English as the medium of education were overruled by Lord Kimberley, the secretary of state for the colonies. Kimberley insisted that Cyprus was a special case and that consequently Cypriots should be taught in one of 'the two ancient languages of the island'.[13] It was a statement of policy that was to have profound and enduring consequences for Cyprus and for Anglo-Cypriot relations up until independence. But at the end of the nineteenth century, with no understanding of the complications that would ensue, Kimberley maintained that 'the rich and varied literature of ancient Greece' proved beyond doubt that Greek afforded 'ample means, not only for ordinary education, but for the attainment of a high degree of mental culture'.[14] This veneration for Classical Greek as the language that underpinned Western civilisation contributed to the failure of colonial education policy in Cyprus and subsequently determined much of the character of the violent struggle for independence during the 1950s.

Kimberley had graduated from Oxford University with a first-class degree in Classics and would have been more familiar than most men of his class with the rich and varied literature he referred to in his landmark policy statement. But while the secretary of state was an exceptional Classicist, all young men who passed through British public schools during the second part of the nineteenth century were required to have a thorough knowledge of the literature and languages of ancient Greece and Rome.

The classical curriculum followed by the privileged youth of Britain may appear far removed from the colonisation of Cyprus, but it formed an essential part of the cultural legacy which the island's civilian administrators brought with them and was to fashion the lens through which they viewed Cyprus and the Cypriots.

The emphasis placed on ancient languages at English public schools was dictated by the entry requirements of Oxford and Cambridge Universities and was also integral to the process by which young men from the elite social classes were themselves 'civilised' and prepared for leadership and public service. Study of the Classics was intended to instil in upper-middle-class youths an awareness of their duty as elevated public servants and of 'the ideal of a noble oligarchy'.[15] This was a potent ideology that shaped public perceptions of British national identity until well after the First World War. For Paul Griffin, headmaster of the English School in Nicosia in 1956–60, to be an English gentleman meant, in ideological terms, to be a Hellene. 'Most Englishmen are culturally Greeks, we are all Philhellenes,' he said; 'I am myself, much as I loved my Turkish pupils.'[16]

Thomas Arnold, the influential classicist and headmaster of Rugby School, believed it was only through studying Classical languages that students could gain proper mastery of their own. 'Every lesson in Greek or Latin', he argued, 'ought to be made a lesson in English.'[17] As late as the 1950s, all pupils at Newham's English School, whether they were Greek or Turkish Cypriot, Armenian, or Lebanese Druze, spent several hours a week studying Classical Greek and ancient Greek history.[18]

Public school classicists were actively recruited for imperial postings and competence in Greek and Latin carried more weight in colonial civil service entrance examinations than a corresponding ability in French or German.[19] As a result, British colonial administrators of the nineteenth and early twentieth centuries had no training in the practicalities of district administration, local customs or religious practices but set out to govern the empire having read, in the original Greek, Thucydides' *History of the Peloponnesian Wars*, the plays of Aeschylus, Sophocles and Euripides, the *Odyssey* and the *Iliad*, along with Aristotle's ethics.

Some schools chose to dilute this mixture with a little more Latin, but this curriculum formed the basis of the education that all university-educated governors and high commissioners of Cyprus received, along with most of their senior administrative staff, until the mid-twentieth century.[20] It was against this background (and the extent to which their subjects conformed to or deviated from their own carefully constructed image of Classical Greece) that most of the colony's administrators viewed their Greek Cypriot subjects during the first 50 years of its existence.

Thus, when Governor Ronald Storrs (1926–32), a Classics scholar of Charterhouse and Cambridge, visited the island's Greek Orthodox Archbishop Kyrillos III, he was disappointed to find the latter's knowledge of ancient Greek to be so weak that 'it would have been defeated by an average sixth form boy in a competition in classical Greek prose iambics'.[21]

This particularly Westernised version of Ancient Greece provided a charter for Victorian imperialism that was enthusiastically embraced by generations of young men. Arnold ensured his pupils understood the special relationship they enjoyed with the Ancient Greeks when he wrote, 'Aristotle and Plato and Thucydides and Cicero ... are most untruly called ancient writers; they are virtually our own countrymen and contemporaries.'[22] Aristotle and Plato may have been Thracian and Athenian respectively by birth, but their genius – their legacy – belonged firmly to the young men of nineteenth-century British public schools.

So, when, in 1889, classical antiquities unearthed at Salamis on the east coast of Cyprus were shipped back to Britain, they found their way not only to the British Museum in London but also to the universities of Oxford and Cambridge, specifically to the public schools of Eton, Harrow, Winchester, Rugby, Charterhouse, Westminster and Marlborough.[23] For Arnold and those of his class, the relics were coming home.[24]

Once appropriated by British imperial culture, ancient Greek civilisation fulfilled an important function within the colonising process. It facilitated the creation of a distance between the rulers and the ruled, 'the notion that the colonists possessed a deep civilization going back to Plato and Aristotle was essential to both their own sense of categorical superiority and the acceptance of this European cultural dominance by local elites'.[25]

But for British colonists in Cyprus it created a particular dilemma: how to reconcile the ideological foundations of empire with a colony where Greek was their subjects' mother tongue? In Cyprus, the Greek-speaking majority appeared to have a prior linguistic and racial claim to 'the well-springs of civilization'. If a major function of the mastery of Classical languages was to reinforce the exclusivity of the governing elite, it must have been disconcerting for the colonists to administer a territory where large numbers of their new subjects, by virtue of being native Greek speakers, also appeared to have access to the same secret knowledge, albeit of the modern, not the Classical, language. The situation was compounded, in the eyes of the colonists, by the Cypriots' obvious inability to live up to the legacy of their classical forefathers. From the colonists' perspective, the islanders' intense poverty, along with the absence of an aristocratic ruling class, placed Cypriot culture lower down in the imperial hierarchy than, for example, that of India, Nigeria or the Gold Coast, where the indigenous aristocracy possessed both money and the distinction of inherited privilege.

The colonists responded to these inconsistencies in a variety of ways. For example, Governor Ronald Storrs saw the Cypriots as a lost people who had effectively lived in the wilderness since the decline of Ancient Greece and needed to be re-connected to their illustrious past. In doing so they chose to ignore those aspects of more recent history which underlined their Greek Cypriot subjects' historical and cultural difference: the Byzantine Empire, the Greek war of independence, and the Greek Orthodox Church were overlooked.

The books held at Nicosia public library today offer insight into this highly selective colonial reading of the island's past. The library, founded by Governor Storrs in 1927, was 'in continual demand (especially owing to its warmth in winter)'.[26] A plain, undecorated single-storey building on top of the Venetian city walls, it was one of the few public spaces where Britons and Cypriots could, in theory at least, meet on equal terms. Many of the original 4,000 volumes acquired in 1927 are still there, in dark dusty stacks at the back of the periodicals room. As the governor of a tiny, impoverished colony, with no cash to spare, Storrs launched a personal appeal for contributions amongst his friends and contacts. As a result, the collection covered almost exclusively the arts and humanities and displayed a particular bias towards those ancient writers taught at Oxbridge and the older public schools.

When the library finally opened, the more prosperous members of the literate Nicosia bourgeoisie – the merchants, lawyers and government clerks – were invited to pay between two and twenty shillings, no small sum, to borrow the works of Plato, Homer, Aeschylus and Sophocles, all in Classical Greek. The pristine condition of these books and the absence of borrowing stamps suggest that none was ever removed from the shelves. Equally unpopular were *The Archaic Inscriptions and the Greek Alphabet*, *Seven Essays on Christian Greece*, translated into English from the original Greek by the Marquis of Bute, and *Select Epigrams from the Greek Anthology*, a volume which the editors hoped 'may be useful in the upper forms of schools and acceptable to lovers of poetry generally'. On the same shelf are three well-thumbed and dog-eared paperbacks dating from roughly the same time and apparently more widely read: *Practical Methods to Insure Success*; *The Cause of In-harmony in Marriage;* and *Control of the Mind*. For Storrs, the library project afforded the opportunity to guide what he regarded as his debased and neglected subjects towards a particularly *British* interpretation of their ancient civilisation. Knowledge of Ancient Greece was, therefore, to be gleaned from the Marquis of Bute and his English translation, rather than the original sources.

A similar process occurs in the writings of the ebullient classicist Harry Luke, who served as ADC to Governor Hamilton Goold-Adams immediately before the First World War. Years after leaving the island Luke attempted to write a brief account of the armed struggle for union or *enosis* with Greece. This was a violent and frightening time that affected all aspects of life on the island between 1955 and 1960 and irrevocably damaged Anglo-Cypriot relations. But Luke was only able to explain the phenomenon in the entirely apolitical terminology of the linguist. *Enosis*, he explained to his readers, as they struggled to understand the reasons for the bloody assassinations and collective punishments that characterised those years, was actually an incorrect transliteration: 'It should really be "*Hénosis*" since the initial short Greek 'E' is preceded by the rough breathing represented by 'H' of the word "Ενωσις" meaning "union".'[27]

The disparity between the academic philhellenism of Storrs and Luke and the realities of early twentieth-century Cyprus should not be surprising. Their classicism was a product of their own Northern European culture. It had scant connection with modern Greece where only the educated minority thought in terms of classical culture and 'it was largely in the west that they found the encouragement to do so.'[28] Nevertheless when applied to a Cypriot context it proved particularly debilitating since it inhibited Storrs and Luke – and other public-school-educated administrators of their class – from engaging with the realities of Cypriot politics. But perhaps the most damaging consequence of viewing Cyprus from the perspective of Ancient Greece was a tendency that emerges in the writings of both Storrs and Luke, to find Greek Cypriots a constant source of disappointment. They were neither exotically Oriental nor did they corresponded to Western ideas about classical nobility and as such always fell slightly short of the mark. It was a disappointment that led to a particular kind of intolerance bordering on contempt.

Thus Storrs recalled the remarks of a legal official who had served in East Africa and complained to the governor ' "I understand a white gentleman ... and a black gentleman, though I don't let him touch me"; the man said, "but these betwixts and betweens I don't want to understand." '[29] In fairness Storrs pointed out to his reader that the 'betwixts and betweens' had often been trained at the inns of court in London and could generally play a passable game of lawn tennis. But a residual sense remains in his writing, that he too saw his Greek Cypriot subjects as occupying a half-way house.

In the same way the writer and illustrator Gladys Peto's description of her own household demonstrates some of the colonists' ambivalence towards their culturally diverse subjects. The exoticism of Turkish Cypriot servants, who waited at table in 'magnificent Turkish clothes, full trousers, a *fez*, a wonderful sash, and an embroidered waistcoat', was a thing to be admired. But Peto's Greek Cypriot parlour maid – with her black frock, white apron and handkerchief round her head, arranged so that 'her hair hangs down in plaits behind'[30] – was actively dissuaded from wearing her own more understated costume. Instead, the maid was encouraged to adopt the dress conventions of the Western European servant, by coiling up her hair and putting on a cap, collar and cuffs, in order to be considered presentable. The maid, not orientalised like the Turkish Cypriot manservant, was expected to assimilate British dress conventions and social norms.

The majority of the Cypriot population was illiterate at the time of the British arrival in Cyprus. Few communities had schools and most families were too poor to finance the education of a child who would remain economically unproductive as long as he was in the classroom. In the decade immediately prior to the British occupation the island's 64 Muslim schools received around £400 a year from the Ottoman administration. The 76 Christian schools, however, were financed entirely by voluntary subscriptions and donations from church funds and monasteries. Virtually all educated professional Greek Cypriots of the nineteenth century, therefore, felt they owed a deep debt of gratitude to the church.

During the centuries of Ottoman rule in Cyprus and Greece, the Orthodox Church had come to view education as its principal, in many instances its only, weapon in the battle for the survival of Hellenism. The cherished dream of one day reuniting Cyprus with Greece could be realised only by fostering a sense of pride in Cypriots' Greek identity. With no common territorial or political base, the only way to achieve this was by developing a shared linguistic heritage. Greek Cypriots were – and would again be – Greek because they spoke and understood the language of aristocratic Athenians of the fourth century BC. To surrender control of the educational mechanism which delivered this doctrine of patriotism was tantamount to relinquishing all hope that the dream would ever be realised.

The arrival of the British in the nineteenth century and the introduction of another foreign administration had no impact on these deeply held convictions. As a result, control of the country's education system became, for the Orthodox Church, one of the most contentious aspects of colonial rule.

Soon after the establishment of Newham's English School, articles appeared in the island's Greek language newspapers discouraging Cypriot parents from sending their children to foreign schools. It was feared they would 'change the national and religious ideas of students',[31] and that children would lose the ability to speak Greek correctly and with it the capacity to 'think with a Greek spirit'.[32]

Britain's education policy in Cyprus has been politely described by one Cypriot historian as 'laissez-faire'.[33] It was a policy born out of a failure to agree on a policy. Formulating one that would be appropriate for what was admittedly an unusually complex colony involved engaging decisively with the issue of who exactly Cypriots were and what part the new subjects were to play in the imperial scheme of things. Were the islanders essentially Oriental hybrids, who should be ruled in an authoritarian manner appropriate to their status, educated according to practical, utilitarian principles and assimilated into the British Empire? Or did the linguistic and cultural Greekness of the majority afford them a special status by virtue of their connection with the classical world? Were they the true inheritors of a culture which was acclaimed in the classrooms of Winchester, Charterhouse and other public schools as 'the first universal civilization ... the cultural ancestor of the Europeans ... the essence of the world itself'?[34]

Much of this confusion over what Cypriots were to be educated for dated back to Kimberley's lofty parliamentary statement of 1881 about the ennobling character of ancient Greek and its suitability as a medium for moulding young minds to embrace concepts of public service and fair play. But his much-cited Philhellenism may just have been a convenient justification for a decision that was actually made on financial grounds. It was cheaper to leave things as they were.

Kimberley went on to tell Parliament in London that government grants to village schools could only supplement the villagers' own contributions and should not lead communities 'to discontinue wholly or partially their voluntary expenditure for the support of education'.[35] If Cypriots were to continue to pay for their children's education themselves, the colonial administration could hardly insist that it should then be conducted in a foreign language.

One result of this was that Greek Cypriot schoolboys in the second half of the nineteenth century spent much of their time reciting the same ancient Greek texts as their counterparts at Rugby and Eton. But when Aristotle, Plato and Thucydides were read aloud in Cypriot village schools they were intended to instil a sense of Hellenic patriotism, specifically of Greek national pride.

As a result Storrs found the teaching of Classics at Cypriot schools 'vulgar and monotonous'. During the course of one college inspection he was intrigued by a locked bookcase at the back of a classroom that appeared to contain a set of Greek classics. When at last the key to the bookcase was found, Storrs was disgusted to find the books had never been opened and the pages inside remained uncut.

After centuries of foreign domination when the principal custodian of scholarship and learning was the deeply conservative church, Greek intellectual life was hardly at its most vibrant. But for the schoolmasters in charge of the locked bookcase of Classics it was perhaps unnecessary for their pupils to be able to read or understand its contents. Its very existence – as a physical presence, a talisman in the classroom – was enough to remind students of their ancient Classical roots. Storrs, who at one level seems never to have reconciled himself to the fact that Greek Cypriots were not ancient Athenians, was dismissive: 'constant as Homer, Aeschylus and Sophocles were on the lips of local orators, it was their names rather than their verses which were cited'.[36]

This uncertainty over the ethnic and cultural identity of the colony was to remain for the entirety of British rule. Policy see-sawed, depending often on the personal inclination and educational background of whoever happened to be in Government House at the time.

William Haynes-Smith, for example, who governed the island for seven years from 1897, persistently attempted to bring elementary school curricula under government control. During official visits to Greek Cypriot classrooms he had been aggrieved to find 'Greek maps describing all Asia Minor and much besides as part of the Greek Kingdom'. Haynes-Smith begrudged the public money spent on 'teaching the young Cypriots much rubbish of a similar kind of inflation'.[37] But his proposals were rejected by the Legislative Council on the grounds that they undermined the influence of the church. The issue was raised – and rejected – every year thereafter until the end of Haynes-Smith's tenure, when the plan was quietly shelved by his more Philhellenic successor, Charles King-Harman.

Subsequent governors were compelled to accept that Greek Cypriot education had effectively 'developed to become a branch of the mainland Greek educational system'.[38] Even in the middle of World War Two, when Greece itself was under Nazi occupation and Cyprus had only narrowly escaped the same fate, the island's education department conscientiously wrote to the Greek government-in-exile in Egypt, requesting permission to reprint copies of *The Greek Reader*, the standard text then used in Greek Cypriot classrooms.[39]

The economic basis on which the island's schools were run – with government funding only matching local contributions, and where donations from the church or from Cypriots abroad were essential – made it inevitable that Greek elementary schools should 'be used largely for fostering the Hellenic idea'. In 1918, the island's chief secretary complained that 'there is hardly a school in the island whose walls are not adorned with portraits of the Greek royal family; Greek flags are displayed on all occasions, and Greek Independence Day celebrated every year with great fervour'.[40]

Occasional concessions were made to Cypriot circumstances, as when locally produced handbooks on hygiene and farming were introduced in the classroom in 1908. Six years later it was stipulated that a map of Cyprus in Greek was to be hung on the walls of every classroom.[41] But this experiment was short-lived. By 1927 Storrs complained that even the brightest Greek Cypriot pupils, though 'always exactly informed as to the distance between Athens and Thebes ... would hazard guesses varying from 120 to 1,500 miles as to the length or breadth of their own country'.[42]

Like others before him, Storrs expressed concern over the absence of portraits of 'English Sovereigns, adorning the walls'.[43] Perhaps as a result, in 1934
an 'anonymous donor' despatched a consignment of 1,050 portraits of George
V and Queen Mary to the colony.[44] These were distributed amongst the
island's 759 schools and two of the remaining 221 portraits can be seen hanging above the stairs at the former residence of the British high commissioner in
Shakespeare Avenue in Turkish-controlled northern Nicosia.

The educational mechanism established under Lord Kimberely and maintained by other public school classicists such as Storrs, Luke, Bertram and their
ilk nurtured the nationalist aspirations of Greek Cypriots and laid the ground
for many of the defining characteristics of the EOKA struggle for union with
Greece in the 1950s. One direct consequence was the number of violent episodes in that conflict acted out in and around the island's schools, with children
at the vanguard.

An ambivalence similar to that which characterised the colony's education
policy was demonstrated in the colonists' approach to the rearing of British
children on the island. Despite the existence of a certain racial and social distance between the rulers and the ruled, many parents hoped that their children would learn Greek, largely because of the language's special status. Some
children, such as Eirwen Llewellyn Jones, whose father managed the Ottoman
Bank in Nicosia during the 1920s, spoke Greek fluently.

In marked contrast to their counterparts in India, colonial parents in Cyprus
expressed no anxiety that their children might become culturally 'contami-
nated' by contact with local children or servants. Elsewhere in the empire large
amounts of energy were expended trying to protect children from the dangers of
cultural or linguistic assimilation with the colonial subjects. For British parents
in India, 'young children's ability to understand and converse in Hindustani
or other tongues with more ease than English was both feared and detested'.[45]
Mastery of Greek, however, even Modern Greek, was considered socially desirable. It is conspicuous that few parents appear to have encouraged their children to learn Turkish. This may have been because, as the minority language,
it was of less practical use, or because, unlike Greek, it was not perceived as the
elevated tongue of classical civilisation but as an Oriental language, which was
accorded a correspondingly lower status in the linguistic hierarchy.

William Battershill, the island's Greek-speaking governor at the outbreak of
the Second World War, was so determined that his children should also learn to
speak Greek that he recruited a Cypriot nanny. The young woman, Ellie, stayed
with the family for many years, regularly teasing her employer for his own poor
Greek pronunciation and 'what she thought was his appalling accent'.[46] The
acquisition of Greek appears to have assumed less significance for Battershill as
his children grew older, when he advertised for an English governess. In 1939,

struggling both to prepare for a possible German invasion and to deal with two boisterous ebullient daughters, he confided in his weekly letter to his mother that he no longer cared what the governess was like, 'as long as she disciplines the children'. The long-suffering governor hoped in vain that his daughters might set an example appropriate to their social situation. They had recently been involved in two 'unfortunate incidents', noisily dropping the collection money on the floor during Sunday church, and kicking the Government House *kavass* (the ceremonially armed Turkish Cypriot guard who stood to attention outside the door of the residence) on the bottom as he bent over to tie up his shoelace. A month after the new appointee arrived, the governor grimly informed his mother that 'the children have locked their new governess in the lavatory'.[47]

A decade later, Ivan Lloyd Phillips, the district commissioner of Nicosia, hoped his young son, Hugh, would pick up basic Greek vocabulary. Lloyd Phillips asked his parents in England to post their grandson a copy of *The Heroes*, Charles Kingsley's popular children's version of the ancient Greek myths.[48] Lloyd Phillips' vague aspiration that Hugh might acquire what would in practice have been colloquial Cypriot Greek appears to have been motivated, not by a desire for his son to communicate with Cypriots, but by a hope that the language might provide him with a route to access the culture of Ancient Greece and all that this implied.

Although most parents were generally more relaxed about limited inter-racial contact than their counterparts elsewhere in the empire, British colonial children growing up on the island had little to do with their Cypriot peers. Growing up in Cyprus in the 1930s, Donald Waterer had no close Cypriot friends and learnt no Greek, despite the fact that his father, who worked in the Forestry Department, socialised extensively with Cypriot families. A generation later, Matthew Parris, who arrived in Cyprus with his family as a four-year-old in 1954, had similar experiences: 'Cypriot children were just there in the background, you saw them playing their own games out on waste ground, but you couldn't speak to them unless you spoke their language. We were completely un-integrated with the majority community.'[49]

But if mixing with Cypriot youngsters was problematic, there would have been no shortage of British children to play with. Despite initial anxieties about the prevalence of malaria in the years immediately after the British arrived, Cyprus was regarded as one of the healthiest of Britain's imperial possessions, and, unlike Africa and parts of India, safe for young families.

In 1926, Gladys Peto, whose book *Cyprus and Malta* offered helpful tips to young colonial wives embarking on new lives in Britain's European territories, reassured her readers that 'children do very well on the island'. Even so Peto warned that 'a continual war must be waged against flies, and you must naturally beware of the midday sun'.[50]

Protecting northern European children from the sun was a constant concern and most were forbidden to play outside without a sola topi. Little Donald Waterer was allowed to accompany his father on forest trips only if he was appropriately dressed in his topi, which, on ceremonial occasions, had to be teamed up with a kilt.

Privileged colonial children spent most of their time outdoors, cycling, swimming, or riding. Horses were the main source of recreation for many. The Waterer children kept their ponies in a field adjacent to the family home in Byron Avenue Nicosia.[51] Some of the old colonial residences on Byron Avenue remain even today – functional stone buildings, designed in the utilitarian tradition of the PWD, fronting on to a noisy, busy thoroughfare. In the 1930s, as Brenda Waterer recalls, 'you just rode out across the old riverbed, and there wasn't a building after that, you could ride straight across country.' Jane Battershill, a contemporary of Brenda's, accompanied her father on early morning rides from Government House to the neighbouring village of Strovolos and, along with both her parents, took part in mounted paper chases across the Messaoria plain on Sundays.

British children in Cyprus, as in other colonies, occupied a middle-ground between the colonisers and the colonised. Members of the elite governing class, they nevertheless spent much of their time in the company of Cypriot servants. Many lived quite separately from their parents. Jane Battershill and her sister occupied an entirely self-contained children's wing at Government House, joining their parents only for set-piece events such as Sunday lunch or Christmas dinner.

Providing 'a normal British Christmas',[52] despite living in a foreign land, assumed great importance to most colonial families, who went to considerable lengths to adapt British Christmas traditions to local circumstances. Some of the conventions they initiated became firmly entrenched in colonial society and were upheld by successive expatriate families over decades. Several generations of colonial children in Nicosia believed that celebrations would not be complete until Father Christmas had ridden along Byron Avenue, mounted on a camel. During the 1930s this role was assigned to Geoff Chapman, the assistant head of the Forestry Department, who 'was piped along the avenue by a Scotsman dressed in a kilt'.[53]

For colonial children in Cyprus, as elsewhere, life carried on in the knowledge that at some point they would be separated from their parents and sent home to England for education and 'the acquisition of appropriate cultural values'.[54] For all its high academic standards and careful cultivation of the ideals of the English public school system, Newham's English School was inherently unsuitable for the children of British civil servants, precisely because it was located within the colony itself. Eirwen Harbottle (formerly Llewellyn Jones)

Geoff Chapman, later Conservator of Forests, about to make his entrance as Father Christmas, c. 1937–41.

[*Reproduced courtesy of the Chapman family.*]

remembers that 'English families didn't send their children to local schools. It wasn't done.'[55] The perpetuation of empire and the British way of life demanded that imperial children should at some stage be sent home in order to ensure they became securely rooted in the British class and racial structure.

Despite the stereotype of the stiff upper lip associated with British colonial rule, families found the separation traumatic. Autobiographical accounts of life in more distant colonies, such as India, contain graphic descriptions of 'weeping mothers [taking] their children down to the great trading ports ... and handing them over to be taken "Home" and brought up by relatives, or in many cases ... strangers'.[56] Such children often did not see their parents again for many years.

By comparison, families posted to Cyprus were fortunate. Closer proximity to Britain meant that children could usually come home at least once a year. Gladys Peto's apparently flippant observation that Cyprus's principal advantage was that it was 'so near home'[57] would have been read more seriously by her female readers, primarily responsible for guiding their families through the frequent separations that colonial life entailed.

While this geographical proximity enabled families to remain in touch, it also served to underline the dilemma the British experienced in Cyprus. Here, the tried and tested techniques of colonial rule appeared not to work. Nowhere in the empire-building rule book were there instructions on how to engage with a mainly Christian population, situated on the edge of Europe, possessing an undeniable linguistic claim to the cultural heritage that underpinned the British empire itself.

The British colonists found the island's inhabitants, the 'betwixts and betweens' who spoke classical Greek badly (such as Archbishop Kyrillos) or wore their hair in plaits in a poor imitation of European fashions (such as Gladys Peto's maid) both disconcerting and disappointing. Cypriots were not sufficiently different from their colonial rulers to be exoticised. Yet the imprint of (an essentially Anglicised) Hellenism that many sought in Cyprus proved so faint, it could be interpreted only as a pale, inferior imitation of the original. This was an issue that the colonists were never to resolve and Cypriots' status within the ideological hierarchy of colonial peoples remained ambiguous throughout the British occupation.

It is perhaps not surprising, therefore, given their profound misgivings about the identity of their subjects, that the colonists felt far more comfortable addressing the issue of how best to modernise and develop the island.

4

Softening Our Rough Peasantry
1900–14

It is Sunday morning on a gloomy February day at the old terminal building of Famagusta Railway Station. A young woman in jeans and a blue shirt is serving Turkish coffee from a circular metal tray. Today's employees are not railway workers but staff of the municipality's housing department, on this particular Sunday they are at work to earn overtime. Two young clerks slowly sip their coffees behind a high counter in what was once the ticket hall. A framed photograph of Turkish Cypriot leader Mehmet Ali Talat hangs on the wall behind them.

The garden in the station forecourt is overgrown, full of yellow Cape Sorrel and purple mallow. Conifers still line the station approach. The clock shows the time as 11.30, although its hands are frozen and its face has long since lost its numbers. The station yard at the back of the building is now occupied by Famagusta Fire Service. The firemen sit outside, opposite the old engine sheds, playing cards. Their equipment is polished and shining, and everything, from the table they sit at to the trunks of two adjacent medlar trees, has been painted white and red.

There is little here today that evokes the atmosphere of a busy railway terminus. But the opening of the Famagusta to Nicosia railway in 1905 marked the beginning of a new period in the colonists' relationship to the island when the first serious attempts were made to leave a British stamp on the territory. The period between 1900 and 1910 saw a burst of development in Cyprus. Roads and railways were constructed, livestock breeding programmes introduced, extensive irrigation projects established and malarial swamps drained – programmes designed primarily to improve the colony's productivity and economic value, but which also constituted part of the reforming, redemptive mission of empire. The co-ordinated promotion of agricultural reform marked the beginning of the administration's relationship with the rural peasantry and a policy of intervention in village life, which continued until independence.

The sudden acceleration in agricultural and economic development which saw Cyprus begin to emerge from the 'stagnation' and 'Rip Van Winkleism'[1] of the previous 20 years was largely due to the combined efforts of Charles King-Harman, the high commissioner in Nicosia, and Joseph Chamberlain, the new secretary of state for the colonies in London.

Chamberlain was a staunch imperialist, arguably just the sort of ally the island needed after decades of neglect and under-investment, and he condemned the 'parsimony displayed [by the government] in every matter where Cyprus has been concerned'.[2]

In 1899 he oversaw the passing of the Colonial Loans Act, which marked a fundamental shift in Britain's relationship with its empire. The act meant that 'the imperial government had finally accepted the principle of responsibility for the economic development of its colonies'.[3] In Cyprus it secured funding for the development of a railway and an expanded harbour at Famagusta.

Six years later, on 21 October 1905, High Commissioner Charles King-Harman stood in front of Famagusta railway station, where the ticket office and engine sheds were draped with union flags and olive branches, to declare the railway line officially open. The single-track line ran from Famagusta to Nicosia, stopping at 18 halts on the way.

The co-ordinated development of Famagusta port and the railway was intended to boost Cypriot agricultural exports. The railway's route would enable the transport of charcoal and timber from the higher altitudes of the Troodos Mountains; citrus, olives, carobs and wine from the foothills; and grain, cotton and potatoes from the Messaoria plain. But there would be other incidental benefits too. Just as the land was being managed, cultivated and controlled, so it was hoped the rural peasantry could also be enlightened and reformed. As early as 1894 the *Times of Cyprus* had observed that 'a railway would do more to educate, civilise and soften our rough peasantry by giving them the opportunities of visiting the large towns of the island than can well be imagined ... the villages on the line of route would improve ... and a new order of things would date from the starting of the first train on the Island'.[4]

The railway's construction was painfully slow and early plans to extend the track up as far as the Troodos Hill Station were soon abandoned as too expensive. In 1902, increasingly frustrated as the costs of the project increased, Charles Bellamy, the director of the Public Works Department, suggested ever more drastic economies, writing in a memo to the Secretariat that 'stations are superfluous, signals not essential'.[5] Although the network did eventually include stations, it managed to function without signals for nearly 50 years, relying instead on the alertness of its 'pointsmen' who were equipped with flags and positioned at the approaches to the main stations.

Despite Bellamy's efforts the railway was not an immediate success and for its first decade it operated at a considerable loss. Trains meandered across the plain making 'an occasional stop, regardless of whether there was a station or not, to pick up or put down passengers' or to allow people on board to sell 'baskets of produce of all kinds'.[6] But the 'rough peasantry' were reluctant to ride on the railway, continuing to use camels, mules and donkeys to transport themselves and their produce. Many colonists were baffled by this preference, indignantly condemning the villagers for being 'content to gape at the passing train, as if it were intended to afford amusement rather than be of use'.[7]

The railway also had an important role to play in the public life of the island, providing the official mode of transport for dignitaries and government officials arriving at Famagusta Port. On such occasions one of the 'miniature engines'[8] would be draped in a Union flag and decorated with bunting, flags were hung above the footplate of one of the 'box cars on wheels'[9] that served as first-class carriages, and a commode was installed discretely inside. The official visitor was then required to stand on the open platform of the carriage for the next two hours waving at 'the curious peasantry', as he 'chugged along backwards'[10] to Nicosia.

Winston Churchill, who visited the island as under-secretary of state for the colonies in October 1907, was one of the first to endure this ritual. Photographs from the King-Harman family album[11] show a slightly nervous young man in a crisp white suit standing on the carriage footplate, preparing to acknowledge the 'large and gay crowds waving hundreds of Greek flags and shouting for union with Greece',[12] which had turned out to mark the beginning of his journey.

As a junior minister, Churchill was in no position to make policy decisions on the island's future, and during his meetings with Greek and Turkish Cypriot delegations he tactfully deflected the question of *enosis* or union with Greece. But his junior status did not deter him from writing a thundering memo to Lord Elgin, the foreign secretary, condemning the continued payment of the Tribute as being 'quite unworthy of Great Britain and altogether out of accordance with the whole principles of our colonial policy in every part of the world, a blemish upon Imperial policy of a particularly discreditable kind'.[13]

While the moral basis of his argument was irrefutable, it did little – in the short term at least – to help the island's situation. The Treasury dismissed the memo as an 'insane minute', while senior civil servants in Churchill's own department criticised him for his 'uncontrollable desire for notoriety' and general 'lack of moral perception'.[14]

Churchill's visit to the island took place against a backdrop of growing Cypriot politicisation. The 'large and gay' crowd that demanded union with Greece from the young under-secretary as he stepped aboard the Nicosia train was itself enmeshed in a bitter and long-standing domestic dispute – over the election of the next Greek Orthodox archbishop. Following the death of the previous incumbent, Archbishop Sofronios in 1900, two rival contenders, the bishops of Kition and Kyrenia, had each claimed the archepiscopal throne. The church election was the only forum in which Greek Cypriots within the island's disenfranchised population could express themselves politically and consequently assumed enormous significance. The bishop of Kition advocated immediate *enosis*, while the bishop of Kyrenia prioritised the gradual democratic reform of the administration's governing Legislative Council. It was in the context of this dispute that the railway did finally play, as the *Times of Cyprus* had hoped, a significant role in introducing Cypriots to modernity, although not in the way the newspaper had envisaged.

In April 1908, 'two hundred partisans' arrived en masse in Nicosia, having come by 'the 11 a.m. train from Famagusta' from the villages of the Messaoria plain – one of the first recorded incidents of the new transport service on the island being used in this way. The 'partisans' marched to the centre of the capital and proceeded to 'riot' in front of the post office. Martial law was declared, troops deployed and 'it was not until much property was destroyed and several heads tapped that [the police] began to regain control of the streets'.[15]

The incident must have been a disappointment for those who had believed that science and technological progress could tame and order the colony, and later generations of colonists expressed nostalgia for the innocence of the pre-railway age. In 1931 a correspondent for the *Cyprus News* imagined himself in Ledra Street in Nicosia several centuries previously, a time when 'no huge dormitory on wheels offends by belching forth evil-smelling smoke. All is as it was ... a happy, jolly, contented people, desirous of living and of letting live, confounding worshippers of that juggernaut of progress'.[16]

The railway symbolised – more strongly than any other British colonial project in Cyprus – the island's introduction to the modern age, dragged by the coal-fired engines of the imperial power. But many colonists felt ambivalent about their desire for progress – particularly economic progress – regretting the loss of both innocence and Oriental exoticism that modernisation brought with it. The 'dormitory on wheels' – obviously not the diminutive Cyprus railway with its boxcar coaches and request stops, but a generic engine of progress – now posed a threat to the natural order of things and the 'happy, jolly contented people' of the island. The innocent peasantry, the *Cyprus News* suggested, now needed protection from the engines of civilisation that the colonists had brought with them.

The process of ordering and reforming the colony had been given new momentum by Chamberlain's Colonial Loans Act, which had also released funds for the development of agriculture on the island. This was a formidable undertaking, one that involved not only technical innovation but also the symbolic domination of the landscape, and, more problematically, the establishment of a relationship with the Cypriot peasant farmer.

Three centuries of Ottoman tax farming had left the Cypriot peasantry in a wretched condition and the island's agriculture neglected. The practice essentially involved selling the right to collect taxes in a particular district to the highest bidder. Putative tax farmers, or *aghas*, often borrowed heavily in order to secure a concession and consequently needed to extract the maximum revenue over the shortest possible time. Without incentive to invest in the colony, its infrastructure was allowed to decay, while extortionate rates of taxation 'impoverished the peasant, involving him in the toils of the money-lender'[17] in order to survive.

The most graphic account of conditions amongst the rural poor during the first half of British colonial rule was written by explorer and agricultural reformer Sir Samuel Baker, who travelled extensively across the island in 1879, one year after the British occupation. Baker encountered villages which were 'mere copies of each other in filth and squalor' inhabited by 'half clad and shivering'[18] children, with the distended abdomens associated with malnutrition, and blind beggars and 'sickly' women, their 'throats and breasts literally covered with ancient and modern fleabites'.[19] He found emaciated cattle 'in a state of weakness that scarcely allowed them, step by step, to ascend the rising ground', and an abject population which exhibited 'a patience and stolid endurance which is beyond all praise'.[20]

Although Baker only passed through Cyprus, staying for little more than a year, his record of the living conditions of the peasantry is unique. Unlike other colonial writers, he did not attempt to romanticise their poverty; his frank descriptions contain a degree of detail and specificity lacking in subsequent accounts of rural life on the island. This may be in part due to the fact that he arrived soon after the start of the British occupation and was, therefore, able to publish his impressions without any implied criticism of the administration.

Baker had been advised that there was no suitable accommodation for travellers in Cyprus, so he procured a 'gypsy travelling van' which enabled him and his wife to 'select a desirable resting-place in any portion of the island, where the route should be practicable for wheeled conveyances'. The travellers were accompanied by their three spaniels and several locally hired retainers, engaged to manage the luggage train, cook meals and act as translators. Not surprisingly, crowds of curious spectators gathered to look at this unusual caravan as it passed; wherever they struck camp 'the lame, the halt and the sick' were brought out in the hope of a cure. The lifestyle of the peasants Baker encountered in 1879 had barely changed by the time the Colonial Development Act sanctioned a loan for the island's first co-ordinated water-management system nearly 30 years later.

The system, completed in 1901, consisted of three reservoirs and 18 miles of 'training banks'[21] and sluices, which between them irrigated an area of 50 square miles in the eastern Messaoria plain. Two of the three reservoirs were subsequently abandoned and the network proved to be an expensive failure. But just as the development of the railway had been expected to civilise and 'soften' the peasantry, so the management and control of the island's water supply was believed to offer moral and spiritual redemption to the colonial subjects. The irrigation system represented an important element in the business of ordering and improving the colony and consolidated the ideological – as well as the economic – foundations of the empire.[22]

Water in the Messaoria was expected to produce not only 'external peace and material prosperity' but also a far more profound personal transformation, nothing less than that 'individual and general moral progress, which is the vital history of the East'.[23] The practicalities of increasing productivity, of growing more potatoes, wheat or barley, were seen as synonymous with the reform of the personal behaviour and ethical conduct of the Cypriot peasant.

The profound symbolic importance the colonists attached to the supply and control of water had been spelled out by Samuel Baker in 1879, more than 20 years earlier. Water, he proclaimed, 'should be the slave of man, to whom it is the first necessity; therefore his first effort in his struggle with the elements should reduce this power to vassalage. There must be no question of supremacy; water must serve mankind.'

This is extraordinary language to use in connection with what would in practice be a system of pipes, ditches and sluice gates, particularly coming from the pen of a practical man such as Baker. It suggests that he was writing not only about H_2O, but also about the need for the colonists to establish dominance over their new subjects. In fact, Baker was clear about the connection between the need to control the water supply and the need to control the Cypriots and their economic productivity: 'The main strength of a country lies in an annual income free from serious fluctuation and the extreme instability of Cyprus is the result of the peculiar uncertainty of seasons. It is therefore incumbent upon the government, as an act of self-preservation to take such measures of precaution as will render certain the supply of water.'[24]

The Messaoria irrigation system was, therefore, significant to the colonists' own understanding of the process of colonisation. But subsequent agricultural reforms, which involved the transformation of both the landscape and its inhabitants, would challenge colonial perceptions of who their Cypriot subjects actually were and how they were to be defined.

Cecil Duncan Hay, manager of Athalassa Farm, with his wife. Their Turkish Cypriot manservant was allegedly employed to 'pick the ticks off the dog', 1890s.

[*Reproduced courtesy of Jean Meikle.*]

In 1902, farming on the island received an additional boost when the government bought a 'model farm' five miles outside the walled city of Nicosia[25] from the Eastern Colonial Company. The company ran three other farms on the island, all managed by a Scotsman, Cecil Duncan Hay. He and his family lived on the Kolossi Estate near Limassol, in a house attached to the keep of mediaeval Kolossi Castle.[26] Hay planted the distinctive Cypress tree adjacent to the keep which now stands taller than the building itself. Most of the vast castle rooms were used to store grain, but one was set aside for use by the family as a badminton court.

The new experimental farm and breeding station was intended to research cultivation techniques and to house stud animals. Those bred at Athalassa were distributed across the island to district stud stables, which loaned boars, bulls, stallions and 'premium donkeys' to local farmers. The district stud stable also served as the local government rest house, part of a network of hostels where administration officials could stay for the night when conducting village inspections 'out in the district'.

As the pace of agricultural reform quickened in the early years of the twentieth century, the colonists attempted to stimulate further interest in improving livestock quality through the introduction of that quintessentially British event, the agricultural show. The concept of competitively showing either farm animals or agricultural produce and handiwork had not initially appealed to Cypriots. Earlier attempts by Kitchener to organise a rural arts and crafts show had failed. After three centuries of government by capricious Ottoman overlords, Cypriots feared that any articles they exhibited would be immediately appropriated by their new British rulers. Kitchener's show had attracted no entries.

By the early 1900s such anxieties had been overcome. The livestock show of February 1906, held below the old city walls of Nicosia in an area that doubled as a military parade ground and a football pitch, was pronounced 'quite the best that has been held'.[27] King-Harman, the high commissioner, distributed prizes. Runner up in the class for dairy animals was a cow belonging to Anton Bertram, the Classics scholar and senior judge, who recorded the event in his photograph album.

But it was towards the Cypriot peasant farmer that the efforts of the agricultural department would be directed for the rest of the colonial period. The business of convincing villagers to change practices that had remained the same for centuries became the cornerstone of British agricultural policy in Cyprus. Unlike their colleagues working in the more politically complex and explicitly ideologically driven sphere of education, colonial agriculturalists enjoyed a straightforward relationship with their work. It was their duty as scientifically trained experts to disseminate information and expertise across the island. By initiating the rural peasant into some of the mysteries of modern science the colonial officer believed he was setting him on the path to prosperity and happiness. For many it was a satisfying job, producing clear and tangible results.

During the course of 1904 the officers of the Agriculture Department ordered manuals on irrigation and meteorology from England, reports on farming experiments from Ottawa, and a uniform and tent catalogue from Burberry's. From the newly founded experimental farm at Athalassa, 'a flood of valuable knowledge'[28] began to spread across the island. In the years that followed, armies of trained officials from the ministry, mostly Cypriot, some British, would visit rural communities bringing with them the latest scientific information. Whether it was the best way to cure olives, the distance at which to space fruit trees, techniques for the extraction of silk, or how to avoid headaches while working in the heat, the ministry official was on hand to advise.

But the advice was not always accepted. Innate conservatism combined with a suspicion of the colonists' motives made the Cypriot farmer a reluctant convert to the 'scientific' new methods. Most retained a deep-seated conviction that they knew better than the educated types sent out from Nicosia. In many cases they did.

Many colonists had been particularly appalled by the islander's archaic ploughing techniques, involving a light wooden plough. This ancient method, believed to have been illustrated 'on the walls of the Egyptian temples', was frequently cited as clear evidence of the backwardness of the peasant class. But the small wooden plough was particularly appropriate for conditions in Cyprus, light enough to be carried easily between fields (few Cypriot peasants had contiguous land holdings) and suitable for ploughing steep gradients or narrow terraces cut into the hillside. Samuel Baker was one of the few who cautioned against 'superseding the native plough with the massive European pattern',[29] which might in the long term be a waste of money.[30]

Baker was always concerned to get value for money and had little time for the romance of lost civilisations that seduced so many of his fellow travellers. Rather than importing expensive 'European inventions' he suggested that cheap aid for the Cypriot farmer could be found in the 'many stone columns lying useless among the heaps of ruins so common in Cyprus'.[31] He argued that if pulled by oxen, the pillars could be utilised as agricultural rollers to even out the soil.

Although agricultural development appeared far removed from the politics of the Legislative Council and troublesome demands for *enosis*, it was in the countryside that the economic exploitation which lay at the core of Empire was felt most acutely by the colonial subjects. Regardless of the efforts of the well-meaning reformers from the ministry, the fundamental injustice of colonial rule was reinforced at least twice every year when officials from the un-elected administration came to each village to take away a proportion of the harvest. One tenth of 'the produce of the land',[32] be it wheat, barley, oats or vetches, was payable to the government in tax.

As archaeologist Michael Given points out, for most Cypriots, their only point of contact with the colonial administration came when 'their hard-won food is removed from in front of them and taken right out of their family, their community... there is the personal humiliation, the knowledge that they are being cheated, if not by the tithe collector then certainly by the regime'.[33] Sticking tenaciously to archaic techniques of crop cultivation, animal husbandry or food production was one small way in which villagers could express resistance to colonial rule and, on a very tiny scale, subvert the imperial administration.

Donald Waterer, whose father Ronald ran the Forestry Department in 1937–1950, remembers one occasion later in the century when villagers outwitted government officials who were attempting to regulate the extermination of vermin. Colonies of rats frequently settled in the boles of neglected carob trees and would systematically eat their way through the young shoots, sometimes destroying entire trees. During a particularly bad infestation which threatened the island's carob crop, the government offered to pay villagers for each rat they killed. Every fortnight an official from the agriculture ministry set up his table at the village coffee shop and handed over money in exchange for bunches of rats' tails. Several villagers soon discovered that the tail of a beetroot was identical to that of a rat and 'had a whale of a time selling beetroot tails to the government'. Waterer recalled that eventually agriculture ministry officials were required to cut every tail in half before offering any payment, 'just to make sure it wasn't a beetroot'.[34]

Although the scientific principles of agricultural reform were straightforward, the delicate matter of relating to the Cypriot peasant could be problematic and, for some, impossible. As late as 1948, after 30,000 Cypriots had fought alongside the British in World War Two, and the concept of racial hierarchy which had once underpinned the empire began to crumble, many colonial civil servants in Cyprus still appeared to view the villagers of Cyprus as a race apart. In a breathtakingly condescending speech delivered at one village agricultural show, the governor, Lord Winster, addressed his audience as if they were a group of recalcitrant children:

> When you make requests to me you must remember that it is not the duty of Governments to do the farmer's work for him. Government must make ... knowledge which it collects from all over the world, available to you and it is then for you and not for Government to put it into action. God helps those who help themselves not those who always ask the Government for help.

The governor carried on to the crux of his speech, the villagers' resistance to the latest scientific techniques of pest control: 'as regards fly on apricots, you have been advised to try five sprays with lead arsenate and sugar bait during the season. Have you done this? I hear that some growers who began this treatment were persuaded to give only three sprayings by stupid people who think they know better than the Department of Agriculture.'[35] The 'stupid people' who presumed to know more than the experts about pest control had not only jeopardised the apricot yield, they were also undermining the entire relationship between the colonial government and its subjects.

The tone of the governor's speech suggests that, like many colonial administrators, he was baffled by the Cypriot peasantry. Although less obviously challenging than the educated urban elite, rural villagers were, at the same time, mysterious, remote and essentially unknowable.

Some administrators, such as David Percival who arrived in Cyprus in 1939, found the contrived ritual of the village inspection, when the commissioner was expected to talk to the villagers 'with pleasant smiles about nothing very much', an ordeal. He was disturbed, too, by his awareness that 'there is never the least hope that one can do any of the things one is asked to do!'[36] Other colonial officials, however, happy not to probe too deeply beneath the surface, found village inspections more enjoyable. Harry Luke, who arrived on the island in 1911, observed approvingly that the villagers, 'remote in their mountains and valleys from the disintegrating influences of town life ... had the natural good manners of the peasant'. Luke also found the villagers pleasingly deferential and noted that 'there were few who did not instinctively dismount as a sign of respect when they encountered the Commissioner on the road'.[37]

During the first decade of the twentieth century, the parameters of the colonists' relationship with their rural subjects were still being drawn. One particularly long-standing dispute between the rural peasantry and the men from the ministry that was influential in formulating the colonists' perceptions of Cypriot villagers concerned the introduction of threshing machines. The traditional Cypriot method of threshing corn involved spreading the crop on the flat, hard surface of a threshing floor or barn; oxen then pulled a wooden board, the underside of which was inset with sharp stones, back and forth across the crop, while the pressure exerted by the stones was increased by someone standing, or more often sitting, on a wooden chair placed on top of the boards.

In 1906 the government imported two machines, both fully equipped with 'straw chopping apparatus' to do the job.[38] For a payment of 6 per cent of the

Governor William Battershill conducts an inspection of the village of Vassa, September, 1940.

[*Reproduced courtesy of The Bodleian Library, University of Oxford.*]

corn's market value the Cypriot farmer could have his grain threshed quickly and efficiently in time to ship it to the Egyptian markets ahead of his competitors while prices remained high.

But centralised, mechanised threshing facilities made it easier for government authorities to assess how much tax should be paid. Far better for the small-scale subsistence farmer to enlist the help of his extended family, who, although they might need the whole summer to do the job, at least did so away from the attention of the government tax man. The old Ottoman system of taxation had actively discouraged Cypriot farmers from adopting new techniques which might have increased productivity. Ottoman assessments of crop production were notoriously arbitrary and often bore no relation to the quantities involved. There was little incentive to cultivate more crops than could be consumed by one's immediate family if all surplus produce was then removed by the tax collector.

To the colonists this reluctance to embrace the benefits of modern technology, was baffling, attributed to the sheer cussedness of the Cypriot peasant who 'clings to the traditions of his forefathers ... and the ancient methods of primitive reaping'.[39] The perceived obstinacy and indolence of the Cypriot farmer soon passed into colonial folklore. Colonel A.O. Green, who visited Cyprus in 1896, found it 'extraordinary how difficult it is to overcome the prejudice of the natives and how loath they seem to adopt any new ideas'.[40]

Resistance to change was usually interpreted as stupidity, or, more frequently, as laziness. The *Times of Cyprus* fumed against 'the native peasant' who did not take the trouble to fertilise his land and was 'in most cases too indolent to take the trouble of collecting stable manure, which is ... in large towns to be had for the asking'.[41]

In this, as in other aspects of colonial life, the Cypriot authorities attempted to lead by example, but the island's size meant practices that had succeeded in other colonies were inappropriate. Unlike the larger African or Australian territories, land in Cyprus had been parcelled into tiny individual smallholdings, so it was never 'available' for appropriation for large-scale agricultural settlement. Consequently, it held no attraction for the class of wealthy agriculturalists or speculators who might develop prosperous estates and thus 'show the natives how it was done'. Attempts were made instead to encourage immigrants to settle on the island. Maltese farmers and East End Jews were granted land in Cyprus, in the hope that they would infuse 'a new spirit among the people, by the introduction of fresh blood'.[42] Before long, cynics came to view the colony as 'a favourite dumping ground of philanthropists who wish to better communities that cannot flourish elsewhere'.[43] Perhaps the saddest were the Dukhobortsi or 'Spirit Wrestlers', members of an obscure Russian religious sect advocating vegetarianism and pacifism, who had been persecuted at home for refusing military service. At the end of the nineteenth century a thousand

Spirit Wrestlers settled near Pergamos in the Larnaca district, but large numbers contracted malaria and died. The survivors abandoned Cyprus for Canada leaving only their rough-haired Siberian dog behind.

The most enduring of these ambassadors of agricultural reform, encouraged by the British to settle in Cyprus, have been the Armenians. In 1897 High Commissioner Sir Walter Sendall supervised the establishment of an Armenian 'silk school' for refugees from the Ottoman massacres.[44] Sendall and others hoped they would act as a bridge 'as the best Armenians do', uniting 'with Western science that comprehension of, and sympathy with Eastern needs and habits, which we Westerns [sic] at first naturally lack and which we can never hope completely to supply'.[45] Silk rules were introduced at 'the rearing places', while 'sericultural stations' provided practical demonstrations of the latest techniques. For many decades silk production flourished. Number 1 Gladstone Street, one of the most imposing houses in Nicosia, was owned by an Armenian silk merchant, whose factory was at the side of the building. Neighbours remember camels lining up there to be loaded with bails of silk before plodding off across the plain towards the port of Famagusta.

By 1906, four years after the government had taken over the experimental farm at Athalassa and with the new threshing machines still unpopular in the villages, the Agriculture Department made another attempt to reach out to the recalcitrant Cypriot farmer by launching *The Cyprus Journal: A Quarterly Review of the Agriculture and Industries of Cyprus*, published in English, Greek and Turkish. It contained articles with such titles as *Facts about Cheese* and *Bees: Are They Friends or Foes?* and provided instruction on how to build a cheap poultry shelter to protect chickens from the summer heat, or improve cotton-picking technique ('Hold the boll firmly with your left hand and remove the seed cotton with your right'[46]).

The journal also carried poignant features on animal welfare, which exhorted Cypriots to be kinder to working animals – particularly donkeys – and appealed for an end to the practice of killing dogs with rat poison. It hoped that if 'some suitable literature on the subject of humane treatment of animals could be made available'[47] the situation might improve. The literature did not work. Rat poison, freely available today, is still used to kill hundreds of dogs each year.

The jolly didacticism of the *Cyprus Journal*, published less than 30 years after centuries of Ottoman neglect had come to an end, must have seemed bizarre to its rural readership. But it is easy to ridicule the journal's breathless enthusiasm – its optimism reflected the widely held belief amongst members of the colonial civil service that they were striving to make the countries of empire into better places.

To a certain degree they succeeded. By 1907, the first co-operative banks had opened in Paphos, affording 'infinite facilities for the villagers'[48] and releasing many from their obligations to the ubiquitous moneylenders. An association to promote the development of the carob tree was established, while the Society for the Prevention of Cruelty to Animals reported it had cared for an unprecedented total of 73 sick donkeys, dogs and horses, 'the majority of which were brought in by the villagers themselves'.[49]

The following year, Cypriot citrus fruit was exhibited for the first time in London at the Royal Horticultural Society's annual Exhibition of Colonial-Grown Fruit, where 'monster oranges of oval shape'[50] caused 'quite a sensation', while that year's harvest 'greatly superseded those of the previous five years'.[51] For the first time since the British occupation began, there was a budget surplus of £70,000.

These tangible improvements provided an obvious and immediate justification for the British occupation; Cypriot agriculture had undoubtedly benefited from imperial rule. Visits to sites of agricultural improvement soon became a popular element in any official itinerary. In 1954, during his first six months on the island, Governor Robert Armitage was taken to see no less than four 'up-to-date orange packing stations and orange groves',[52] as well as flood control works, irrigation projects, experimental pig farms and modern fruit-canning plants that could turn out 'two hundred cans a minute'. He inspected the export potato crop, toured an innovative poultry farm and drew lots for 'fifty Holstein heifers in calf' to be allocated to local farmers to test their suitability for milk production in the Mediterranean climate.

Yet despite these achievements, for most of the time that the British occupied Cyprus the rural peasantry remained wretched and poor. When Rider Haggard stayed at a rest house at Khirokitia near Limassol in 1900, he was confronted with dramatic evidence of the harshness of rural life when he assumed his twenty-six-year-old hostess to have been 'around sixty years old'.[53]

Few Britons had direct dealings with the rural peasant class, with the notable exception of Forestry Department officials who, along with their families, were required to live in remote forestry stations. For most, the peasantry remained exotic specimens, observed from a distance but never really understood. To that extent the experience of most colonists did not differ significantly from that of travellers to the island, both in their own way were tourists making brief excursions into an unknown and unknowable environment.

The failure of the colonial project – certainly during the first 30 years of British occupation – to improve the lot of the island's rural poor meant that colonial depictions of the Cypriot peasant became complicated and problematic.

This did not prevent the colonists from appropriating the landscape and making it comfortingly English. In 1878, Esme Scott Stevenson found that 'the whole country was as green as Richmond Park',[54] while 30 years later Gladys Peto observed that the ruined mediaeval abbey of Bellapaix was 'exactly like the kind of thing one is taken to see in England or France with Gothic ruins and carving'.[55]

A closer inspection of a more particularised countryside would have revealed the miserable shivering children and blind beggars whom Samuel Baker encountered in his eccentric gypsy caravan and whose continued presence in the landscape, after 30 years of British stewardship, inhibited the colonists' proper 'enjoyment' of the rural scene.

This disquieting vision was replaced in many colonial accounts of the peasantry by a jolly theatrical caricature of the rural Cypriot, someone who was cheerful, childlike and prone to spontaneous outbursts of singing. When, for example, Colonel Green encountered a party of men with their camels at a khan he observed that 'they would have made the fortune of an impresario in want of a select parcel of brigands for "Fra Diavalo[56]", for a more truculent-looking lot of scoundrels it would be difficult to imagine'.[57] In the same way Gladys Peto compared customers at the village coffee shop to 'stage bandits, owing to their predilection for scarlet handkerchiefs and sashes'. Peto savoured the contradiction between the villagers' ferocious appearances and her knowledge that they were, in fact, 'quite harmless', playing not 'the exotic and dramatic gambling game that one would expect to see, but "rummy," just as one might do oneself at home'.[58] Similarly Green was anxious to point out that there were 'few other places in the East where one could wander about unarmed in such absolute security and be dependent for assistance and supplies on the inhabitants of the country as in Cyprus'.[59]

For colonists and colonial visitors alike, the island, by contrast to other colonies, provided a faint whiff of the exotic which could be enjoyed in a safe and unthreatening environment. The familiar Cypriot peasant, recognisable by his ubiquitous colourful clothes, was easily reduced to a stereotype. In this respect the colonist's cast of theatrical characters also conformed to long-established patterns of Western perceptions of the Orient in which the 'patently foreign and distant' was represented as 'more rather than less familiar'.[60]

The character of the indolent, child-like villager incapable of either managing his own affairs or controlling the landscape he inhabited became ubiquitous. Not only did he need protection from the vagaries and harshness of the natural world, the British argued, but he also needed shielding from his urban compatriots, the predatory moneylenders and lawyers who threatened both the harmonious rural order and the legitimacy of British rule. The stereotype was to become particularly entrenched during the violent final years of the British occupation, at the time of the EOKA armed struggle, when the simple, loyal Cypriot peasant was often depicted as being manipulated by his treacherous urban compatriots.

But the enduring appeal of the image of the jovial Cypriot peasant, pictured in the colonial imagination perpetually travelling 'the roads of the plains...driving before him a number of greatly be-panniered donkeys',[61] derived from the fact that it sustained the colonists' vision of their own paternalistic role. It was a picture that, by implication, cast them as agents of progress, guiding the neglected island and its benighted inhabitants towards modernity, prosperity and happiness.

5

Clauson Will Do the Best He Can
1914–18

Punters at Nicosia racetrack sit on grubby white plastic chairs in the centre of a cavernous high-ceilinged room with glass walls. Television monitors hang from the ceiling and one wall is entirely occupied by betting kiosks. The men – there are no women – are mostly unshaven and dressed in open-necked shirts. Several pace around the perimeter talking furtively into their mobiles, betting by phone to avoid paying taxes. One man rises from his seat to shout angrily at a jockey as he walks past. These gamblers are not here for an entertaining afternoon out; their tense faces suggest an internal compulsion – or financial need.

Gambling is big business in Cyprus. The Nicosia municipality of Ayios Dhometios where the racetrack is situated derives almost half its annual revenue from the proceeds of horse racing. But local officials complain that their income is now threatened by organised crime syndicates who 'manage' the risks involved in each bet, bribe jockeys to lose races and undercut licensed betting shops who avoid tax. It is not uncommon for racetrack officials to find small bombs under their cars – the traditional method of registering dissatisfaction with a result.

The racecourse itself seems to be part of a different world from the bleak and shabby betting hall. Elegant and compact, it is bordered by royal palms and eucalyptus trees. An oasis of green topiary marks out the island at the centre of the track. From the stand, race-goers have a view of the distant Kyrenia Mountains. As the afternoon's racing progresses the mountains are gradually washed in a rosy light from the setting sun, turning them from pink to purple, to black. It is a memorable view that British colonial race-goers in Cyprus gazed on for decades and doubtless carried away with them to bungalows and retirement homes in England.

While racing in Cyprus is obviously a legacy of colonial rule, there is no evident link between the desperate anxious faces in the betting hall and the exclusive,
hierarchical institution that the British first established in the early years of the
twentieth century. The early colonists had hoped that horse racing would foster 'a
great bond of fellowship and goodwill between the English and the natives',[1] but
within expatriate society itself, success on the racecourse – or, at the very least,
enthusiastic participation – was always a serious and important matter. An individual's social standing, even his career prospects, could be dealt a severe blow by
a lack of interest in the field; more bookish colonial officials were not always welcomed. Claude Cobham, the district commissioner for Larnaca, 'a scholar and a
gentleman',[2] preferred digging for antiquities at Salamis to racing or polo. When
he retired in 1908 after 28 years service, the *Anglo Cypriot* newspaper lamented
the 'long inactivity and dull existence' that had been imposed on the district by
Cobham's lack of interest in the saddle and expressed the hope that 'dances and
horse racing'[3] would be introduced by his successor.[4]

It was during the rule of Sir Hamilton Goold-Adams, who governed Cyprus
from 1911 to 1915, that 'licensed' racing assumed its pre-eminent place in the
colonial social calendar. The most important race of the year was, inevitably,
the Jubilee Cup.[5] As in other colonies, the patronage of the ruling class made
the sport attractive to many of the leading Cypriot families of Nicosia, and
meant that 'only the social elite took part in racing and only the very best families owned their own horses'.[6]

Goold-Adams himself was less interested in demonstrations of social status and more concerned with agricultural development and practical improvements to animal welfare. Said to possess 'all the Irishman's love of a horse and
instinctive knowledge of horseflesh',[7] he was also an irascible man, 'inclined
to be hasty both in action and in speech',[8] who was deeply unpopular amongst
Greek Cypriots, presumably because of his 'strong anti-Greek sympathies'. He
is still remembered in some quarters today for spending a sixth of the island's
entire annual budget on a thoroughbred stallion. This was at a time when the
majority of Cypriots were living in primitive conditions in acute poverty, and
the island's roads and infrastructure remained seriously under-developed.
Questions were asked in London about whether this was a responsible act, but
in the end Goold-Adams escaped censure. The stallion, Temeraire, was sta-
bled at the government stud farm in Athalassa, in a building for which Goold-
Adams had laid the foundation stone during his first year in Cyprus. Temeraire
went on to sire generations of outstanding horses. His progeny were exported
to Egypt and Greece, where they enjoyed such racing success that both countries eventually prohibited the import of Cypriot-bred horses.[9]

Goold-Adams wrote regularly to the Colonial Office in London about
equine matters such as the quantity of government forage granted to the horses

of junior administrative officials, or pension arrangements for the widows of mounted policemen. But on all other subjects he demonstrated an intense dislike of administration and bureaucracy, entirely failing to master the technique of the well-crafted diplomatic despatch. The content and phrasing of this official communication that was sent back to the Colonial Office in London often determined the course of a man's career. The ideal despatch was brief and ultimately reassuring; even as it drew attention to a dilemma, it should propose a series of solutions that would make the problem disappear – without the need for action from London. The high commissioner's communiqués by contrast were vague and verbose and were dismissed by the permanent under-secretaries of the Colonial Office as 'mediaeval'[10] and 'stupid'.[11] Despite such reservations about his abilities, the Colonial Office continued to allow Goold-Adams to govern the sleepy colonial backwater and its docile subjects and for the British administrators of Cyprus life had a pleasing, undisturbed rhythm. With London at least a five-and-a-half-day journey away, and the nearest British administration at Port Said over 19 hours distant, the colonists were cocooned from the rest of the world. Each year was much like the next, punctuated by the annual three-month sojourn up in the cool of the Troodos Mountains.

This was where Goold-Adams and the Cyprus government were stationed on 4 August 1914, at the outbreak of the First World War. Communications between London and Mount Troodos were slow and it was to be a full 10 days before Goold-Adams finally contacted the Colonial Office. When he did so, his response did not take the form of an official despatch, but a peevish handwritten letter sent on his personal writing paper. It was primarily concerned with the island's chief secretary, Captain C.W. Orr, who was due to return to his post in Nicosia after a period of absence. Goold-Adams complained to the Colonial Office, 'I am sorry that you thought it necessary to send back Orr. Bolton, who is acting, is so calm and quiet...and in anxious times like the present is delightful to work with. Orr on the other hand is highly strung. With a jerky anxious manner whose presence is itself slightly worrying to myself and those who serve under him.'[12]

For the previous three decades, since the British occupation of Egypt in 1882, Cyprus had been a strategic backwater. With the outbreak of war the island's military significance changed overnight and its status suddenly became uniquely complicated. Under the terms of the Cyprus Convention Britain had only acquired the right to 'occupy and administer' the island. Technically, therefore, it remained part of the Ottoman Empire, an empire with which Britain was about to go to war. The Colonial Office grew increasingly concerned about the allegiance of the island's Muslim minority, which it was feared would 'rise in revolt'[13] if Cyprus was annexed and incorporated into the British Empire and might even incite Greek Cypriots to join the rebellion. It recommended that since 'nearly two thirds of the police are Turks, it would be necessary that some troops should be sent to the island, over and above the company which are there'.[14] At the same time, the island's proximity to Turkey and those territories of the Ottoman Empire that encompassed modern-day Syria, Lebanon, Jordan, Palestine and Israel placed it on the front-line and enhanced its strategic value as a wartime refuelling station. Famagusta in particular became an important 'coaling and victualling'[15] depot for the French navy and for British sea planes. In this politically complex and potentially volatile situation Goold-Adams's idiosyncratic correspondence could hardly have done more to generate unease in London.

A week later, as millions of men were being mobilised across Europe and the British army prepared for 'its first major battle on European soil since Waterloo',[16] the high commissioner sent another 'furtive handwritten letter'[17] which began not by discussing the war or its possible impact on Cyprus but by expressing acute anxiety about the health of the island's chief accountant, Mr Greaves, who had a badly fitting wooden leg. The unfortunate Greaves could not have hoped for a more sympathetic employer, but as Europe prepared for all-out war, this was not what the Colonial Office wanted to hear. The permanent under secretaries were unimpressed.

Finally Goold-Adams addressed the subject of the war, writing less in the tone of His Majesty's representative overseas and more as if corresponding with an elderly relative: 'I wonder when we shall hear of any really important engagements on the Continent? Presumably the first will be along the France Belgium border in which our own people must take part. I do hope that everything will be as we wish and that many of our people may not be killed. Trusting you are fit and well and not over worried. I certainly don't bother you much.'[18] To make matters worse, Goold-Adams continued governing the island from his summer headquarters on Mount Troodos. During July and August, when the intense heat of the plains around Nicosia would have virtually brought all work to a standstill, this was not unreasonable. But by October, when Goold-Adams had still not left Mount Troodos, London was forced to conclude that 'he cannot be depended on for energetic action in an emergency'.[19] It was at this time that the British administration in Cyprus began to acquire a reputation in the Colonial Office for containing a high proportion of 'people who had either defects in their character or their minds'.[20]

Although any fighting still seemed very distant, ripples from the conflict soon reached the island. The announcement of war with Germany led to 'panic amongst bank depositors' of the Nicosia branch of the Imperial Ottoman Bank, who immediately withdrew their savings. Although its majority shareholders, like its senior management, were British and French, the bank's head office was in Constantinople, making it, in the event of war with Turkey, 'an alien enemy'. As a result the bank found itself with 'only four thousand pounds in cash left in its coffers'. The administration declared a month-long moratorium on further withdrawals, during which time it was hoped that public anxiety would diminish and some of the cash would be re-deposited. Bafflingly, however, Goold-Adams took no steps to safeguard the government's own deposits at the bank. It was not until three months later, 24 hours before Britain declared war on Turkey, that London received a querulous telegram from the high commissioner explaining that 'the position of the Imperial Ottoman Bank in the event of war with Turkey is causing me considerable anxiety'[21]; £40,000 of Cyprus government cash remained at the Nicosia branch, an amount which, as Goold-Adams correctly surmised, could not be 'withdrawn or decreased without inconvenience to depositors', and which, he painstakingly explained, would be adversely affected if communication between the branch and head office in Constantinople ceased with the outbreak of hostilities.

The civil servants at the Colonial Office could barely contain their exasperation, writing on the cover sheet of one despatch, 'Why on earth the Cyprus government left forty thousand pounds in the local branch so long I cannot say.'[22] A week later, all branches of the Ottoman Bank were granted special permission by the government in London to 'keep open their doors for the payments of cheques and drafts ... on condition that no transactions shall take place with their establishments in, or with persons resident in, enemy territory'.[23]

In fairness, despite his failings as a despatch writer and what might be described today as poor presentational skills, Goold-Adams had risen to the occasion and initiated several wartime measures. On 5 August 1914, the day after Britain's declaration of war on Germany, he had introduced martial law and established a defence committee to deal with any 'measures of extraordinary internal administration' necessary during wartime. The committee concluded that in the event of invasion, defence of the island with the tiny British garrison would be impossible and that there were 'political obstacles to calling upon the native population to take up arms'. It did not, therefore, waste time with useless military preparations but concentrated on 'preserving as far as possible, normal conditions on the island'.[24] It posted British troops to Larnaca, Limassol and Famagusta in order to requisition enemy merchant vessels docked at the ports; it introduced telegraphic censorship, imposed fixed prices on various essential foodstuffs and prohibited the export of cereal, animal feed and livestock unless the British government in Egypt made specific requests. Finally, in an effort to prevent the export of gold and silver coins Goold-Adams proposed the introduction of the island's first paper currency. Sending money from England would take too long, so the notes were hastily produced by the Government Printing Office in Nicosia. Goold-Adams, along with Harry Luke, who had been appointed secretary of the defence committee, spent 'some twelve hours daily on five consecutive days'[25] during September 1914, painstakingly signing

£35,000 worth of notes in denominations of £5 and £1. (They subsequently proved so easy to copy that the notes had to be withdrawn and the government was forced to pay nearly £100 in compensation to people in possession of forgeries.)[26]

The high commissioner's business-like account of these measures went some way to restoring his reputation in London, where it was admitted that an 'absence of fuss' in his previous correspondence had been 'mistaken for lethargy'. It was even suggested that a letter should be sent from the secretary of state to 'express ... satisfaction with the manner in which he conducted the administration of the island'. Goold-Adams also had his supporters within the administration in Cyprus, particularly Harry Luke, his 'energetic and tactful'[27] private secretary, who commended his former boss for being 'completely honest, and a man'.[28] Their friendship seems an unlikely one – the bluff military officer who lived for racing, horse-breeding and hunting and was interested primarily in the implementation of agricultural reform, and the witty, effeminate linguist who devoted his spare time to the conservation of Nicosia's historic monuments. Perhaps they both shared a love of Cyprus and were sufficiently different to appreciate each other's qualities.[29]

It was Luke – no doubt because of his diplomatic manner – who had been called on to announce to leading Turkish Cypriots Britain's annexation of Cyprus and the severance of the island's 400-year link with the Ottoman Empire. On 5 November 1914, following 'a busy day at the Secretariat getting out the necessary Proclamations in English, Turkish and Greek', Luke attended the engagement ceremony of the eldest son of the mufti, Mehmet Ziyaeddin Efendi, known as Munir Bey. The ceremony took place at the mufti's house, immediately opposite Arab Ahmet Mosque in northern Nicosia.

That building has long been demolished, but Munir Bey's summer residence remains. 'Beautiful and unpretentious in the old Turkish style', it was built outside the city walls in an area known as *Kosklu Ciftlik*, where 'fields and gardens' contained date palms, cypresses and eucalyptus, and there were 'no more than a few scattered and isolated houses'.[30] Remarkably, the house, whitewashed, with a thick privet hedge over the gate, is still home to the mufti's descendents, a living link with the island's Ottoman past.

The mufti was the highest Islamic religious figure on the island, elected by Turkish Cypriots, with his position ratified by the caliph. He supervised the religious life of the community and had the right to pronounce on issues related to Islamic law. Although in practice by 1910 his role had become primarily symbolic and he no longer had a seat on the Legislative Council; he still assumed ceremonial precedence over the Greek Orthodox archbishop. His appearance at the annual official opening of the council was spectacular. Luke describes him as dressed in violet ceremonial robes with a white turban

around his fez over which 'was laid a band of gold brocade of width varying according to rank, with a tail of white linen, gold-tipped, hanging down
the back'.[31] The office of the mufti had fulfilled an important function in the
public expression of a shared religious identity, one that bound all Muslims to
the Ottoman Empire, from the borders of Europe in the west to the Arabian
peninsula in the east.

Now this old Ottoman world order, where individual and societal identity was defined by religion, was being replaced by the emerging ideology of
the nation state. Ottoman suzerainty on the island was at an end and Cyprus
became part of the British Empire. Luke commented that his hosts 'took the
news, which was not unexpected, with dignified resignation'.[32] It fell to both
Goold-Adams and his successor John Clauson to deal with the consequences
of this abrupt change in status.

For the British, as much as for the Cypriots, the new relationship required
some adjustment. On the day of the proclamation the Home Office in London
issued instructions concerning the treatment of 'enemy aliens of Ottoman
nationality' which specified that all Ottoman subjects able to prove they had
been born in Cyprus were from now on 'to be regarded as being British subjects'. The instructions were swiftly followed by a corrective from the secretary
of state for the colonies, Lord Harcourt, which stressed that 'in view of the
annexation of Cyprus, persons born in the Island are not only to be *regarded* as
British subjects, but are *in fact* British subjects'.[33]

The issue of nationality became increasingly slippery as the war progressed,
and the terms under which British citizenship could be acquired were continually reviewed as more exceptions and anomalies emerged. It was soon recognised that Cyprus also contained 'many persons of Ottoman, Armenian, Greek
and Syrian race' who did not qualify for British citizenship. Technically, many
of them were now enemy aliens, required to declare in writing that they would
not harm Britain or her allies and to obtain government permission to leave
the island. But as Goold-Adams explained to the Colonial Office, their numbers included 'several trusted servants of the Government', along with 'others
anxious to acquire British citizenship at the earliest opportunity'. In such cases,
he argued, Foreign Office regulations concerning their treatment 'should be
interpreted in as liberal a spirit as possible'.[34]

Travelling abroad created further problems for the new British subjects.
The old Ottoman-style passports, written in Arabic script on a scroll of paper
which the holder unrolled as required, were now obsolete and the administration's early attempts to provide replacements were not a success. Several British
consulates in Europe complained of difficulty in identifying 'persons presenting passports issued in Cyprus',[35] since the documents contained only a name,
without photograph, fingerprint or signature.

Passports or not, the extension of British nationality to all Cypriots made little impression on the Turkish Ministry for War, which continued to view them as Ottoman subjects, conscripting Cypriots living in Constantinople into the Ottoman army.[36]

For its part the Colonial Office could, when political expediency required, be equally selective in its interpretation of the obligations that accompanied the island's annexation. In 1916 it received a copy of a petition that had been forwarded to the Grand Vizier in Constantinople from the unfortunate sheikh of the mosque or *tekke* of the Mevlevi Islamic sect in Nicosia. The petition appealed for backdated payments of the sheikh's food allowance, suspended since the outbreak of war, without which he was living 'in a miserable condition' and was subject to 'the utmost distress'. The office's response to the sheikh's plight was a vague and supercilious minute: 'What exactly a sheikh of a tekke may be I cannot discern... if the Turks will pay, so much the better.'[37]

While both the British and Turkish governments obfuscated the island's new status when it suited them, most people were genuinely confused about it. Cypriots had overnight exchanged government by one empire for subjugation to another, more geographically distant and certainly more culturally alien. Since their arrival in 1878 the British had been scrupulous in their observance of Ottoman diplomatic protocol. Cyprus might be tied to the Porte by only the loosest of bonds, but many of the trappings and public rituals of the Ottoman Empire were still maintained. Every year the sultan's birthday was celebrated with a series of military salutes, fired off throughout the day to coincide with each of the five times of Islamic prayer. At night the minarets of 'Ayia Sophia' mosque in Nicosia were illuminated.[38]

Similarly, the Ottoman mounted police force, the *zaptiehs*, became the public face of the British colonial police. For the first 20 years of the British administration the *zaptiehs'* official uniform included a *fez*, with a white turban wrapped around the outside. By the turn of the century the turban had disappeared (prompting the alarmed newspaper headline 'Zapts Lose Their Turbans!'[39]), but the distinctively Ottoman *fez* remained. The annual *zaptieh* sports day – held, like all such contests, in the moat of the old walled city of Nicosia – included sports such as 'tent-pegging'.[40] A variation of *jirit*, a kind of polo played by the elite Ottoman *janissary* corps, it involved horsemen galloping at speed towards a series of wooden pegs driven into the ground in an attempt to carry one off on the tip of a lance. This quintessentially Ottoman sport offered an opportunity both to display the skills of the colonial police force and to demonstrate the island's continued connection to the Ottoman Empire.

It was a connection which could not be unravelled overnight. There were Cypriots (defined by the new proclamation as anyone born in Cyprus) living and working in all the major cities of Egypt, the Levant and Asia Minor. Many were traders with business interests in Alexandria, Beirut, Izmir, Athens or Constantinople. For its part, despite the early scares of the war, the colonial administration still kept its money in the Ottoman Bank in Nicosia.

The loyalty of the empire's newest 'Mohammedan' subjects was brought into question in the first months of the war by an event which became a source of acute anxiety to the authorities in both London and Nicosia. Over the previous decade, as the disintegration of the Ottoman Empire accelerated, Britain, France and Germany had each sought to establish their own sphere of influence within the Turkish armed forces. For the best part of a century 'the powers' had competed with each other in 'the great game' of securing a share of those territories that would be potentially available when the Ottoman colossus finally keeled over. With this ultimate objective in mind Germany maintained an influential military mission (which ultimately led to Turkey's participation in the war), France supervised the gendarmerie, and Britain 'advised' the Turkish navy. Turkey's war minister Enver Pasha had been impressed by the latest innovations in British naval technology, particularly by the revolutionary new dreadnought, 'more robustly and rationally armoured than any ship afloat'.[41] In an attempt to bolster Turkey's international prestige he launched a high-profile public subscription campaign to finance an order for two super-dreadnoughts from British shipyards. When, as war approached, Britain appropriated the vessels, still under construction in British shipyards, there was uproar in Constantinople and the Porte accused Britain of breaching international law. The sense of outrage was contagious and quickly spread to the Muslims of Cyprus where 'acts of disloyalty occurred amongst the members of the Police'.[42]

Goold-Adams managed to tear himself away from the racetrack for long enough to write an open letter to Irfan Bey, a senior Muslim member of the Legislative Council. In it he outlined the British government's legal justification for appropriating the ships and rather disingenuously expressed his confidence that 'His Majesty's Government were unaware of the fact that the Turkish ships had been subscribed for by the Moslem world'. Unlikely though it was that either Irfan Bey or his colleagues would have been convinced by these arguments they nonetheless reassured the high commissioner of their loyalty and agreement that British action had been entirely justified and expressed the hope that the island's annexation would see 'the inhabitants so released from Constantinople intrigue'.[43]

The Muslims of Cyprus now occupied a delicate position. They continued to be closely connected to the Ottoman Empire by ties of religion, language, commerce and culture. The *fez*, 'the hallmark of the Turkish male',[44] remained the distinctive headgear of the mounted *zaptiehs* and would continue to be worn on the streets of Nicosia until the middle of the 1930s. But as British subjects,

Cypriot Muslims were collectively – and in some cases individually – at war with Turkey. As a result they were highly vulnerable to accusations of treason, espionage and collaboration with the enemy and, under martial law, were at risk of being interned at any time without trial. Leading members of the Kenan family, for example, who ran an import/export business, trading with Syria and Turkey, suddenly found themselves accused of smuggling petrol to the enemy and were imprisoned in Kyrenia Castle. Health worker Mehmet Aziz, who was later to make an immense contribution to the development of the colony, recalled that 'it was easy to lose your job and position: the Turks really had to keep quiet'.[45]

The conservative Turkish Cypriot middle classes of Nicosia, most of whom were employed in government service, tended to support the old monarchist order, but Turkish Cypriot society as a whole was divided. Many supported the Young Turk triumvirate whose Committee of Union and Progress now controlled the Ottoman Empire. In August a clerk in the land registry in Nicosia was dismissed for intrigue and for corresponding with the office of a member of the triumvirate in Istanbul. This proved to be an isolated incident, but it caused Goold-Adams to prohibit any public ceremony to mark Britain's annexation of the island in case it provoked a violent response from Turkish Cypriot residents of the capital.

In its concern to 'keep the Moslem population of the island quiet at times of acute national feeling',[46] the British administration became increasingly dependent on the influential Turkish Cypriot legislative councillor Irfan Bey. Although he was frequently criticised for being more interested in his own advancement than the well-being of his community, Irfan Bey nevertheless assumed considerable importance to the British administration and came to be regarded as 'the sole expounder of the Turkish view'.[47] Goold-Adams had particular reason to appreciate Irfan Bey's conciliatory presence when, less than two weeks after the annexation, the caliphate declared a holy Islamic war on Britain, France, Russia, Serbia and Montenegro and condemned any Muslim who fought against the Ottoman Empire to 'the fires of hell'. Cypriot Muslims responded by making conspicuously generous donations to the Cyprus branch of the Red Cross Society. By December 1915 the society had raised nearly £1,500.[48]

These financial offerings were significantly more practical than the high commissioner's own contribution to the war effort – a donation of such startling uselessness that it confirmed the Colonial Office's worst fears about Goold-Adams and quite possibly set the seal on his demotion. Goold-Adams offered His Majesty's government an unsolicited gift of 3,000 tons of salt, from the Larnaca salt lake. Like its Ottoman predecessor on the island the British government in Cyprus enjoyed the monopoly of salt collection. Disposal of the salt became a time-consuming and irritating problem for the Colonial Office, which could find no use for it but did not wish to risk offending the Cypriot members of the Legislative Council who had endorsed the gift, by appearing to reject the offer.

Correspondence about the 'useless gift' continued for several weeks while the Colonial Office desperately tried to find someone who would take responsibility for it. As the folder marked 'Gift of Salt' grew thicker, Sir John Anderson, the permanent secretary at the Colonial Office, commented wearily that 'Cyprus has rather a knack for suggesting inconvenient gifts'. Eventually the gift was politely refused and it was suggested to the high commissioner that he might like to offer goats as an alternative since 'the Indian soldiers use them for food'; 1,200 goats were duly shipped to Malta 'for the victualling of the Indian troops'.[49] The salt debacle was to be one of Goold-Adams's last actions on Cyprus. By January 1915, six months after the outbreak of war, he was on his way to take up the governorship of Queensland, demoted to a less demanding post, well out of harm's way.

Goold-Adams's successor, John Eugene Clauson, could not have been more different. The Colonial Office, generally content to allow the administration of Cyprus to drift aimlessly, somehow managed to provide the island with capable and incisive rulers at times of crisis when British military interests were threatened. Clauson was a military high-flyer who, in his early twenties, had designed a revolutionary pontoon bridge subsequently adopted by the army. He had spent six years as assistant secretary of the Committee of Imperial Defence, during which time he had gained a thorough understanding of the workings and internal politics of both the Colonial and War Offices. He also had considerable knowledge of Cyprus, having been the island's chief secretary between 1906 and 1911, during Charles King-Harman's commissionership. Significantly for both Clauson and for Cyprus, given the immense challenges that lay ahead, he possessed the mental clarity that his predecessor had lacked. Officials of the Colonial Office were particularly delighted with his lucid and fluent writing style, commenting approvingly that his 'despatches read admirably'.[50] This was just as well. As a high commissioner governing a colony at war, with the disintegrating Ottoman Empire on its doorstep, Clauson would be confronted by uniquely complex situations of which neither he nor his superiors in London had previous experience and which required him to improvise policy on the hoof.

Although no fighting took place in Cyprus during the First World War, its geographical location meant that it was perforce heavily involved in the conflict. Over 10,000 Ottoman prisoners of war were incarcerated on the island, thousands of sick and injured allied soldiers were transported to military convalescent homes on Mount Troodos, while the island's forests were almost entirely obliterated in the effort to provide timber for the Allied war machine in the

Middle East. Clauson oversaw the recruitment of some 13,000 muleteers and the despatch of 7,000 Cypriot mules for the Macedonian and Egyptian fronts. He authorised the provision of food relief for thousands of starving Cypriot refugees trapped in Asia Minor, arranged for the reception of thousands more in Cyprus and headed off serious challenges to his authority from British military intelligence in Egypt. For security reasons, much of this responsibility fell to him alone, generating a workload that would have exhausted the most energetic of high commissioners.

One of Clauson's first duties concerned nine Ottoman-registered ships, known as 'enemy bottoms', detained at Famagusta harbour, which, under international law, could be claimed by the colonial administration. In August 1914, these vessels were detained at Famagusta harbour, pending a decision by a specially convened Prize Court. Most were small schooners or caiques, which transported Cypriot oranges and pomegranates to Syria and Egypt and came back to Cyprus for re-fitment at the beginning of each summer. Many of their crews had families on the island, while any sailors who happened to be in the colony on 5 November 1914, the date of the annexation, had automatically become British subjects. Clauson managed to arrange the release of five of the boats and their crews and quietly did nothing about instituting Prize Court proceedings against the remaining four. The Colonial Office continued to fret about the ships over the following months, but Clauson managed to keep them at bay, and finally the matter was dropped.

The colony's main role throughout the first year of the war was as a 'military convalescent depot'.[51] A camp capable of accommodating 500 recuperating soldiers was established on Mount Troodos and managed by the Cyprus PWD. Troops who had been treated at British military hospitals in Egypt and were considered almost fully recovered were shipped to Cyprus and transported up to the Troodos Convalescent Home, by 'railway or motor', for two weeks respite amongst the pine trees, before being sent back to the front. The majority were Allied survivors of the Dardanelles campaign.

The colonists, proud of the new facility and the contribution the island could now claim to be making to the war effort, donated £400 via the Red Cross for 'comforts for the convalescents', while Lady Clauson appealed for donations of tobacco, cigarettes, razors, combs, slippers, stationery and books for 'the wounded warriors'.[52] Back home the Church of England's 'Scripture Gift Mission' donated 500 New Testaments.[53] Less than a month after the first consignment of troops had arrived, an anonymous article entitled 'Our Wounded Soldiers' appeared in the weekly magazine *The Near East*. It described the new establishment and its modern facilities in glowing terms and went on to give precise details of the specially constructed landing facility for receiving the soldiers at Karavostassi, along with its exact geographical location, 'at the southern end of Morphou Bay, on the west of the island'.[54] This was potentially disastrous. Transport ships lay anchored off Karavostassi for several days and nights, during which time they were an easy target for German submarines. The officer commanding British troops in Cyprus observed bitterly that 'no more useful information to the enemy could possibly have been published'.[55]

Clauson launched an investigation. It revealed that the 'objectionable material' had been written by the newly appointed head of the Agriculture Department, William Bevan, a man considered to be a 'mixture of brilliance and stupidity'.[56] On 22 October 1915, Bevan stood before a secret tribunal comprising the high commissioner, the king's advocate, the chief secretary and the treasurer and expressed pain and 'profound regret' for his actions. The Tribunal was lenient. The head of the Agriculture Department received a severe reprimand and was judged to be an 'honest but feather brained person who is wanting in judgement and common sense'.[57]

Troops continued to be sent to the Troodos camp until the end of October 1915, when it was considered too cold for invalids to remain there. The following January Allied troops were evacuated from the Dardanelles. Pressure on Egyptian hospital facilities eased and the fortnightly troop transports to Cyprus never resumed. Instead, as the Allies began to establish a military base in Salonika and to launch a series of operations in Bulgaria, the island developed an entirely different wartime role.

The failure of the Gallipoli campaign, compounded by the stalemate of trench warfare on the Western Front, had convinced the British prime minister, Lloyd George, that the Balkans would be a suitable site for another, more decisive offensive. If such an operation was to succeed, it needed the support of the Greek monarch, King Constantine. Convincing the king to join the Allied cause was to become one of Britain's key diplomatic objectives for the rest of the war.

Lloyd George's opening gambit involved shipping 150,000 French and British troops to northern Greece. It was hoped that the presence of the soldiers, ostensibly there to defend Serbia, would demonstrate to the Greek king that Britain took its commitments to its allies seriously and was honouring an earlier treaty obligation to provide military aid. When these measures failed to impress Constantine Britain took the unusual step of offering to cede Cyprus to Greece. The offer remained open for three days in October 1915, after which it was withdrawn, never to be repeated.

Relations between the king and the British government deteriorated thereafter and Greek military co-operation with the Salonika Expeditionary Force was withdrawn. The mountainous geography of northern Greece, together with poor infrastructure and a primitive rail network, had made the force almost entirely dependent on locally supplied pack animals for transport. Without local mules and muleteers the operation was at a standstill and, as Constantine sought to distance himself from the British, Greek sources gradually started to dry up. Soon Clauson began receiving a series of anxious telegrams from army directors of supply in Macedonia, requesting the immediate despatch of mules and muleteers.

Recruitment began immediately. Muleteers did 15 days basic training at a vast camp outside Famagusta where mules were tethered to trees in military lines, before being transported in requisitioned Egyptian cargo boats to Salonika. Once there the recruits underwent further training in how to handle weapons. By contrast, the small number of Greek muleteers who served with the British army until July 1916 were not armed and carried no ammunition, a reflection of the prevailing uncertainty surrounding Greece's loyalties during the conflict. The issue of allegiance remained a potentially awkward one. At least 400 of the Cypriot muleteers on the Macedonian Front were Muslims, who would have come into direct contact with enemy Ottoman soldiers. Perhaps they now considered themselves to be British subjects above all else, or perhaps they viewed their arbitrary allocation of nationality with bemused scepticism. Whatever an individual's thoughts on his own identity and nationality may have been, it is likely that the prospect of regular army wages, paid for up to a year at a time, was too tempting to ignore. Cyprus was still a predominantly agrarian society and for many Cypriots this would have been their first experience of contracted wage labour.

For the colonial administration the recruitment operation was almost too successful. Over the next six months 4,060 men were sent to Salonika, along with another 4,000 mules and donkeys. By the end of the First World War as many as 13,000 men had joined up, approximately one in every 26 Cypriots. The removal of large numbers of able-bodied men led to a rural labour shortage and – a universal feature of war – placed a greater burden on women at a time when the island's resources were already stretched. As the war progressed the army in Macedonia become so dependent on Cypriot muleteers that the British military authorities in Salonika demanded the introduction of conscription in Cyprus to guarantee a continued supply. Such an unpopular measure would almost certainly have led to political unrest and – equally importantly – have made it virtually impossible for the island to maintain agricultural self-sufficiency. Clauson refused, insisting that compulsory military service was 'unnecessary and inadvisable'.[58]

During this time Cyprus was not only cultivating crops to feed itself but was also supplying provisions for the Allied armies in Egypt and Macedonia. Between 1914 and 1918 the military authorities bought up the island's entire annual crop of carob beans, approximately 60,000 tons,[59] to provide forage for horses and pack animals. Together the Salonika and Egyptian Expeditionary

Forces bought 100,000 tons of wheat and barley[60] every year for the duration of the war, along with tens of thousands of goats and hundreds of thousands of eggs. The demand for cigarettes meant that tobacco began to be cultivated for the first time. The standard of living of the rural peasantry rose significantly and many peasant farmers received 'record prices for their crops'.[61] Some even managed, for the first time in generations, to emancipate themselves from debt.

But if life became easier for those living off the land, the German submarine blockade of Mediterranean merchant shipping meant that for the urban population the cost of living rapidly increased. The British Admiralty had been wrong-footed by the speed with which Germany adapted to unconventional naval warfare and was completely unprepared for Germany's devastating deployment of its fleet of submarines. Over the course of 1916 German submarines sank an average of 500,000 tons of Allied shipping every month.

As a result, colonies such as Cyprus were forced to become virtually self-sufficient. Tithe wheat from the government grain store – wheat taken as taxation revenue which would under normal circumstances have been exported to Britain – was released for local consumption. Prices of the 'necessities of life' – wheat, macaroni, coffee, petrol and sugar – were fixed by the colonial administration and exports of essential materials became illegal. The list of prohibited exports published in the *Cyprus Gazette* was long. It included cattle, sheep, pigs and poultry, along with beeswax, bladders and sausage skins, bones, caustic soda, cotton rags, guano, Neat's Foot oil, 'projectiles of all kinds' and railway wagons.[62]

Despite these measures town dwellers and white-collar workers struggled to cope with rising prices. Clauson was particularly concerned about 'working men' and 'lower middle class officials' within his administration, many of whom were forced into debt. He complained to the Colonial Office that men with families were 'burdened with the gravest anxieties...and are unable to lay by funds to provide for leave, insurance or other benefit for their widows and the education of their children'.[63] Like senior colonial officials in other territories Clauson also feared that excessively low salaries also made British civil servants susceptible to bribery and the impartiality of their 'official relations to the public'would be jeopardized. Despite the colony's impoverished status he managed to convince London to sanction a series of salary increases which he hoped would 'relieve much heartburn'.[64]

Communication between London and Nicosia could be erratic. Fuel shortages jeopardised the Cyprus mail service, presenting both Clauson and his predecessor Goold-Adams with a challenge that each man responded to in characteristic – and very different – ways. Increases in the cost of coal had forced the Khedivial Steamship Company, which transported the post between Cyprus and Egypt, to increase its charges by 50 per cent. When Goold-Adams refused to meet the increases, the steamship company announced that it would operate the steamers only 'as opportunity offers'. Concerned, Goold-Adams vowed to maintain the service, 'by means of sailing vessels'.[65] Regrettably he left the island before his picturesque solution could be implemented. Clauson's business-like response, by contrast, involved re-negotiating the contract with the Khedivial Line so that increased costs were absorbed by the more remunerative export of military supplies to Egypt.[66]

Wartime conditions also meant that numerous other responsibilities which under normal circumstances would have been delegated to government departments had to be handled personally by the high commissioner. Clauson was expected to adjudicate on the fate of a consignment of Italian ox-hoof combs, insured with a German agency and subsequently detained at Larnaca on the grounds that they were of 'enemy origin'.[67] He was required to authorise the loan of two translators, their typewriters and a 'small hand printing press suitable for printing proclamations'[68] to the British naval base at Mudros for the Gallipoli campaign. He also found time to nominate two young men for an award from the Royal Humane Society after they rescued a man who fell off Limassol pier trying to catch his hat, explaining that their 'prompt and courageous action' was particularly noteworthy 'in view of the fact that natives of Cyprus are not accustomed to sea bathing'.[69]

Private morals were also considered a matter for the high commissioner. When rumours began circulating that the medical officer at Nicosia Hospital, Dr Cooke, was having an extramarital affair with one of the nurses, Clauson insisted that he should be transferred to Larnaca, arguing that suggestions of infidelity had a bad effect on British society in the capital and that 'an imprudent married medical officer with an absent wife is out of place'.[70]

At least in terms of the island's domestic politics Clauson had an easier time than most of his predecessors. Britain's offer of Cyprus to Greece had fundamentally changed Cypriot perceptions of British rule. The imperial power had, for the first time, declared that its presence in Cyprus was conditional on political expediency and, therefore – ultimately – negotiable. Greek Cypriots interpreted the gesture as an overdue acknowledgement of the island's essentially Hellenic character, while Turkish Cypriots, fearful that, like the Turks of Crete, they would be forced to leave their homeland if they came under Greek rule, submitted lengthy protests to London. Despite this, members of the Legislative Council, aware that the island's future could not be resolved during wartime and that precipitate action now could jeopardise any post-war settlement, agreed to defer discussion of 'any measures of domestic legislation that may call for prolonged deliberation or might be regarded as controversial'.[71]

This was probably just as well, since Clauson was fully occupied with another difficult challenge: attempting to define who exactly Britain's Cypriot subjects were and what rights their new status gave them. From 1914 onwards a succession of ships arrived in Cyprus bringing refugees from Asia Minor. A number of these were men who claimed a Cypriot connection and were escaping conscription into the Turkish army, often leaving families and dependants behind them. Others were Christians or Jews of the Ottoman Empire, fleeing the chaos that erupted as the fragmentation of the old multi-ethnic society accelerated under the pressures of war. Many, like the shipload of Maltese from Smyrna, were simply despatched to Cyprus as a convenient holding station until they could be moved elsewhere. Clauson, like Goold Adams before him, struggled to deal with the immediate practical demands of these sudden influxes of needy refugees. The responses of both men were inevitably framed by their own Western European concepts of identity and nationhood, concepts which were entirely alien to the majority of refugees now flooding into the island.

The old Ottoman *millet* system had categorised individuals as belonging to religious communities, each under the jurisdiction of spiritual leaders, but it did not recognise the idea of a coherent national identity – or even of national boundaries – in the way that such concepts were understood in Europe. This traditional social structure, which extended even to the construction of an individual's sense of who he was and his personal relationship with the state, had been at the point of collapse for some time. The war now brought it crashing down.

The impact and enormity of the societal changes under way in the countries of the disintegrating Ottoman Empire were profound. Suddenly, Levantines who might have been born in Limassol or Salonika but lived in Beirut or Smyrna and were used to trading or travelling freely throughout the region were confronted by the concept of nationality. A passport, no longer merely a travel aid that facilitated a smooth journey, became a vital document which defined a man and his family and could determine their very survival.

Goold-Adams, compassionate but muddle-headed, became particularly concerned about the fate of the 'distressed Cypriots' of Asia Minor. He allocated £1,000 for their relief, to be distributed by the British ambassador in Constantinople. The Colonial Office commented cynically that the arrangement was 'probably useful at present to demonstrate the advantages of British protection'.[72]

As the war progressed the high commissioner's initial response developed into an extensive, ongoing relief operation, one that was conducted by inexperienced officials with limited funds, inadequate information, and no idea of how long existing levels of need would continue. Money was sent to approximately 1,200[73] Cypriots in Constantinople, Smyrna, Aleppo and Mersin. Cypriots 'stranded' at Athens were also granted 'relief necessary to avert starvation'.[74]

It was an impossible task, exacerbated by the Cyprus government's inability to confirm whether any of the recipients were, in fact, Cypriots as defined by the administration's new criteria. Many, it was acknowledged, were 'apt to claim Ottoman or British nationality indifferently, as may suit their convenience from time to time'.[75]

Even today, the quantity and thickness of the Colonial Office files with titles such as 'Relief of Distressed Cypriots in Asia Minor', 'Destitute Cypriots at Smyrna' 'Armenian Refugees' or 'Destitute Maltese' are daunting. Many of the marginal comments made on Clauson's despatches indicate that London, too, was overwhelmed by the scale of this unfamiliar problem. Insulated both by distance and by the de-personalising scale of the suffering, the civil servants at the Colonial Office offered little support to their men on the ground. They confined themselves to hoping that the humanitarian crisis might somehow be solved through success on the battlefield and that 'if we occupy Smyrna and the surrounding district, the position will be altered in so far as the Cypriots there will no longer be pressed to register as Turkish subjects'.[76]

For Clauson, closer to the suffering, it was not possible to adopt the same resigned fatalism as his colleagues in London. The high commissioner would have been aware of the massacre of millions of Ottoman Armenians in 1915. He would also have read reports from British intelligence officials in the Greek islands, where refugees from Asia Minor had fled and where 'there was nowhere one could walk but a small emaciated hand would pluck at one's sleeve and point mutely to an empty hungry mouth'.[77] It fell entirely to the high commissioner to create and implement a refugee policy that was both morally justifiable and economically sustainable in a country with such limited resources.

Clauson originally stipulated that only holders of Cypriot passports who had resided in Cyprus 'within say the last two years' should be entitled to repatriation to the colony at the government's expense. But as the difficulty of determining precisely who was entitled to a Cypriot passport gradually became apparent he adopted a more pragmatic approach, informing the Colonial Office by telegram that he now proposed to arrange for 'repatriation of persons born in Island and their families as special war measure at costs of Cyprus funds and irrespective of difficult question of nationality'.[78]

The first group to arrive on the island in March 1915, a party of 210, consisted not only of Cypriot repatriates but also Maltese and British Jewish refugees from Smyrna. Clauson had originally requested that the Maltese refugees be sent elsewhere since accommodation was scarce, 'food supplies are insufficient... substitutes for wheat flour being largely in use and prices high'. But on learning that they were already on their way, he telegrammed

London: 'Will make best arrangements possible. Have already obtained permission Government of Egypt importation limited amount flour weekly.' The Colonial Office, relieved at not having to handle the problem, filed a brief note alongside the high commissioner's telegram, 'Clauson will do the best he can.'[79]

After being processed at the Laranaca quarantine station, refugees were distributed amongst *khans* or inns in the town. Clauson's administration arranged for those refugees who arrived with their own bedding to be accommodated free of charge, while those who required beds paid 3 copper piastres[80] each: 'In this way accommodation was obtained for many more than the number for which payment ... was being charged.' But the rates soon had to be reduced, after none of the refugees, apart from a few lace makers, was able to find work, 'owing to distress and want of work amongst Cypriots, especially at Larnaca'.[81]

'Superior families' were initially offered accommodation in a small hotel nearby, but they too encountered the same difficulty finding jobs. The Cremona family of Beirut was typical. A British citizen, William Cremona arrived in Cyprus with his two sons, his sister Adele, sister-in-law Julienne and her 'numerous children'. Cremona had been forced to abandon his wine business in Beirut, and his brother, previously the steward of the Beirut French Club, had been interned there. None of the adults obtained jobs in Cyprus, where preference was 'naturally given to the numerous Greek girls who are working cheaply',[82] and they attempted to live on small hand-outs from three or four charitable funds.

The sudden fragmentation of the Ottoman world view that resulted from the First World War meant that groups of individuals who might previously have lived together relatively peaceably were now regarded as if they personally were representatives of warring nation states. Could Armenians fleeing the Turkish genocide be securely accommodated amongst Turkish Cypriots? Would it be safe to billet Serbian refugees with Greek Cypriot families, given Greece's refusal to honour its treaty obligations to Serbia and defend it against Bulgarian attack?

These were the practicalities that confronted the high commissioner as the ideological tectonic plates that underpinned the old order shifted and the Ottoman world collapsed. When the war began Cyprus was a forgotten backwater administered by the abstracted and ineffectual Goold-Adams. By 1918 it was enmeshed in the reconstruction of the post-Ottoman Levant. Clauson was required – much of the time single-handedly – to deal with the consequences of the most profound changes to affect the region since the Ottoman conquest. It is to his credit that throughout this period he not only responded to various wartime contingencies but also ensured that relations between the island's different religious and cultural communities remained calm.

Such responsibilities were daunting enough, but the high commissioner had another important task: to supervise the island's development as a base for regional espionage, a hitherto little-known aspect of the conflict that began two years into the First World War.

6

Showing Benevolent Neutrality
1916–19

Visitors to Cyprus who travel inland and drive across the Troodos Mountains are sure to notice Mount Olympus. At 6,404 feet it is easily the highest peak in the range, but it is made even more conspicuous by the enormous white sphere that sits on the summit – popularly referred to as 'the golf ball'. The ball's casing contains sophisticated electronic equipment. Today the uppermost tip of Mount Olympus is occupied not by Greek gods, but by a British long-range radar and radio-receiving station. Signals picked up on the mountain are transmitted to a British receiving post at Ayios Nikolaos near Famagusta and from there to Government Communication Headquarters in Cheltenham. According to the terms under which Cyprus gained its independence in 1960, Britain retains the right to use Mount Olympus in perpetuity, a reflection of the island's continuing importance to British intelligence interests in the region to this day. It was during World War One, while John Clauson was high commissioner that Cyprus first became a regional centre for espionage – a status which almost cost the high commissioner his post and very nearly led to the introduction of direct military rule on the island.

In the aftermath of the disastrous Gallipoli campaign, British military intelligence in the Mediterranean was reorganised and the Eastern Mediterranean Special Intelligence Bureau (EMSIB) established to co-ordinate military and local police intelligence-gathering work. The author Compton Mackenzie, who later wrote *Whiskey Galore*, ran the Athens branch of EMSIB. He found the organisation highly territorial and commented that it fought its battles 'with a ferocity and endurance which could not but evoke the admiration of readers, were the prime inspiration of such struggles a little more admirable'. The bureau was headed by a former military consul, Major Samson, a man 'wedded to the notion of secrecy for the sake of being secret',[1] who instructed his agents never to leave the office without first incinerating their used blotting paper in a cast iron flower pot.[2] Samson based his organisation in Alexandria and in the spring of 1916 Cyprus was placed within its field of operations.

For his part, the high commissioner (like his predecessor Goold-Adams) believed that despite its ethnically mixed population Cyprus posed no risk to security and offered 'little or no opportunities to the working of the enemy's secret service'. Since all Ottoman subjects born in Cyprus were now in any case British, there were only 31 'enemy aliens' resident on the island, mostly Austro-Hungarian mining engineers.

The high commissioner believed the keen new arrivals from EMSIB in Alexandria would have little to do in Cyprus and he frequently ignored their communications or forgot to reply to them. Even so it is hard to feel much sympathy for the officious and curiously gullible EMSIB officers who rampaged across the island over the next two years. They were to run their own operation with farcical ineptitude while making repeated attempts to undermine civilian authority in Cyprus.

The activities of the Cyprus bureau were divided into 'A' Work, 'the acquisition of information about the enemy' undertaken mainly in Asia Minor and Syria, and 'B' Work, essentially counter-espionage, which involved 'safeguarding the existence of agents and their landing places in Cyprus'. 'A' branch headquarters were in Famagusta (along with the regional offices of British Naval Intelligence) with sub-agencies in Aleppo, in Damascus, and Rayak in the Bekaa Valley and 'constituted an essential part of the service of information on Palestine'. The Famagusta bureau reported to a Captain Smith based at Port Said. Agents were regularly conveyed to the enemy coast by Cypriot trawlers or caiques, or occasionally by French vessels stationed on the tiny island of Ruad – present-day Arwad—off the coast of Syria. The 'A' intelligence network extended to no less than three wireless telegraph stations on the island. There was a British intelligence station at Larnaca, a British naval intelligence facility at Famagusta and a third terminal at Limassol used by French naval intelligence for secret communication with the flotilla stationed at Ruad.[3]

In Cyprus, as in Greece, the intelligence services initially relied on recruiting agents from the huge numbers of multi-lingual Levantine refugees flooding into the island. But these destitute, traumatised men, desperate for work, did not prove reliable sources of information and their collaboration with over-imaginative British intelligence officers with an inflated sense of their own importance often produced episodes of sheer lunacy. A typical message received by Mackenzie at the Athens bureau read, 'the minerals of Mounichia cannot be explored because the wild boar brings itching to the body. Have met and talked with the commander. Compliments Mary the Virgin'.[4] Predictably, early results in Cyprus were disappointing and Clauson was forced to telegram an admission that 'despite the utmost endeavours ... to establish [agents] in Syria and Cilicia, refugee and Cyprus agents have proved worthless'.[5]

'B Work' headquarters were in Nicosia, where a team of three men worked under a zealous officer called Captain Scott. Between them they were responsible for safeguarding the island's oil and fuel depots and preventing sensitive information from Egypt being passed to the enemy via Cyprus. New recruits were issued with comprehensive EMSIB guidelines on how to handle local informers. But since agents were paid only for information provided, the system inevitably leant itself to obscure and often entirely fictional reporting. In tacit acknowledgement of this the EMSIB handbook cautioned that an 'ornate report' was usually suspect and 'generally supplied by worthless agents who wish to impress those engaging them'.[6]

When not engaged in supervising unreliable local agents 'B' branch officers were required to complete 'Personalities Forms', detailing the careers of leading politicians, businessmen or 'those of general social importance', and to provide fortnightly reports 'on matters of general interest'. If there was nothing to report, the EMSIB guidelines doggedly explained, then 'a note to this effect should be forwarded'.[7]

For Captain Scott in Nicosia this was seldom necessary. His reports catalogue a succession of conspiracies, plots and dangers, any one of which he argued could pose a grave threat to Allied success in the war. EMSIB Nicosia became particularly disturbed when the commander in chief of the Egyptian Expeditionary Force, Lieutenant-General Sir Archibald Murray, decided in August 1916 to send 3,500 Ottoman prisoners of war to Cyprus. A vast prisoner-of-war camp capable of accommodating 6,000 prisoners was erected at Famagusta. The high commissioner boasted that it was 'admirably equipped with all accessories including several mosques' and provided 'excellent' food.[8]

Clauson believed that the existence of the camp would have a beneficial effect on the island's Turkish Cypriots, 'by shaking the idea of German invincibility in their slow minds and showing them British treatment of a gallant adversary'.[9] The notion of leading by example, so important to the island's early administrators, persisted. The long-standing imperial rivalry between the European powers which had led to the war was articulated in microcosm through the Famagusta POW camp. For Clauson, it provided an opportunity to denigrate Germany (as opposed to the Ottoman Empire, where the prisoners actually came from) while demonstrating to Cypriot subjects the specific benefits of colonisation by a people – as the colonists saw themselves – of such intrinsic decency as the British. But whether any of the 'slow-minded' Turkish Cypriots cared to decipher this public enactment of British colonial legitimacy was another matter.

If some did, others at least remained unconvinced. In May 1917 an excitable communication from EMSIB Nicosia explained that letters and bottles of brandy were being concealed in a hole in the ground outside the camp by 'Turks in the town'.[10]

The clandestine letter writers were later identified as four men from Famagusta. They were arrested and prosecuted but subsequently acquitted when the intelligence agent giving evidence against them was discredited. The defendants were, however, 'adjured by the court to be more circumspect in their behaviour in the future'. Captain Scott was appalled by the verdict and submitted a lengthy report to his colleague Smith in Port Said, stressing 'the need for better control in Cyprus'. On this occasion Clauson seems to have concluded that EMSIB's objections could not be ignored, for he overruled the court's decision and, in a rare demonstration of his executive powers, interned two of the accused men in Kyrenia Castle.

Of particular concern to 'B' Branch in both Nicosia and Alexandria was the extent of the island's contact with Egypt: 14 Cypriot caiques regularly traded along the eastern Mediterranean coast, 10 of which were licensed to trade with Egypt, while another 33 boats based on Ruad Island were licensed to trade on the same route. The intelligence bureau feared that information about troop movements through the Suez Canal or about military operations in Palestine was being leaked through Cyprus to the Turkish mainland. In this case their concerns were not unreasonable. In January 1917 General Sir Archibald Murray was preparing to move significant numbers of troops northwards from Egypt into Ottoman Palestine and launch his assault on Gaza. It was crucial that details of the operation were not leaked to the enemy. But as usual EMSIB's response was clumsy and heavy handed.

Samson immediately condemned all commercial traffic between Cyprus and Alexandria as 'a menace to the welfare of operations on the Eastern Frontier'[11] and instructed Captain Scott to draft new regulations designed to prevent enemy agents from stealing boats and sailing them to Syria or Anatolia. Fishing vessels were to be brought into port at night and placed under guard. Access to the quayside would be restricted to military officers or those with passes, and every porter should be 'stripped to his shirt and thoroughly searched'.[12] Clauson initially resisted the proposals, arguing that they disrupted normal fishing work while achieving little. But he finally acquiesced and the regulations were reluctantly put into force in April 1917. Still Scott was not satisfied. He insisted that crews from Cypriot vessels arriving at the port of Alexandria should be forbidden from disembarking, while the crew of the regular Khedivial Line mail steamer the SS Kossier, which made a weekly round trip from Cyprus to Egypt, should also be refused shore leave in Cyprus. The mail boat was viewed with particular suspicion on the questionable grounds that it had not yet been torpedoed 'in spite of the recent activities of submarines'.[13] Scott demanded that an agent be permanently retained on board the *SS Kossier*, to sail tediously back and forth between Cyprus and Port Said and monitor the crew's activities. Scott and his officers were also concerned by the frequent trade between Cyprus and Ruad island. 'B' bureau in Nicosia believed the route had become 'a likely source of leakage of information' and demanded that the high commissioner should arrange for the wholesale evacuation of the inhabitants of Ruad to an unspecified location in Cyprus – possibly to 'a village near Larnaca'.[14]

Clauson chose to ignore this far-fetched proposal and calmly explained to the Nicosia bureau that although he did not object in principle to the deployment of permanent officers on board *SS Kosseir* it was doubtful whether their presence would have the desired effect 'as messages could still be secreted in packages loaded or unloaded'. Relations between Government House and 'B' Branch remained cool and Scott submitted a series of highly critical reports about Clauson to EMSIB Alexandria. As a result the high commissioner was accused by British military intelligence of being 'far too lenient',[15] largely because of his refusal to intern 'enemy alien' Austrians who worked at the Amiandos asbestos mine in the Troodos Mountains. Cyprus was judged to have made inadequate contributions to the Allied war effort and was damningly dismissed as being little better than 'a foreign country showing benevolent neutrality'.[16]

Matters deteriorated further following an incident in June 1917 when an 'A' branch agent was shot and killed while attempting to land by night on the Anatolian coast. Scott and Smith suspected that a Cypriot lighter called *Dolphin* had leaked information about the expected landing. Some days earlier the *Dolphin* had left Famagusta heading for Limassol but had never arrived and was presumed to have defected to enemy territory. Judging by the experiences of EMSIB in Athens it is likely the boat was doing nothing more sinister than 'plotting to smuggle hashish into Egypt',[17] but that did not deter Scott and Smith. Together they demanded that Clauson should secretly 'prohibit all Moslem Cypriots from working on ships or boats', measures, they insisted, that must be implemented without 'raising the suspicions that such an order had been issued'. Not surprisingly this unworkable proposal 'did not commend itself to his Excellency', who declined to take the recommended action.

Scott and Smith responded by submitting a particularly damning despatch to Captain Samson in Alexandria. They complained that their work was impeded by lack of support from the Cypriot authorities and that their recommendations were only implemented 'in so far as they do not affect the interests or convenience of the administration of the people and the inhabitants'. They were particularly incensed by Clauson's continued insistence that he alone should retain the right to authorise internment, and then only if it had been proven 'to the satisfaction of a Martial Law Court' that an individual had been assisting the enemy.

Fortunately Clauson enjoyed better relations with naval intelligence services on the island, presumably because the security threats they identified were
more tangible. Consignments of petrol sent from the Vacuum Oil Company in
Egypt sometimes arrived up to 40 cases short, and it was feared that Cypriot
customs officials were being bribed to divert fuel to German submarines in
the region.[18] Clauson placed the island's coastal depots under armed guard
and implemented an intelligence proposal for an island-wide telephone system,
with Famagusta as its hub, so that submarine sightings could be reported to the
British naval intelligence station there, 'and thence by wireless to the French
patrol vessels'.[19] The system was eventually completed in July 1917, but the war
office insisted that costs should be met by the Cyprus administration and argument over who was to foot the bill continued long after the war was over.[20]

None of these measures deterred EMSIB from continuing to interfere in
Clauson's management of the island's affairs. The next challenge came, unex-
pectedly, from the former head of the agency's Salonika bureau – Harry
Pirie-Gordon, a contemporary at Oxford of both Harry Luke and Compton
Mackenzie, who had been appointed to the bureau in August 1916. Two months
later the Greek prime minister, Eleftherious Venizelos, arrived in Salonika
where he established a 'Temporary Government of National Defence'. Possibly
as a result of conversations with Venizelos, with whom he was known to be
on good terms,[21] Pirie-Gordon submitted a startling proposal to the Colonial
Office for the forced relocation to Cyprus of no less than 20,000 Macedonian
Turks on the grounds that, amongst other things, 'the newcomers by reason of
their dislike for the Greeks would naturally become supporters of the British
Administration'. Clauson's response to yet another hair-brained scheme for
wholesale population transfer was calm. He pointed out that the island administration 'scarcely needs the support of the Moslems of Cyprus against the Greeks,
and would I think be very unwise to seek it'. In conclusion he drew the Colonial
Office's attention to the difficulty of feeding such a large influx without heavy
'initial expenditure on housing, well sinking, animals, implements and seed',
adding, with understatement, 'the proposal seems very impracticable'.[22]

Despite the reasoned tone of this official response it is clear that Clauson's
patience was exhausted and his frosty relations with EMSIB soon came to
a head. At 6.57 pm on 11 August 1917 the Colonial Office forwarded a telegram to the high commissioner requesting his observations on its content. It
contained a message from General Allenby, who had replaced Murray as the
general officer commanding in Egypt, proposing that Cyprus should immediately be placed directly under military control, more specifically under his own
command. At this stage in the conflict Allenby was involved in detailed planning for his campaign in Palestine the following autumn and was concerned
to ensure that details of the operation were not be passed to the enemy. His

claim to Cyprus was based on recent intelligence which showed 'some leakage of information and other undesirable activities of the enemy'. In fact, Allenby's proposal had been prompted by Smith's and Scott's latest report on Clauson which had been forwarded up the chain of command to GHQ Cairo. This was potentially devastating for the colonial administration and was tantamount to a redundancy notice for Clauson himself. The introduction of military control on the island would have involved the subordination of all officials in the colonial civil service to army officers, men who had no previous knowledge of Cyprus and who were answerable to their own chain of military command. Clauson and his senior staff would, in effect, have become superfluous.

It is not clear when exactly the telegram arrived on Clauson's desk but he wasted no time in responding. His reply was wired off at 1.30 a.m. on 13 August. It is another model of dignified, almost magisterial, reasoning; but Clauson no doubt needed a few stiff drinks to get him through its composition. The high commissioner argued respectfully that General Allenby could not be expected to have local knowledge of Cyprus, or to appreciate that recent military intelligence reports were entirely hypothetical and based on discredited local sources. It was not until the end of his telegram that Clauson mentioned Captains Smith and Scott, alluding to the possibility that their criticisms of his administration had been filed maliciously after he had rejected their demands to detain all Turkish-speaking fishing crews ('a groundless provocation of boat captains and a political blunder'[23]).

Clauson's ability to draft a knock-out despatch, a talent which his predecessor, Goold-Adams, had so conspicuously lacked, won the day. His former colleagues at the Colonial Office clucked around his telegram vexatiously, each anxious to pencil in his comments of support. 'It is clear', one wrote, 'that the proposal came from the Army Captain in Port Said, after Clauson rejected his advice.' Others followed, 'I cannot imagine a much less suitable field for the exercise of military control than Cyprus with all its local problems and complexities ... I entirely agree. The jack-boot would be much out of place in Cyprus.'

The threat had been defused. Four months later Captain Scott was recalled from Cyprus. The following February (1918), as part of a general overhaul, most of his agents were dismissed and approaches made instead to 'various persons of standing and reliability with a view to obtaining their voluntary assistance'.[24] From that point on relations between EMSIB and Government House improved dramatically and two months later, at Clauson's suggestion, a Captain Mervyn, a former police commissioner in Nicosia, was appointed to supervise 'B' work on the island.

On 11 November, a week after the war in Europe ended, Clauson submitted a request for six-weeks leave on full pay, to be spent within the colony, on the grounds that he was suffering from 'fatigue and loss of voice'. The extraordinary burdens of the war would have exhausted a man in the best of health; but throughout his time in office Clauson had been suffering from latent pulmonary tuberculosis. He died at Government House on 31 December 1918, aged 52. Clauson was buried at the Anglican cemetery in Nicosia where his grave is marked by a horizontal stone of white marble and is hidden away at the back of the cemetery, behind later, grander tombs. The inscription, usually concealed under an accumulation of pine needles and cones, says that he died in the service of his country.

The colonial machine continued ticking over. The island's chief secretary, Malcolm Stevenson, took over management of the administration and subsequently succeeded Clauson as high commissioner. In early 1919, Alfred Milner, the new secretary of state for the colonies, received a genial personal letter from an Oxfordshire J.P. called Sir Paul Makins, in which he enquired whether his sister, Lady Clauson, might receive a pension from the Colonial Office since her husband's death was 'largely due to the continued strain of his work in Cyprus during the last four years'. Milner forwarded the letter to his permanent secretaries who concluded that there were no official funds available for such a purpose and that in any case 'with £800 a year she is not badly off even in these times'. The last official word on Clauson's life and career in Cyprus was scrawled awkwardly on the cover sheet of his files, ordering, perhaps in embarrassed haste, that the advice of the permanent under secretaries be heeded: 'As proposed. Get off quickly.'[25] Thus one of the more creditable pages of British colonial history was turned and largely forgotten.

7

Gentle Somnambulance
1918–26

Business is slow inside Nicosia Post Office on the northern side of the divided capital, where, on this particular Monday morning, the Turkish Cypriot staff outnumber the customers by nine to one.

An elderly man leans heavily on a sloping wooden writing desk attached to the wall, painstakingly addressing an envelope. The desk must have been fixed to its space below the window long before the invention of the ballpoint: a series of square indentations in the surface marks spaces that were once occupied by inkwells.

At the counter opposite, the solitary woman customer is buying stamps, while the clerks and cashiers chat together in Turkish. On the wall above them is the usual image of Mustafa Kemal Attaturk, the father of modern Turkey (a legal requirement in all public buildings in Turkey and Northern Cyprus), along with photographs of past and present Turkish Cypriot leaders.

In the street outside, a man selling *simit*, the hard, circular bread covered in sesame seeds that many Turkish Cypriots eat for breakfast, wheels his covered trolley to his usual position at the corner of the building. Above him, the clock over the main entrance, the work of H. Williamson Ltd of London, has stopped at 10 minutes to four.

In the decades when the postal service provided the only link with the outside world, walking past the clock on Thursdays or Fridays when the mail steamer made its delivery was 'like attending a family gathering, with the town's merchants and professional people clustered round the post office or in nearby coffee shops while the mail was being sorted. The hopes of remittance men, expecting this and that, doctors expecting formulae of the latest patent medicines all gave the proceedings the appearance of a lottery, with broad smiles or long faces depending on the luck of the draw.'[1]

Despite the presence of taller, modern office blocks nearby, Nicosia Post Office still seems a monumental building. Constructed in 1925, its ostentatious neo-classical columns seem ridiculously inappropriate for a colony as small and impoverished as Cyprus, an enduring demonstration of administrative hubris.

The post office was one of a series of grandiose public buildings erected between 1918 and 1926, the period when Malcolm Stevenson served first as high commissioner then as governor of Cyprus. Although Stevenson himself was obviously not responsible for the buildings' designs, it is tempting to see in the overblown style of Nicosia Post Office in particular an architectural reflection of the pomposity and sterility that characterised his government of Cyprus.

Stevenson was not a high flyer. Widely recognised by his contemporaries as having been promoted beyond his abilities, he was described by former high commissioner Charles, King-Harman, as 'very incompetent'. He was an unsympathetic man, who failed entirely to address the alarming economic and social problems confronting Cyprus in the aftermath of the First World War. In fairness, these were particularly complex and would have challenged a more able man. But Stevenson's inept response, in particular his attempts to manipulate Legislative Council elections, generated enormous bitterness amongst Cypriots and irrevocably damaged their faith in colonial government.

The appointment of such an ineffectual high commissioner was particularly harmful for Cyprus in the immediate aftermath of the First World War when the island's political and economic future was under debate. Although, for the colonial authorities on the island, the fighting ended in November 1918, for the emerging nation states of Greece and Turkey it was to continue for another four years during which time the balance of power shifted dramatically between them as each claimed territory at the other's expense. Ultimately this had little direct impact on Cyprus, but it contributed to a prevailing climate of uncertainty over the island's future, in particular over the question of whether it might be ceded to Greece.

In the years directly following the armistice a succession of Greek Cypriot delegations travelled to London, hoping to press their case for union with Greece in the context of the general dismemberment of the Ottoman Empire. Encouraged by Britain's wartime offer of Cyprus to Greece, and by Lloyd George's warm relations with the Greek prime minister, Eleftherios Venizelos, the first deputation spent almost a year in London, hoping (in vain) for an audience with the British prime minister. Around this time letters from Philhellenic academics appeared in *The Times*, urging that 'Cyprus, which was offered to Greece in 1915, should now be transferred to her keeping'.[2] Their views were taken seriously and renewed doubts over government plans for the colony meant that for the next two years the Anglican church was unable to recruit clergy to serve in Cyprus because of 'uncertainty as to what was going to happen there'.[3]

Greek Cypriot hopes came to an end on 26 October 1920, when the London delegation was finally granted an interview with Leo Amery, the under-secretary of state for the colonies, and told that no change in the island's status could be contemplated. Preoccupied with drawing up a new map of the world, neither Lloyd George nor Venizelos had regarded Cyprus as sufficiently important to bring to the conference table, and, more significantly, neither enjoyed sufficient domestic political support to be able to broker a deal in the face of opposition. The British public first became aware of the delegation's meeting with Amery six days later via a startlingly imperialist headline in *The Times*, which, alluding to Richard the Lionheart's brief occupation of the island in 1191, reported, 'Cyprus Remains British, King Richard's Conquest Retained.'

The retention of Cyprus might have been a negotiable issue in Lloyd George's eyes, but within both the admiralty and, equally importantly, the air force the conviction was growing that the island might, after all, be of considerable strategic importance. The arguments were broadly similar to those put forward 40 years earlier. Although Cyprus was less valuable as a station for peace-time air operations than nearby Egypt, had the regional political landscape changed for the worse, it might have played a significant role. It would, therefore, have been unwise to jeopardise this potential by ceding it to a foreign power. The chief of air staff, Air Commodore S.M. Steele, concluded that although 'we do not propose to use Cyprus as a base in peace time … it is of vital importance that no other power should be allowed to do so and therefore we must retain control of the island'.[4] Once again Cyprus was pushed to the back of the imperial arsenal until a rainy day, not important enough in itself to attract money or resources, but too much of a threat in the hands of a hostile power to be given away.

While Cyprus lapsed into a decade of political and economic stagnation, neighbouring Asia Minor was in a state of flux, the site of a war that was to change forever the demographic character of the Levant, leaving the island even more of a colonial peculiarity in an increasingly ethnically homogenised region.

The Greco-Turkish war, during which more than a million non-Muslims fled their homes in Smyrna, had been characterised by atrocities against civilians on both sides. As a result, the 1923 Treaty of Lausanne, which marked its end, required the two new nation states to arrange a compulsory exchange of populations. Around 2 million people were forced to leave their homes and since the criteria for exchange were exclusively religious, over 1 million 'Greeks', many of whom spoke only Turkish, found themselves uprooted to present-day Greece, while hundreds of thousands of Muslims were forced to re-locate within the frontiers of modern-day Turkey. Cyprus, with a mixed population that until then had been typical of the multi-ethnic nature of the Levant, became an anomaly.

These developments could not leave the island entirely unaffected. An estimated 1.5 million (mainly Greek) Christians were expelled from Asia Minor, around 2,400 of whom subsequently sought refuge in Cyprus.[5] Concerned at this sudden depletion in manpower, the Kemalist government in Ankara encouraged Turks living outside the borders of the new Turkish Republic to emigrate to Turkey. Turkish Cypriots were particularly welcome since they were considered to be 'accustomed to western cultural orientations as well as free from religious fanaticism'.[6] The Turkish government optimistically authorised the entry of up to 20,000 Cypriot Turks into the country and established a consular office in Larnaca.[7] Between 1924 and 1926 just over 9,000 Turkish Cypriots applied for Turkish citizenship, but no more than 5,000, most of them poor farm workers, are thought to have emigrated. Many later attempted to return, disillusioned because the land and property they had been promised never materialised.

Ankara nevertheless declared that all Turkish Cypriot applicants – even those who had never left Cyprus – legally retained their Turkish nationality. For its part, London, fearing that the policy might lead to the creation of a Turkish colony on Cyprus, on behalf of which Turkey might subsequently intervene, maintained that any automatic right to Turkish nationality had now lapsed. The status of the 9,000 putative Turkish Cypriot emigrants became a complex and politically loaded issue over the years that followed, as successive administrations attempted to come to grips with yet another consequence of the fragmentation of the Ottoman world.

A sharp decline in the fortunes of the Turkish Cypriot community after the First World War must have made the prospects of a fresh start in Anatolia particularly attractive. But for all Cypriots life on the land was becoming increasingly harsh.

The war years of relative prosperity were followed by global economic recession resulting in a decline in demand for Cypriot exports and a corresponding drop in the prices they commanded on international markets. The slump in the international economy hit the Cypriot farmer, who habitually spent most of his life in debt, particularly hard.

Rural indebtedness had been endemic amongst the Cypriot peasantry in the centuries before the British occupation, but the complex Ottoman system of land management meant that although debtors frequently served prison sentences and were often forced to bequeath their debts to their children, they were seldom actually dispossessed of their land. The British administration applied radically different concepts of land ownership, based on the sanctity of private property. The new legislation changed the basis on which debts could be recovered and the administration ensured, through efficient policing, that its strictures were enforced thoroughly. As a result, at times of hardship, or after an indifferent harvest, the peasant farmers grew increasingly dependent on urban money lenders – merchants and lawyers, whose power and influence grew accordingly.

Some colonial civil servants were aware that many of their early land reforms had, in practice, created more hardship amongst the rural poor than the feudal Ottoman system. Soon after the start of the British occupation, in 1886, the district commissioner of Paphos admitted that although 'from the point of view of our western civilization' the old laissez faire Ottoman system of debt collection appeared to be unsatisfactory, 'when it is considered that in a country like Cyprus about 90% of the population get into debt more or less every winter, and these are the peasant proprietors who are the backbone of the country and provide the greatest proportion of the revenue, it will be seen that there is some reason for government protecting them as much as possible'.[8] But comprehensive measures to alleviate rural indebtedness would have challenged one of the fundamental principles that underpinned the empire: the inviolability of private property. Not surprisingly, successive administrations ducked the issue and failed to address its causes, casting themselves instead as the disinterested defenders of the rural poor, whose efforts to relieve economic distress were obstructed by the duplicity and cunning of the money lenders.

Previous attempts to protect 'the illiterate and those who worked with their hands from oppression by the shrewd quick-witted money lender' had ground to a halt in the face of the island's Legislative Council. It was claimed that 'nearly all the Greek elected members are advocates and usurers... inclined to use their position to block legislation on the subject'. The administration hoped it could bypass the council and appeal directly to the rural peasantry, arguing 'if the people understand the bills they will be able to exert a pressure which the members of the Legislature will be unable to resist. The people, no doubt look to the Government for help ... If however the Government fails they will all revert to a state of apathy and resignation and the debtors to their patient subjection to their old masters.'[9] Feelings, even in the distant metropolis, against the 'villainous' money lenders often ran high. One Colonial Office official regretted the passing of an earlier, less regulated age when the hard-pressed peasant had the freedom to 'administer a dose of shot',[10] if the usurer's demands became too onerous.

This image of a villainous Greek Cypriot legislature motivated purely by self-interest, exploiting the vulnerable peasantry while at the same time acting as a barrier between the 'real Cypriots' and their government, became increasingly established in the rhetoric of the period. It was a damaging stereotype that endured until the end of the British occupation.

The impact of the post-war economic recession was exacerbated by a succession of failed harvests. As levels of debt increased, money lenders began to foreclose on their loans and in 1924 alone there were over 3,000 forced sales. Land values plummeted, and properties sold for a fraction of their previous value. A new class of dispossessed peasantry came into existence, and by 1927 it was estimated that there were 11,000 landless families dependent on 'the miseries of casual labour'[11] with an income of £12 a year or less.

Stevenson was not immune to the sufferings of the rural poor, but he and his staff were not sufficiently competent to legislate effectively to alleviate them. The introduction of no less than four laws during the course of his governorship, each intended to ameliorate the problem of rural debt, merely exacerbated the problem. As successive attempts to alleviate the economic crisis failed, Stevenson both alienated the urban class he so despised and lost the confidence of the rural peasantry.

Arguably the most successful initiative to remedy rural distress during this period owed as much to the private sector as to Stevenson's bureaucratic and inefficient government. In December 1924 Stevenson began discussions with Hugh Llewellyn Jones, manager of the Ottoman Bank in Nicosia, on the establishment of an agricultural bank that would lend money at fixed rates of interest to agricultural co-operatives. By June of the following year the Agricultural Bank of Cyprus was offering fixed-rate loans at an interest rate of 4 per cent. Twelve months later only 62 co-operative societies had applied for loans. For many of the most needy farmers the repayment terms were too short, but the bank's formation nevertheless represented the most serious attempt to date to address the crisis of rural indebtedness.

One enduring source of disaffection, viewed with increasing resentment, was the British government's insistence on extracting £92,700 each year from the colony – around six shillings per head of population – in payment of the Turkish Tribute. Under the terms of the 1923 Lausanne Treaty, all former Ottoman territories were obliged to 'contribute towards the debts formerly contracted by the state to which they belonged'.[12] Technically Cyprus was not included in this obligation since Britain had annexed the colony at the outbreak of war, placing it overnight on the winning side. But in a remarkable demonstration of legalistic manipulation and mean-spiritedness, London insisted that Cyprus should continue to pay. In lieu of this, the deduction of the 'Tribute' remained in place.

Stevenson submitted a detailed despatch to the Colonial Office proposing that the island be exempted from further payment. He requested that a proportion of the budget surpluses accumulated between 1914 and 1922 be returned. This amounted to around £40,000, money that could be spent on water supplies, schools and the provision of small loans to municipal authorities. The

Colonial Office responded pedantically that Stevenson had disregarded 'the liability of Cyprus to bear a share of the Ottoman debt'.[13]

A more resolute and confident high commissioner might have persisted. But not only was Stevenson himself a man of limited abilities, his administration was staffed by 'misfits and incompetents', men lacking 'in intellectual and social attainments' who were unable to 'mix with other races without detracting from the dignity of the ruling class'.[14] As a result, far less social contact took place between members of the colonial administration and the local elite than in other colonies. Gladys Peto noticed in 1926 that despite the presence of 'Turkish and Greek judges … all of whom speak English', it generally took 'some time for the English residents to get acquainted with those people of other races, which is a very great pity'.[15]

A large number of the island's most able wartime officials had moved on, replaced by former army officers, recruited by a Colonial Office determined to 'give preference to those who had seen active service in the armed forces'.[16] The newcomers, many of whom exhibited a 'contemptuous arrogance'[17] and continued to refer to themselves by their military rank, often had little colonial experience and even less understanding of the complex situation that had existed in Cyprus during the war years. Anxieties over social status contributed to a particularly authoritarian style of government. Many colonial officials, particularly those 'escaping from the lower orders in England' who found themselves in positions of authority in Cyprus, were 'determined to take on the mantle of the lord of the manor, if they could possibly seize it'.[18]

The mediocrity of the Stevenson administration became a standing joke, and visitors noted that officials tended to 'take the line of least resistance and regard serious constructive work as an encroachment on their elevenses'.[19] The pace of work was certainly leisured. When the colony's financial secretary, Clive Watts, submitted a flimsy handwritten memo to the chief secretary requesting permission to leave the office early on three days a week so that he might play golf, the scrawled reply came back 'no objection'.[20]

The indifference of senior administrative personnel inevitably filtered down to more junior (Cypriot) staff. When Stevenson's successor, Ronald Storrs, attempted to invigorate the lethargic administration and increase the working week by five more hours he was faced with a succession of 'objections not less ingenious than varied'[21] before he was finally able to force the measure through.

The relaxed pace of life was also noted by the young Gilbert Harding, who subsequently gained fame as the irascible participant of the early British television programme 'What's My Line?'. Harding, who taught English at a number of schools on the island, described his daily routine as one of 'gentle somnambulance'. Work began at 7 a.m. and finished at 11.30 a.m., when he retired to the English Club for a pink gin. After that, he returned to school for 'a pleasant lunch of cheese and salad, washed down by the good wine of the island'. Harding then took a siesta, rising in time to change and 'stroll back to the English Club for a weak whisky and soda, followed, in God's good time, by dinner and bridge'.[22]

The administration's post-war torpor was occasionally enlivened. Charles Hart-Davis, the new commissioner for Nicosia, and his wife, Vivian, found that their responsibilities included care of Hussein bin Ali, the elderly king of the Hejaz, the western part of modern-day Saudi Arabia. As the sharif of Mecca during the First World War, he had been encouraged by the British to lead the Arab Revolt against Ottoman rule. Later, having declared himself king, he had been forced to flee and seek refuge with his former ally after the cities of Mecca, Medina and Jeddah were captured by his rival, Ibn Saud. The king arrived in Nicosia with numerous servants, several horses, 'who were brought into the dining room for tit-bits at the end of the meal', and his pet ostrich, 'a cross bird that snarled at everyone'. With his colourful clothes, his menagerie, and his 'huge black slaves',[23] Hussein became an object of fascination to Nicosia society. He appears to have played up to the role of the exotic Oriental, riding across lawns during society garden parties 'on a prancing grey Arab',[24] and, more poignantly, lending his ceremonial gold and silver robes and 'exquisite headdresses' to his hosts for a government fancy dress party. Eventually the Foreign Office packed the king back to his sons in Transjordan (today's Jordan). He was despatched from Nicosia railway station in the 'cleaned and carpeted' luggage van of the train, which, after several 'thuds and jerks got off at last'.[25]

Unthreatening, aristocratic and colourful, the king was embraced by the colonists as the last flourish of an obsolete world order. But there were other indications that elements within the tiny British community regretted the dismemberment of the Oriental Levant and the creation of a region of modern nation states. Glady's Peto's guide to Cyprus reflects this ambivalence. Her writing combines a cultivated modernity and worldliness, with periodic lapses into passages of melancholia and wistfulness, such as her description of a garden in Nicosia where she had previously met King Hussein.

Groups of chrysanthemums and pink climbing geraniums grew among the cypress-trees. The fountain dripped and tinkled. Below in the moat two teams of black-haired Greek boys were playing football. One side had lemon-coloured shirts, the other emerald green. They wore tight, much abbreviated shorts, which gave a sort of Russian ballet effect. They cheered and shouted and leapt upon the ball … it appeared to me a curiously unreal and stage-like kind of performance. The setting sun gleamed upon the little houses on the wall – they seemed to be cardboard houses upon which the limelight shone. Then suddenly the game was over, the football players shouted themselves away, and we went in to tea.[26]

The sense of transience that the young footballers, like many of the Cypriots Peto encountered, were almost an illusion, one that would eventually disappear altogether, is reminiscent of nineteenth-century travellers to the Orient. But in Peto's case there is the added complication that she was writing about a British colony, an enterprise that involved the rationalisation and modernisation of the Levant, of both the exotic king of Arabia and the unreal 'stage-like' world and the 'cardboard houses' inhabited by the balletic jumping boys.

Despite the private misgivings of a few individuals, the cogs of the imperial machine cranked on. On 1 May 1925 Charles Hart-Davis stood in full dress uniform on the dais in front of the law courts in Konak Square in Nicosia.[27] Looking out at a mass of Union flags, hung from balconies and draped around the columns of the post office,[28] he announced that Cyprus was now a crown colony and that Malcolm Stevenson, the island's high commissioner, was from now on to be referred to as its governor.

This change in status enabled the administration to introduce long overdue reforms to two of the island's most important Ottoman institutions, the *Evkaf* Charitable Foundation and the *Sharia* Courts. Both were inefficient, but the heavy-handed manner in which changes were implemented undermined the status and self-esteem of the Turkish Cypriot community so fundamentally that it never fully recovered.

The *Evkaf* Foundation supervised the numerous Islamic charitable endowments established on the island over the preceding 400 years and used much of its income to fund philanthropic and public works. Under the reforms the foundation was effectively converted into a government department, but one that was expected to be self-financing, meeting additional administrative costs from its own revenues, a measure which severely reduced its ability to maintain its religious and educational function.

At the same time, the jurisdiction of the traditional *Sharia* Courts over domestic and family matters within the Muslim community was significantly reduced, and the power to appoint and dismiss *Sharia* judges vested in the governor. But the measure that caused greatest alarm within the Turkish Cypriot community was the merging of the *Evkaf* administration with the *Sharia* Courts. *Sharia* judges, it was announced, were to be considered as *Evkaf* agents, their tribunals would be held within the *Evkaf* offices and their salaries drawn from *Evkaf* budgets. For many Turkish Cypriots this not only threatened the impartiality of the judges but, more importantly, also demeaned them in the eyes of those on whom they would be passing judgement.

In fairness to the British administration, similar changes had already taken place in Turkey, where, in the context of Attaturk's sweeping modernisation programme, both *Sharia* Courts and the caliphate had been abolished. But the small Turkish Cypriot population, cut adrift from the establishments that had shaped daily life for generations, was not part of the Kemalist revolution. It was left instead with the impression that the institutions that had once underpinned the community's existence had been destroyed merely to balance the colony's books. It is not surprising, therefore, that the transition of Turkish nationalism into a broad-based political movement in Cyprus can be traced to this point.

With the previous uncertainty over the island's status resolved, it was hoped that resolution of the island's sovereignty would not only result in greater efficiencies in moribund Ottoman institutions but might also attract a new breed of speculators and commercial settlers to generate wealth and invigorate the stagnant administrative class. A letter to *The Times* from a retired British resident of Cyprus insisted that while 'every encouragement should be given to Englishmen wanting to settle here … we want the right sort'.[29] The 'right type of settler', it was believed, would do 'more to show the Cypriot the proper way of English life than any amount of propaganda can – and at no cost to the Government'.[30]

In the event, the settlement of Cyprus was a more gradual, piecemeal affair. Among the first of the post-war agricultural colonists were Phillip and Evelyn Newman who had both seen active service in the First World War, were 'tired of the mud and trenches, rain and cold' and wanted 'somewhere near the sea … sunny and colourful'. After assurances from the Colonial Office that Cyprus would always be British and that they could 'live there for generations to come', the Newmans bought nine *donums*[31] on a small promontory to the west of Kyrenia near Karavas. The previous owner, Kosta Haji Stephani, a victim of the rural debt crisis, was 'in a bad way financially'[32] and had been forced to sell up. The Newmans gradually established a successful dairy farm and a popular café, which until the early 1950s was one of the few places on the island where it was possible to obtain fresh milk.[33]

Whatever Kosta Haji Stephani may have felt about the new British settlers and the circumstances under which they had acquired his land, at least they lived and worked alongside him. Unlike the office-bound administrators of the Secretariat, commercial colonists like the Newmans were in regular contact with and surrounded by Cypriots. But they were a minority. The tiny business community on the island – mostly family-run import agencies such as that of the Hays, who imported cars, whisky, tea and cigarettes, or the Petrides and de Glanvilles – was never sufficiently large or prosperous enough to challenge the dominance of the stagnant administrative cadre. As in other colonies, direct involvement with the production of wealth was considered vulgar and those who engaged in it were viewed as socially inferior. In Cyprus, these class tensions were heightened by the insecurities of the under-achieving inter-war Cypriot administrators, resulting in 'an incredible categorization within colonial society'.[34] Eirwen Harbottle remembered that although her parents, Mr and Mrs Llewellyn Jones, were well-liked members of the Nicosia Club, and stalwart members of the congregation of St Paul's Anglican Church, as a banker her father was still considered 'just slightly below the salt'.[35]

It is ironic that one of the few administrators during this period who was *both* entirely committed to his work and enormously energetic became a figure of hate on the island, a man so reviled that villagers spoke his name – Mr Unwin – as a threat to delinquent children.[36] He also succeeded in single-handedly inflicting greater damage on the Cypriot peasant's relationship with the British administration than almost any other individual in the colony's history.

George Unwin, the chief forestry officer, was a small man with a goatee beard and 'hair sticking up in all directions',[37] who 'loved his trees like human beings, only a good deal more'.[38] Instantly recognisable by his habit of wearing several sun hats one on top of the other, Unwin toured the island's forests on foot at great speed, leaving exhausted subordinates trailing behind.[39] Despite his numerous eccentricities Unwin was highly respected within the colonial forestry service for his work in Canada and Nigeria and was the first to develop a strategic plan for the protection and development of Cyprus's neglected forests. He was also inflexible, 'not blessed with a good public relations spirit',[40] and entirely unable to relate to the thousands of Cypriot villagers whose support he badly needed to implement his programme.[41]

An autocrat both at home[42] and at work, Unwin expected new recruits, whether Cypriot or British, to 'rough it and see whether they could stand the treatment. It was the old Nigerian idea – you break the weaklings on their first tour.' Geoff Chapman, who joined the Cyprus Forestry Department in 1930, was taken on an initial reconnaissance tour of the Paphos Forest by his new boss and was 'astounded' by the way he spoke to a local Cypriot forester. 'He sort of nagged at him and shouted at him. It gave me a very bad impression, but apparently he always talked like that.'[43] Unwin's peculiarities became legendary amongst his staff. His deputy, Ronald Waterer, regularly invited his boss for Sunday lunch at his home in Byron Avenue in Nicosia. Waterer's son Donald recalled that 'he kept eyeing up the curtains in the sitting room. They had a white and green stripe, and eventually my father said to my mother, "He's got his eye on those curtains, you're going to have to give them to him".' Finally Mrs Waterer gave way 'and the next time we saw old Unwin he was wearing the curtains as a suit, with this green and white stripe going lengthways down the leg. They were quite loud stripes too.'[44]

Dr George Unwin, former head of the Forestry Department, speaking in retirement, at the annual Arbour Day celebrations, in the 1950s.

[*Reproduced courtesy of the Cyprus Department of Forests.*]

At the time Unwin arrived in Cyprus in 1921, the future of the island's forests hung in the balance. One-sixth of Cypriot woodland had been felled during the course of the war in an effort to supply the Allied campaigns in Egypt and Palestine. The head of the Forestry Department during the war years had been Alfred Bovill, an affable man, patriotic and keen to contribute to Britain's war effort. But he was not a trained forester (his main qualification for the job having been his relationship to a former chief justice in the colony) and in attempting to meet the insatiable demands of the British army he had devastated the island's woodlands. Policies introduced decades earlier to facilitate reforestation had been waived and any attempt at sustainable forest management abandoned. Bovill introduced sawmills to process the timber more rapidly. But there was still no adequate system of tracks or roads within the forest that could be used to transport the cut trees. As a result Bovill's felling strategy was dictated by a plantation's proximity to the few existing roads, rather than the maturity of the trees within it. The Paphos forest, in particular, was thus dramatically over-felled, with young trees 'rolled down off the steep mountainsides to the valleys'[45] and transported by rough, hand-cut tracks down onto the plains. A constant stream of boats from Paphos, Limassol, Larnaca and Morphou had delivered timber to the waiting cargo ships at Famagusta, until the end of the war, by which time 100,000 tons of Cypriot forest had been shipped to Egypt.

Extensive re-forestation was now urgently needed to prevent large-scale soil erosion and a consequent reduction of dry season water supplies which would lead to 'the speedy ruination of the country'.[46] But this remained impossible as long as the island's forests continued to be used as a grazing ground for goats which 'did incalculable damage to the young trees, nipping off the opening bud, the shoot piercing the bark, the seedling pushing up from the ground'.[47] Omnivorous goats, the 'irreplaceable means of subsistence for the very poor',[48] were the last resort of the Cypriot peasantry, their single reliable source of food in times of hardship. The growing numbers of dispossessed peasants might have lost their fields, their olive and carob groves, but with a small herd of goats grazing for free in the forest, they could still survive. Now, they too appeared to be under threat.

From the earliest days of British administration repeated attempts had been made to limit encroachment on designated forestry land. Initial enthusiasm to save the island's woodlands was so great that legislation had been passed prohibiting the felling or pollarding of *any* trees, including those on private property. The island's neglected forests became a compelling focus for what the colonists perceived as their redemptive role on the island, saving Cyprus both from 'the blighting influence of the Turk'[49] and from its own 'careless and indigent peasantry'.[50]

As early as 1879, visitors to the island had been 'overcome with anger and dismay at the terrible exhibition of wanton and unwarrantable desolation' caused by 'the Cypriote with his unsparing axe'.[51] Alongside the axe-wielding villager, goats were identified early on as the major villains in the story, and it was claimed that Cyprus contained 'more goats in proportion to its area and population than any country in the world'.[52] As farming practices changed and land cultivation increased, more and more lowland villages expelled goats from their district, in an attempt to prevent crop damage,[53] resulting in an increase in the number of herds grazing on areas of state forest. Goat husbandry became associated with laziness and indolence and was contrasted with the consistent, regular labour required in the cultivation of the soil. Restoration of the forests, therefore, was considered to contain the key to the restoration not just of the island's agricultural fertility and economic prosperity but also of the moral well-being of its population.

Unwin's determination to protect the forests went beyond nurturing saplings and new plantations: it had all the elements of a moral crusade, a mission to protect the colony from the damage inflicted upon it by those he castigated as irresponsible natives. Initially Unwin tried to buy shepherds out, offering a *donum* of land for every 10 goats, along with a year's supply of seeds, a shed and a plough. But despite an encouraging early start the overall response to his initiative was poor.[54] So the chief inspector of forests resorted to the vigorous enforcement of pre-war grazing restrictions which compelled shepherds to buy the rights to graze designated areas of forest. Shepherds were either charged exorbitant sums for grazing permits[55] or refused them altogether. Those who broke the law and continued to graze their flocks were prosecuted – in enormous numbers. During the latter part of Unwin's time in office prosecutions for illegal grazing ran at around 5,000 every year. By way of comparison, similar cases in the Indian United Provinces, an area with eight times the forest area of Cyprus, averaged 129 annually. It was left to the local officials, British and Cypriot foresters who lived in remote forest stations, often side by side with the villagers they were policing, both to implement Unwin's draconian policies and to deal with their consequences.

The brief diary entries of Gilbert Sale,[56] the officer responsible for the Paphos Forest between 1922 and 1928, reflect the weight of responsibility on the forester's shoulders. Sale, like all forestry officers, had received basic first-aid training and was often called on to treat injured villagers living in remote areas. During one routine patrol, he spent an entire day treating the 'poisoned or wounded hands' of villagers who had not seen a doctor for several months. When he was not providing rudimentary health care for deprived villagers Sale attempted to develop the inferior western end of Paphos Forest by a programme of planting. But his efforts were 'made hopeless because of the grazing', often carried out by the very same people who so desperately needed his medical attention. All too often Sale arrived at villages only to find that 'the villagers have no permits, but they live almost entirely by grazing, and obviously must keep all their goats in the forest'.[57] Donald Waterer remembers a similar degree of dependency on goats and one particularly wretched village near Paphos where '14 families all lived in caves. All they had were their sheep and goats, so when they were faced with losing their livelihoods they just became frantic.'[58]

In the summer of 1924, pushed to the limits of their endurance, the villagers who grazed their animals within Paphos Forest responded to Unwin's increasingly intransigent approach to goat control by a series of arson attacks,

setting fire to the forest at eight separate places. It was left to Sale to co-ordinate fire-fighting efforts. Fire-fighting in Cyprus at that time was conducted
with minimal resources. The steep gradient in both the Paphos and the
Troodos forests made it impossible to create permanent firebreaks without
causing extensive soil erosion. Firefighters, therefore, relied almost entirely
on the risky strategy of establishing a series of small back fires ahead of the
main blaze in order to deprive it of combustible material. This was exhaust-
ing work and, if the wind suddenly changed direction, extremely dangerous.
A team of fire-fighters would be lined up, each with a box of matches, and
'when the forest guard blew his whistle they all stepped over the ridge lit a
fire and then stepped back pretty sharply'.[59] The first fires broke out in the
western Paphos range close to the village of Pomos on 16 July 1924. Sale and
his forest guards eventually brought them under control, but by the end of
the day 'excellent young woods', including 'nearly the whole growing stock',
had been destroyed.

Two weeks later fires broke out again. Sale set up an operations base on
a mountain ridge from where he despatched runners with instructions to the
teams of forest guards. Arriving at the blaze, they found 'thick patches of excellent young woods' in flames, but the 'variable and gusty' wind made it too
dangerous to intervene. That night the wind died down, but efforts at 'trace
felling', removing trees that stood in the path of the flames, were hampered by
a shortage of axes and a lack of bread to feed the fire-fighters. Attempts to use
the felled trees to start a back fire had to be abandoned when the wind changed
direction. Sale and his team 'retired in haste' but eventually succeeded in making a trace fire further away. When finally the fire was damped down Sale and
his men, who by this stage had been without food for nearly 24 hours, hoped to
rest, but runners brought news of a second fire nearby. 'All the labourers were
demanding bread, but we managed to hustle them up the hill,' Sale noted in his
diary, adding that the operation reflected 'great credit on the Forest Guards
and officials who carried it out with tired hungry men.' Finally, with the main
danger passed, Sale looked down at the smoking ruins of the woodland of the
Ayia Marina Valley which had previously contained 'several thousand acres
of young woods about the best and most regular in Paphos', and where now
'practically every tree in the valley was burned'.[60] A total of 18 square miles of
forest had been lost.

The forest fires were started primarily in response to an economic threat
from the government authorities; but they also reflected an emerging anti-
colonial sentiment that began to make itself felt towards the mid-1920s. The
Stevenson era had opened with considerable possibilities. The clarification of
the colony's status, after years of uncertainty, opened the way for long-term
investment and development. But these opportunities were largely squandered

in an atmosphere of lethargy and ineffectiveness, the climate of 'gentle somnam-bulance' that pervaded the colonial administration. The smouldering resent-ments felt by Cypriots towards an administration that was by turns indifferent or heavy-handed led to the destruction of much of the Paphos Forests. But this was merely a prelude to a spectacular eruption of resentment that would con-vulse the island in the next decade.

8

No More Mixed Tea Parties
1926–38

Sunday services at the church of St George in the Forest in Troodos take place only during the summer. Visitors arriving at other times must ask for the key from the British military base on the opposite side of the winding track that leads off Troodos Square. Bordered on three sides by dense pine woods, the church seems to belong in a Brothers Grimm fairy tale. Today the church exterior is dominated by its steeply sloping roof of bright red corrugated iron which runs from the apex of the building to its windows, and which partially obscures its architectural merits.[1] But at the time of its construction in 1928, St George's represented an architectural coup.

The building, designed by the eminent ecclesiastical architect William Douglas Caroe, incorporates many elements of the Arts and Crafts movement.[2] Caroe suffered from poor health and spent his winters amongst the burgeoning community of retired Britons in Kyrenia, where he designed a substantial house for himself.[3] He waived his fee for the work on St George's, but in keeping with Arts and Crafts tradition, he insisted that the church interior should form part of a single coherent architectural design. The church committee, presumably unused to having an architect of Caroe's stature at its disposal, was overawed and minuted that 'no gifts of furniture shall be accepted except those made to the design of the Architect or approved by someone representing him'.[4] Virtually all the congregants' donations, including the altar, a copper cross and candlesticks, and the church weather vane, conformed to Caroe's aesthetic criteria. The single exception, mounted on a balcony above the west door, was a flamboyant eighteenth-century icon of St George, depicted astride a prancing white horse, his sword raised in an arc above his head, his red cape billowing out behind him. This was the donation of Ronald Storrs, the cultured, well-connected new governor who had a profound and enduring impact on the island and whose time in Cyprus was to be as spectacular and dynamic as the picture he donated.

Storrs was ambitious, erudite and charming, with a taste for theatricality and display. He spoke six languages, amongst them Greek and Arabic, and had enjoyed a distinguished and influential wartime career, first as oriental secretary to the British consul general in Cairo and later as governor of Jerusalem and Judea. According to Harry Luke, who succeeded him as oriental secretary in Egypt, Storrs possessed a 'discriminating taste, a Voltarian cynicism, a lucidity of thought ... and a wide but critical and discriminating appreciation of the good things in life'.[5] He was also a vain man anxious to display his learning and appear cleverer than he actually was,[6] a relatively harmless shortcoming, but one which ultimately contributed to the breakdown in his relations with those he governed.

Storrs came bursting into Cyprus full of ideas and proposals to 'overhaul every aspect of administration including agriculture and archaeology as Lord Curzon did in India'.[7] His career on the island has subsequently been overshadowed by its dramatic and violent conclusion, but his arrival in Nicosia, via the laborious engines of the Cyprus Railway, was initially greeted with enthusiasm by the British and Cypriots alike. Storrs was a man in a hurry, for whom the development of the island and of his own career went hand in hand. In his first 12 months, he established the island's first Chamber of Commerce, set up a music school, and founded a public library, persuading his influential friends to donate up to 4,000 books. He inaugurated medical and chess societies, which, since Cypriots were excluded from the racially segregated English Club, 'provided common ground upon which British and Cypriots could meet on equal and non-political terms'.[8] Government House, embellished by Storrs's extensive library, his collection of antiquities, icons and works of art, now hosted dinners, receptions, dances and concerts, as the new governor socialised eagerly with Cypriots. During his first year in office Storrs toured over 100 towns and villages, deliberately 'courting the good opinion of the Cypriots, especially of the Greek Cypriots', and aimed to restore 'the old warmth in Anglo-Cypriot relations which ... had marked the High Commissionership of Sir Charles King-Harman between 1904–11'.[9] Along with his wife, Lucy, he established a 'Social Hygiene Council', which aimed to address problems as diverse as the spread of venereal disease, cruelty to animals and the welfare of apprentice boys.[10] The new governor's energy was infectious and irresistible and the moribund government administration was suddenly infused with renewed energy and purpose, fuelled by the belief that at last the island's fortunes were about to change for the better.

But Storrs's greatest coup, for which, had his post in Cyprus ended less controversially, he would still be remembered, was the abolition of the Tribute. Like the men who had governed the island before him Storrs was in no doubt as to the iniquity of the 'black pall of the Tribute', arguing that Britain should either 'recognise that we have done and are continuing to do a great wrong to the Islanders or get out'.[11] Unlike his predecessors, Storrs found the tide of political opinion in his favour. The man who had appointed him, Leopold Amery, the dynamic new secretary of state for the colonies, was an advocate of colonial development. Amery believed that since the question of British sovereignty in Cyprus had now been definitively resolved the time had come to take the colony in hand. In this he was at odds with the mighty Treasury Department, which, under Chancellor Winston Churchill, argued that the repeal of the Tribute was a question that 'the British tax payer cannot be asked to reopen ... at the present time'.[12]

Knowing that the majority of his colleagues and even King George V supported his views, Amery brought the matter to a Cabinet meeting on 20 July 1927. He had yet to convince the chancellor, who, ironically, after his short visit to Cyprus 20 years earlier, had produced the most eloquent and commanding arguments ever written against the Tribute. In a shrewd manoeuvre, Amery quoted at length from Churchill's own memorandum until, 'largely on the strength of the convincing eloquence'[13] of his own words, 'Churchill himself had to join in the laughter of his colleagues and come to terms.'[14]

On 31 August 1927 the government adjourned from its summer seat on Troodos to take part in an extraordinary meeting of the Legislative Council in Limassol Court House. After imparting his 'momentous and memorable' news to the Greek and Turkish Cypriot elected members, Storrs was cheered and applauded before sailing off from Limassol harbour for a holiday in Rhodes. Back in Britain his reputation also seemed assured, with former incumbents, such as Charles King-Harman, praising him for 'a splendid piece of work'.[15]

Storrs' arrival in Cyprus had coincided with Amery's own comprehensive reform of the Colonial Office, including its recruitment policy. New recruitment practices were to produce a class of trained specialists capable of initiating development policies. As a result, the number of imperial appointments to departments such as agriculture, land survey or forestry rose sharply.[16] In Cyprus, the first results of Amery's policy were seen in the appointment of two highly capable forestry officers: Ronald Waterer and Geoff Chapman. Waterer, a congenial countryman, believed it was 'the duty of the local forester to make sure he was on damn good terms with everyone, because if you wanted to do anything you had to have the villagers on side'.[17] Chapman, by contrast, approached silviculture from a more academic perspective, drawing up ambitious five- and ten-year management plans. These two products of Amery's reformed, meritocratic colonial service formed a strong bond, united by their abhorrence of the racism they often saw amongst their colleagues and by a shared vision of how the island's forests could be developed. Between them the two men succeeded in securing the future of the island's forests, and in restoring much of the trust of the villagers which the Unwin administration had destroyed.

Buoyed up by his early success over the Tribute and encouraged by the personal support of the reformist colonial secretary, Storrs indulged his instincts for promotion and display. The year 1928 was the fiftieth anniversary of the British occupation of Cyprus and the governor 'determined ... to extract from this Jubilee something of the publicity which the Colony so sorely needed'.[18] He began by issuing 'a remarkable series of postage stamps ... a historical and topographical picture gallery nicely calculated to soothe local religious, racial and linguistic rivalries'.[19] Storrs went on to order the issue of a commemorative five-shilling silver coin and even persuaded the influential London art dealer Joseph Duveen to donate a portrait of Catterina Cornaro, the last queen of Cyprus, to the colony. The picture, now darkened with age, hangs in a wide gold frame, high up on the walls of the library of Cyprus Museum in Nicosia. From the ground, only Caterina's chalk-white hands and face are visible.

In the spring of 1928 the Greek-elected members of the Legislative Council had made another of their periodic requests for constitutional reform along with 'a responsible and effective share in the administration of the island',[20] arguing for the introduction of a Maltese-style constitution, which would give full powers over local affairs to the indigenous population.[21] As on previous occasions their request had been defeated by the combined British and Turkish vote. Not surprisingly, when confronted by Storrs's enthusiastic plans to commemorate 50 years of colonial rule, the Orthodox Church and the majority of the Greek Cypriot leadership declined to participate, arguing that they could not 'celebrate what does not give satisfaction to the people'.[22]

Storrs, irritated by the 'absurder counsels' of this 'unreasoning minority'[23] and the shadow it threatened to cast over his self-congratulatory pageant, steamrollered on. But without Greek Cypriot participation his plans for a gala programme of sporting activities soon degenerated into farce. Mixed cricket and football fixtures had to be hastily re-arranged. The island's mainly Turkish Cypriot police force was called on to step into the breach, and a contingent of troops moved to Nicosia from Polemidia in order to make up numbers.

Celebrations culminated in a ball at the racially exclusive English Club in Nicosia. Storrs recorded with relief that the absence of Greek spectators at the horse races, the one sporting event which had a cross-cultural appeal, was counterbalanced by 'a special train of Moslem sportsmen from Famagusta'.[24]

The article that subsequently appeared in *The Times* commemorating the anniversary had all the characteristics of Storrs's flowing, sardonic style. The 'special correspondent' to whom it was attributed anticipated that the administration's ongoing promotion of Cyprus would attract 'capital from other parts of the Empire' and that since the island had now 'escaped from the nightmare of the Tribute', it could at last benefit from 'the sympathetic attention of the world and commerce and finance outside'. The language grew increasingly flowery as the writer warmed to his theme, arguing that 'the fairy godmother has taken the long neglected Cinderella by the hand and she is emerging from the Turkish torpor and Greek parochialism in which she has hitherto been sitting while her ugly sisters have been playing politics at her expense'. At this point, the author suddenly descended into precocious public school humour. The Greek Cypriot desire for *enosis*, or union with Greece, was depicted as an absurd fantasy animal, the '*Enosis sterilis*, a mule-like creature of uncertain parentage', which was 'chiefly hunted by the higher ecclesiastics and literati among the Greek-speaking islanders' and 'usually found in the nest of a *hippalectryon* (a cock horse) in the romantic *Nephelococcygian* (cloud cuckoo land) mountains, which loom so large on the horizon of some Cypriots. Here it may be insulted with impunity, as in Cyprus the *Enosis* is bovine in its mildness'.[25]

It is possible that Storrs may not have been the author of this supercilious article. It could equally have been the work of his ADC, Rupert Gunnis, but it was clearly written by someone within the island's administration and could certainly not have been published without the governor's prior knowledge. Not only had Storrs persisted in staging a series of official celebrations of British rule against the wishes of the majority population, but he had also sanctioned the ridiculing in print of strongly held local political beliefs. Not surprisingly, the goodwill that had accompanied his appointment rapidly began to evaporate, to be replaced by 'a mutually felt alienation between nationalists and Governor'.[26] Storrs's conspicuous cleverness, his compulsion to demonstrate his erudition and linguistic ability at every opportunity, began to arouse suspicion within the Legislative Council. Many members feared he would prove untrustworthy and 'that they could not fully grasp the implications of the policies of their "resourceful and ever-moving Governor"'.[27]

In this they were not alone. Storrs's reputation for evasiveness, even downright duplicity, began to take shape during his period as governor of Jerusalem. Although the governor maintained that he was strictly neutral on the question of Palestine, 'not wholly for either, but for both',[28] he harboured anti-Zionist feelings. The chief political officer in Palestine during Storrs's period there commented decades later that he had 'for twenty years been paying lip-service to Zionism ... playing a double game ... it had taken all these years ... to find out'.[29]

The gradual shift in attitude towards Storrs on the part of the Cypriot Legislative Council did not immediately dampen the governor's enthusiasm. Despite a period of illness brought on by overwork, Storrs continued to press ahead with his plans to develop the island and overhaul its administration. Incompetent officials, many of whom had spent decades in the colony were gradually prised from their positions to be replaced by better qualified men. At the governor's insistence, changes were made to the outdated antiquities law, allowing the first foreign archaeological missions to conduct controlled excavations on the island, while in an attempt to 'bring about a diminution of [venereal] disease',[30] a specialist nurse was recruited to the colonial administration and brothels were abolished.

From the time of his arrival in Cyprus Storrs had recognised the colony's potential as a tourist destination, along with the necessity of improving communications. He argued plausibly for the development of both until his 'hotel and tourism file swelled to portentous dimensions'. He had been shocked to learn that while the rest of the world 'had reached the air age ... no aeroplane or seaplane had arrived in Cyprus since the end of the war',[31] and that the 'emergency landing ground'[32] outside Nicosia remained undeveloped. In 1927 he began lobbying Imperial Airways to substitute Nicosia for Alexandria as one of their refuelling stops on their Iraq and India route. In September 1930 the airline finally began experimenting with an air-mail service between Famagusta and Alexandria via Haifa, but the venture was short lived. In an effort to entice Imperial Airways to land their 'great airboats' at Akrotiri Salt Lake, Storrs proposed a typically ambitious scheme to double the lake's depth by using 'an ancient Venetian dyke', to create 'a safe landlocked *thalassodrome*'. Although these plans too came to nothing, the rudimentary landing facilities outside Nicosia were developed after a fashion. Pilots were warned that although there was a telephone at the airfield, 'Nicosia West 44', it could be used only 'if notice of arrival has been given in advance'[33] and was not available for emergencies.

One of the first aviators to brave these rudimentary landing facilities was Jean Batten, the record-breaking long-distance pilot, who stopped at Nicosia to refuel her Gypsy Moth on her solo journey from England to Australia. The flight from Athens had taken eight hours and as she attempted to land Batten had to contend with strong upward currents of hot air which caused the Moth to gain over 1,000 feet in less than a minute, 'only to bump down hundreds of feet the next'.[34] Donald Waterer, taken as a child by his forestry officer father to witness the historic event, waited alongside George Ridgeway, the Shell agent on the island and his wife Phyllis. George, 'well over 20 stone, very tall and very fat', subsequently 'perched precariously on the wing' to refuel the plane with 60 gallons of petrol poured from four-gallon tins handed up to him one at a time. Phyllis Ridgeway, meanwhile, supplied her celebrity guest, whose face had been burned by the sun in the open cockpit, with large quantities of Pond's cold cream.

Despite the publicity generated by Batten's fuel-stop on her record-breaking flight and the experimental summer service to Palestine, tourist traffic to Cyprus remained negligible. Storrs had already authorised the production of a tourism brochure, *Cyprus the Garden of the Near East*, which promoted the island as a safer, watered-down version of the exotic east. Prospective visitors were promised 'the peace and quietness of the Orient', without the inconvenience of being 'importuned by hordes of rapacious *baksheesh* collectors'.[35] Storrs believed that while the 'peach-fed and jazzing Riviera tourist' would always seek his pleasures elsewhere, the discerning visitor 'in search of beauty, tradition, antiquity and, above all quiet'[36] would find the colony attractive. In the view of the governor, the greatest deterrent to tourists was the shortage of adequate hotels, a deficit that was remediable only by private capital investment. Nonetheless by the end of his term of office he could boast that Kyrenia, Limassol and Famagusta each had one hotel, while there were at least three in Nicosia offering 'modern comforts and sanitation'.[37] According to the travel writer Freya Stark, Storrs was also responsible for designing the monstrous Berengaria Hotel in the hill village of Prodromos. This menacing stone building, reminiscent of a nineteenth-century asylum, is now derelict, but it still lours gloomily over the single-storey village houses beneath it. On the walls of the hotel basement the faded silhouettes of chains of dancing figures suggests that, much as Storrs might have disapproved, a certain amount of 'jazzing' did take place at the Berengaria. Despite persistent letter writing and the organisation of several 'exploratory visits' the governor failed to attract the Swiss and Egyptian hoteliers whom he hoped would invest in the island.[38] In this, his timing was unfortunate.

The Wall Street crash of 1929 and the subsequent global economic collapse inevitably had an impact on the Cypriot economy. The island's traditional export markets began to contract. At the suggestion of a mixed British, Greek and Turkish committee Storrs cut his own salary, imposing similar reductions on other officials within the administration. Typically he responded to the crisis by redoubling his efforts to promote Cypriot produce and to find new outlets for it in Britain. Small quantities of Cypriot oranges had already been exhibited to the British public at the Empire Exhibition of 1924, along with wine, sponges, dried fruit, oil and 'carpets for which the island is famed'.[39] Storrs now used his personal connections to introduce Cypriot cigarettes to the bars of the House of Commons and 'several of the larger clubs'.[40] This represented the first co-ordinated attempt to raise the colony's profile within Britain since the occupation, and it prompted several interested enquiries. Some were '1,000 miles wrong in their guesses as to its locality', Storrs wrote gleefully, 'others being in doubt as to whether it is inhabited by whites or blacks'.[41]

Yet in his way Storrs was equally out of touch with his colonial subjects, choosing to ignore those political movements that did not correspond to his own vision of the island. The 1920s had seen a widening of the division within the Turkish Cypriot community between those who supported Kemalism and the more pro-British old guard. Elections to the Legislative Council in 1930 saw 'the "new Turks" of Cyprus'[42] returned to all but one of the Turkish Cypriot seats. Storrs' administration refused to accept the result as a genuine reflection of Turkish Cypriot political will, attributing it instead to personal animosity towards Mehmet Munir, an influential council member and the Evkaf representative. Successive governors insisted on regarding Munir, who was approvingly described as '100 per cent pro-British',[43] as the only legitimate representative of Turkish Cypriot political aspirations.

But neither recalcitrant Turkish Cypriots nor the economic recession was able to diminish the prevailing conviction at Government House – which filtered down to the administration – that the island's fortunes had now changed and that Cyprus was at last on the brink of great prosperity. A loan secured from Amery's Colonial Development Fund, supplemented by another smaller advance from the admiralty,[44] enabled Famagusta Harbour to be extended. There were other tentative indications that good times might at last be just around the corner. In 1929 Nicosia gained its first bus when Michalakis Efthyvoulou began operating a shuttle service to the railway station. Passengers needed to be both agile and determined since the early vehicles had no built-in seats, just ordinary free-standing chairs.[45] The drinks company Kia Ora established a factory in Famagusta and the mines at Amiandos and Skouriotissa were expanded. The discovery of a life-sized bronze statue of the Roman emperor Septimus Severus in a field near the village of Kythrea reinforced the general impression that the island's wealth was about to be revealed and its untapped resources realised.

The enterprising spirit that Storrs brought with him was reflected in *The Cyprus News*, which ran articles with titles such as 'Why the English Are Great Colonisers'.[46] Times were good for those men and women who might have glanced through the local paper as they sipped their sundowners on the balcony. Life at home, even for the most junior civil servants, continued to be made comfortable by large quantities of cheap domestic labour, while newcomers to Nicosia generally found themselves accommodated in a 'modern flat upon the edges of the town',[47] the result of Malcolm Stevenson's programme to build 'modern houses suitable for occupation by English people'.[48] Their suitability was largely based on the inclusion of flushing lavatories, still unavailable in even the most distinguished houses inside the city walls. But managing this transition from more traditional methods of sanitation was difficult. Many of the new-style lavatories lacked regular water supplies and flushed only irregularly, with the result that, in the case of the newly arrived Hart-Davis family, 'it became quite awful ... the landlord purred with pride and we all got upset tummies'.[49]

Occupants of older buildings still relied on the 'thunder-box', a portable wooden structure which required sawdust to be sprinkled liberally through the hole after use. Twice a week the 'thunder-box' would be replaced and the soiled latrines, collected from the narrow streets of the old city by donkey cart in the small hours of the morning, often created a major obstacle for party-goers returning home. It was 'always a great joke amongst the young subalterns who'd been out partying, whether they might get stuck behind one of the night soil carts'.[50]

But even the most well-appointed new houses lacked running water. When their inhabitants wished to take a bath, hot water 'heated on a wood burning Dover stove' was carried laboriously by servants in old kerosene cans, to fill a tin hip bath on the bedroom floor. Houses in Cyprus were heated by wood, with coal used only for industry. Supplies of firewood were delivered by cart, along with bundles of *throumbi*, 'the scented camel thorn which grows wild, and starts fires beautifully'.[51] Newcomers were cautioned that creeping modernisation in Cyprus meant that servants had abandoned the traditional use of *throumbi* as a firelighter in preference for kerosene.

For some new arrivals, adjusting to different hygiene practices in a country where water was at a premium, pots and pans were cleaned with sand, and the floor was washed with a damp sack, took time. 'It seemed all pretty dirty to me when I first went out there', Vivian Hart-Davis wrote in her journal, 'but when I came to learn their reasons, I think they managed pretty well.'[52] Most of the 'houses suitable for English people' did, however, boast electric light, but since the supply was centrally controlled and 'not available until the municipality considers it to be really dark enough ... the evening is usually started by candle-light'. 'Progress' and the movement away from exoticism towards functionality and convenience, a process that was for many the justification of colonial rule, continued to disturb the writer Gladys Peto. She lamented that her new home lacked 'romance' but was consoled by the prospect of spending 'the hours after dinner ... very pleasantly' on the balcony with friends, 'while the moon shines through the trees and the moths flutter and fall round the hanging lamp'.[53]

Women who were about to leave England to set up home in Cyprus were warned against bringing 'a good deal of paraphernalia' out with them. But shopping in the colony had to be approached with caution. Gladys Peto's advice manual for colonial wives includes a detailed account of the items for sale in Cypriot shops, underlining the significance of the concept of good taste in the delineation of the British class structure. While the colourful exotic Orient was desirable from a distance or when incorporated selectively into a colonial context, the brightly painted iron bedsteads sold at the drapers in Nicosia and decorated with 'swans and rosebuds in gay colours with pieces of looking glass inset' were unacceptably vulgar. In the same way, Peto rejected the draper's stock of 'pink and mauve and emerald ribbon edged with silver and gold', explaining to her reader that she had searched unsuccessfully for 'plain white or rose ribbon', the more 'tasteful' alternative, the selection of which confirmed her own place within the British class structure. Peto was similarly unsuccessful in her efforts to buy writing paper, available commercially in Cyprus for the first time in the 1920s. Cypriot shopkeepers, uninitiated into the subtle code by which demonstrations of 'good taste' acted as badges of class and status, stocked the wrong sort, offering either 'the type that has been made up in a floppy pad and called "English Linen Bank"' or 'the sort that lives in a box and has envelopes lined with gold paper, and gold rose buds as a letter heading'.[54] An upper-middle-class woman such as Peto could use neither without betraying her class and causing social embarrassment.

This, in a nutshell, was the central problem that bedevilled much of the administration's attitude to Greek Cypriots during this period. They were not quite different *enough* for that difference to be celebrated, controlled and exoticised. The brightly coloured mirrored bedsteads, like the detested native lawyers educated at the Temple Bars of London, were understood to be inferior imitations, situated outside the complex network of privilege, economics, education and aesthetics which expressed social and political power through the public demonstration of good taste. Both lawyers and bedsteads were considered *inherently* vulgar, their mimicry perceived as posing a much greater challenge to British cultural hegemony than if they had been more obviously different and unfamiliar.

Social embarrassment could, however, be generally avoided if local craftsmen were instructed to copy existing British designs. The newly arrived colonial administrator, anxious to look smart at the office, was reassured to learn that Cypriot tailors, if supplied with cloth from England, 'could copy a well cut suit marvellously',[55] while a woman with a knitting machine in Famagusta produced excellent socks at one shilling a pair. Most shoemakers could create 'an admirable pair of brogues' for around 30 shillings along with evening shoes from 'a particularly pleasant gold leather'.[56] Women with young children generally invited the local dressmaker to bring her machine and 'live in' for a week, when, provided with pattern books obtained from the *Army and Navy Catalogue*, she would create several sets of children's clothes that would last until the following year. A fabric known as *idare*, a mixture of silk and cotton,[57] was a particular favourite for girls' summer dresses, along with Cyprus silk, remembered by Jean Meikle, as being an 'off-white, colour, so it was always dyed'.[58]

It was not necessary to venture far to obtain any of these items. Silk, lace, and even occasional consignments of antiquities were brought by donkey for sale at the kitchen door, along with the daily delivery of food. Without refrigerators, fresh food had to be bought and consumed on the same day. Itinerant yoghurt sellers, promoting their produce with calls of 'yogurtcu-u-u', would deliver small earthenware bowls of yoghurt, which were kept in a wire meat-safe. The affluent kept theirs in zinc-lined ice chests, replenished every week, which also provided ice for the evening sundowner. Milk generally arrived in the form of a herd of goats 'that trotted round to the back door and the shepherd asked how many pints you wanted and just pulled it off'.[59] Those who insisted on cow's milk for their porridge could either add water to imported Nido milk powder or order supplies from the government farm in Athalassa close to Nicosia.

During the shooting season the colonist's diet might be varied by partridge. Forestry official Ronald Waterer, an enthusiastic hunter, made every effort to keep 'all the English people of Nicosia in game'. Waterer would return from early morning expeditions to the Larnaca salt flats with as many as 50 brace, which were then laid out across the sitting room carpet before being distributed to colonial families across the city. Poultry was also delivered to the kitchen door, alive and squawking, 'in big long baskets'[60], but its purchase could involve protracted bargaining. Some women, such as Vivian Hart-Davis, who claimed to have taken three hours negotiating over a turkey, enjoyed these transactions. Other intrepid wives, equally confident of their abilities to drive a hard bargain, cycled to market every day, 'but of course the local tradesman usually saw them coming and would add the price on before they started'.[61] Such women usually ended their expeditions with a visit to Spinney's, a 'magnificent provision shop', at the top of Ledra Street. Established by an entrepreneur from Palestine, it was one of a chain of outlets that operated across the Middle East selling imported food and drink, English hams, Huntley and Palmers biscuits, Camp coffee, potted meats, Gorgonzola cheese, along with 'wonderful Greek and Turkish delicacies'. Customers were given a chair, 'a glass of iced lemonade or a chocolate according to the temperature', and their attention drawn to 'a newly opened barrel of caviar'.[62] The shop was synonymous in the minds of most colonial children with Christmas and birthdays. When young Donald Waterer walked past Spinney's one day in late November he was captivated by 'a fantastic grey castle, decorated with painted lead soldiers, beautifully painted, Red Indians, all sorts, I thought it was wonderful'. His mother Nora immediately attempted to drag him away. Unbeknownst to Donald the castle had been specially made as his Christmas present, but 'the chap was so proud of it he'd put it in the window'.

The majority of women chose to leave the daily market expedition to their kitchen staff. The more transient administrative officials and those attached to military stations inherited their cook, along with the rest of their household staff, from their predecessors, with the result that 'the life-history of the servants ... is generally known to all the older residents upon the island, and all their talents and failings also'. Gladys Peto found that this had advantages, as when 'you arrange a dinner for the friends whom you have known perhaps a year, the cook, who has known them for 10 years or so, will be of great assistance. "No, the doctor never eats curry ... and madame likes very much the cheese cakes ... Shall I make cheese cakes for this evening?" '[63] A 'good man cook' in Nicosia in 1927 could expect to be paid £5 a month, while his female counterpart could command wages of £2 10s. The primitive kitchen equipment they were obliged to use made their work particularly arduous. Even in the modern bungalows erected during the Palmer administration the kitchen stove consisted of no more than 'a row of square holes in a built up block of stone',[64] into which burning charcoal would be placed. For baking or roasting, an oven was improvised from an empty kerosene tin, placed upside-down on top of the glowing charcoal, a technique that was still in use in British homes in Cyprus in the late 1950s.

Senior members of the Secretariat and heads of department usually kept at least three servants, sometimes as many as five. Phyllis Ridgeway, whose husband earned £35 a month, managed a staff consisting of a cook, a housemaid, a gardener who doubled as a groom, and a servant who did the shopping.[65] Domestic staff were frequently related and were often accommodated in a series of outhouses at the back of their employer's home. Some households had as many as four family members working together so that 'it was like a little community round the back of the house'.[66] Although government officials received only three quarters of their salary until they had passed exams proving fluency in either Greek or Turkish, this requirement did not extend to government wives. The ability to speak English was a prerequisite for domestic employment in a colonial household.

Cypriots employed within the culturally Anglicised space of the colonial household were expected to conform to British social norms. Occasionally Gladys Peto's maid failed to do so, as when she persisted in 'shaking hands with guests at the front door, so engagingly that one can hardly bear to correct her'. Although Peto wrote with amusement about her occasional encounters with Cypriot village women who 'have a most curious habit of patting you upon the cheek when they take leave', her maid's far less intrusive hand-shake was condemned as being over-familiar, because it took place in the context of Peto's own home. Other instances of cultural faux pas committed by the housemaid included the habit of airing the bed clothes from the front bedroom window 'like flags at a festival'. To anyone who has ever sweltered through an August night in Nicosia without air-conditioning, this seems an eminently hygienic measure, but Peto was careful to explain that although the practice was widespread amongst Cypriots it was not condoned in houses 'belonging to English people'.[67]

Outside the home the focus of expatriate social life for the colonial establishment and for those who wanted to advance within it was 'the club'. Each of the major towns had its own club, and none was more class-ridden and hierarchical than that in Nicosia. In its heyday the Nicosia Club had two tennis courts, a swimming pool, a library, a dance room, two bridge rooms and a bar. Today the building is in ruins, visited only occasionally by patrols of Turkish troops checking the Green Line that partitions Cyprus. The building was abandoned in 1974 when the Turkish army invaded Cyprus in response to a Greek military coup. Its tall chimney stacks are just visible from the Metehan-Kermia bypass, beyond a Turkish military exercise ground.

By 1928 women visitors to this exclusive institution were grudgingly allowed access to 'a curious dark little sitting room', but, as Gladys Peto complained 'the rest of the club may not be desecrated by female feet'.[68] Only Grade 'K' officials and above were invited to join, and even then membership was not automatic. Men such as Frank Hopkins, the superintendent of Nicosia Central Prison, who occupied a senior and responsible position within the administration, could not be considered for membership because he was lower-middle class. 'Remittance men', individuals who had been forced abroad to avoid disgrace at home and were supported by remittances from their families 'to make sure they kept quiet and out of harms' way,'[69] were also blackballed, while any applicant suspected of homosexuality was excluded as a matter of course. Rupert Gunnis, the governor's extrovert aide-de-camp, appears to have been a notable exception to the club rule: 'People whispered behind their hands that he was a 'a "bi-sort of you know"... but he was a colourful character, so he just brazened it out'.[70]

An erudite and cultured man, Gunnis wrote *Historic Cyprus*, a definitive guide to the churches and historic monuments of Cyprus. After retiring from the colonial service he went on to produce a definitive reference book on British sculptors. But despite his public ebullience Gunnis felt ambivalent about the British community in Cyprus, confiding in a colleague that he found 'everything ... so petty here ... self-centred and untrustful'.[71]

In the end Gunnis had the last laugh. Unlike the derelict Nicosia Club, once the exclusive bastion of the British establishment in Cyprus, the magnificent mansion he built for himself in Shakespeare Avenue, in what is now North Nicosia, is still in use today. The large grounds of this stately Italianate building contain the results of their original owner's occasional architectural pillages. For all his scholarship and genuine love of antiquities Gunnis was not beyond purloining a marble column from Salamis and a mediaeval sandstone arch reputedly from the palace of Catterina Cornaro.

Today, the house is owned by the British Foreign Office, which uses it for occasional diplomatic functions, including the annual charity band concert, held amongst the fountains and clipped green lawns of the gardens. Gunnis would have relished one particular concert held in the spring of 2007, when, with the encouragement of a very camp conductor of the band of the Royal Electrical and Mechanical Engineers, the 400-strong audience of retired British expatriates enthusiastically took to their feet to perform the actions to the gay anthem 'Y.M.C.A.'.

Absurd though many of the rigid social conventions of the Nicosia Club may seem today, they reflected the extent to which the hierarchy of the colonial administration dictated the terms of an individual's social and personal life. Seating at Sunday services at St Paul's Anglican Church, for example, was organised strictly according to a man's ranking within the administration. Even comparatively informal social situations were infused with anxiety about status. Peto noted that 'even if you only have four quite intimate friends to dinner, whom you call by their first names, and see twice every day, you must be extremely careful to consider the proper precedence in your seating arrangements, otherwise somebody will be extremely affronted and will call the next day to explain your mistake'.[72]

The importance attached to professional precedence, even at private social events, served to remind administrative officials that they were public servants, expected to adhere to exemplary moral and behavioural standards in their private lives. Officials and their families were not allowed to accept gifts (even for Christmas or birthdays) from Cypriot friends or acquaintances in case they might be bribes or possibly perceived to be so. According to Donald Waterer, who still remembers the dismay he felt as a child on learning that his father had to return an unexpected gift of two turkeys, 'it was like an obsession, they could think of nothing else but stopping corruption'.

Keeping up appearances was equally important on the golf course, which in Cyprus featured greens made of sand, with 'a gentleman with a *fez* acting as your caddie'. The particularly eccentric course at Famagusta included several shots that had to be played from the top of the old city walls. When the author Rider Haggard visited Nicosia in 1900 the course was maintained and weeded by veiled Turkish women. Like the fox-hunting administrators of 30 years earlier, Haggard was conscious that his game was being observed by the colonial subjects and of the need to behave appropriately. The presence of these veiled female labourers, so inaccessible and unknowable to Haggard and his peers, prompted him to speculate, not about the arduous reality of their daily lives, but rather about how *they* perceived *him*. 'What in their secret hearts', he mused, 'do these denizens of the harem think of us?'[73]

Golf, along with tennis, swimming and riding, helped to structure the days of sporty colonial wives such as Phyllis Ridgeway who 'spent her life riding' and took her horse, Gaza, for daily hacks along Ladies' Mile Beach near Limassol. Those women who did not share this enthusiasm for the outdoor life found their days filled by lunches, tea, bridge, dinner parties and 'a hell of a lot of social calling'.[74] Visitors to Nicosia who belonged to the correct social class were required, on arrival in the capital, to write their names in the Government House visitor's book, kept on a table in the hall next to a stuffed moufflon.

Social encounters between colonisers and the colonised involved particularly complicated protocols. 'Mixed tea parties' at Government House, held to entertain Greek or Turkish Cypriot officials, were stiff occasions, where 'the British sat rigidly at one end of the room; the Greeks and Turks at the other'.[75] The governor's wife hosted similar events for wives, thereby providing Turkish Cypriot women – who continued to cover their faces in mixed company long after this was prohibited in Turkey[76] – with the opportunity to socialise unveiled. These too were generally 'rather an ordeal, so frightfully formal' but were an essential part of colonial social obligations. The guests obviously felt the same way since they generally ate little. After the women had left, the district commissioner's wife was expected to help Lady Storrs to gather up 'the untouched cakes and put them in tins for the household'.[77]

For those Cypriots unfortunate enough to be invited to socialise with the British, the anxiety generated by the risk of a social or sartorial faux pas was intense. When Suha Faiz's parents learnt at short notice that the dinner they had been invited to that evening would be a black tie event, they embarked on 'an afternoon drive all the way back to Larnaca [from Nicosia] at what seemed to me an almost terrifying speed in order to change before returning to the party'.[78]

Little wonder, then, that government officials often longed for quiet evenings at home. Chief Secretary William Battershill spent his 'off duty' time mastering the latest Gershwin tunes on the piano, while others tuned in to one of the early BBC overseas broadcasts through the new Phillips All Electric Radio Sets being imported to the island.[79]

The congenial, insular life of the British civil servant assigned to administer the 'happy and contented populace'[80] of this most sleepy of imperial outposts was not to last. It was disrupted by an event so entirely unexpected and so traumatic for the British community that even 14 years later, new arrivals to Cyprus complained that it continued to dominate conversation. The deliberate destruction of Government House on the night of 21 October 1931 traumatised the British community on the island and sent shock waves throughout the Empire. The incident led to a fundamental change in British perceptions of their Cypriot subjects and meant that until independence, 30 years later, the island was governed as an autocracy, its inhabitants ruled by decree. From that day on even the most obscure and far-flung of Britain's colonies was to enjoy greater political autonomy than Cyprus.

It is one of the most tantalising paradoxes of British rule in Cyprus that this catastrophe took place at exactly the time when the Colonial Office had at last sought to develop the island, and during the governorship of the man who had finally abolished the hated Tribute. But despite Storrs's fluency in Greek and his programme of increased social contact with his subjects, he was not a popular figure. Articles such as the *enosis* hunting story which appeared in *The Times*, coupled with the governor's compulsion to demonstrate his erudition, particularly his mastery of classical Greek, gave Cypriots the impression that they were being mocked. As a result there was a 'complete distrust of his sincerity'.[81]

When Storrs arrived in Cyprus his much vaunted Philhellenism had generated hope among many Greek Cypriots that the governor's personal affiliations would translate into political action – notably the ceding of Cyprus to Greece. In 1929, after a delegation led by the Bishop of Kitium returned from London empty-handed, its claims unconditionally rejected, the Greek Cypriot press began to express doubts about the governor's motives. Storrs obviously lacked the power to grant the delegation's demands; but even if he had possessed the authority to single-handedly unite the island with Greece, it is most unlikely he would have done so. For Storrs, a benevolent British autocracy in Cyprus was not incompatible with his reverence of classical Greek civilisation. In fact, seen from his perspective, the two complemented each other. It would only be through a period of enlightened British government that Greek Cypriots could rediscover the values that underpinned their classical past – concepts of civic duty, public obligation, self-discipline and honour – from which they had been alienated for so many centuries. For the Orthodox Church and for Greek Cypriot members of the Legislative Council this amounted to nothing more than a hypocritical justification of imperial domination – and personal ambition.

In certain respects Storrs was just unlucky. His term in office coincided with the global economic recession. By 1928, 82 per cent of the agricultural population was in debt, owing on average £36. This was an impossible amount for rural peasants – earning an average wage of £1 a week – to repay.[82] To make matters worse, the island's biggest employer, the Cyprus Asbestos Company, reduced its workforce by two-thirds, putting more than 2,000 employees out of work.

As exports fell and government revenue declined, Storrs, anxious to avoid a budget deficit, proposed an increase in taxation. In an unusual display of solidarity, Greek and Turkish Cypriot members of the Legislative Council combined to reject his new proposals in the spring of 1931. Unmoved, Storrs exercised his executive powers to impose the new legislation, sweeping aside Cypriot council members.

The following July, Storrs's standing amongst his subjects sank even lower when a chance question in the House of Commons in London revealed that his greatest triumph, the abolition of the Tribute, was not quite the unmitigated success the governor had led people to believe. Contrary to Cypriot expectation, an accumulation of overpayments made by the islanders over the previous 50 years, amounting to over £1million, was not, after all, to be returned to the colony.[83]

This was the last straw. Greek Cypriot members of the Legislative Council were appalled and on 17 October 1931 the fiery Bishop of Kition resigned his seat on the council, summoning a mass meeting in Limassol three days later. There he called for a programme of civil disobedience and urged his audience to 'strain every nerve' to be rid of 'this abomination which is called English occupation'. It was stirring stuff. The men, and very few women, who heard the Bishop of Kition speak that day were radically different from the audience who might have attended such a meeting even five years earlier. The post-war economic slump and the increasing wretchedness of life in the countryside had forced thousands of Cypriots to migrate to the towns in search of work. Once there they became increasingly politicised, many formed trade unions or joined the embryonic Communist Party. The bishop may not have convinced every member of his audience of the need for action but those who heard him were, to an unprecedented degree in Cyprus, aware of the possibilities afforded by organised political resistance and collective action.

News of the bishop's speech reached Nicosia the next day, in particular it reached members of the newly formed National Radicalist Union, an organisation of young Greek Cypriots impatient for union with Greece. In what was, with hindsight, a decision of crucial importance, the district commissioner of Limassol considered the previous evening's rally to have been of only minor importance and did not pass on details to either the Secretariat or Government House.

The Radicalists responded swiftly and convened their own meeting at the Commercial Club in Ledra Street in the old city of Nicosia on the afternoon of 21 October. Soon a crowd of around 3,000, summoned by the ringing of church bells, gathered outside the building to hear emotional speeches of resignation from the Greek Cypriot Legislative Councillors and to witness the priest of Phaneromeni Church unfurl a Greek flag, shouting as he did so, 'I proclaim revolution.' When one of the councillors referred to Storrs's imminent departure to England, 'the cry arose, "To Government House" ', and soon thousands were marching out of the walled city towards the governor's official residence. As they passed the government timber yard, men 'helped themselves to sticks of various sizes' and 'tore up the wooden tree-guards along the roadside', before marching on through the outlying village of Ayios Omologites. Today, Ayios Omologites has been swallowed up by Nicosia, its traditional stone and mud-brick buildings hemmed in by high-rise blocks and dual carriageways. Despite this, it manages to retain something of the tranquil atmosphere of a village, and many traditional houses have been restored. On that Wednesday evening in October 1931, the impact of several thousand protesters forcing their way through its narrow streets, bearing 'sticks ... lanterns ... and huge banners',[84] must have been electrifying. But although Government House provided an obvious focus for the demonstrators' frustration and anger, crucially the marchers lacked clearly defined objectives about what to do once they go there.

Storrs, who was about to travel to Britain to discuss his next posting, had spent the evening wrapping Christmas presents for his staff. On being alerted that 'a disorderly demonstration'[85] was approaching, he followed Colonial Office regulations and placed the district commissioner, Charles Hart-Davis, in charge. Five mounted and eight foot police with batons were placed at the entrance to the driveway. But the horses stampeded 'and the crowd poured into the drive'. Hart-Davis, along with Andrew Wright, the acting chief secretary, and Albert Gallagher, the inspector of police, then attempted to address the demonstrators, asking them to 'withdraw to a respectful distance',[86] but the officials were forced back onto the porch, their words drowned by the chants of '*enosis*'. Stones began to be thrown, and windows were broken. It was clear the small police patrol had lost control, but according to Storrs's detailed account of the night's events the district commissioner refused to give the order to open fire due to the large number of students and young people in the crowd. In an attempt to persuade the rioters to disperse, the remaining Greek Cypriot members of the Legislative Council, 'realizing they had no control, and fearing the consequences',[87] left the scene. Large numbers of people followed and for a while it appeared as if order would be restored, when suddenly an outburst of 'violent stone throwing', with 'rocks larger than coconuts', broke all remaining windows and shattered the masonry of the porch. The police retreated inside through the empty window frames, prompting the rioters to begin an assault on the front door, using a length of timber as a battering ram. Wright's car was overturned and set alight, together with three police cars that had brought reinforcements from Paphos Gate Police Station. It was only when burning material began to be thrown through the broken windows that the district commissioner gave the order for the Riot Act to be read, and police opened fire. 'Almost simultaneously the flames from the curtains at the west corner of the frontage of the house spread to the roof and took hold of the whole building.'[88] Five minutes later Government House – 'Lord Wolseley's old tinder barrack'[89] and the official residence of Britain's imperial representative in Cyprus – was destroyed. Lost in the flames too were Storrs's 1,500 books, his antiquities, his icons and his works of art.

The British community was stunned. Cocooned by privilege they were detached from the social and political tensions within Cypriot society and for the most part ignorant of the extent of economic deprivation. This explosion of violence on the part of their previously docile and deferential subjects was all the

The ruins of Government House as seen in Britain by readers of the *Illustrated London News*, 7 November 1931.

more shocking because it appeared to have emerged from nowhere. Overnight the malleable, easily governed Cypriots had turned into a braying, angry mob. Many assumed it to be part of a co-ordinated island-wide rebellion that would continue over the coming weeks. Eirwen Harbottle (formerly Llewellyn Jones) remembers that her parents 'were really frightened that night, it just came absolutely out of the blue'. A curfew was immediately imposed and troops summoned from their summer quarters on Mount Troodos. The permanent British garrison, which, much to the distress of the Greek Cypriot community, had been reduced to a token presence in 1894, now consisted of just three officers and 123 men.

Later that night with British troops still eight hours drive away, members of the regular police force were despatched to guard the capital's public buildings, the Secretariat and the house of the district commissioner. All expatriate officials were summoned to Paphos Gate Police Station, where Gallagher swore them in as temporary constables, issuing each man with a pistol. British women and children were escorted to the Palace Hotel in Gladstone Street, a building that was considered easy to defend, since it was on open ground. For the women staying at the hotel it must have been an acutely anxious night. The attack on Government House was in itself shocking, but the speed and total unexpectedness of events served as an ominous reminder to the colonists that any subjugated race was intrinsically unknowable and always, therefore, a potential threat. As they waited for news of their husbands and fathers, out patrolling the streets, the two great horror stories of imperial Britain, of the atrocities committed against British civilians during the Indian and Boxer rebellions, must have preyed on their minds. For children, however, the experience was an exciting one. Jean Meikle remembers that the hotel 'had these little tiny cakes of soap. They were so small I thought they were lovely, and I started to collect them and rolled them up in my jumper ready to take them home with me. But when my mother found out she made me put them all back again.'

The first platoons of Royal Welch Fusiliers reached the capital from Troodos early the next morning and reinforced the police pickets outside public buildings. A pair of naval cruisers accompanied by two destroyers embarked for Famagusta from their base at Suda Bay in Crete. Military reinforcements also began to arrive by plane from Rainileli Aerodrome in Alexandria. Laboriously, in small groups, troops were flown in tri-planes to an emergency landing ground on the outskirts of the city. Donald Waterer watched the planes arrive, 'three damn great wings on top of each other, huge things'.

Meanwhile, children at the Froebel School on the road into Kyrenia observed troops being transported slowly along the main road towards the harbour in 'two very curious looking machines ... like tin boxes on wheels'.[90] Several of the reinforcements from Egypt were billeted in the Ottoman Bank building in Nicoisa, in anticipation of a possible assault on the bank. The young Eirwen

Llewellyn Jones became 'frightfully cocky with all my friends, because I had soldiers living in my house, sleeping in our downstairs hall. I used to tip-toe onto the top landing and look down on all these soldiers' feet as they slept'.

As news of the riots in Nicosia spread, disturbances broke out at various points across the island. Noisy meetings took place in Larnaca, Limassol and Famagusta. The district commissioner of Famagusta ordered the immediate evacuation of British women and children to the safety of the Khedivial Line steamer that happened to be in harbour. When the commissioner's house in Limassol was set alight the next day, with the commissioner, his wife and 12-year-old daughter still inside, the government became convinced that it was dealing with a co-ordinated, island-wide rebellion. This was very far from the case, but, as news of the assault on Government House spread, many Cypriots were encouraged to instigate their own local acts of rebellion. Geoff Chapman, the young forestry officer serving at the Paphos Station of Stavros Tis Psokkas, remembered that 'when the news came through ... it started to excite the villagers of Kambos'. The villagers attempted to sabotage the rudimentary telephone line between their village and Nicosia. This would not have been difficult, the line was no more than a length of galvanised wire pinned to tree trunks, powered by batteries in conjunction with vigorous hand cranking. It was also the most tangible manifestation of colonial rule in the village, available exclusively for forestry officials wanting to contact departmental headquarters in Nicosia.

Rumours reached Chapman that the villagers were planning their own arson attack on the forest station and surrounding plantations. He led the station horses away to the safety of a neighbouring village, locked his passport and valuables in a metal box which he lowered down the latrine and, with two fellow foresters, set off for Nicosia, 'glancing back over our shoulders to see if we could see a glow in the sky caused by Stavros forest burning'. After being issued with rifles and a machine gun and allocated half a platoon from Polemidia Garrison for support, Chapman returned to Kambos accompanied by Chief Veterinary Officer Robbie Roe, 'the oldest and most experienced among us'. The men had orders from Gallagher to 'shoot if you have to, and when you shoot, shoot to kill'.[91] In the end the rumours of arson came to nothing, the forest was not burned and the villagers meekly retrieved the buried sections of telephone wire and repaired the line. In Kambos and the rest of the island, the rebellion had run out of steam.

The intensity of the uprising, 'a combination of nationalist verbal agitation and spontaneous peasant riots',[92] had also come as a shock to the Greek Cypriot political and religious leadership. Unprepared for mass mobilisation on such a huge scale its response had been disorganised and un-co-ordinated. Most significantly, it failed to translate the militancy into any kind of political advantage.

In his sombre report to London on the events of that night Storrs recorded that six Greek Cypriots had died and 30 more had been wounded.[93] Ten men were banished, including the bishops of Kition and Kyrenia, and, in the weeks that followed, over 2,000 people were imprisoned. The destruction of Government House – the public manifestation of the king's authority on the island – was a huge psychological blow for the British community and for imperial prestige globally, severing the fragile links that had begun to develop during Storrs's term in office between the colonists and a small section of the Cypriot elite. The short-lived experiment in inter-racial fraternisation was over. Storrs noted rue-fully the advice of the officer commanding the detachment of reinforcements from Egypt: 'If I might suggest, Sir, no more mixed tea parties.'[94]

Storrs himself was broken and his career shattered. From being on the point of securing an appointment to the governorship of Bombay, he was effectively exiled to Northern Rhodesia, to be invalided out of the colonial service two years later. His Philhellenism remained unshaken to the last. But perhaps this is not so surprising, it was after all the product of Storrs's own class and cultural values and had little to do with governing Cyprus. His own account of the burning of Government House ends, typically, with a quote from Euripedes' *Medea:* 'What the gods ordain, no man foresaw, what we looked for is not ful-filled: the gods bring unlooked-for things to pass.'[95]

The administration's response to the crisis bore all the characteristics of British rule on the island. It was cumbersome, inappropriate and suffocating. A collective fine of £35,000 was immediately imposed on all Greek Cypriots, with the exception of civil servants, in order to finance the re-building of Government House. The constitution was suspended, the Legislative Council disbanded, never to reconvene, and the governor was granted absolute power. Political parties were forbidden, municipal elections banned and the press cen-sored. In short, 'from then until 1960 Cyprus was ruled by decree'.[96] For the rest of the colony's existence the Colonial Office maintained that Cypriots should be excluded from all aspects of government, 'until the shadow of union is finally removed from the political horizon'.[97] Symbols of Hellenism were outlawed; it became illegal to fly the blue and white Greek flag, to play the Greek national anthem, or even for more than five people to gather in one place. In 1937 the vice-mayor of Larnaca applied unsuccessfully for permission to host a dinner party for 12. Habeas corpus was suspended and the police were given power to conduct random searches of people and property. As historian Doros Alastos observed, 'it was a policy that excluded all possibility of an understanding and which led, ultimately, to stalemate and the disturbances of 1955.'[98]

Turkish Cypriots who had played no part in the uprising but were also affected by the restrictions felt they were being unfairly punished for the actions of their compatriots. Unsuprisingly support for Kemalism increased.

The movement was no longer perceived primarily as a vehicle for modernisation and secular reform, but equally importantly as a counterbalance to British intransigence and Greek Cypriot support for *enosis*.

For Cyprus, the long-term consequences were devastating and in many ways continue to be felt to this day. The curtailment of political and democratic freedoms which remained in effect for several decades stunted the development of Cypriot civic consciousness. Although free speech and the right to elect local municipal officials were gradually restored over the years that followed, it remained true that immediately prior to the island's independence in 1960, Cypriots enjoyed fewer democratic rights than other colonial subjects. This was a direct legacy of the events of 21 October 1931. It meant that the generation of leaders who assumed power in 1960, leaders who were required to navigate a path through a complex web of ethnic and nationalist interests, had negligible experience of consensus government and virtually no comparable historical precedents to draw upon.

The Government House riots and British reaction to them still feature largely in the minds of many Cypriots today. In November 2007 the then president, Tassos Papadopoulos, unveiled a memorial to those Cypriots killed in the incident. At the ceremony, he expressed opposition to a partnership agreement that Britain had signed the previous month with Turkey and suggested that the agreement may have been motivated by a spirit of vindictiveness arising from the events of 1931 and the subsequent EOKA uprising of 1955.

The events of October 1931 marked a profound transformation in British attitudes to Cypriot culture. From that point on, the administration sought to promote 'Cypriot' nationalism, an identity that would transcend cultural and linguistic affinities towards Greece and Turkey and pose no direct threat to British rule. Radical changes to the education system were forced through, concentrating greater control over finances, appointments and curricula in the hands of the governor. The teaching of Greek history was forbidden, religious officials were excluded from educational administration, and classes were orientated towards British university entrance exams.

A new English-language history of the colony was commissioned, written by Phillip Newman, who ran the dairy farm near Kyrenia. It was written with 'the youth of the island' in mind and sought to provide an 'even-handed account' of the role of 'barbarian or classic legend'[99] in the island's past. In doing so it attempted to downplay any of the real or imagined connections with Ancient Greece that had so delighted previous generations of administrators, classicists such as Storrs, Cobham, Luke and others.

One of the British schoolteachers employed to oversee this transformation in cultural and political allegiances was Gilbert Harding, who taught English at Limassol Gymnasium in the mid-1930s. He noticed what he described as a 'rather disagreeable atmosphere', both at the school and in

Limassol as a whole. Shortly after his arrival the new teacher was taken to inspect the town's prison, where he encountered a young detainee described as a 'prize Communist' whose 'crime' was the possession of 'a stenciled Greek transcription of Shaw's "Intelligent Woman's Guide to Socialism".'[100] Soon after, Harding, an outspoken, confrontational man, was expelled from the English Club in Limassol after the club's president, the trigger-happy Colonel Gallagher, who had supervised the military response to the Government House riots, overheard him comparing British rule in Cyprus with that in fascist Italy.[101] The comparison may not have been too far off the mark. Even the Colonial Office complained that under Storrs's successor, Richmond Palmer, 'the governments of Cyprus are becoming more and more autocratic... imbued with the political philosophy of Mussolini and are thoroughly afraid of criticism in any shape or form'.[102]

For his part, Governor Palmer believed that 'the normal model of colonial government, to which we are accustomed, cannot with safety be initiated in Cyprus, until at least a sound British sentiment has been built up'. Palmer's rule was bitterly resented by Cypriots who referred to his period in office as the *Palmerokratia*, the dictatorship of Palmer. His numerous (British) critics claimed that 'few people since Disraeli can have done more to try and fetter Cyprus to Britain than Sir Herbert Richmond Palmer, but perhaps no one so far has done more than Sir Herbert to make Cypriots want to belong to Greece'.[103] Reading the governor's description of the people he had been sent to govern it is easy to see why. In a lecture to the Royal Central Asian Society in London, he explained that 'several thousand years ago a lady called Aphrodite landed in Cyprus, and the island has never quite recovered'. He went on to point out that 'the people of Cyprus make a luxury of discontent and always pretend that they do not like being ruled, and yet, like the lady I have mentioned as a prototype, they expect to be ruled, and, in fact, prefer it'.[104]

This belief presumably sustained Palmer as he set about systematically restricting civil freedoms in the colony. His more liberal chief secretary, William Battershill, wrote darkly in his diary, 'I never liked an Autocracy and that is what this government is.'[105] The governor's autocratic policy was founded on a fear that Greek and Turkish Cypriot nationalists would one day join forces against British rule, an assessment based on a profound misunderstanding of Turkish Cypriot aspirations. The Kemalists had no desire to see the British leave but rather sought greater communal autonomy and a climate more receptive to modernisation and reform. By making this spurious connection the governor merely succeeded in alienating the more progressive elements within the Turkish Cypriot community. As a result there was a revival of Turkish Cypriot interest in emigration and in October 1934 over 100 families from the Karpas region set off for Anatolia by steamer. After Palmer introduced a substantial passport fee in an attempt to discourage any more members of the 'hardworking, albeit poor, Moslem community'[106] from leaving, young Turkish Cypriots began escaping quietly – and illicitly – from the island's north coast, on small fishing vessels bound for Turkey.

The composition of the population of Nicosia also changed in the aftermath of the riots. Many nervous expatriate families were calmed by a decision to establish a permanent British military presence in the capital, an unmistakable symbol of colonial authority. The main garrison at Polemidia was abandoned and the troops were housed in the buildings of Canon Newham's English School. Newham obligingly moved his boys to temporary premises in Kyrenia, but the school never returned to the original building, which is used today by the capital's Greek Cypriot population as law courts. The Anglican chaplain who had served the Polemidia garrison from Limassol was dismissed. From now on troops and civilians would jointly use St Paul's Anglican Church on Sunday mornings. Government families were allocated pews on the right of the aisle, while the soldiers stood on the left. The final moments before Sunday morning services began were usually characterised by much crashing and clattering as the soldiers dropped their rifles at the porch.[107]

But the decampment to Nicosia brought unexpected complications. The men were soon found to be suffering from an 'abnormally high' incidence of venereal disease, the result, it was believed, of their exposure to 'very strong and persistent temptation'[108] in the capital. The officer in command of the platoon believed the solution lay in 'licensed and inspected houses', but since Storrs had succeeded in making brothels illegal during his own time in office, this would have required new legislation, which would have reflected poorly on Palmer's defended administration. The vicar of St Paul's, who had strong moral reasons for rejecting the measure, attempted to address the problem by encouraging parishioners to arrange regular tea parties for the men, while Rupert Gunnis, head of the Antiquities Department, arranged a series of 'expeditions to interesting places in the neighbourhood'. Meanwhile, a Miss Tristram organised and ran 'The Victory Club', which provided soldiers with 'a quiet place just outside the confines of the barracks where they can read and play games', along with a canteen, 'where they can get a simple supper without going to the public restaurants in the town'.[109]

The presence of British soldiers on the streets of the capital sent out an unmistakable message about the military strength that lay behind the British occupation, but reconstructing the prestige of the civil administration, in the form of Government House, proved a much slower process.

Initial ambitious plans were abandoned as being too expensive and ornate and bickering over the cost, style and method of construction continued for several years, during which time governor, architect and Colonial Office were all at odds with each other. The building, which functions today as the official residence of the president of the Republic of Cyprus, was an attempt at an architectural hybrid, an expression of the fusion of cultural traditions which the colonial government wanted to believe defined Cyprus, with a deliberate under-playing of Hellenic influences. The new building also contained elaborate features such as 'a tiled swimming bath' surmounted by Roman arches and 'a sliding interior wall', fixtures that the majority of Cypriots would never set eyes on, but which every adult male Greek Cypriot had paid for through the 'punishment tax' levied on those not in government service. The ingenious sliding wall in particular delighted subsequent generations of colonial children attending the annual Government House Christmas party, when it would be raised to reveal Father Christmas in the adjoining room.

But there was another strand to Palmer's response to the public humiliation suffered by British authority as a result of the attack on Government House.

Governor Richmond Palmer presents Chief Secretary William Battershill with an award to mark King George V's Jubilee, at a parade beneath the Venetian walls of the old city of Nicosia. 6 May 1935.

[*Reproduced courtesy of Jane d'Arcy.*]

At the same time as taking steps to repress civil rights and freedoms he also enhanced the status of the district commissioners, 'the most important agents of contact between the Government and the people',[110] while reinforcing imperial authority by placing renewed emphasis on strict protocol and precedence at public occasions.

From the perspective of a colonial administrator such as Palmer the social structure of the colony presented particular problems. Cyprus lacked an aristocracy which the British could co-opt as nominal partners in the process of government. Elsewhere in the empire the office and rank of hereditary leaders were respected, and the support of princes, kings and maharajahs actively sought in an effort to maintain order and control. But in Cyprus, like the rest of the Ottoman Empire, there had been no hereditary governing elite. The Ottoman system, in which the right to govern and collect taxes was bought and sold at great expense, was designed to pre-empt the emergence of a hereditary aristocratic class that might one day threaten the centralised authority of the sultan. When the holder of a high office died, any rights or privileges his family might have enjoyed generally died with him.

Palmer's concentration on the role of the district commissioners, the representatives of the crown at regional level, and his efforts to inject a greater element of formality and pomp into public demonstrations of imperial authority was an attempt to compensate for this perceived gap in the tiers of imperial power.

In 1936 the governor drafted his own new table of precedence for his officials, which he submitted for approval to the Colonial Office in London. At first sight it seems absurd that a man charged with restoring order and addressing the island's acute economic problems should devote time and effort to something so seemingly irrelevant. But the close attention given to the order in which officials arrived and left at public functions suggests that, for Palmer at least, this formed part of his strategy for controlling the colony. The section addressing the order of precedence for government officials to board visiting naval vessels was typical: 'The commissioner should call in uniform, and should, where ever possible, be accompanied by the mayor – the latter in morning dress. The following procedure will be adopted:- The commissioner will enter the launch from the pier after the person who may be accompanying him, but he will precede them up the gangway of H.M. Ship. After the commissioner has paid his official call, he will be preceded down the gangway to the launch by the persons who may be accompanying him, but will disembark from the launch before them on arrival at the pier.'[111]

Chief Secretary Battershill, a man with a scrupulous sense of social and ethical propriety, was appalled. He believed the new table undermined the position of the Secretariat, the administrative centre of colonial government, and wrote solemnly in his diary, 'had they known the implications [of this] at home, they would never have passed the table'.[112] Gilbert Harding, one of only a small number of Britons in

Cyprus who were not engaged in government service, observed that there was 'a good deal of fuss about precedence, agriculture leaving before public works, and so on'. Unlike in other colonies there was no influential landowning or trading class and those British residents, who, like Harding, were non-government, were placed 'at the bottom of every list, the last to enter and the last to leave'.[113]

Etiquette and social hierarchy became increasingly rigid as colonial society became more entrenched. The British distanced themselves from their subjects and terminated all contact with 'Cypriots suspected of promoting union with Greece'. By 1936 Battershill found that he was unable to see 'certain Cypriots, as people would say I was hobnobbing with Cypriots who did not agree with Government policy'.[114] Even the Anglican church found that 'the situation is so complicated and so wrapped up with politics that it is considered inadvisable ... to have any official dealings with the responsible Orthodox authorities'.[115]

Bizarrely, the governor appears to have made occasional exceptions to this policy by making periodic visits to the Chanteclair Cabaret in Nicosia, in the company of, 'several officials of the secretariat, the commissioner of Nicosia, and the mayor'. The Chanteclair – where for a cup of coffee costing a shilling it was possible to watch 'indifferent artistes', many of them women 'fleeing from Hitler' – had become 'a kind of government annexe'. Palmer's visits appear to have been made as part of a misguided attempt to gain popularity with his Cypriot subjects. In fact, as Battershill noted in his diary, it 'created consternation' amongst the capital's elite, as it was known that 'the mayor is a great womanizer. The inference made by many Cypriots was that the mayor was producing women for [***][sic].'[116] The highly principled chief secretary was particularly distressed because the cabaret visits had taken place during the period of formal court mourning for King George V.

Increased segregation following the Government House riots exacerbated the racist attitudes that many colonial administrators brought with them from other postings and contributed to alienating them still further from their Cypriot subjects. Jean Meikle remembered that while mixed socialising was the norm for her mother's generation, when she herself was growing up in the years following 1931 'one never had a very close Cypriot friend'. The vicar of St Paul's Anglican Church in Nicosia would have endorsed Meikle's childhood experiences, for he noted in a lecture to Anglicans in the Holy Land that 'friendship between the British community and the Cypriots is the exception rather than the rule'.[117]

The laudable requirement that British civil servants in Cyprus should speak either Greek or Turkish had done little to facilitate greater social integration or even contact between the colonised and the colonisers. Relations, no matter how polite, were on the whole restricted to the purely functional. Although the manager of the Ottoman Bank in Nicosia, Hugh Llewellyn Jones, prided himself on being 'on very good terms with his Cypriot and Armenian customers', none of them were ever invited to his home.[118]

Inevitably in such an environment, inter-racial marriage was discouraged. The ethnic and cultural fluidity reflected in the roll call of names in the register of Canon Newham's English School in 1901 was long gone. Administrative officials who looked as if they might be about to commit the social transgression of marrying a 'native' were generally sent on distant postings elsewhere in the empire.

In 1938 Eirwen Llewellyn Jones found herself pushing at the boundaries of racial prejudice when she suggested inviting her friend Mona Papadopoulos to a Christmas party at the Nicosia Club. Papadopoulos's father was a member of the Royal College of Surgeons with practices in London and Cyprus, while she herself was 'a highly intelligent girl, beautifully educated'. Llewellyn Jones' social plans floundered when her brother-in-law protested, saying, ' "But sis, you can't ask her, she's a wog!" And this was very much what people thought.'

But although the social climate following the riots was certainly conducive to the development of racial bigotry and suspicion, British officials in Cyprus had long demonstrated a particularly depressing, small-minded strain of racism. Storrs encountered several such instances of racial prejudice during his period as governor and recorded how 'the wife of an officer excellent in his work, told me with pride on the eve of his transfer that they had been in Cyprus 14 years, and never had a "native" inside their house; and was genuinely shocked when I reminded her that she owed to Cypriots the food she was at that moment consuming (at Government House) and the clothes on her back'.[119]

Officials whose previous experience of colonial government had been gained in Africa often found it particularly difficult to adjust to life in Cyprus, where there was no obvious indigenous aristocracy. Today, Eirwen Harbottle feels uneasy at the part she played in the perpetuation of such attitudes when, as a teenager, she took part in a revue at the Papadopoulos Theatre. The performance ended with a rendition of 'There'll Always Be an England', a song that was 'so strong and exciting, and I was on stage singing my heart out with the rest of them, "Red, white and blue, what does it mean to you? Surely you're proud, shout it out loud, Britons awake!... Freedom remains, these are the chains, nothing can break!" I remember looking at the Cypriots in the audience thinking, "They're not looking awfully happy down there." Looking back on it now I don't know what they must have thought.'

The exception to this trend appears to have been the Forestry Department, possibly because British and Cypriot foresters were compelled to work and live alongside each other in remote and occasionally dangerous circumstances. Forestry was 'a world apart, like a mini-estate'.

The disastrous forest fires that resulted from Unwin's policies had convinced his successors, Ronald Waterer and his deputy, Geoff Chapman, of the importance of listening to popular opinion in rural areas. As a result 'the lower grades of the department, the forest guards, were given a lot of freedom. They were encouraged to spend many hours in the coffee shop, talking to the villagers, and finding out what they thought about things, what was going on.'

Both men had been disturbed by the racial and social segregation they encountered on board ship during their journeys to Cyprus. The P&O line deposited Cyprus-bound passengers at Port Said, before continuing with its longer-haul passengers to India. Waterer, fresh out of university, was shocked to discover 'this very stratified society, and how those who were referred to as *chi-chis* were treated'. Perhaps as a result both Waterer and Chapman made considerable efforts to establish friendships with Cypriots, amongst not only the senior staff within their own department but also 'businessmen, traders, people who dealt in timber for example'.[120]

One professional relationship in which Ronald Waterer invested particular time and energy was with the Abbot of Kykko Monastery, Chrysostomos. The chief forestry officer spent many years winning the abbot's confidence, offering assistance with problems that arose in the surrounding forests and convincing him that his approach to the goat problem was radically different from that of his predecessor. During this time Waterer secured sufficient funding for his department to purchase a small amount of land to provide a livelihood for several landless families who depended entirely on their goats for survival. The families were re-settled and 'established themselves as farmers, growing three to four crops a year on same bit of ground'.[121] Waterer's plan extended to the offer of £7,000 in compensation to Kykko Monastery, owner of the island's biggest single flock, if the abbot followed suit.

Gaining the abbot's support was critical, since if Kykko relinquished their goats, others would follow. For Waterer, who, unlike many of his colleagues in the Forestry Department, was only a moderate drinker, this involved no small effort. As an honoured guest at the monastery, Waterer's glass was kept permanently filled whenever he visited, until 'he believed he must have drunk enough Cypriot brandy to send most people mad.' When his 17-year-old son Donald accompanied him on his visits to Kykko he received the same treatment: 'They all said *yiamas* and knocked it back, so I knew I had to do the same. I tipped my glass back and it went down and the whole lot came up. I was sitting in a whicker chair at the time and I went so rigid trying not to cough that my hands went straight through the back of the chair!'

Today the spluttering 17-year-old is a genial open-faced countryman, living in a farmhouse in Somerset, where he grows mistletoe and holly, and willow for cricket bats. One of his most valued possessions is the ecclesiastical staff, which Abbot Chrysostomos presented to his father to mark the occasion in 1939 when Kykkos Monastery withdrew its rights to graze the monastery's 3,000 goats in the Troodos Forest. The 'goat wars' at least were over.

9

Bread Stuffed with Raisins
1939–41

The black-and-white Pathé news footage shows soldiers in shorts carefully disembarking at Famagusta Port in 1941, their rifles and kit bags over their shoulders. On the quayside below, large wooden boxes of equipment are being loaded onto trolleys, while behind them a line of lorries waits to transport the cargo. As the soldiers march out of the harbour towards the camera, the reassuring voice of Bob Danvers Walker informs the viewer that 'any German attack on Cyprus will indeed prove a hazardous adventure'. Finally, the camera, pans up to a white lighthouse, standing on top of the thick Mediaeval walls built for the defence of the old city.

Standing in front of the lighthouse on a grey day in March, as the *khamseen* wind covers everything with dust, the visitor needs considerable imagination to think back to the time when as many as 20,000 Allied troops landed at this point. Swallows fly low over the earth embankments that now cover large sections of the walls. An old woman with a plastic bag hunts for wild asparagus amongst the poppies and long grass. The port is silent, the only sign of life a brown and white dog chained up at the entrance gate.

Famagusta Port was crucial to Cyprus's involvement in the Second World War, playing different roles as the conflict unfolded. In 1941, when it was feared that Cyprus would, like Crete, be occupied by German forces, the wives and children of all British government officials were compulsorily evacuated en masse from the port. As they left, soldiers of the Durham Light Infantry were rushed across from Egypt to defend the island, their kit unloaded with such speed that much of it ended up in the water. More discretely, from 1942 until the end of the war, small fishing boats or caiques carrying radios, sabotage equipment and secret agents regularly left the port for special operations in Turkey, occupied Greece and the Italian-controlled Dodecanese.

Throughout this period, timber, men and mules were also exported in unprecedented numbers from Famagusta Harbour, following the pattern established during World War One. Thousands of tons of pine from the forests of Troodos and Paphos were shipped to North Africa for use in trenches and fortifications and to provide matches for the Eighth Army's cigarettes. At the same time, steaming carefully out of the narrow harbour mouth, troop ships carrying soldiers of the Cyprus Regiment, along with their pack animals, sailed for Greece, Italy and Sudan.

When war was declared on 3 September 1939, the Cyprus Government was at its summer capital on Mount Troodos. William Battershill, the new governor, had been sworn into office only two months earlier. At 43, he was the youngest governor in the Colonial Civil Service. As he and his staff prepared to return to Nicosia he confided in a letter to his mother, 'war has shattered all my hopes and plans for Cyprus'.[1]

Battershill, who had served as chief secretary from 1935 to 1937, had a strong affection for the island and its inhabitants and had been frustrated and disturbed by the policies of his predecessor, Richmond Palmer. Many at the Colonial Office in London had come to share Battershill's frustration. Officials wrote candidly about the 'Colonel Blimp regime' in the colony and looked forward to Battershill's arrival, when 'the Cyprus government will acquire a new angle of vision'.[2] The new governor was highly regarded by his colleagues in London and was understood by British residents to have been appointed precisely because 'he was not in agreement with the policy of Sir Richmond Palmer'.[3] One of the few British rulers to speak fluent Greek, Battershill had planned to revoke much of his predecessor's more repressive legislation, to hold municipal elections and legitimise trade unionism. Now, wartime emergency measures would take precedence over his plans for democratic reform.

For Cyprus, like Britain, the declaration of war was followed by several months of anxious waiting, when nervous energy was directed into meticulous defensive preparations. David Percival, a junior official at the Secretariat complained that 'we are doing precisely nothing here, very fussily and inefficiently – and say regularly that the navy will protect us. It is a tiresome business, worrying a bit, nothing particular to do about it, and yet unable to go on with the ordinary routine on the grounds that it will be wasted'![4]

Preliminary measures included the installation of air raid sirens, from England, in the minarets of 'Ayia Sophia' mosque and on the roof of Paphos Gate Police Station. In parts of the city where sirens were not audible, street wardens, mounted on bicycles with the letters 'ARP' painted in white on the frames, were instructed to use trumpets, drums 'or any other handy device for creating a noise'.[5] Residents of the capital living outside the boundaries of the old city were expected to construct their own shelters in their back gardens. Those within the city walls were to take cover in one of several slit trenches dug by the PWD, which, the department claimed, could accommodate nearly 17,000 people. The sudden surge in demand for wooden planks to support the underground shelters meant that unprecedented quantities of timber had to be rapidly brought down to the plains from the forestry plantations in Troodos and Paphos.

Air raid preparations at Government House however, were less successful. An alarm installed on the roof of the building was so loud that the governor could not be heard when he tried to issue subsequent instructions by telephone. In an unusually intemperate directive Battershill wrote to his chief secretary, Andrew Wright, 'I cannot stand it any longer ... the siren must go.'[6] Battershill soon discovered that the protocol accompanying his official position made rapid reaction to enemy attack particularly difficult. Whenever the governor left his official residence a ceremonial guard was obliged to line up and present arms while a bugler sounded a formal farewell. Battershill's daughter Jane remembers, 'we had this dummy air raid run to the shelter when the gentlemen at the front door presented arms, and blew a bugle and then we all climbed into the car and drove off into the wilds of the garden, and leapt into the slit trenches. We then realized just how long it had all taken'.[7]

The first air raid drills in the capital were chaotic, as panicked residents rushed indiscriminately for shelter. Handbills entitled 'How to Act During an Air Raid' were subsequently distributed in Greek and Turkish, instructing people not to 'panic, shout or run about'. Those who were more than 60 seconds away from a trench were told to 'stay STILL and not move about in the open', and everyone was admonished against 'looking for trouble'. Motor vehicles, even bicycles, were legally required to stop when the siren was sounded and to remain stationary until the raid was over. Anyone unlucky enough to be caught driving a horse or donkey cart during a raid was given the questionable advice to un-harness the animal and tie it sideways across the cart in an attempt to prevent it from bolting. But the sirens quickly lost their ability to terrify, largely due to several false alarms, when a succession of friendly aircraft were mistakenly reported as hostile. Six months later, in April 1940, a senior RAF officer complained of 'the present state of complacency and apathy so noticeable amongst the Cypriot people',[8] whenever the siren was sounded.

Battershill supervised plans for the voluntary evacuation of Cypriots living in Nicosia. In the event of enemy attack they were to be encouraged to return to their native villages and remain there for the duration of hostilities. It was estimated that as many as 5,000 evacuees would need to be 'shepherded to the roads leading to their villages' by ARP wardens. Meanwhile the island's coastal surveillance network was expanded to include lighthouse keepers and police

Governor Battershill, in dressing gown and sola topi, relaxing on the beach with an unknown friend, in the early 1940s.

[*Reproduced courtesy of Jane d'Arcy.*]

constables on horseback (4th Class) who continuously patrolled the shore line. Any suspicious sightings were passed on to teams of waiting motorcyclists, 'primed and at the ready',[9] who would in turn relay information via the nearest telephone. Battershill also oversaw the establishment of a military recruiting office in Nicosia. The first eager volunteers to be accepted were despatched to Egypt, where they were equipped and trained as transport drivers.

Once basic precautionary measures had been taken the familiar routine of colonial life began to reassert itself. Percival complained that 'except for a few trenches, one or two "emergency schemes" and a vast amount of pomposity and hush-hush among high officials, Nicosia is completely unchanged since before the war!'[10] While the British community in Cairo, where Middle

East Command was headquartered, acquired a reputation for cosmopolitan hedonism, their counterparts in Cyprus enjoyed more innocent pleasures. The conscientious governor, who relaxed by reading *The Complete Nonsense Verse of Edward Lear* or cultivating tomatoes in his greenhouse, set the tone for the rest of his administration. So, as the German army advanced across Poland in September 1939, the Nicosia gramophone concert circle began its autumn programme, the chess club resumed its meetings, and a small singing group began meeting weekly to practice madrigals.

Thorough and meticulous though Battershill was in his defensive planning, he did not allow the outbreak of war to deter him from his pet project of converting the lawns at Government House into a polo pitch. Members of the administration were encouraged to acquire their own polo ponies, although some were sceptical since 'no-one here has any suitable animals or knows the first thing about it'.[11] This did not dampen the governor's enthusiasm, and he observed with satisfaction that 'the local people are getting well into the swing of it'. He had particular hopes for the mounted police constabulary. 'When they get into the game', Battershill wrote, 'they should be really good.'[12] But his experiment lasted little more than a year and subsequent plans to establish a second polo ground on the site of Nicosia race track had to be abandoned after it was requisitioned for wartime food production.

In 1939 the number of potential spectators at the governor's polo matches would have been greater than ever before. There were now just over 600 Britons living in Cyprus. During the course of the previous two decades a community of 200 or more retired colonial officials from other imperial outposts, all fiercely patriotic, had gradually established itself in Kyrenia. Since the British first occupied Cyprus in 1878, the picturesque harbour, which reminded many visitors of a Cornish fishing village, had been considered to have potential as 'an excellent invalid resort, better in some respects than even the most popular localities in France and Italy'.[13] Subsequent generations of retired colonial administrators discovered that in Cyprus their pensions went further, labour was extremely cheap, and they could continue to enjoy an enhanced status merely by virtue of their race. These were perks and privileges that would be lost if they returned to Britain, a country which, after a lifetime spent in the colonies, they hardly knew. The nucleus of this highly stratified, introverted little society was to be found in the tea rooms of the Dome Hotel, where the seating was carefully arranged to reflect social status. Those with titles, such as Lady Lock, Lady Chenevix Trench, or Lady Murphy, were afforded precedence, while the untitled lady was seated in accordance with her husband's final ranking in the Indian Civil Service. An exception to the seating plan was made in the case of the formidable Mrs Pocklington, Lady Chenevix Trench's mother, who sat with her daughter. Mrs Pocklington, who occupied a suite of

mauve painted rooms at the Dome, insisted during her annual summer retreat
to the tented hotels of Mount Troodos that the interior of her own tent should
be similarly decorated with swathes of mauve fabric. The most senior member of this expatriate enclave was Major General Sir Courtney Manifold, who
had retired from the medical service of the Indian army and occasionally took
the salute on the king's birthday parade. Manifold's house, Harbour Heights, a
'veritably tiny palace',[14] is now a bar and nightclub. Turkish Cypriot rock bands
play in the room that was once Manifold's library, panelled at great expense
with Indian teak. The wealthy Manifolds were a source of fascination to the
expatriate community of Kyrenia. It was rumoured that it had taken no less
than two ships to transport their library and antiques to Cyprus and that Lady
Manifold retired to bed each night weighed down beneath her valuable collection of jewellery in order to prevent it from being stolen. The insular retirees of
Kyrenia, the largest single British community on the island outside the administration, had virtually no contact with Cypriots apart from their own servants.
One new arrival noted wryly that Manifold and his compatriots believed there
was 'little wrong with Cyprus, only the Cypriots: and except for a few, [they]
take frequent opportunities for saying so'.[15]

The inhabitants of Kyrenia were not alone in their low opinion of Cypriots.
Although encouraged to enlist in mule and transport companies they were
considered by several senior military figures to possess a 'poor physique and
a relatively low mental capacity'[16] which made them unsuitable for combat.
Nonetheless, the first 700 Cypriots who joined up in September and October
1939 were the subject of considerable media interest. Together with an Indian
mule train they constituted 'the first colonial contingent to land in France' and
were filmed for a short Pathé documentary which showed them feeding, shoe-
ing and exercising their mules.

Altogether 30,000 Cypriot volunteers served in the British army, forming
mule and general transport companies, mobile laundry units and a battalion
of engineers. They were to fight with particular bravery in Greece and North
Africa, at Keren in today's Eritrea and at the Fourth Battle of Monte Cassino
in Italy. Their courage under fire led to a rapid reassessment of previous preju-
dices and by the end of the war Cypriot troops who had served overseas were
applauded for having 'distinguished themselves and earned warm praise from
[their] Commanders'.[17]

Throughout January and February 1940 however, Nazi radio propaganda,
broadcast in Greek on shortwave, justifiably accused the British of considering Cypriots 'only fit as muleteers and slaves'.[18] The governor responded by
announcing the formation of a 'fighting battalion', to be known as the Cyprus
Regiment. The chief secretary, Andrew Wright was appointed colonel, and
regimental recruiting offices at Nicosia and Polemidia were 'besieged'[19] by

volunteers, prompting Battershill to assure the Colonial Office that conscription on the island would be entirely unnecessary. He added that its introduction in a colony where the inhabitants had virtually no democratic voice would have been both morally questionable and politically provocative.

Cypriot enthusiasm for enlistment arose primarily from economic necessity. 1939 and 1940 were characterised by widespread unemployment and industrial unrest. Volunteers accepted into the regiment were paid two shillings a day, around three times what a labourer could expect to receive for a day's work. Many volunteers were unemployed miners, recently laid off by the American-owned Cyprus Mines Corporation (CMC). This was the island's largest single industry which had employed large numbers of the landless poor and accounted for 60 per cent of Cyprus's entire exports. In June 1940, when Italy entered the war all mining operations were suspended. Thousands of miners were without work. The loss of European mineral markets was compounded by the shortage of shipping, which prevented agricultural exports from being transported to outlets within the Middle East and Eastern Mediterranean. Miners laid off by the CMC returned to their villages to find that agricultural work too had dried up.

Until 1939, Cyprus's principal agricultural export had been carobs. After war broke out sales plummeted, and only occasional shiploads were to leave the island over the next six years. In an effort to prevent widespread and serious economic distress, the government agreed to purchase the entire annual carob and raisin crops at a fixed price for the duration of the war. Battershill, meanwhile, made imaginative attempts to find new regional markets for the island's citrus crop, proposing that it should be exported to British troops in Egypt. In the summer of 1940, the men of the Seventh Armoured and the Fourth Indian Divisions were bracing themselves to repel Mussolini's Italian Blackshirts as they advanced across the Western Desert from Libya. Battershill suggested that they should be supplied with a daily Cyprus orange as part of their rations. But the governor's representations failed when the War Office, anxious to avoid upsetting the Egyptian authorities, ruled that 'only Egyptian-grown oranges could be bought by the army'.[20] Cypriot orange exports stopped entirely for the rest of the war and farmers were forced to plough their crop back into the soil. There was, however, more success in finding a market for Cypriot silk. This was a cottage industry, generally operated by women who kept trays of silk worms under their beds; 15 tons of silk were sold to the Ministry of Supply during 1943–44 to be made into parachutes.[21]

By May 1940 over 3,000 Cypriots had registered for relief work; 1,300 of them in Nicosia alone, where they earned basic subsistence wages[22] working on road repairs organised by the PWD. Most of the men were labourers and miners, but the list included tailors, shoeblacks, confectioners and even a few interpreters and clerks.

Italy's entry into the war had more profound repercussions for Cyprus than the disruption of its export markets. For it brought the conflict closer to home and turned the Eastern Mediterranean and North Africa into a potential theatre of combat. In 1940, Turkey and Greece, Cyprus's immediate neighbours to the north and west, had both declared an uneasy neutrality. Neither had yet fully recovered from the devastation of the First World War and both were desperate to avoid being drawn into another conflict.

Turkey, in particular, still coming to terms with the loss of its empire and determined not to find itself once again on the losing side, was to sign treaties with both Britain and Germany during the course of the war. Despite initial promises to assist Britain and France in the event of conflict in the Mediterranean, it subsequently elected to support the Allies from a position of what Prime Minister Ismet Inonu memorably described as 'theoretical belligerence'. Germany's non-aggression pact with Turkey's old adversary, Russia, signed in the summer of 1939, and the spectre of further, closer alliances between the two countries had caused alarm in Ankara. 'What we would really like', one Turk is alleged to have remarked, 'would be for Germany to destroy Russia and for the Allies to destroy Germany.'[23]

For its part, Greece was equally anxious to do nothing that might incite German or Italian aggression. Aware that Mussolini hoped to establish another Italian foothold in the Mediterranean, the Greek dictator General Metaxas studiously avoided responding to Italian provocation. At the same time, throughout the summer of 1940, he discretely accelerated his programme of modernising the Greek army and embarked on an extensive scheme of road and rail works in frontier areas. Six days after Mussolini's invasion of Albania, Britain and France offered Greece a guarantee of military support in the event of a threat to its independence. While accepting the guarantee in principle, in the interests of preserving his neutrality, Metaxas endeavoured to keep offers of British military assistance at arm's length.

Meanwhile in Cyprus itself Battershill stepped up his preparations for attack. He established the Cyprus Volunteer Force (CVF), the colony's equivalent of the Home Guard. A total of 70 officers and 1,300 men were employed in demolition and bomb disposal tasks along with 'general field engineering work', under the command of Stafford Foster-Sutton, the attorney general. Forestry Department staff formed their own separate company, stationed at Troodos, ready to deploy as a fire-fighting force should the enemy drop incendiary bombs 'to create diversionary forest fires'. The network of forest fire lookout stations doubled up as observation posts reporting sightings of enemy planes.[24]

Throughout the spring of 1940, as the prospect of war with Italy had increased, Battershill became concerned about the island's feeble defences and the likelihood of aerial attacks from the Italian-controlled Dodecanese about 200 miles distant.

On 4 June 1940, just six days before Italy at last declared war on Britain, there were only 165 regular troops stationed on the island, supported by 'members of the police force'. Cyprus was a soft target, one that would be attainable, even by the Italian air force, with a minimum of effort. Battershill believed that the 50,000 gallons of aircraft fuel stored at Nicosia aerodrome, along with the island's potential as an air base from which the enemy could attack Beirut and Haifa, made it an attractive prospect. He pointed out to the Colonial Office that 'the loss of prestige we would suffer from a successful enemy occupation would be serious'. The governor and the officer commanding troops on the island proposed increasing the strength of the garrison by one battalion, which would at least be capable of withstanding attack until the arrival of reinforcements. The War Office endorsed the proposals, but General Archibald Wavell, the commander in chief of Middle East Forces, did not. Wavell's resources were already stretched, and he feared he would be unable to repel the anticipated Italian advance into Egypt. By contrast, the chances of an attack on Cyprus, he argued, were small. Battershill was duly informed that no further troops could be spared.

But the French commander in chief in the Levant, General Eugène Mittelhauser, concerned to protect French territories in Syria and Lebanon, did not endorse Wavell's view. Throughout May, as German troops swept effortlessly across Belgium and France, Mittelhauser pressed Wavell for permission to deploy his own troops in Cyprus. Battershill was now in a dilemma. Desperate for the island's defences to be augmented, he questioned the advisability of using French troops to defend a British colony. Cypriots would, he argued, interpret the presence of a French contingent as proof that Cyprus was not 'considered of sufficient importance to be defended by British troops'. He feared that any resentment would increase 'if the French colonial coloured troops were sent … in view of local feeling on the colour question'. Even a small detachment of British troops, he repeated, could be sufficient to deter any Italian incursion.

Wavell, a thoughtful man, whom Batterhill considered 'a good friend' after they served together in Palestine, may have been swayed by these arguments. On 6 June 1940, as German troops began to break through the French defensive lines that stretched east-west from Rheims to the Somme, the company of Sherwood Foresters already garrisoned in Cyprus was expanded to full battalion strength. It was assigned to Nicosia and Larnaca aerodromes, where the men set to reinforcing the defences. After Mittelhauser again requested permission to send a battalion and a 'flight of aeroplanes,' Wavell telegrammed that he had no objections 'provided battalion was a white one'.[25] A small French force was eventually sent but stayed for only a short period, until France's surrender to Germany on 22 June 1940.

Battershill, meanwhile, had been forced to direct his energies in another direction. In 1939, the BBC had begun transmitting its first broadcasts in Greek to Greece and Cyprus. The evening broadcasts 'made people feel more friendly towards the British'[26] and rapidly assumed great significance, being 'followed with great attention in towns and villages throughout the island'.[27] Undeterred by the 10 shilling annual radio-receiving licence, a significant number of Cypriots bought their own Phillips set. By 1940, around 3,000 sets were in use across the island, most of them installed in village coffee-shops. In some areas villagers regularly walked long distances to hear the bulletins, which opened with the familiar phrase 'This is London'.

But this new and attentive audience was also specifically targeted by Nazi propagandists. Regular broadcasts in Greek were transmitted from the occupied Polish city of Wroclaw, identified during the war by its German name of Breslau. Unlike the BBC's Greek service, which was aimed primarily at a mainland Greek listenership with occasional references to Cyprus, the Breslau broadcasts were intended specifically for a Cypriot audience. Some of the earlier bulletins suggest a questionable judgement on the part of the German propagandists. One programme solemnly announced that 'the bloodthirsty government of Cyprus has decreed the early closing of shops',[28] while another accused the administration of doing irrevocable damage to the bowels of its Cypriot subjects by force-feeding them the surplus orange crop. But such blunders were rare. The majority of the material from Breslau was informed, accurate and topical. When the network announced the formation of the Cyprus Regiment in February 1940, the day before the news was made public within the colony, Battershill's suspicions were confirmed. Information was being passed to the enemy, 'probably by letter, taken by hand on board Greek (and possibly Italian) ships'.[29] The Breslau transmissions hit the administration at its weakest spots. Broadcasts regularly assured listeners that a German victory would bring the people of Cyprus 'their own union with their Greek fatherland'[30] and enable them to 'throw off the British yoke'. Even more damagingly, they referred in detail to the restrictions on civil liberties that had remained in place since the burning of Government House in 1931. Why was it, asked a broadcast in February 1940, that a people 'so faithful to empire' had not yet been granted the right to choose their own local authorities, elect their own archbishop, display the Greek flag or congregate in groups of more than five at a time?

These were all questions which exposed the contradictions inherent in the British administration of Cyprus and to which Battershill was hard pressed to provide satisfactory answers. Despite the enthusiastic response to military recruitment campaigns which had prompted more than 6,000 Cypriots to volunteer for army service, the governor was forced to acknowledge that the Breslau propaganda constituted a challenge to both the legitimacy of his own government and Cypriot loyalty to the crown. Winning the battle for hearts and minds at home was to be a priority for the rest of his time in office. In a typically understated telegram he advised London that the broadcasts were beginning to have 'a harmful effect' on public opinion. The Colonial Office agreed, in a world-weary reply, that the broadcasts were likely to 'find a more fruitful field in Cyprus than in other colonies whose roots are more firmly established in British traditions'.

Battershill was aware that short of a wholesale reversal of British policy, his hands were tied. He wrote to the Colonial Office: 'There is nothing we can say or do, which will weigh in the balance against Hellenistic sentiment cleverly played upon from within Cyprus itself and from without.' But this didn't stop the governor from embarking on a lengthy campaign to convince the BBC to use the Greek service broadcasts to appeal to a Cypriot audience. He requested that the 8.10 p.m. bulletins should be transmitted earlier in the evening, so that villagers, many of whom 'retire early to bed', could 'listen in' before they left the coffee-shop in the evening, but received a terse response explaining that technical reasons made this impossible. Undeterred, he pointed out that 'the cold formal manner of the BBC announcer...does not appeal to the Cypriot,' and that listeners had complained about the speed of the announcers' delivery, requesting that they should speak 'more slowly and distinctly'.

The BBC's Greek section, based at Bush House in the Strand, was staffed mainly by sophisticated, urban Athenians, many of whom regarded their Cypriot audience, with its provincial dialect, as an irritant. It explained that its three Greek announcers had all 'earned much favourable comment from Greece' and added, with a dig at the rural peasantry of Cyprus, that it was 'very difficult for a cultured Greek to speak his language slowly'.[31] Battershill persisted, requesting that the broadcasts should contain more frequent references to Cyprus. In this recommendation he was, at last, successful. A meeting was held between members of the Orwellian-sounding Anti-Lie Unit and a substantial contingent of BBC management, including the Empire news editor, the overseas news editor, the European news editor, the Arabic editor, and a Mr Cummings of Editorial Liaison.

As a result it was agreed to broadcast a biweekly 'letter from Cypriot soldiers serving overseas' at the end of the Greek news. The programmes would contain 'as much news of the daily life of the Cyprus contingents as would convey no information to the enemy'. They would be read, initially, by soldiers from No. 1 and 2 pack transport companies, recently evacuated from Dunkirk and garrisoned in Swindon and Melton Mowbray, and would be supervised by Richard Wayne of the Cyprus Office in London[32]. The programmes began in July 1940 and became very popular. Listeners in Cyprus submitted requests, via the Secretariat, for speakers from their particular village. Villagers in the Karpas region in the north east of the island were particularly persistent, but despite Wayne's best efforts at trawling the Karpasian community in Britain for suitable contributors, he had to conclude that 'all the Karpas villagers are either too bashful or have nothing to say'.[33] Wayne was soon forced to cast his net wider and subsequent contributors included Greek Orthodox priests, a Cypriot ARP warden talking about air raids in the East End of London and the young Glafcos Clerides[34] speaking about his service in the RAF.

The difficulties that Battershill had encountered in his struggle to combat Nazi propaganda and obtain wartime radio programmes specific to Cyprus were symptomatic of Britain's enduring ambivalence about the island. The colony was not considered sufficiently significant to merit its own dedicated radio broadcasts and was only reluctantly accommodated after its subjects had been specifically targeted by the enemy and attempts were made to undermine their loyalty to the crown.

Any residual hopes that a conflict in the Eastern Mediterranean might be avoided came to an end when Italy declared war on Britain on 10 June 1940. In London, the subsequent internment of over 4,000 Italians, many of them waiters in cafés and restaurants, was to create unexpected job opportunities for Cypriots in the capital.

For the inhabitants of Nicosia, Italy's declaration of war meant that the hitherto distant conflict now impacted on their daily life. A full blackout was immediately imposed on the city, where, fortunately for the inhabitants, the weather was unusually cool for the time of year. Battershill wrote to his mother that 'black out in intense heat with the windows closed and the curtains drawn isn't going to be a bit pleasant'.[35]

Just over a week after Mussolini's declaration, Battershill addressed the Advisory Council and announced that as Cyprus was now a potential battle zone, emergency measures allowing for the arrest and detention of fifth columnists had been introduced, along with the strict control of cameras and wireless receiver sets, the imposition of food controls and petrol rationing. The governor, mindful of his responsibility to set an example and perhaps having read Churchill's directive to all senior civil servants to 'maintain a high morale in their circles',[36] told the Council, 'this is the gravest crisis through which any of us have lived, but there is no reason here for despair or despondency'.[37] Privately, he wrote to his mother that 'I have done all I can think of, though I often wonder if I have done enough and correctly'.[38]

Food control was amongst the most contentious of Battershill's emergency measures; despite the government's control of the purchase and distribution of essential items, it was unable to prevent shortages, food hoarding and profiteering. White sugar disappeared completely, to be replaced by grape sugar, which was also rationed, with the result that, as Battershill's daughter Jane recalled, 'we each had a jam jar with our name on it and this treacly stuff at the bottom, not very nice, and if you put it in tea or something it was quite revolting'. Seven government distribution centres were set up, while at village level rationed goods were given out by the local Co-operative Society. The success of the scheme, implemented at village level by the *mukhtar*, varied across the island. Limassol municipality in particular was frequently accused of favouritism, with complaints that clothing had been allocated to 'dead men and then their relatives'.[39]

Cyprus had relied heavily on imported arable crops and despite wartime increases in the wheat and potato acreage, it became necessary – to the governor's regret – to plant crops on Nicosia race course and in the dry moat surrounding the old city walls of Nicosia. The government attempted to control distribution by buying all locally grown wheat and barley not required for the grower's private consumption and even requisitioned village threshing floors. In 1942, 35 per cent of the crop was purchased by government.[40] In an effort to dispose of the surplus grape and carob harvest, the administration also made attempts to incorporate them into bread. Carob bread proved highly unpopular and did not last long, but 'bread stuffed with raisins' became a staple food for the rest of the war, with bakers obliged to add a specified quantity of raisins to every kilo of dough. The government issued robust assurances that the bread was 'no less wholesome than before',[41] and it gradually came to be grudgingly tolerated.

Shortages of cotton and petrol were particularly acute. Clothing grew so scarce that it became impossible 'for an even distribution to be made', as around half the motor vehicles on the island were requisitioned for military use. Petrol rationing was so stringent that the 700 cars that remained in private hands were seldom used.[42]

On 22 June 1940, with three-fifths of France under enemy occupation, the French government in Paris surrendered to Germany. Vichy-controlled Lebanon and Syria, the territories geographically closest to Cyprus, were now potentially hostile bases. Britain and her colonies faced Germany alone. Hitler, for whom air superiority was a prerequisite of a successful land invasion of Britain, began a programme of sporadic daylight raids on strategic British targets. At the time, Britain had only 600 serviceable fighter planes, well below the 1,000 considered to be the minimum defence requirement. The Ministry of Aircraft Production appealed to the public for donations of aluminium, promising to turn pots and pans into Spitfires, Hurricanes and Wellingtons. In Cyprus, the English language newspaper *The Cyprus Post* launched a 'Speed the Plane' fund, which collected over £4,000 for the cost of a Spitfire 'in the defence of England'. A further £3,000 was donated by a Mr Demetriou to pay for an aircraft to be called 'Larnaca'. In Britain meanwhile, the governor's mother established a comforts fund to provide cigarettes and other small items for Cypriot troops serving overseas.

For the British residents of Cyprus, particularly those with children in England, the summer of 1940 was agonising. Radio reports of the Battle of

Britain were followed by the even grimmer news of the London Blitz. 'You cannot imagine how much all of you in England are in our minds now,' Battershill wrote to his mother. 'Every time I hear of a raid on a south west town I think of home. It is very trying to put it mildly to sit here and listen to the radio news and feel that one's relatives are putting up with all sorts of hell and that one cannot be there oneself. Sometimes it makes one want to curse.'[43] As the delivery of letters became increasingly disrupted, the colonists became heavily dependent on the radio for news of what was happening at home. 'The wireless is very depressing' complained Percival, 'which does not prevent everyone spending hours a day listening to it.'[44]

As the blitz on London and the south west wore on, Battershill launched a public subscription in Cyprus for mobile canteens to provide food for those in Britain who had been made homeless. By the end of November the fund amounted to more than £3,000. The colony paid for no less than 12 canteens, allocated to London, Plymouth, Taunton, Stroud, Swindon and Trowbridge. 'If you are in London and see one with Cyprus on it,' Battershill wrote to his mother with justifiable pride, 'I hope you will go and have a snack.'[45] Funds established by the Red Cross, St John's Ambulance and the British Legion between them received £25,000 raised by contributions from the colony, a phenomenal sum considering that in 1939 the British population did not number more than 700 and the average Cypriot wage was a little over £20 a year. During this period of the war the relationship between colony and metropolis was publicly depicted as a symbiotic one of mutual support in the face of a common enemy. But it was also a narrative that had a particular personal resonance for the governor, and his understanding of his own role. In September 1940, when news reached Cyprus that Buckingham Palace had been bombed, Battershill recorded with satisfaction that his subjects had been 'deeply moved' and that the news 'had been heard with indignation'.

Throughout the summer of 1940, while Britain was bombarded from the air and Cyprus was targeted by Nazi propaganda over the airwaves, Greek ships were being systematically harassed by Italian planes. Finally at 3 a.m. on 28 October 1940, a date which is still commemorated in Greece and Cyprus, the Italian minister in Athens presented General Metaxas with a humiliating ultimatum demanding that the Greek government should consent to the immediate occupation of the country by Italian troops. The terms were impossible to accept and the general immediately rejected the ultimatum, knowing that by doing so he was bringing Greece into the war.

Cyprus was electrified. Battershill telegraphed the Colonial Office that a 'spirit of excitement bordering on hysteria persists. British, Turkish and Greek flags (the last in the majority) fly everywhere'.[46] Crowds gathered outside the Greek consulate in Nicosia and the offices of the district commissioners in Larnaca and Limassol. A steady stream of applicants called at the Greek Consulate volunteering for service in the Greek army. Bishop Leontios, the locum tenens, or acting archbishop, addressed a meeting at Larnaca draped in the British, Greek and Turkish flags.

For Greek Cypriot nationalists, such as the locum tenens and the exiled Bishop of Kyrenia who both supported *enosis*, these were exciting days. It was assumed that Greek support for Britain would be rewarded in peace time by the gift of Cyprus, an impression which both Churchill and Eden periodically encouraged. The Bishop of Kyrenia's idealised account of the atmosphere in Kyrenia following the declaration of war was highly emotional and politically charged. 'From every door, from every window, there sprang a [Greek] flag, waving proudly in the breeze. Once again, over mountain and sea, the Race was united.'[47] In fact, the bishop was very far from Kyrenia, he had been exiled for his part in the Government House riots and did not return to Cyprus until after the war was over. In the context of the fascist doctrines being espoused in Nazi Germany his depiction of a select and ethnically distinct racial group of Hellenes, 'the Race', might seem chilling to a contemporary reader, but it was one that in 1940 had enormous resonance for Greek Cypriots.

The British administration in Cyprus was in a delicate position. Greece now stood alongside Britain against the Axis, the only country in Europe to do so. Its entry into the war was undoubtedly welcomed; Churchill described it as the nation's 'finest hour'. But at the same time, the patriotism this evoked in Cyprus stimulated loyalty to Greece, not to Britain or the Empire. Until October 1940 expressions of Greek patriotism had been actively discouraged, particularly so during the long years that followed the Government House riots, when it had been illegal for Cypriots to fly the Greek flag or to play the Greek national anthem. Not only were these symbols now permitted, they were utilised by the British in an attempt to aid recruitment. But exploiting Greek patriotism as part of the war effort was a double-edged sword, as Battershill explained in a telegram to the Colonial Office in London, 'enthusiasm for war and G.B. is genuine but is based on the entry of Greece into war and the hope that now Greece is an ally local "oppressive" laws will be repealed'. Privately, Battershill complained that support for the Greek fighting fund meant that 'there will be less money for any British war charities'.[48]

Now that Greece was an active combatant, the BBC's Cyprus broadcasts were suspended. Those sections of the Greek Service's airtime previously assigned to talks by Cypriots were now dedicated exclusively to news of the war in Greece. But for Battershill, concerned that Cypriot loyalty to Britain's newest ally should not overshadow its allegiance to the Empire, it became more important than ever that Cyprus should have its own dedicated broadcasts. He argued that the locum tenens and the Orthodox Church in Cyprus were

> supporting the war which Greece is fighting for freedom and the self determination of small nations, not the war which the British Empire is fighting for these principles. They are in short trying to make the Cypriots regard themselves as striving for the liberation of Greece and not for the survival of Britain. The BBC broadcasts in Greek for Greece are naturally designed to emphasise the general unity of purpose of Great Britain and Greece. But the broadcasts in Greek for Cyprus are specially designed to strengthen the bonds between Cyprus and Great Britain. The two things are very far from the same[49]

The weekly five-minute talks for Cyprus were resumed some weeks later, but this time with the specific intention of reinforcing the link between Britain 'as the centre of the Empire and Cyprus as an inherent part of it'. Until now the BBC's broadcasts had been intended primarily to neutralise German propaganda and to maintain communication between troops and their families. From now on they would also have the clear ideological function of encouraging Cypriots to 'think of themselves as part of the British Empire'.[50]

After some weeks of deliberation the Colonial Office eventually endorsed Battershill's view that the contents of broadcasts to Cyprus must 'be entirely different from those of broadcasts intended for persons of foreign and particularly Greek, nationality'.[51] From October 1941, the biweekly 15-minute Greek language broadcasts to the colony were removed from the corporation's European network and transmitted instead via the memorably titled 'Empire Greek Network'.

Italian violation of Greek soil on 28 October 1940 had brought Britain's guarantee of military support to Greece into force. Four bomber squadrons arrived at Suda Bay in Crete the next day. Churchill continued to press Metaxas to allow a British expeditionary force to land in Greece in an attempt to block German advances into the Balkans. But the general feared that the forces proposed would be inadequate to hold a front successfully and might provoke a reaction from Germany. He rejected the approaches.

Despite the constraints Metaxas placed on overt military assistance from Britain, New Year 1941 was a time of optimism for the allies in the Mediterranean. Within a few days of the general's rebuttal of the Italian ultimatum, the Greek army had seized the initiative and pushed Mussolini's army back into Albania. At the same time, the British army in North Africa was having similar successes against the Italian divisions in Libya, Eritrea and Abyssinia. Then, at the end of January 1941, General Metaxas died, prompting Britain to reiterate its offer to send ground troops to defend Greece.

Anthony Eden, the British foreign secretary, hoped that the prospect of Britain honouring its treaty obligations to Greece might encourage Romania and Turkey to join the Allies. Eden, accompanied by General John Dill, the chief of the Imperial General Staff, and General Wavell, travelled to Athens on a mission to convince Metaxas's successor, a mild-mannered banker called Alexander Koryzis, and his chief of staff, General Papagos, to permit a British expeditionary force to land on the Greek mainland.

The British delegation accomplished its goals on 22 February, with both ease and considerable incompetence. A misunderstanding arose at the meeting at the royal palace of Tatoi, outside Athens, which proved disastrous for the Allied war effort and threatened to have momentous political repercussions for Cyprus. As a result of the misunderstanding, General Papagos left the negotiating table with a vision of the combined strategy which differed dramatically from that being pursued by the British. But the communication breakdown did not become apparent until some weeks later when Eden returned to Athens expecting to see elements of the programme already in place. Hoping he might yet salvage some political advantage from the ensuing tactical confusion, Eden arranged an impromptu meeting with his Turkish counterpart, Sukru Sarajoglu, at Government House in Nicosia on 18 March 1941. There, he renewed his attempts to convince Turkey to throw in its lot with the Allies. But the meeting was inconclusive, and for the second time Eden failed to convince Turkey to abandon its neutrality. For the governor, making 'rather intricate arrangements' for the foreign secretary's visit at short notice proved problematic. Battershill complained to his mother that 'we cannot order up something from the cold storage at a moment's notice'. However, for the hosts at least, 'it all seemed to pass up all right', particularly for Jane and Anne Battershill, who were 'very excited over obtaining the autographs of our distinguished visitors'.[52]

The delays that resulted from Eden's obfuscation at Tatoi meant that when German forces finally launched their attack on Greek territory from Yugoslavia on 6 April, Allied troops were disorganised and deployed too thinly on the ground. Their attempt to hold a defensive line along the course of the River Aliakhmon, south west of Thessalonika, failed. The city fell and it was clear that the entire country would soon follow suit. On 12 April, as Australian troops attempting to hold the Aliakhmon Line were pushed further south, the Defence Committee was forced for the first time to consider what action to take in the event of an Allied defeat, including, how it might safeguard the Greek royal family. Churchill telegrammed General Maitland Wilson, commander of the British Expeditionary Force in Greece, with instructions that if King George and his government were forced to leave Athens, they should base themselves first in Crete, and then, if that island was overrun, in Cyprus. The directive was not well received by the military, concerned that the presence of the Greek royal family in Cyprus would require further reinforcement of the colony. For its part, the Greek government responded by boldly requesting some 'territory in Cyprus over which they could exercise jurisdiction', even if it were 'only one small village in Cyprus which they can call their own'.[53] The Foreign Office spent some time weighing up this request for territorial concessions, eventually demurring less because of their implications for the future sovereignty of the colony and more out of concern that 'it might also create difficulties with other allied governments now resident in Great Britain who would be receiving less favourable treatment'.

The suggestion of conceding even 'one small village' to Greece, in a colony where the single greatest threat to the continuation of British sovereignty was the Greek Cypriot demand for *enosis*, must have been shattering news for Battershill. The governor, however, agreed to accommodate the Greek exiles, numbering around 100, in Platres but warned that accommodation in the island was 'of low standard and not in the least comparable to that commonly associated with European capitals'. He added, with studied casualness, that it should be explained that the Greek king's presence in Cyprus would inevitably 'render position of this Government almost impossible'. Greek Cypriots would, he continued, consider the king and his government to be the de facto government of the island, and the expectation that Cyprus would be ceded to Greece after the war would gain credibility. This could only exacerbate tensions between the Greek and Turkish communities, tensions which were increasing 'as the result of the failure of Turkey to enter the war'.[54]

Four days later, General Papagos pressed Britain to withdraw from Greece to save his country 'from complete devastation'.[55] Commonwealth troops moved back to the southern ports of Monemvasia, Kalamata and Nauplia and awaited rescue by sea. Priority in the order of evacuation was given to combat troops, with the result that 2,500 Cypriot supply and transport troops were abandoned and subsequently taken prisoner. A few members of the regiment avoided capture by passing themselves off as Greeks, later making their way back to Cyprus slowly by boat.[56]

As Britain's position in Greece deteriorated, the plan to evacuate King George and the government to Cyprus was re-assessed. On 20 April the secretary of state telegrammed Battershill that 'for defence reasons apart from the embarrassing political reactions, HMG would much prefer that they should not, repeat not, go to Cyprus', but he added that nothing had yet been concluded. Four days later Greece capitulated to Germany. By the end of April, the Allied military withdrawal, undertaken under cover of darkness, was complete; 50,000 troops, approximately 80 per cent of the expedition, had been evacuated from the mainland, the majority taken to Crete. Large quantities of valuable equipment had been destroyed during the withdrawal, including

8,000 vehicles, reluctantly relinquished by Wavell who had hoped to use them in the conquest of Libya. In North Africa, Rommell had seized the opportunity created by the diversion of Allied resources to Greece to recapture Benghazi. By the middle of April he had Tobruk under siege and showed every prospect of being able to continue his advance into Egypt.

Cyprus was now more vulnerable than ever. The significant Axis advances to the west and the south meant that it could no longer be considered a safe home for the Greek government in exile. A move to the colony, the Foreign Office acknowledged, would hardly enable the government or the royal family to 'escape the danger to which they are exposed in Crete'.[57] On 29 April 1941, most of the royal household, accompanied by Otto, the royal dachshund, left Crete for exile in Egypt and subsequently in Britain.

10

Stripped for War
1941-42

Events in Crete were followed intently in Cyprus. On 24 May 1941
Battershill wrote to his mother that a victory there would 'mean all the
world to the people in these parts'.[1] Six days later he was forced to acknowledge that things were looking 'extremely serious', adding 'Cyprus, like Crete,
is an island between the Germans and their advance eastwards. There is no
disguising that fact.'[2] Allied commanders in Nicosia, Cairo and London now
feared that Cyprus, a strategically important point in the British line of defence
between Tobruk and Baghdad and a potential constraint on German expansion
in Africa or Asia, was likely to be the site of the next Axis attack.

Once again British military strategists were confronted by the same dilemma
that had troubled their predecessors in the 1880s. Although Cyprus might not
in itself be strategically valuable enough for scarce resources to be allocated to
its defence, if it fell into enemy hands it could represent a threat to the vital Suez
Canal. The military leaders of 1940 also had another source of anxiety, one that
had not troubled their counterparts in the previous war: the prospect that the
island could be used as a regional air base by Italian or German forces to launch
attacks on the Middle East or North Africa.

Over the preceding six weeks, as the news from Greece grew worse, the
geriatric community in Kyrenia had been gradually packing up and retreating
east to Simla, Darjeeling and Baghdad. Nicosia, Famagusta and Limassol meanwhile began to 'take on a military appearance', with the arrival of Australian
troops who 'roused the islanders to enthusiastic demonstrations of hospitality'.[3]
The Times correspondent, in a stirring piece of propaganda, described their
arrival: 'Along the roads where the English crusaders of Coeur de Lion once

trod, there now march British and Australian troops, and where English archers once caused havoc, modern troops hope to prove themselves equally valiant.'[4] The reality, as Wavell and Dill were aware, was that the island's existing garrison was too small to be capable of mounting more than a token defence. Without substantial reinforcements the flat plains of the Messaoria and the coastal regions would be impossible to defend in the event of a coordinated air and sea attack.

It has only now become clear how close Cyprus came to being totally abandoned by Britain. In the spring of 1941, the British government decided that it would, if necessary, relinquish Cyprus, putting up only minimal resistance in the face of a concerted Nazi assault. On 27 May 1941, as British troops in Crete once again prepared for evacuation, Churchill summoned his Defence Committee to determine the fate of the island if Hitler continued his advance south-eastwards. For Battershill their conclusions were sobering. Defending Cyprus was less strategically important than attacking Syria and Lebanon. Both territories were under the control of Vichy France, which retained around 35,000 troops there. If Hitler's advance eastwards towards the oil fields of Iran and Iraq was to be blocked, it was vital to secure control of the French garrisons in the Levant. By the same token, if Syria became a forward base for German forces in the region, any defence of Cyprus would become hopeless. It was therefore decided that in the event of a co-ordinated air and seaborne attack on the island no reinforcements should be sent to relieve the garrison, even, the minutes of the meeting added chillingly, when 'the inevitable appeals materialise'. Although a small military presence was to remain to defend the aerodrome at Nicosia against 'air-borne raiders' and ensure that 'the Germans do not get the island for a song', the island was effectively to be abandoned. When the anticipated 'Battle of Cyprus' began expatriate women and children were to be evacuated to the Troodos Mountains. British troops would 'fight a slow retreat to the foothills',[5] from where they would dig in at a series of 'keeps' in preparation for a 'last ditch stand'. When, as was predicted, this was also lost, they were to be 'handed over to the Germans under a flag of truce carried by Northcote, the old and very doddery Commandant of Police from Famagusta'.[6] The 'white elephant' colony and its occupants were, once again, expendable. Churchill appears to have had some qualms about this bleak strategy, adding in a subsequent minute that although Britain should not 'fritter away' its forces in defence of Cyprus, 'if it should be found possible to spare two or three Fighter Squadrons, these should be sent'.[7]

Unknown to Battershill, the Australian and Indian battalions in the region, which he might have reasonably expected to see deployed in Cyprus, were already marching towards Damascus and Beirut. It fell to the officer commanding troops on the island, Brigadier Rodwell, to inform the governor of the Defence Committee's decision that Cyprus would not be relieved and that a commando battalion garrisoned on the island was about to be withdrawn.[8] Battershill appears not to have been aware of the imminent Syrian action. After he had so recently hosted the British foreign secretary on his mission to coax the government of Greece to accept British military assistance, he must have wondered why more could not be done for the defence of a crown colony.

The governor immediately lodged a forceful protest with the Defence Committee. He argued that its strategy was 'fraught with consequences of such gravity for 380,000 persons in this colony' that he had a duty to spell out all its implications. The token defence envisaged would inevitably involve 'destruction of main towns and villages with much loss of life'. If the short delay this might cause to the German advance was vital to Britain's war effort then, he acknowledged, 'sacrifices must be accepted'. But if not, the proposals were merely 'a half measure' which would gain nothing and cause 'untold suffering to civilian Cypriots'. Instead, Battershill urged that the colony should be 'turned into an island fortress', one that would 'give us at least a sporting chance of defeating a determined attack' and would raise morale amongst Cypriots 'to steel them to the coming suffering'.

The governor, a man who was 'not easily rattled', was held in high regard both at the Colonial and the War Office. He had distinguished himself in action during the First World War and was seen as 'one of our best colonial governors, keen, sensible and reliable'. His concerns were taken seriously and were discussed again at length by the Defence Committee on the night of 5 June 1941.

But a 'half measure', as Battershill put it, was exactly what the Defence Committee, hedging its bets on the outcome of operations in Syria, needed. Even a short and ultimately hopeless resistance of the island might disrupt German deployments sufficiently to create valuable time 'for the completion of operations in Syria or elsewhere'. If this were so, the committee concluded, then 'the wholesale slaughter and destruction which the enemy would bring about in attacking the colony' could be justified on military grounds. However, it added that the 'useless destruction and slaughter of the civilian population' was to be avoided. Responsibility for determining at precisely what point either destruction or slaughter became useless and when British forces should abandon the island fell to General Wavell. The secretary of state represented the case rather more diplomatically to Battershill, reiterating that although the defence of the colony depended on developments in Syria, 'the instructions to prepare plans for guerilla warfare if Cyprus is attacked must hold'. He sweetened the pill by passing on Churchill's 'warm expression of his confidence in you in what he realises is a very difficult situation'.[9]

Battershill had effectively been abandoned. He began to arrange for the urgent evacuation of British civilians and other vulnerable groups. The entire evacuation programme was expected to take 10 days and would involve three round trips to Haifa. The first group to be sent to safety were Poles, followed by Jewish refugees from Eastern Europe, who were transported to the East African territories of Tanganika and Nyasaland, and lastly, the British dependants of government officials.

The 500-strong community of 'politically compromised Poles' consisted of members of the Polish intelligentsia, who had fled to Cyprus in the autumn of 1940. The refugees had been housed in the Helvetia Hotel in Platres, where they produced their own newspaper and formed a choir which sang regularly at Red Cross benefit concerts where 'Chopin's Polonaise and rousing national songs were thundered forth'. In the event of a German invasion it was considered they 'would have been the first for the chop',[10] so, for 'humanitarian and security reasons', Battershill insisted they must leave first. The Poles left Famagusta for Egypt, 'singing defiantly as the steamer pulled away'.[11]

For the Poles, as well as the wives and children of British government officials, evacuation was compulsory 'with no exceptions to be made'. For the 400 'foreign Jews' residing on the island, along with non-government Britons and the 20 Cypriots whose 'support for the government and the war effort'[12] placed them in particular danger, it was optional. Over the preceding decade a colony of around 200 Jews had settled in the Famagusta region, where they established citrus farms in conjunction with the Cyprus Palestine Plantation Company Limited. But by 1941 the majority of Jews in Cyprus were refugees from Europe. Most, like the Viennese professor who 'won a precarious existence by sausage-making',[13] attempted to eke out a living as best they could. A few had found employment as nannies and domestic servants in the households of colonists or forces' personnel.[14] The refugees were each permitted to take only one small case. Elsie Slonim, whose husband David owned the Fassouri citrus plantation near Limassol, remembered a night-time voyage, on board a converted cattle transporter, the SS Hannah. All lights on the ship were extinguished as the Hannah sailed slowly towards Haifa, occasionally turning abruptly to avoid mines. On either side of Elsie women sat weeping silently.

As other small groups of exiles made their way towards Famagusta they passed large numbers of Cypriot women and children on the roads, all following the governor's orders to leave the towns and return to their villages. The Times correspondent noted that 'buses crowded with a strange medley of the goods and chattels of people moving their households to the country are a familiar sight in the streets of the main towns'[15]; 5,000 were evacuated from Nicosia alone, at an estimated cost of £15,000.[16]

Finally, it was the turn of the dependants of British officials, around 60 families who travelled, via Port Said, to South Africa. Battershill was adamant, despite appeals by the Red Cross on behalf of two wives who ran auxiliary hospitals, that *all* British government dependants must leave. In their case the luggage restrictions imposed on the Jewish evacuees did not apply. Jane Wynne-James, who left with her mother, her nanny and three sisters, remembered 20 pieces of luggage accompanying them on their voyage. Non-government personnel, such as the American managers of the Cyprus Mines Corporation and their families, joined them, abandoning, as they did so, 'expensive cars and other valuable property'.[17] Private individuals who wished to leave but were unable to 'maintain themselves anywhere other than Cyprus' were granted financial assistance if they signed a pledge to repay any loans in full after the war was over.

Geoff Chapman, the young forestry officer, and his wife Esther, who had both arrived on the island in 1930, spent their last day together swimming at Kyrenia. That evening they joined other couples, including the governor and his wife, for a 'farewell dance given by moonlight in defiance of enemy raiders'. *The Times* correspondent noted that women were 'wearing evening frocks for perhaps the last time for some weeks', and that husbands were 'claiming from their departing wives a final waltz'. Chapman remembered it as 'a rather sad evening and we didn't dance'.

The next day the Chapmans and their small son Mark managed another swim at Famagusta before driving to the port in time for the evening departure of the *S.S. Fouadiah*. *The Times* correspondent observed that 'although the alert sounded during the embarkation, no panic disturbed the orderly arrangements, and the people remained calm'.[18] But *The Times* omitted to report that as the families lined up along the quayside an RAF plane crashed into the harbour, '20 yards away from the ship'. Chapman recalled the horrified reaction of bystanders when 'a man hooked up the sandy haired scalp of the pilot which had been shaved off his head'. After the goodbyes were over and the boat had left, Chapman drove to 'a point on the road, a few miles north of Famagusta. I sat in the car and watched the boat sail over the horizon and disappear'.[19]

On 13 June 1941 Battershill telegrammed the Colonial Office that the final consignment of evacuees, 164 British women and children, had left that day at 18.00 local time. He wrote to his mother that his family had been 'amongst the last to go and are now safely in Egypt. They will have to remain in Cairo until they can get a passage to South Africa'.[20] *The Times* observed that 'the island is now stripped for war and prepared for all eventualities'.

Some of the men left behind in Nicosia, wandering around houses that now seemed too big for them, attempted to raise their spirits with a trip to the capital's open-air cinema. The film being screened that week was a patriotic documentary about the blitz, *London Can Take It*. When the king and queen appeared on screen the audience broke into spontaneous applause.

Wartime economic distortions had forced the cost of living up dramatically and for lower-ranking civil servants at the bottom of the salary scale the cost of supporting two (or for those with children in England, three) homes now became 'frankly impossible'. Battershill proposed the introduction of a separation allowance of £7.10s a month to officers whose wives and children had been compulsorily evacuated. The Colonial Office agreed, largely out of concern that it would be 'extremely undesirable that these relatives of British officials in Cyprus should be compelled to live in Africa at a level which is inconsistent with the prestige of white people in the eyes of the native population'.[21]

In Cyprus, husbands economised by sharing accommodation with colleagues. Chapman formed a 'mess' with two other men from the Secretariat; all three brought their individual servants with them. For Chapman, this 'very pleasant arrangement', in which the men had their own bedrooms and shared a common living room, was reminiscent of time spent at university. Between them the mess mates usually consumed 'a good half bottle' of Cyprus brandy each night[22] and 'used to entertain a lot and had some very merry parties'.[22] Others found that the similarities between their new bachelor existence and university or boarding school became even more apparent with the sudden appearance of old school friends on the island. One junior official was delighted to come across a man 'who was Pooh-Bah to my chorus at Harrow',[23] while Charles Potts, the army chaplain, discovered two men from his house at Fettes, 'one was two years senior to me, the other was one of my fags'.[24] Chapman's account of this period is certainly full of undergraduate humour. Christmas presents despatched to his long-suffering wife, Esther, were wrapped in sheets of paper on which he had written a long letter in secret ink. Esther soon discovered that 'the secret ink turned out to be urine', enabling Chapman to explain with boy scout relish that 'all you have to do with urine letters is dip them in 2½% solution of potassium permanganate and the writing suddenly appears as dark brown characters'.[25]

Chapman brought his dog Demon, a descendent of one of the original pointers imported by the chief vet, Robbie Roe, into the mess. Dogs, in particular, were a source of great comfort to men far from home without their families. Some soldiers arriving at Famagusta from East Africa were distressed to find that quarantine regulations in the colony forced them to leave dogs which had been with them on the front line at the port. Chaplain Potts was given several dogs during his time in Cyprus, including a Jack Russell which he named Little Audrey. The governor, who felt the absence of his noisy, rumbustious daughters particularly keenly, was seldom seen in public without his black spaniel Bruce in tow. Bruce attended meetings of the Executive Council and accompanied his master on swimming expeditions and to the cinema, where, on one occasion, he 'disgraced himself at the start by giving a couple of loud barks, but after that relapsed to silence'.[26]

Other colonial administrators joined army officers in seeking consolation at the popular Chanteclair Cabaret, just outside the city walls[27] where the Hungarian dancers who provided the 'floor show' could be purchased as dance partners at a cost of four shillings a dance. Soldiers of lower ranks frequented the Empire further down the road. The 40 or so Hungarian cabaret dancers who provided this service, both at the Chanteclair and at other night spots across the island, were interned after Hungary entered the war on the side of the Axis powers. Several cabarets nearly went out of business as a result, but the dancers' internment also proved a serious setback for many of the more affluent members of the administration who had, in the absence of their wives, begun affairs with the women. Their dilemma became 'one of the big jokes'[28] at the English Club, and it was widely reported that several senior officials would despatch their chauffeurs to the internment camp each evening to collect their girlfriends, returning them again with the same panache the next morning. After some weeks of this inconvenience, 'the resourcefulness and adaptability of British administration ... manifested itself, and without any fuss or bother all cabaret girls were freed from internment, to the great relief of several British officials, [and] to the delight of great numbers of the British Forces'.[29]

Cyprus was now a front-line posting. Discussions began on the feasibility of moving the seat of government to the monastery of Ayia Varvara near Larnaca[30] and the officer commanding troops, Brigadier Rodwell, stepped up preparations for attack by developing Troodos Keep. Here, stragglers from the anticipated 'Battle of Cyprus' would be re-equipped and trained to carry out acts of sabotage and guerilla warfare. The success of the plan depended on the establishment of a chain of arms and supply dumps from the foothills upwards to the area around Mount Troodos itself, which could be utilised during the withdrawal. From the mountains it was hoped that the British 'would be in a position to carry out quite a stern guerilla warfare'.[31] Cypriots, however, were to be excluded from plans for sabotage work owing to their 'inherent apathy and untrustworthiness'.[32] Battershill, still concerned that the Breslau broadcasts may have undermined support for British rule on the island, was conscious of the damage Nazi propaganda had done to French morale in 1940. One senior judge on the island, George Griffith Williams, claimed that several Greek Cypriots in the villages surrounding Troodos had already begun learning German in anticipation of a Nazi conquest, while some even feared that 'the Cypriots may become actively hostile when the enemy gains control of the island'.[33]

Some members of the CVF, such as Chapman, maintained that a further retreat into the more remote Paphos hills following a German invasion would buy survivors from the 'Battle of Cyprus' more time and facilitate the establishment of an escape route, via small boats, from Paphos Harbour. A coordinated military relief operation had been ruled out because 'the naval forces had taken such a battering during the evacuation from Crete',[34] so Chapman began to investigate the possibilities of an improvised Dunkirk-style departure. A Turkish Cypriot from whom he had previously hired boats agreed to provide him with one of his best vessels, 'fully fuelled and ready for immediate sailing with provisions for a number of officers and men'. Unusually for provincial Turkish Cypriot society, Chapman was introduced to the man's veiled female relatives, who were instructed to shield him from the enemy in the event of a Nazi occupation.

Unknown to Chapman, reinforcements were at last being despatched to the island in the form of three battalions of the Durham Light Infantry. This was a turning point in the defence of Cyprus, one where, as always, the interests of the colony were subordinated to other regional strategic considerations.

The brief campaign in Syria – in the course of which the defence of Cyprus had been abandoned – had been a success. The Vichy French forces had been defeated and the Allies had gained control of the strategically important Syrian airfields. General Claude Auchinleck, who replaced Wavell as commander in chief in the Middle East on 5 July 1941, was keen to consolidate the recent gains. He feared that a 'friendship' treaty signed between Turkey and Germany in Ankara in June 1941 might enable German forces to establish bases in Turkey and from there to advance on Syria. In a reversal of previous military assessments of the colony's value, Auchinleck now considered that 'consolidating the newly won position in Syria necessitated making Cyprus secure against attack. On 12 July, as soon as hostilities in Syria ceased, he accordingly decided to send a complete Division of troops to the island'.[35]

The troops were shipped to Famagusta from Alexandria in July and August 1941 at break-neck speed. Following the bruising experience of the naval evacuation from Crete, the commander of the Mediterranean Fleet, Admiral Andrew Cunningham, was anxious to minimise the risk of further losses. As a result *HMS Latona*, a state-of-the-art mine-layer, and a light cruiser, *HMS Leander*, steamed across the Mediterranean under cover of darkness in record time, prompting one observer to comment that 'the wash was the most incredible sight'.[36] Below deck troops were told about their destination only a few minutes before disembarking; few had heard of Famagusta.

Unloading was carried out with equal haste. Long wooden chutes were levered over the side of the ship and the cargo thrown down the slides onto the quayside. 'Our stores were just chucked off', one soldier recalled, 'including our Brens, still in their boxes, thank God.'[37] Much kit and equipment ended up in the sea and the men speculated that local divers 'went down and retrieved it for financial reward – it was even suggested that the navy and the divers were in cahoots'.[38] Once disembarkation was complete the ships 'shot back again to Alexandria, they didn't waste any time at all'.[39] They had good reason not to hang around. On 7 August, as Lance Bombadier Edward Stirling and his artillery company were disembarking, Italian raiders struck the harbour, sinking the ship alongside theirs, the *Admiral Lacaze*, and blowing up the petrol dump.[40]

Loaded onto military transports, the men were driven through the orange groves close to Famagusta. Many had never seen citrus trees before and memories of 'ripe oranges ready for picking' – of piles of citrus fruit sold at the roadside for two pence a dozen, 'much less than they were in England' – remained vivid decades later. Fruit that was scarce or exotic at home, even in peacetime, was cheaply available. As a result, the men found that their ubiquitous desert sores, small wounds that had failed to heal due to aggravation by sand and insufficient vitamin C, rapidly disappeared.

Troops bound for the aerodromes at Nicosia or Lakatamia were transported by the single-gauge Cyprus railway. Private John Rogers of the 9th Battalion Durham Light Infantry carried with him a lucky haul of tinned peaches, a luxury somehow acquired during the journey. As the train rocked slowly through groves of fresh fruit, Rogers and the rest of the company managed to distribute the tins between the carriages by hooking them into their lanyards: 'We swung the lanyard to the next carriage and they took the fruit out and it came back and we sent the fruit along to the lads that were in different carriages that way.'[41]

Anxiety increased on the island throughout the spring and early summer of 1941. The extent of the damage inflicted on German forces during the battle for Crete was still unknown and Hitler appeared to be advancing unstoppably towards the oil fields of Iran and Iraq. Invasion was expected daily. The defence of Nicosia aerodrome and the prevention of enemy landing became vital.

On arrival, the men of the Durhams were issued with picks and shovels and urgently deployed in digging out defensive trenches around the aerodrome. But the rocky ground made progress frustratingly slow and sappers often had to be called in to blast a route forward. The first structures were basic, as there was no time even to build interlinking communication trenches. As one soldier recalled, 'we worked on the defences, ate and slept'.[42] To avoid alerting enemy reconnaissance flights most of the initial work was done at night, with men withdrawn at first light and the trenches covered in camouflage nets. After breakfast the troops slept until lunch, before resuming work again in the evening. The digging continued uninterrupted in an atmosphere of growing tension, relieved on one memorable occasion by the arrival of a comfort parcel from Sunderland Corporation, containing Oxo cubes, razor blades, socks, and a picture of a tram car. The men slept in the completed trenches, throwing their bivouacs over the top. 'That was our billet for the time that we were there ... spread the dirt over the top for camouflage and that was it.'[43]

Troops remained on full alert, with companies alternately extending the defences, keeping fit by five-mile route marches in full kit ('pretty hellish because of the heat') or with shooting and grenade practice. One company was kept in reserve, to be deployed in the event of possible incursions in the Paphos region, the point of the island geographically closest to German-occupied Crete.

Cypriots, too, were digging; 20,000 people were now being employed 'on attractive wages',[44] on defensive works throughout the island. As a result, applications for enlistment in the Cyprus Regiment plummeted, a reflection of the economic pressures that had previously compelled men to sign up. The most ambitious of these defensive works was the construction of tens of thousands of anti-aircraft mounds, stretching for miles across the Messaoria Plain. Five-foot high, built of earth around a stone core, the 'hummocks' were intended to discourage enemy aircraft from landing. If that failed, it was hoped the obstacles would delay any attempt to construct runways on the plain by as much as three hours, the time taken to clear the mounds away. Work was carried out by unemployed workers of the Cyprus Mines Corporation and by village women, who transported the earth by donkey pannier and were paid per pyramid. Several soldiers, unfamiliar with the sight of women labourers, commented on the use of 'Cypriot girls', for the purposes of 'carting rocks'. Many of the 'Cypriot girls' were now receiving a steady income for the first time in their lives. Earnings from their defence works, combined with the regular wages received from husbands and fathers in the Cyprus Regiment, enabled many women to build their own houses. As the late George Lanitis remembered, 'many many houses were built during the war, it really helped the village people'.[45]

The building scheme, supervised by the PWD, cost around £65,000 'roughly the cost of two heavy bombers' – a price considered small 'in comparison with the advantage it brings'.[46] But the defensive value of the cones or koukos was disputed and subsequent officers ordered their partial demolition. As a result, Freya Stark, who visited the island in 1942, described a confused strategy in which 'some ground was fortified and some not, and paratroop invaders could shelter behind the cones after landing on the open ground behind them'.[47]

In the early hours of Saturday 22 June 1941, as many of the women who laboured over the defensive koukos were starting to prepare breakfast for their families, the BBC broadcast the news that German planes had bombed the

Geoff Chapman darning his socks on Mount Troodos, as he hears news of the German invasion of Russia on the radio. Cyprus is no longer in the frontline. June 1941.

[*Reproduced courtesy of the Chapman family.*]

Soviet cities of Minsk, Odessa and Sevastapol. Hitler's long planned 'Operation Barbarossa', the invasion of Russia, had begun and Cyprus was now out of immediate danger. In a radio broadcast made the same day, Churchill told the Empire that the news 'was no surprise to me'. But it did come as a surprise to the inhabitants of Cyprus, where 'the sigh of relief that went out was almost audible throughout the whole island'.[48] Edward Sinclair, stationed with the

Royal Army Medical Corps at Prodromos, recalled feeling merely 'very surprised and mildly relieved';[49] but all British soldiers and civilians on the island
remembered precisely where they were when they heard the news. Chapman,
seated on a deckchair in the Troodos camp, darning his socks as he listened to
the radio, realised that this meant 'the end of the German "underbelly attack
strategy"... and that we should have a breathing space and there would be no
danger of [them] coming on to us'.[50] For the moment at least, the fascist threat
had receded and the island was safe.

But this did not mean that Cyprus was entirely out of the firing line. The
Italian air force stepped up its hitherto lackadaisical bombing raids over the
island, launching a series of coordinated 'nuisance' attacks on Paphos, Morphou,
Nicosia Airfield, Wolseley Barracks and Famagusta Port, killing at least nine
civilians.

The raids made it difficult to obtain Cypriot labour to work in either Nicosia
Airfield or Famagusta Port, where, the governor noted, 'danger of air attack
is used as a lever to secure higher wages'. There had been several cases of
labour unrest during the early part of the war. In February 1940 electricians
and mechanics employed in the workshops of the PWD had gone on strike
demanding higher wages and shorter hours. The following April, 'serious disturbances' in Nicosia led to a number of arrests, and the confinement of 'agita-
tors' to certain villages, which they were not allowed to leave.[51]

Following Battershill's introduction of more liberal labour laws in 1939, the
number of trade unions in the colony had increased from 14 to 30. But terms of
employment remained poor, with most men working between 52 and 60 hours a
week,[52] and between 1939 and 1945 there were around 30 labour disputes every
year involving the newly formed trade unions.[53]

An instinctive supporter of the underdog, Battershill was not, in principle,
unsympathetic to workers' demands. By the government's own estimates the
cost of living for manual labourers had increased by as much as 30 per cent since
the outbreak of war. But industrial relations at Famagusta Port in particular
appear to have been managed badly, and communication between the men and
the superintendent of the railways was poor. A previous strike by gangers and
railway labourers in June had been successfully resolved after the government
agreed to increase the wages of unskilled labourers from 31 to 54 *piastres* a day.
Then, on 1 July 1941, the 'artisans and men of the Locomotive Department'[54]
submitted demands for a 50 per cent wage increase, downing tools immediately
and bringing the railway to a standstill.

This was a potentially disastrous situation. Heavy armaments and supplies
for the island's defence were now arriving at the port daily and accumulating
on the quayside, just as Famagusta was being subjected to increasing bom-
bardment by the Italian air force. It was 'only great good fortune', Battershill

pointed out, that had 'preserved the stores already there'. On 2 July, under increasing pressure from the general officer commanding, who demanded that Royal Engineers be despatched immediately from Alexandria to replace the striking men, Battershill declared the railway to be a service of public utility, essential for the prosecution of the war. The government would consider the men's demands if they returned to work, but anyone failing to do so immediately would face prosecution and prison. Over the following week Italian planes bombed a ship carrying Greek refugees off the coast of Cape Greco and blew up the fuel stores at Nicosia aerodrome, but miraculously the supplies that sat undispersed in the freight sheds at Famagusta remained untouched. It was only after three of the strike leaders were given prison sentences of a year and a fine of £20 was imposed on each of the six other activists that the striking men returned to work on 11 July. In the end, a settlement was reached and the wages of skilled artisans increased from 48 to 84 *piastres* a day.

In the aftermath of the labour crisis the army assumed responsibility for stevedoring. Chapman, promoted to captain within the CVF, was seconded to coordinate working parties of Palestinian Pioneers and a company of the Cyprus Regiment. As the only Greek-speaking officer he was called on to resolve misunderstandings between Cypriot troops and NCOs who were often unable to make themselves understood by their men.

Work was regularly interrupted by air-raid sirens, when 'the men came tearing out of the ships' holds, down the gangways, and raced across the quay to shelters'. The colonel in overall charge of the operation, an officer of the Sherwood Foresters, ordered that during air raids officers were not to join their men in the shelters but should parade up and down the quay to set an example and maintain morale. 'Whose morale we could never quite make out', Chapman wrote later, 'because there was nobody else except us officers walking up and down the quay.'[55]

On 12 July 1941, in the most intense raid of the war, seven Italian planes dropped a total of 30 bombs. But by now the railway was operational again, supplies were being dispersed, and the bombs did relatively little damage. Six days later the governor was able to telegram the Colonial Office triumphantly, 'one enemy aircraft shot down into sea by our fighters. The first confirmed destruction of enemy aircraft in raids on Cyprus.'[56] Privately he wrote to his wife Joan in South Africa, 'it was great bagging one of them wasn't it?'[57]

But Battershill's brief governorship was already virtually over. He had been asked to relinquish his appointment and return to the Colonial Office in London to succeed Sir Alan Burns, as assistant under-secretary of state for the colonies. The governor, who spoke fluent Greek and probably loved Cyprus and its people more than any of its other British rulers, was devastated. He reluctantly consented, believing that 'in war time one should go where the authorities want one to go'. On 27 August the governor wrote to his mother: 'Just a line to let you know that I left Cyprus on the 25th and almost broke my heart.'[58]

With Battershill's departure Cyprus lost a capable governor, a man of the utmost moral rectitude and an instinctive liberalism. Despite being in office for just two years his legacy was considerable, and it is tempting to speculate on what Battershill might have achieved had his work not been so abruptly terminated. He passed legislation allowing for the election of municipal councils, believing that the organisation of successful local elections would strengthen the argument for wholesale constitutional reform and pave the way for elections to a central legislature. His plans were frustrated when Germany's invasion of Crete forced their postponement until 1943, but he had continued working on a report on the introduction of extensive constitutional change up until his departure from Cyprus. During his brief time in office Battershill also introduced comprehensive trade union legislation, along with a worker's compensation law, and supervised the drafting of new laws sanctioning the formation of political parties.

Around the same time as Battershill – a man of fierce, compulsive honesty, almost pathologically incapable of deceit – prepared to leave Cyprus, an officer of 'A' Force, an organisation dedicated to subterfuge, cunning and pretence arrived. 'A' Force operated out of Cairo, under the direction of Brigadier Dudley Clarke, 'the *éminence grise* of WW2 strategic deception'.[59] Clarke's plan to save Cyprus involved the creation of a network of bogus airfields across the island. It was hoped that the 'special' airfields would both exaggerate the state of the island's defences for the benefit of enemy reconnaissance planes and divert hostile fire away from genuine aerodromes. Clarke also created an entirely artificial order of battle, involving fictional divisions and codenamed 'Cascade'. The Cascade Battle Plan was planted on a double agent, Lena Moray, on 19 July 1941, in the hope that it would fall into enemy hands.[60] But agent Moray's efforts may have been unnecessary, the previous week the German military attaché in Ankara had revealed that he believed Cyprus to be far more heavily defended than Crete.

Work on Clarke's strategy began the following autumn. Nicosia Airfield, the only airbase in constant use, was reinforced with 'special personnel' in the form of mannequins that were positioned around the runway, supplemented by plaster heads, balanced on top of sandbags above shallow trenches. The 'specials' were deployed on a rota basis, being placed in position on Mondays and returned to stores again on Thursdays, when the direction of the dummy guns was also changed. Elsewhere fresh runways were cleared and marked out with strips of calico, ready to be equipped with 40 specially constructed mock-ups of Hurricanes and Bofors anti-aircraft guns imported from the army camouflage centre in Helwan in Egypt.

Artificial air bases were constructed at Dhekalia and Yerrolakas to deceive the enemy in daytime. In order to keep the sites 'fresh' small groups of eight men at a time were seconded to each dummy air base to maintain the deliberately unconvincing camouflage and make regular adjustments to the position of dummy equipment. The duties of these lonely maintenance parties included marching daily around the living quarters to keep paths well trodden, sleeping in a different camp hut every night and driving their ration truck back and forth over the parade ground and the football pitch to stop weeds from growing.

Artificial keeps were dug at Lysi, Trikkomo, Ayios Seryios, Ayia Marina and Morphou. The sleepy town of Polis on the north western coast, occupied by a single platoon, became the site of particularly elaborate works, equipped with 34 dummy anti-aircraft guns.[61] Meanwhile, battalion commanders drove along the region's dusty unmade roads boldly flying the flags of brigade commanders on their cars. Brigade commanders in turn would have deceived any villagers who happened to have a working knowledge of the British military hierarchy by flying the flags of larger divisional commands on their vehicles. Booby-trapped dummy pill boxes were constructed, demolition plans drafted and misleading German road signs distributed, in the hope that paratroopers could be led 'to positions where they could be wiped out'.[62]

Actual defence positions surrounding the airfield at Paphos, a strategically important installation near the Tombs of the Kings with 'valuable facilities for long range recce',[63] were cunningly concealed as agricultural workings. Pill boxes were made to resemble well tops by erecting water wheels on top of them and it was proposed that during harvest time Bren gun posts could be concealed within 'long sheaves of flax'.

More ambitious schemes included draining Larnaca Salt Lake, which, with the aid of 'dummy horse tracks etc.', could be made to appear, to an approaching enemy aircraft, dry enough to land on. But the line separating audacious deception from downright nuttiness was occasionally crossed. In the event of enemy landings it was proposed to confuse German or Italian patrols by broadcasting gramophone recordings of the CVF on the march from mobile loudspeakers mounted on the backs of trucks.

It is doubtful whether any of these measures influenced Axis strategy at this point in the war, but an Italian map of Cyprus captured around this time certainly suggests that the enemy had a confused impression of the island's defences. It estimated the number of troops on the island as being between 30 and 35 thousand, when the actual force was closer to 19,000, and recorded the existence of 17 aerodromes (including one, improbably located, on the rocky summit of the Kyrenia mountain range) when in reality there were just 10.

As the threat of imminent invasion disappeared, troops were able to appreciate the benefits of their posting. For those stationed at coastal aerodromes, where they often camped on the shore or in olive and eucalyptus groves, this was an idyllic period of tranquillity. Peter de Martin stationed at Limassol remembers 'we were able to bathe, the nightclubs and restaurants were working – it was a super life for a young officer and for the men. They loved it.'[64] The stifling army-issue bell tents, which had been so unhealthy for Wolseley's troops in 1878, had been superseded by Indian-pattern ridge tents, 'like small marquees with a fly sheet to keep an air vent so there was air going all round'.[65] Men used their army-issue Flit guns, provided to combat infestations of desert flies in North Africa, to zap the relatively milder Cyprus mosquitoes.

The troops soon discovered that wine and spirits were comparatively cheap. Both sold at a shilling a bottle, at a time when a brandy and soda in a London pub cost six pence. Predictably, for the first week after a new regiment's arrival 'the effect was disastrous. The guard room was absolutely jammed full of drunks every night when they came back.'[66]

Cafés in Larnaca and Nicosia began offering English staples such as egg and chips. Despite being presented with 'Cypriot food to try and tempt us',[67] the men generally resisted local dishes. Sergeant George Self was appalled when, during a stay at Nicosia Hospital, he was presented with a breakfast of olive, cheese 'and this dark bread that they eat'.[68]

By the end of 1941 21,000 allied soldiers were stationed in the colony. At least 7,000 of these were from India. Mary Taylor, who lived with her parents and sisters in a house overlooking Wolseley Barracks in Nicosia, remembers being impressed by the Sikh troops on parade in the moat, 'looking so handsome in their turbans'. Her sister Jane, who was eight when war broke out, used to play gramophone records loudly at her bedroom window for the benefit of the troops below and was rewarded by being thrown bars of chocolate. This was a time when there was also an unprecedented level of interaction between soldiers of empire and Cypriots; inevitably, the nature of these informal encounters varied enormously. For some soldiers, their main contact with Cypriots came through their dealings with the capable Mrs Ioannides who ran the Cyprus Arts and Crafts Shop in Onasagorou Street and provided discrete assistance in choosing affordable presents for wives and girlfriends. But several men remembered individual acts of kindness, friendships formed with particular families, invitations to meals in Cypriot homes and, more rarely, to village weddings. Such favours could, on occasion, be returned but still required those involved to negotiate a path through the complex nuances of class and race, often with no shared language. Edward Stirling, who following drunken nights out was regularly smuggled back into camp by a Cypriot guide, repaid the man by securing him a job as 'a native foreman'. This did not prevent Stirling from ending his deployment in Cyprus with a broken cheekbone after a fight 'with a gang of natives' who had been 'looking for trouble with the British soldiers'. Scraps between soldiers and young Cypriot men, 'who would knife you as soon as look at you',[69] were a regular occurrence in the clubs and bars of Nicosia, Limassol and Larnaca and fatalities were not uncommon. Men setting off for an evening out in the capital were instructed to take their rifles with them, along with 'five rounds in your magazine'.[70] Eric Hooper remembered receiving an order instructing his men to 'refrain from referring to the locals as "effing Cypriots" '.[71]

Apart from cheap spirits, the main attraction for soldiers on a night out, whether in Nicosia or one of the coastal towns, was cheap sex. In the spring of 1942, it was estimated that 740 women were working as prostitutes across the island, the majority in Nicosia, Famagusta and Limassol. Every major town on the island – with the notable exception of Kyrenia – had its own venereal clinic. In addition 12 prophylactic centres were established, along with a 200-bed venereal disease ward at the general hospital in Nicosia.[72]

Prostitution had been the focus of periodic expressions of moral indignation and prurient outrage since British colonists first arrived in Cyprus.[73] Although the Colonial Office, for its part, argued that there was 'no evidence to suggest the problem is greater in Cyprus than in other comparable colonies',[74] Cyprus retained a reputation as 'a rather notorious island'.[75]

Prostitution in British colonies was more tightly controlled than in Britain itself. Not only were 'inferior' subject races believed to lack self-control and to be at the mercy of their incontinent sexual appetites, but also unregu-lated sexual encounters carried the danger of inter-racial liaisons and even of mixed-race offspring. Since the Empire's existence was predicated on the assumption of intrinsic racial superiority this prospect threatened the very bedrock of the imperial structure. An in-depth analysis of imperial anxieties about prostitution in Cyprus is beyond the scope of this book. But it is pos-sible that in Cyprus in particular, where Levantine women conformed more closely to conventional northern European criteria of physical attractiveness, the threat of inter-racial relationships was feared to be greater than in other parts of Empire. The recurrent concern that prostitution and disease were more widespread on the island than in other colonies may have been in part due to deep-rooted fears about miscegenation, the dilution of Anglo-Saxon racial purity and the specific threat that Cypriot women in particular were feared to pose.

'Public women' had long been required to register with the municipality. A copy of the 1916 registration booklet for Larnaca, containing numbered pho-tographs of the town's prostitutes, survives in the town museum. Dressed in traditional striped fabrics, their hair braided in neat plaits, the women stare blankly at the camera. By 1931, Governor Ronald Storrs had succeeded in making brothels illegal, but during wartime, when a robust heterosexuality was considered essential for the exercise of an appropriately manly aggression towards the enemy, exceptions were made, and even the Bishop of Jerusalem, conceded that a case could be made for 'licensed and inspected houses'.[76]

Once again the colonists' perceptions of their Cypriot subjects were flawed and contradictory. At one level the island's geographical proximity to Egypt and its visible cultural links with the Levant made it part of the exotic, sexually charged Orient that needed to be controlled and disciplined if it was not to sap imperial strength and masculinity. In 1946, military surgeon Robert Lees castigated both Cyprus and Egypt as being dominated by 'flies and whores',[77] while one visitor to the island in 1934 observed that 'the standard of sexual morality among the native population is pitifully low'.[78] The popular perception that prostitution was a natural activity that provoked neither moral censure nor social stigma amongst locals is illustrated by one soldier's curious observation that although certain villages on the island were 'riddled with VD' this was in turn cured by the raging temperature that accompanied malarial attacks, 'so one week they had VD – the next they had malaria and it cured itself. Sounds horrible to me, but they didn't seem to bother about it'.[79]

In an effort to limit the spread of the disease ('an ever present source of inefficiency in the garrison')[80] the army medical corps introduced a card system, as it did in other parts of empire. In 1941, the 300 'public women' who registered as prostitutes were issued with identity cards and subjected to daily inspections at government medical centres. Those found to be clear of disease had their cards stamped, while the cards of the infected were withheld while the owner received treatment. For their part, soldiers were instructed 'not to consort with women who are not in possession of properly stamped cards'[81] and were required, before visiting a brothel, to attend one of the prophylactic centres, where they were supplied with condoms and ointment. After intercourse they were expected to return to the clinic and submit to an eye-watering procedure, involving an antiseptic solution being pumped into the penis. This did not invariably prevent disease, but it did at least provide insurance against a military reprimand and was no doubt distressing enough to act as a deterrent in itself. There must have been many like George Iceton who concluded that 'as far as I could see it wasn't worth it'.[82]

Chaplain Charles Potts attempted to reduce rates of disease by providing the men with more wholesome places of recreation. Known in his home town of Stoke on Trent as 'the fighting parson', because of his boxing skills, Potts was a resourceful man who later won the military cross in action with the 1st Battalion, the Buffs (Royal East Kent Regiment) in Libya. Potts spent 18 months in Cyprus and gave a detailed account of his work in daily letters to his fiancée, Pamela. Potts's duties as an army chaplain were varied and provide a valuable insight into social conditions on the island. His primary function involved taking communion services for the various regiments, for which purpose he travelled between camps by motorbike, carrying with him his communion set, ecclesiastical robes and up to 100 hymn books. Other duties included hospital visiting, often ministering to men injured in knife fights with locals, attempting to 'disentangle' an officer from a 'very serious affair that he has been having with a local girl', and arranging a series of Christmas parties for 150 of 'the poor children' of Nicosia. Light relief came in the form of occasional expeditions in a flying boat, such as the occasion when Potts and his RAF friends 'landed on the sea, and had a glorious bathe and then lay on top of the plane sun bathing'.

Potts aimed to establish a recreational club for the troops where they could play cards, have debates and listen to talks. To finance the project he established a magazine, *Tin Hat*, profits from which he hoped would cover the start-up costs. The magazine, marketed under the memorable slogan 'To Keep "A" Company out of the brothels', sold reasonably well, making an average profit of around £20 a month. By the beginning of October 1941, as Hitler's armies advanced on Moscow, Potts found he had sufficient funds to rent premises for his club. The building, 'a quaint old place with stone floors', was opposite Arab Ahmet mosque in an area of north Nicosia now inhabited mainly by Turkish and Kurdish migrants. Today the building is a dilapidated private house, the spotless lace curtains in the windows contrasting with the crumbling exterior and rubbish-filled garden. In 1941 the garden contained a large date palm, which Potts excitedly mistook for a coconut tree. The house was owned by a respectable member of the Turkish Cypriot bourgeoisie, Kiazim Bey, who occupied the house next door. Each morning (to the delight of Pott's batman) six female members of the household would 'walk down to the bottom of the garden ... very scantily clad and wash in a bowl by the pump and comb their long hair'. Potts, whose experience of the Middle East was no doubt based on the stories of the Arabian Nights, pondered whether they were 'all Kiazim Bey's *harem* or whether one or two of them are his daughters'.

The chaplain busied himself establishing a canteen selling beer, cakes, cigarettes and chocolate, he cadged books for a library from long-term British residents and set up a rest room that boasted papers, magazines and card tables made locally to his own design. He persuaded the Royal Engineers to make an altar for the chapel, which was subsequently consecrated by the Bishop of Jerusalem. By the end of the month the club, now 'very comfortably furnished ... with a lovely log fire burning in two rooms', was officially recognised by the military authorities. Potts persuaded officers and men to give weekly lectures. Early highlights included 'Head hunting savages', 'The Gestapo' and 'Tramps and the way they live'. Charles Potts left the island in the spring of 1942, hoping that he had 'left something worthwhile behind me'.[83]

Winter 1941 saw troops, long starved of entertainment, able to enjoy more than just Potts's lectures on head-hunting savages, when an ENSA revue,

'Hello Happiness',[84] made a short tour of the island. The revue's Cyprus tour prompted a sheaf of appreciative letters thanking the performers for bringing 'laughter and happiness to thousands of troops' and providing 'a close up view of such marvels of feminine beauty'.

As British and Commonwealth troops watched girls in short silky dresses and jaunty hats dancing 'The Donkey Serenade' and 'Waltz of My Heart', boat-loads of Greek refugees began arriving on the island's western coast. During the winter of 1941–42 Athens was starving. The occupying German army had requisitioned food for the Afrika Korps with the result that people were dying in the streets of the capital at the rate of 300 a day. In the port of Piraeus, bodies were collected in trucks and flung into huge trenches. Thousands attempted to escape to Cyprus, crossing the Mediterranean in small fishing boats. Most landed 'more dead than alive', at Morphou Bay, where observers recorded, they 'rush at food like animals and are half naked'.[85] Others came ashore at the mining harbour of Xeros on the north west coast. The pit head baths at the pyrites mine at Mavrovouni was converted into a reception and quarantine centre, where refugees remained for 10 days before being dispersed to camps across the island. While the refugees washed and received medical attention, their clothes were placed in oil drums and sterilised with steam created by one of the engines of the government railway.[86] During the fumigation process women were issued with pyjamas and men with shorts and under shirts sewn by two welfare workers employed by the Cyprus Mines Corporation.

As boat-loads of starving Greeks arrived in Cyprus, the island's sovereignty once again became an international bargaining chip amongst the more powerful countries of Europe. The quisling Greek prime minister, Georgios Tsolakoglu, toured his country proclaiming that the reward for Greek cooperation with the Nazi occupation would be the restoration of all Greek territories, including the Dodecanese and Cyprus. In the context of widespread famine, *The Times* recorded that 'his blandishments leave the Greek people unimpressed'.[87] Over the next three years it was estimated that as many as 15,000 Greek refugees passed through Cyprus en route to Palestine, just over half of them from the Dodecanese.

Battershill's successor had arrived quietly on the island in November 1941. Charles Woolley flew directly to Cyprus from Nigeria, where he had been chief secretary. Wartime luggage restrictions had forced him to abandon the ceremonial dress adopted by his predecessors and the new governor was sworn in at a modest ceremony at Government House wearing just a morning suit for the occasion. Like Battershill, Woolley was a capable, humane man, whose appointment supported the theory that the Colonial Office could select able men to fill the island's top job in times of crisis.

Woolley's arrival coincided with a brief period of relative calm. During this time he introduced compulsory ARP service for anyone between the ages

Despite snow on Mount Troodos, Governor Charles Woolley and unnamed guests picnic outside a sandbagged Government Cottage. The dog begging for scraps is Battershill's spaniel Bruce.

[*Reproduced courtesy of The Bodleian Library, University of Oxford.*]

of 18 and 45 living in the towns and rationalised the distribution of wheat and grain, appointing Robbie Roe, the chief vet, as cereal controller. For the next 12 months the fate of the colony would hang on the progress of the war being waged in North Africa, and during December 1941 there were signs that the tide might be about to turn in Britain's favour. Auchinleck had forced Rommel and his desert corps westwards out of Cyrenaica, successfully withstanding an eight-month siege on the Libyan port of Tobruk. Then, in 'the single most decisive act of the second world war',[88] the United States entered the conflict, ensuring that the vast quantities of American military hardware already being directed towards North Africa would soon be supplemented by troops.

The colony that Woolley took over in the late autumn of 1941 was far better defended than it had been the previous January, when Battershill first voiced his concerns to London. It now had 21,000 Commonwealth troops on its soil, including regiments from India and Australia, the largest garrison of any time in its history. *The Times* observed that 'nearly the whole Empire seems to be represented in the Cyprus garrison'.[89] Military headquarters and the island's signals base were at Athalassa outside Nicosia, where the Cyprus National Guard has several substantial training camps today. The various Indian divisions were billeted at Larnaca, the Household Cavalry at Kondea, and an armoured regiment, the Yorkshire Hussars, divided between Kokkinotrimithia, Nicosia Aerodrome and Wayne's Keep. The island's (genuine) airfields at Nicosia, Larnaca, Limassol and Paphos were all heavily fortified against aerial attack. Since Allied forces had gained control of Syria and Lebanon in the summer of 1941, these airfields could, if necessary, be augmented by RAF fighters stationed at Syrian airfields only 150 miles away. The defence of Nicosia Aerodrome became a strategic priority, a reflection of the increased regional importance of the base.[90] The previous plan for the Battle of Cyprus, which had envisaged a last desperate stand on the top of Mount Troodos, was abandoned. In its place a 'mobile and aggressive garrison'[91] was developed for deployment wherever the enemy landed. The east coast near Famagusta was considered particularly vulnerable to seaborne attacks if the Germans attempted to establish a bridgehead from which they might launch an assault on the airport.

But it was only a brief respite. By January 1942 the British position in North Africa had deteriorated. The gains of the previous month had been eroded, largely because of Churchill's insistence that experienced troops and valuable equipment should be withdrawn from the Middle East for the war against Japan. Seizing this opportunity, Rommell launched what soon became a steady, relentless advance across North Africa towards Egypt, a movement which continued throughout the spring and into the summer. It was feared that if the Germans conquered Cairo, assaults on Palestine, Syria and Cyprus would be next as Rommell drove on towards the vital oil supplies of the Persian Gulf. The diversion of resources to the Far East had necessitated a redistribution of the remaining forces in the region, and, for Cyprus, 'the acceptance of certain risks'. The island's garrison was reduced and the 10th Indian Infantry Brigade left Larnaca for deployment in Iraq, with the Household Cavalry and the Yorkshire Hussars taking its place. To speed embarkation at Famagusta, large quantities of heavy equipment were left on the island.

After the disastrous surrender of Tobruk on 21 June 1942, when 30,000 allied troops were captured, Britain's hold on North Africa appeared increasingly fragile. As Rommell pushed Auchinleck's men back to El Alemein, only 60 miles west of Alexandria, panic spread through Cairo. The Mediterranean fleet withdrew from Alexandria to the Red Sea and the chief of the Imperial General Staff, General Alan Brooke, began discussions with Churchill about retreating from Egypt and North Africa to establish a garrison further east around the Persian Gulf. A detailed programme for the military evacuation of Cyprus, codenamed 'Arcadia', had been drafted the previous April. It now looked as if it might be time to put it into practice. In order to conceal preparations from the public and prevent leaks, a curfew was to be enforced and the possession of carrier pigeons by civilians made illegal. The governor was asked for details of all vessels that could be used during the operation, along with details of volunteer civilians capable of handling them. The plan allowed for the evacuation of just 1,000 civilians.

In the event of evacuation the British fleet would provide cover for the departing convoys and maintain anti-submarine surveillance. But its ships could not be exposed to the risk of open sea by daylight, so the time available for loading and embarkation was reduced to just three hours each night. The process would be slowed still further by the narrow harbour mouth at Famagusta, which meant that only four ships could be accommodated at a time. Men would also have to be picked up from designated beaches at Larnaca, Limassol and Paphos. Units would be directed to arrive at rendezvous points close to the places of embarkation at night and remain there for a day, during which they would demolish their vehicles before embarking the following night. Steps were taken to 'thicken up' the anti-aircraft defences at Famagusta in anticipation of sustained attack from Italian and German aircraft during the evacuation. Additional protection could be provided initially by RAF fighter aircraft from the island's own air bases, but in the final stages this would have to be provided from bases in Syria. It was, therefore, considered 'desirable' that the decision to evacuate should be made while Syrian aerodromes were still in Allied hands. Yet even in favourable conditions, with good weather and no enemy interference, it was estimated that the programme would still take up to 38 days to complete.

The final stages of the evacuation scheme involved the infliction of an extensive programme of destruction on the island's infrastructure. The runways at Nicosia, Lakatamia, Larnaca, Limassol and Paphos, all primed for demolition, were mined at intervals of 250 yards and troops were given 'detailed instructions' on how and where to lay charges. Directives were issued for the destruction of the asbestos mine at Amiandos and other mines at Troodos and Limni. If all else failed, troops were instructed to remove all useful parts, 'destroy remaining machinery and do as much damage as possible'.[92] Finally, after the majority of troops had been safely evacuated from the island, demolition schemes were to be put into action to destroy the ports at Famagusta, Larnaca and Limassol and the harbours at Kyrenia and Xeros. Those men who could not be evacuated would, it was hoped, join up with a guerilla force of saboteurs operating from Troodos Keep.

In the first week of July 1942, as tension on the island rose once again, Chapman, the assistant conservator of forests and a fluent Greek speaker, was summoned to Cairo to the Middle East headquarters of Special Operations

Executive (SOE) to be briefed for a secret mission. Arriving in the glamorous capital in his utilitarian CVF uniform Chapman was hastily advised to change into smarter-looking 'civvies' and taken to the offices of Force 133, as the Cairo branch of SOE was known. There, he spent several days being sounded out with 'general chats about Cyprus, myself and my career',[93] before being recruited as a special agent with responsibility for post-occupation resistance in Cyprus. Chapman, now promoted to major, would be known henceforth as Force 133 Field Commander, Cyprus.

At Shepherd's Hotel, where he was relieved to find 'modern plumbing', Chapman met other intelligence officers with experience in Greece and Crete. Over sundowners they provided advice on 'how one set about organizing resistance, the snags, and so on'. He also met up with the wives of colleagues from Cyprus, evacuated the previous summer by Battershill and now employed in 'top secret jobs'.[94] The phrase 'special duties' was widely used, 'so if someone said that, one did not enquire further'. At the Mohamed Ali Club, Chapman was introduced to the exiled King of Greece; this was a sophisticated, glamorous environment, far removed from the madrigal singers and chess clubs of Nicosia, and further still from the remote forestry stations where Chapman spent much of his time. As Eirwen Harbottle, recalled, there was 'all this excitement in Cairo – there were mad people there. It was an extraordinary time, and so exciting'.[95]

Chapman was provided with basic training in how to cut telephone wires, blow up bridges and apply limpet mines known as 'toys'. On his return to Cyprus he was alarmed to discover that both his promotion and his posting to Force 133 had been erroneously published in the official *Government Gazette*. He attempted to cover his tracks by telling friends and colleagues that he was now involved in underground propaganda, but he took his boss at the Forestry Department, Ronald Waterer, into confidence, thereby beginning a remarkable story of wartime cooperation.

11

The Levant Fishing Patrol and the Angelic Scheme 1942–45

It is Sunday lunchtime at the Forestry Station of Stavros Tis Psokkas. Around a dozen families on an outing to the mountains have come to the café. They sit at wooden tables beneath the pine trees, plates of blackened *souvla* or pork kebab, lemon halves and raw onion rings before them. A skinny girl feeding pistachio nuts to an overweight Cyprus poodle is reprimanded by her grandmother. She runs off to play on the swings, which, like most Forestry Department accessories, are painted green. Some way off from the picnic area stands a substantial stone building with a wooden verandah around the first floor. This was once the residence of the assistant conservator of forests who enjoyed uninterrupted views far down the valley towards the sea. Today the house is closed up and there are no signs of life. A hollowed out log, whittled into the beginnings of a bowl, lies discarded outside the back door.

There are no sounds apart from a faint breeze in the pines and a lazy, buzzing fly. Yet this silent shuttered house played a crucial role in British plans for resisting German domination of the region and, thanks to the unique wartime partnership that existed between Geoff Chapman and Ronald Waterer, became the supply centre and putative headquarters of a clandestine network of guerilla fighters.

Waterer had also been recruited to Force 133, and after Chapman's return from Cairo and his appointment as field commander, Cyprus, the two men effectively shared Forestry Department duties with operational assignments for the force. They agreed that the nucleus of any post-occupation resistance should be based at the Stavros Forestry Station.

Ironically, the meticulous preparations made by Chapman and Waterer for a guerilla led resistance to the German occupation began at a time when the threat to Cyprus had passed. Any thoughts the German high command may have had of taking the island in their eastward sweep towards Persia had evaporated. The crisis of 1941 would never be repeated and, with the threat of imminent invasion lifted, the war, for the two forestry officers at least, began to resemble a *Boys Own Paper* adventure.

The efficacy of a post-occupation resistance force depended on the establishment of a series of secret supply dumps where food, clothing, ammunition and sabotage equipment could be stored. The dumps had to contain supplies for as many as 1,000 men for a period of up to six months. With Waterer's help the house at Stavros was 'filled to the ceiling with SOE stores' and placed under armed guard by the Forestry Company of the CVF. A smaller store was established at the disused monastery of Prophitas Elias near Lythrodontas, now occupied by George Unwin, the irascible former forestry chief who had retired there with his wife. Additional dumps were established in the northern mountain range at Epikho and inside a deep cave near the village of Aghirda, where after 'squeezing through a hole no bigger than a foxhole'[1] Chapman installed a rope ladder, hurricane lamps and paraffin. Between them the dumps contained 1,000 pairs of boots, 4,000 socks, 1,000 cardigans and 500 rifles.[2] Additional supplies of food, intended for use by officers operating in the northern range, were to be stored in Kyrenia in premises being used by the English School, which had been evacuated from Nicosia. In the event of invasion all stores were to be transported unobtrusively by donkey.

By the middle of October 1942 the first sabotage equipment arrived at Famagusta and was driven to the forestry station at Platania, for sorting and distribution. It was subsequently decided that it would be safer to store the largest consignments of ordinance near the village of Lefka in one of the underground storage chambers used by the Cyprus Mines Corporation for controlled explosions. Meanwhile at Stavros, an instructor sent from Cairo began training the first batch of 12 recruits in demolition techniques, use of small arms 'and general commando work'.

The work was done in secret, with virtually no co-operation from the garrison on the island. General Rumbold, who had taken over as officer commanding troops in Cyprus, refused to discuss any plans for post-occupation guerilla activity 'from the point of view of morale', so Force 133's planning had to be done 'without the knowledge of the military forces'.[3] Chapman established the agency's Nicosia bureau in a house in Parthenon Street in the Anglicised residential area of Ayios Andreas outside the city walls. The top floor was occupied by a wireless operator, who maintained direct radio communications with Cairo via one of SOE's specially designed 'suitcase radio sets' that could be

Two of Geoff Chapman's friends prepare to explore Aghirda Cave, subsequently used for concealing secret supplies in the event of invasion.

[*Reproduced courtesy of the Chapman family.*]

charged by bicycle generator. On the second floor Chapman installed a care-taker, with responsibility for maintaining security, and carried out surprise checks to ensure the building was never left unattended.

The formation of an effective resistance force also depended on the crea-tion of a network of 'rally officers',[4] who could guide escapees from the Battle of Cyprus to one of three keeps in the mountains. Chapman began recruiting expatriate CVF reservists who could act as collectors and guides, moving the escapees into the Kyrenia and Troodos Mountain ranges, passing them along via agents in the Paphos Forest area to resistance headquarters at Stavros. With this in mind, a series of potential collection points in the Kyrenia and Troodos Mountains were identified, places where survivors of the battle would be likely to congregate.

Each 'collector' was given control of a designated area and allocated two assistants. The men had to be fit and 'capable of long marches through the mountains'.[5] But more importantly they had to learn the geography of their area in detail, familiarising themselves with the routes along which men would be passed and memorising potential hiding places where 'stragglers' from the battle might be concealed, ranging from caves in the limestone mountains of the Kyrenia range to Roman mine workings in the south of the island. To do this they needed help and information from local villagers. So in an attempt to explain their sudden interest in particular aspects of regional topography, the 'collectors' claimed to have established a club, The Cyprus Speleological Society, dedicated to exploring the island's caves.

Chapman now had a series of bases and a network of field agents. It was time to test them out. For this he needed the co-operation of the Levant Fishing Patrol. The patrol consisted of a fleet of small Mediterranean fishing vessels or caiques which had been re-fitted with powerful Matilda tank engines for greater speed and with false bulkheads where arms and supplies could be concealed and unloaded rapidly without disturbing the legitimate cargo. It also included two bogus schooners, which were, in fact, RAF speedboats camouflaged by the British magician Jasper Maskelyne, another recruit to 'A' Force, so that they 'would pass as Greek fishing vessels, but doing 40 knots'.[6]

When, in 1940, the Greek dictator General Metaxas had declined British military assistance in defending Greece against Germany his refusal had prompted British intelligence to arrange for more discrete infiltration of the Greek resistance movement. The boats of the Levant Fishing Patrol began operating clandestinely from Alexandria, Haifa and Famagusta, transporting agents, radio equipment and ammunition to the Greek islands. Famagusta, where it was considered that the presence of visiting caiques excited 'less suspicion and curiosity than elsewhere',[7] became an important refuelling station. On arrival, vessels anchored at the harbour entrance to avoid becoming embroiled with customs or quarantine regulations and waited for a dinghy to bring out provisions and fuel supplies stored at a secret dump outside the port. The role played by British intelligence services in Greece during the Second World War was colourful and, latterly, highly contentious and is certainly beyond the scope of this book. But from 1943 onwards until well after the end of the Greek civil war, Cyprus developed into a key base for maritime intelligence operations in the region.

One of those who helped ensure that vessels left Famagusta with adequate supplies was Eirwen Llewellyn Jones, who was employed as a secretary in Nicosia, working in what she described as 'the secret department, for the filing of secret things'. Initially Eirwen was unimpressed by operational security. 'The cupboard in the secret department had no back to it,' she remembered, 'but never mind, we locked it very carefully from the front.' The 'secret department' was actually MI9, an organisation responsible for bringing escapees with 'knowledge that was valuable to intelligence'[8] out of enemy territory.

The activities of the Levant Patrol, some of whose members were also connected to 'a reasonably sound smuggling organization' on the island, had prompted Chapman and his minders at Force 133 in Cairo to conclude that the best way to test 'the post-occupational life line in pre-occupational times'[9] was by setting up their own smuggling agency. Contraband would be brought into the island at secret landing points by fishing patrol vessels, transported to the main 'keep' at Stavros and from there to agents in the field who would sell it on the black market.

Chapman recruited a ship's chandler and steamship agent in Famagusta as Force 133's chief maritime contact at the port. The agent, Fred Murat, was fluent in Greek, Turkish and English and was a familiar figure at harbours across the island. On Murat's advice an initial consignment of cigarettes, silk stockings, whisky, gin and cartridges was ordered from Cairo. A stern memo from Force 133 in Cairo, which appeared to have a poor opinion of Cypriot smuggling skills, insisted that it was 'essential to practice this scheme now in order to get the reluctant Cypriot interested and accustomed to it'. Chapman took the precaution of informing the chief secretary about the exercise, but it was understood that any agents who were caught would 'have to take what punishment is meted out' since 'in NO way can the "firm" be involved'.[10]

The initial test run resembled an elaborate boy scout camping trip. Supplies arrived at Famagusta in sealed petrol tins and were transported by Murat and his agents in motorised caiques to the island of Yeronisos off the Akamas Peninsusla. A dozen of Chapman's 'rally officers' swam out and stacked the contraband in a quarry cut into the seaward side of the island. With the trial run completed, the men 'lay on the beach ... lit fires, cooked what food we had brought with us, had some drinks and finally got to sleep'.[11] The next day the goods were unloaded to be distributed on the black market by Murat's agents. Other 'trials' followed and Chapman and Waterer, who always maintained particularly good relations with their Cypriot colleagues in the Forestry Department, appear to have relished joining forces with this network of Cypriot black marketeers 'testing' their supply lines and outwitting their own administration.[12]

Any incidental profits made by Force 133's smuggling operations were sent on to SOE in Cairo, which also occasionally benefited from other unconventional sources of funds. When a captured enemy caique, containing a consignment of fish intended for German garrisons in the Aegean, was towed into Famagusta Harbour, Colonel Patrick Lefoy, the extrovert head of 'A' Force in Cyprus, held a 'lively and successful auction'[13] from a soapbox in the harbour, raising over £200 for SOE finances.

As the irregulars of Force 133 in Cyprus organised hi-jinks, the Cairo bureau (which in the first of many name changes was now known as MO4) began preparations to accelerate resistance activities in the Italian-controlled

Dodecanese and the more distant islands of the Aegean. The capture of these territories – or at least their infiltration to 'carry out a piratical war on enemy communications in the Aegean'[14] – became an issue of almost obsessive concern to Churchill, who hoped it might induce Turkey to finally throw its lot in with the Allied cause. Any elements of 'piracy' would depend on a small number of irregulars operating clandestinely in the region.

As a result the role of the Levant Fishing Patrol expanded. As demand for deliveries of supplies and agents increased Murat, Chapman and Waterer took part in numerous caique operations, with the two forestry officers alternating 'three weeks on and three weeks off, forestry and SOE runs'.[15] Chapman was also responsible for distributing payment to Greek field agents, made in the form of gold sovereigns, since hyper-inflation had made the drachma virtually worthless. Significantly less valuable, but according to Chapman, more fun, were the consignments of sabotaged donkey droppings that were laid carefully in the anticipated path of German army transports. The droppings contained caltrops, devices consisting of three erect spikes designed to puncture tyres.

The increase in traffic between Famagusta and the Greek islands required the establishment of a safe house for agents embarking on and returning from missions. Chapman rented a secluded bungalow in a large orange grove outside Famagusta at a site called Freshwater Lake Plantation. A small number of Greek refugees had, on arrival in Cyprus, been recruited by Force 133 and trained as wireless operators for secret missions in the Dodecanese. One of these men was now installed at the Freshwater Plantation. He worked undercover as a waiter in Famagusta, supplied with a cover story by Force 133 which explained his 'non attendance with the Greek army' as being due to 'slight epilepsy'.[16]

In mid-February 1943, following directions from Cairo, Chapman drove overnight to Paphos, arriving at first light to meet two Greek agents returning from an operation in Rhodes and escorting them to the safe house at Famagusta. One of them, George Kazaris, was a sponge-boat captain from the island of Simi. Kazaris had been despatched, without papers, to the north coast of Rhodes, an island where he knew no one and where, as a stranger, he feared he would rapidly attract suspicion. He had refused to land and was returned to Cyprus. Kazaris convinced Chapman to help him make a second attempt to infiltrate Rhodes, by landing this time at a remote location on his native island of Simi where he knew both the people and the terrain. Kazaris believed that the abbot of the monastery of Panormitis would shelter him and co-operate in establishing a forward wireless base from where operations could be run on Rhodes and even the Greek mainland.

But Chapman first had to convince the abbot that the mission was genuine, by meeting him in person. The meeting, approved by Force 133 but ominously codenamed 'Erratic', was scheduled for the next moonless night. Chapman, anxious that his first active operation should be a success, prepared for the trip by learning his speech to the abbot by heart, checking his Greek pronunciation with Murat.

Chapman and Kazaris set off, accompanied by a wireless operator, a native of Rhodes who had recently completed Force 133 training in Cairo. Their boat, the *St Nicholas*, was crewed by Greek refugees and flew the Turkish flag, with the Turkish star and crescent painted on boards hung on the vessel's seaward side. At one point as many as 78 Turkish-flagged caiques operating out of Famagusta were stationed at various points along the southern Turkish coast, liaising with military intelligence's forward base on the Çeşme Peninsula.[17] Patrols by German sea planes meant they could sail only at night and were forced to put in at inlets on the south west coast of Turkey by day where the crew bribed inquisitive Turkish coastguards with four-gallon tins of Cypriot *ouzo*. The plan was for Kazaris and the wireless operator to land on the south coast of Simi and walk to the monastery of Panormitis. There they would make contact with the abbot and bring him back to meet Chapman at the landing spot five days later. Chapman and the crew of the vessel, meanwhile, would anchor at one of the Turkish inlets.

After the initial drop, the meeting between Chapman and the abbot was fixed for the night of 1 June. Dressed in his major's uniform to avoid being shot on sight if he was caught, and with hand grenades and a pistol in the pockets of his army trench coat 'in case we had been betrayed', Chapman was rowed across in the darkness to Simi. The journey took two hours. Once they heard the chug-chug of a motor vessel. Night sailing between the Italian-controlled islands had been banned and the men's suspicions were aroused. They lay on their oars and waited silently for the boat to pass them in the darkness. Finally the crew spotted the abbot and two of his monks 'all in Greek orthodox robes and tall hats' waiting in the shelter of bushes just above the beach. Chapman was 'dumbfounded' when the abbot embraced him passionately, planting three kisses on his cheeks. 'He had an enormous white beard and this very nearly suffocated me,' Chapman wrote later. 'However it was a good start.' With the monk's cloaks acting as a screen to shield their torches, the two men scrutinised 'a sort of mediaeval map[18]' which nevertheless contained valuable references to Simi's coastguard positions and police stations. The abbot had also brought samples of German travel documents, to be sent to Cairo for copying.

With the mission behind them, Chapman and the crew spent the journey back to Cyprus sunbathing on deck and watching dolphins. The sailors introduced Chapman to the technique of bomb-fishing, stunning shoals of fish with home-made bottle bombs. Five nights later the *St Nicholas* was back in Kyrenia with Chapman back in his office at the Forestry Department the next morning.

The resistance cell established by Chapman was subsequently expanded by Ronald Waterer. Simi became an important distribution and supply centre for cells in north west Rhodes and on the islands of Carpathos, Nisiros and Seskli, necessitating monthly trips from Cyprus with ammunition and sabotage equipment.

Following Mussolini's overthrow in July 1943, Churchill pressed for British forces in the Mediterranean to gain control of the Italian-held Dodecanese and induce the demoralised Italians to surrender, before the islands were overrun by German forces. In September 1943 irregulars of the Long Range Desert Group and the Special Boat Service operating in and around the islands from bases in Cyprus and Turkey established bridgeheads for Allied troops deployed from Cyprus. Simi in particular was the scene of fierce fighting, but the operation was a failure and by the beginning of October German troops had taken control of the islands. The Abbot of Parnormitis and a radio operator based at the monastery were both killed in 1944.

Intelligence work in Cyprus could take bizarre forms. In the summer of 1942, while Chapman was preparing for the post-occupation resistance, another officer recruited by Force 133 arrived on the island and moved into the house in Parthenon Street. Captain A.L. Dray had been appointed to operate a 'whispering organization' for the oral distribution of subversive propaganda that would 'sustain morale and belief in an ultimate Allied victory'.[19] His initiative was known as the 'Angelic Scheme'. Dray and the colonial administration believed that Nazi sympathisers had long been disseminating rumours and lies designed to undermine British rule. By dispersing his own 'whispers, talking points...and other forms of lie calculated to direct public opinion where required', he planned to tackle 'this menace [of Nazi rumours] on its own ground'.[20]

Oral propaganda was considered to play a valuable part in influencing public opinion in the Middle East where literacy was low. Dray, whose knowledge of Cyprus appears to have been based on briefings by the chief secretary, John Shaw, believed that Cypriot cynicism about the government, which still exercised certain restrictions over what its colonial subjects were allowed to read and say, meant that it could also play an important role in Cyprus. Although the more draconian constraints imposed in the aftermath of the October 1931 riots had been lifted, the government retained control of the use of printing presses and there were strict licensing laws surrounding publication. Dray argued that this had discredited the press in the eyes of most Cypriots, and meant that any printed material was 'tainted with authority'.

Dray also had the support of the district commissioners, and it is likely that he benefited from their local knowledge, for very soon after his arrival he recruited two intermediaries, a lawyer, George Rossides, codenamed 'Gunner', and an Anglophile travel agent from Larnaca, Odysseus Wideson,[21] known as 'Constant'. They were instructed to establish cells, no more than 15 strong, drawn from across society and including 'the bourgeoisie intelligentsia, agricultural peasantry, communists and mine workers, Turks'. Gunnner and Constant began 'scouting for likely whisperers' and managed to recruit 26, including a mineral water manufacturer from Larnaca and a farmer 'with a strong tongue' from the village of Skarinou. Each received a payment of between two and eight pounds a month.

Only Gunner and Constant knew that the scheme was the work of British intelligence. Others were told an elaborate cover story about a club 'of big Allied personalities, Greek, Cypriot, and Turk, so appalled at the islanders ignorance of the realities of this war, they feel it their bounden duty to enlighten them'. The club's unconventional tactics, it was explained, were necessary to avoid the colonial administration's strict censorship.

Rossides and Wideson were instructed to listen to the daily BBC news broadcasts and introduce 'talking points' based on their contents, which would be embellished twice a week with material invented by Dray. A list of numbered rumours was drawn up, each one to be disseminated in a different part of the island on a different date. Dray's stories ranged from the plausible, the arrival of two American divisions in the Middle East, to more imaginative claims that Mussolini planned to populate Cyprus with ousted Italian colonists from Libya and 'ship Cypriots and other Islanders to North Africa in the desert'.[22] Whisperers were instructed to attach credible sources to their stories and preface them with casual remarks such as 'I read in the papers' or 'I heard in a broadcast from X'. It was useless, Dray stressed, for an illiterate man to claim that he read something in the papers, or for a waiter to say he was 'told by the British ambassador'.

It is impossible to assess whether Dray's stories had any impact on public opinion on the island and there is an absurdity to his methodical dissemination of numbered rumours in different towns on a strictly rotational basis. But traffic between Dray and his network of oral propagandists ran in both directions, for they were also expected to keep their ears to the ground and pass on information about what was going on in the island.

The justification for this was that in the event of enemy occupation a newspaper of resistance would be produced by SOE in Cairo and dropped onto the island by plane, for distribution by the whisperer network. If its stories were to appear credible, they would need to contain items of authentic local news. The journalist and intelligence agent Sefton Delmer adopted a similar technique in his German black propaganda radio broadcasts from London, interspersing fictional information with accurate local detail. Dray's whisperers were also expected to organise a post-occupation go-slow movement and it seems reasonable to assume they would have been expected to inform on Nazi collaborators.

Wideson began submitting reports to Dray in October 1942 and continued conscientiously until the war was over. Although not a reliable source of historical fact they provide a unique insight into Cypriot concerns of the time. Wideson claimed that 'enemy cells' disseminated Axis propaganda in the island's towns and alleged that the villages of Arsos, Mandria, Platres and Omodhos were all strongly pro-German. He reported that corruption in government departments was widespread, and that soldiers' wives in the Limassol district had not received their husband's pay for the previous two months because the district paymaster was a drunk and a gambler. Other reports range from observations about the unpopularity of the British Institute staff, who were alleged to have 'a very bad moral reputation', to complaints about the price of straw, which had jumped from 6 shillings a camel load to 11 shillings in the space of a month.

In 1943, in the face of Churchill's refusal to renounce his unconditional support for the King of Greece, British efforts to reconcile the Greek resistance collapsed and violence broke out between right- and left-wing groups. From this point on Wideson's reports primarily contained dramatic accounts of plots allegedly being hatched by the recently sanctioned Cypriot Communist Party, AKEL; 2,000 armed men, Wideson claimed, were waiting to start a revolution at a sign from AKEL, reporting in the same conspiratorial language that Percy Arnold, editor of the *Cyprus Post*, was rumoured to be a member of the British Labour Party and had even once stood as a parliamentary candidate.

It is likely that the contents of these reports were generated mainly in the imaginations of agents anxious to secure their monthly £2 retainer. But the fact that they were taken seriously by Dray and Force 133 in Cairo reflects their growing concern about the acrimonious split that had developed within the Greek resistance. Ironically the 'Angelic Scheme' itself was to pose a far greater potential threat to the establishment of democracy on the island than the activities of AKEL members. Dray's curious system for distributing tall tales and rumours took on a far more sinister dimension when it attempted to influence Cypriot public opinion to the benefit of the colonial government.

In January 1943, after the island's trade unions called for a general strike, Dray initiated a rumour that if the strikers did not return to work by the following Monday the government would conscript them into labour camps. He noted smugly that 'our little game seems to have had admirable effects', for the strike ended on Sunday evening. A year later Chapman submitted a proposal that the 'Angelic Scheme' should continue to operate in peace time when it could actively seek to influence opinion on the island so that it assumed 'a much more sympathetic and co-operative attitude not only towards the local government but towards regional and international aims in the peace to come'. For the first time it was being suggested that British intelligence should become actively involved in domestic Cypriot affairs, in order to bolster support for the colonial government. Chapman and Dray even sought the support of Hugh Foot, the island's new chief secretary and later governor. Astonishingly, Foot agreed that the proposal 'has possibilities'[23] and recommended approaching the head of Force 133 in the region.

In the event the plans came to nothing, probably because SOE began to focus on developing its wider post-war role in the Middle East and the establishment of a wireless station of a 'completely clandestine and secret character' in Cyprus for communication with Near Eastern countries and the Balkans. Pending a final decision about the future of intelligence services in the region Chapman relocated Force 133's wireless operators to Navy House in Famagusta, where they blended in unobtrusively with the navy's own communications system.[24]

After the war was over Chapman and Waterer received the MBE and the CBE respectively for their work with the Greek resistance. When they also recommended Fred Murat, SOE's chief maritime agent in Famagusta, for an MBE, they were told that 'with the liberation of Europe SOE has opened the floodgates of awards for foreign nationals'.[25] Like the colony as a whole, Murat would have to wait some time longer for his reward.

Official British involvement in the Levant Fishing Patrol came to an end in August 1945, but many of the crews carried on using their specially adapted boats with their high-performance tank engines for commercial smuggling operations. Cyprus continued to be an important point in a network that transported illicit goods, including fur coats, from Alexandria to Piraeus.[26] Ten years later, the smuggling of arms into Cyprus, quite possibly using former Levant Fishing Patrol vessels, became an essential element in the EOKA campaign to overthrow British rule on the island.

12

The Great Liberator
1945–55

The single unequivocally beneficial legacy of British rule in Cyprus has been almost entirely forgotten. There is no plaque, no monument, no grandiose public building to mark the achievement, which came about when the colonial government was about to enter its final bitter phase, and which has subsequently been overshadowed by the story of the armed struggle for independence.

In 1949, after a three-year campaign spearheaded by the island's chief health inspector, Mehmet Aziz, and paid for from the Colonial Development Fund, Cyprus became the first of the world's malaria-infested countries to totally eradicate the disease from its shores. Aziz, a Turkish Cypriot and a sufferer from recurrent malarial attacks since childhood, had witnessed the deaths of 'many young people, many children' in his own village. Those who survived were often incapacitated for life. As Donald Waterer recalled in the 1930s and 40s 'an awful lot of youngsters never made it, others were not fit to do a day's work after contracting the disease'.[1]

The early colonists had struggled to understand what might cause malaria. In 1886 the medical officer Dr Heidenstam suggested that it was more prevalent amongst 'those who indulge in an over-abundant diet of cucumbers, melons and fruits'. Recognising the prevalence of malarial fevers in marshy areas, Heidenstam and his contemporaries speculated that it could be caused by 'invisible effluvium...particles so minute as to escape not only the human vision, but the highest power of the microscope'.[2]

It was not until 1899 that Ronald Ross, the pioneering Scottish malariologist, established a connection between the disease and the anopheles mosquito.

In 1913 he visited Cyprus, taking the young Aziz under his wing. But lack of funds meant that preventative work remained limited. By the mid-twentieth century Cyprus was considered one of the most malarious places in the world, with around 10,000 cases each year.

In 1946 Aziz, by then chief health inspector, secured a grant from the Colonial Development Fund to eradicate the anopheles mosquito from Cyprus. He planned his campaign along military lines, dividing up the entire island according to a grid plan into 556 blocks. Each block could be covered by one man over the course of 12 working days. Aziz's team worked systematically, metre by metre over the entire island, spraying 'every pool and stream and area of water-logged ground' with insecticide. Drinking wells, even the hoof prints of animals, 'wherever water and breeding places could be found',[3] were treated. Men waded into marshes and were lowered by ropes into caves on the sides of cliffs. Treated areas were checked on a weekly basis for evidence of mosquito larvae and sprayed repeatedly until they could be classed as clean. The campaign began on the Karpas Peninsula and moved westward, and while it lasted all traffic travelling from unclean to clean areas of the island had to be sprayed with insecticide.

Unbeknown to Aziz, the Italian authorities had begun a similar project in Sardinia. In December 1948, the Government of Cyprus accepted a challenge from the Sardinian high commissioner: whichever territory eradicated the anopheles mosquito first would be rewarded by the other with 100 litres of wine. By February 1950, Cyprus was officially declared malaria free and the men of the anopheles eradication service received their casket of Sardinian port.

Aziz, acclaimed by the London *News Chronicle* as 'the Great Liberator', and his team of Greek and Turkish Cypriot health workers ('front line fighters in the anti-malaria battle') were invited to London. There, the secretary of state for the colonies, Arthur Creech Jones, applauded them for winning 'fame among doctors and scientists all over the world'.[4] Aziz was awarded the MBE, yet this remarkable public servant and his genuinely historic achievement remain unknown to the majority of Cypriots today.

The anopheles eradication campaign took place at a curious crossroads in the island's colonial history. In the decade after the end of the Second World War Cyprus experienced unprecedented material development, and many colonial accounts of the time express an enthusiasm redolent of the early settlers of the 1880s. But this was also a time of political failure, when the prospects of negotiating a peaceful path towards self-government or union with Greece (in the words of one historian, 'one of the biggest lost opportunities in the Cyprus dispute'[5]) finally disappeared. Confronted with growing evidence that both the policy and, at an individual level, the personal attitudes of many British colonists remained unchanged, Cypriot frustration turned to bitterness.

Mehmet Aziz, 'the Great Liberator', as pictured in the *Cyprus Review* of February 1950 in front of a poster promoting the malaria eradication campaign.

The end of the war and the election of a Labour government in Britain in 1945 had led many Cypriots to believe that the island could soon cast off the shackles of colonial rule. In Britain the creation of the welfare state, the extension of social democracy and the ascendancy of a newly self-confident working class were all developments that were essentially incompatible with the ideology of empire. Precisely which factors were the pre-eminent contributors to the decline of the British Empire is the subject of much debate, but by 1945 it was clear that the theories of racial superiority that had underpinned it had been fundamentally undermined and that 'empires and colonies had become less respectable'.[6] Economically, Britain was virtually bankrupt, dependent on American aid for food and basic supplies and forced to extend rationing of essential goods for another nine years. It could no longer afford to maintain substantial troop numbers abroad or economically unproductive colonies. But in the case of Cyprus, strategic considerations overrode both economic and social ones.

Britain's military bases in the Suez Canal had grown so unpopular in Egypt that 'as the war ended, the Egyptian people were clamouring for the British to leave their country'.[7] Cyprus's potential as an alternative garrison made it a special case. As historian Robert Holland explains, increasing pressure on British interests in the Middle East enhanced the significance of Cyprus as a military base and meant that 'the imperial value of the island was rising rather than falling'.[8]

As a result, the secretary of state for the colonies concluded that 'when imperial strategic needs have to be served', difficult decisions would have to be made about 'what limits must be imposed on the people attaining responsible self-government'.[9] In October 1946, Creech Jones unveiled a twin-pronged strategy for the future of Cyprus, one that encompassed both a 10-year economic development plan and the introduction of a more liberal and progressive form of government.

The man appointed to steer through both measures, the new governor, Lord Winster, was a career politician. A Labour peer and former minister for civil aviation, Winster had no experience of colonial administration, an omission which in the context of Cyprus may have been a good thing. He was quick to absorb a brief and had a logical and thorough approach which made him popular with his senior administrative officers. As one former civil servant recalled, 'if you sent a report in he read it all through and made comments down the side and wanted to know more about things'.[10] The new governor arrived in the spring of 1947, a month after Italy had ceded the islands of the Dodecanese to Greece and while the negotiations that would ultimately lead to independence for India, Pakistan, Ceylon and Burma the following August were already underway. Cypriots began to feel that their moment in history had come and was in danger of passing them by.

In November 1947, Winster presided over the first meeting of the Cyprus Consultative Assembly at the English School. It was hoped that the assembly would agree on a constitution to re-establish the island's legislature for the first time since 1931. But the discussions barely began. The Greek Cypriot right, led by the church, refused to consider measures that did not include union with Greece and boycotted the meeting. Those who did attend, politically weakened by nationalist accusations of selling out, found the proposals too limited and concluded that they would not win public support. After months of stalemate the government announced its own plan for a representative assembly where, for the first time, the Greek Cypriot majority would no longer be blocked by a combined British and Turkish Cypriot vote. But because it fell short of full self-government the assembly rejected it outright.

The consultative assembly was dissolved in August 1948, three months after Britain relinquished its mandate in Palestine, leaving Cyprus the only territory in the Eastern Mediterranean still under British sovereignty. Holland argues that 'the crisis of trust which impregnated the final years of British rule on the island started at this point'.[11] Three months later Winster announced his resignation, referring bitterly to 'the action of certain members of the Assembly, in refusing what was possible because they were not given what it would have been disastrous to grant'. The governor believed that the members had made an error of judgement which in his view indicated that they lacked the 'fitness to exercise the powers they were demanding'.[12]

In some ways Winster's assessment, despite its blunt phrasing, was correct. The long-term impact of the uncompromising Palmer regime was now evident. The generation of politicians and church leaders the governor had been hoping to win over had, for the previous 16 years, been politically infantilised by the colonial administration and systematically excluded from playing a role in the political or civic affairs of their country. They had been addressed, particularly during the lengthy years of the Palmer administration, as if they were obstinate children. Some, such as the recently elected Archbishop Makarios II, who as Bishop of Kyrenia had spent the previous 15 years in exile, had been allowed to return to Cyprus only in 1946. During his absence the Cyprus communist party had become a significant political force – one which potentially threatened the archbishop's own power base. Once in office, undermining the left became one of his principal political objectives.

Small wonder then, given the distortion of the Cypriot political landscape which resulted directly from British policy, that the assembly members were disinclined to pursue an incremental approach and accept the constitution on offer.

Winster was a plain-speaking pragmatist and, like many British administrators before and after him, he totally failed to comprehend the appeal of *enosis*. His enthusiasm for the newly announced 10-year development plan was, in part, due to a belief that material and economic improvements could be an adequate counterweight to the attractions of union with Greece. Subsequent governors attempted in vain to explain to their subjects how much better life was under British rather than Greek rule and, like Winster, remained baffled by the apparent irrationality of the desire to unite with an economically destitute, war-ravaged country that was still locked in a bitter civil conflict. In an attempt to convince the public of the 'substantial material improvement' that was already under way, and how much 'Government was doing on its behalf', the governor appointed a public information officer to publicise government works.[13] Winster himself frequently challenged his subjects to compare their homeland with 'other countries in the Mediterranean, and ask where more is being done about soil erosion, about water, forest and health. Let our critics tell us where things are better. I shall not be afraid of the comparison'.[14]

Winster made few friends amongst Cypriots and from the patronising tone of his public addresses it is easy to see why. But his speeches also convey the frustration of a man who was utterly baffled by the tenacity with which Greek Cypriots clung to what appeared to him to be an irrational, sentimental attachment. This in turn contributed to a failure to believe that the movement could be an authentic one with an organic basis amongst the rural community.

The confusion expressed by Ivan Lloyd Phillips, the district commissioner for Nicosia in 1949–51, is typical of that of many colonial officials. 'It is difficult to attempt an estimate of how deep-seated the *"enosis"* movement really is,' Lloyd Phillips wrote to his father in England. 'Much of it is clearly emotional, but it lacks economic inducement and in the countryside, apart from a display of Greek flags, one sees little positive desire for it.'[15]

Evidence of Winster's 'substantial material improvement' and the benefits of the 10-year plan were not hard to find. Extensive development was already in progress. Mains water and electricity were brought to remote villages, new roads were built, while 'in the towns hundreds of fine new stone houses and blocks of flats are arising'.[16] The make-up of the expatriate community, dominated until now by government officials, had begun to change as a result. The profusion of construction and building projects attracted large numbers of transient workers, men employed on short-term contracts working on Colonial Development Fund projects, and their families. The Anglican vicar responsible for Larnaca and Famagusta complained that 'while they are here' the contract workers 'do not attach themselves to the life and institutions of the country'.[17]

Ironically, as the prospects for dialogue between London and Nicosia declined communication between the two places became easier. In December 1947, Cyprus Airways, the colony's new airline, owned jointly by the Cyprus government, local subscribers and British European Airways, began its first regular service between Nicosia and London. It was a journey of 16 hours, with an overnight stop in Rome. Cyprus Airways' beginnings were modest, and its first secretary was obliged to balance the airline's single typewriter on the kitchen stove, 'owing to shortage of furniture'.[18]

Two years later, on Empire Day 1949, the governor opened a new terminal at Nicosia Airport. The complex ('second to none in the Middle East') included a restaurant, the 'Happy Landings', along with lavatories that were 'as comfortable as they can be made'. Gone was the grass strip of pre-war days, Nicosia Airport now staked its claim to be the 'aerial cross-roads of the Middle East'. Ten minutes on the tarmac would see 'a BOAC. York from Tehran; a Cyprus Airways Dakota from Athens; an Australian National Airways emigrant liner with a load of Italians bound for a new continent and a new life'.[19]

For Lloyd Phillips, as the commissioner of the capital, the development of regular air routes to Cyprus brought distinct disadvantages. The numbers of visiting dignitaries who needed to be officially welcomed at the airport and subsequently entertained increased significantly. For some, like the prime minister of newly independent Pakistan, Nicosia became a convenient stopping point on a journey further west. But a new generation of affluent and well-connected Britons were also now starting to come to the island on holiday. Typical arrivals met by the commissioner included the Duchess of Wellington, 'a most

Passengers at Nicosia Airport climb aboard the aircraft 'Alasia', the fifth plane
to be added to the Cyprus Airways fleet. April 1950.

[© *The Collection of the Leventis Municipal Museum of Nicosia.*]

extraordinary old trout with the mentality and appearance of 1750', Charles
North, an MP whose 'chief interest in life appears to be the Emperors Augustus
and Tiberius'[20], along with numerous officials and ambassadors on leave from
Egypt, Libya and Sudan.

Efforts to establish the colony as a holiday resort for wealthy Britons were
enhanced the following October when 'one of the finest hotels in the Middle
East – the Ledra Palace' – opened in Nicosia. The hotel, which had cost
£25,000 to build, had 93 en-suite bedrooms, a swimming pool, lounges, bars,
tennis courts 'and other amenities such as are provided by the best European
Hotels'.[21] Lloyd Phillips attended the hotel's inaugural ball and found it 'better
than I expected, though a bit garish in design inside'.[22] Today, the hotel, in serious need of renovation, serves as the barracks for the British contingent of the
United Nations peace-keeping force, a major landmark in the buffer zone that
divides the island in two.

Soon Limassol, Famagusta, Kyrenia, and even quiet Paphos all boasted
three- and four-star hotels. But holidays in Cyprus remained the preserve of
the elite. A return trip from England with a month's stay on the island was estimated to cost as much as £150 – a considerable sum for most post-war Britons
struggling to cope with food and housing shortages.[23]

This was a curious, schizophrenic time in the colony's history. Although professionally it was apparent to members of the colonial administration that fundamental change was inevitable, in all other respects life for the majority of Britons continued virtually unaltered.

The significant official rituals of imperial life also reinforced the message that the political balance of power in the colony would remain unchanged. Empire Day was still celebrated as a public holiday, and official functions at Government House continued to demand that guests wore white tie and decorations. The highlight of the year remained the King's Birthday Celebration, a lengthy procedure which began with a military parade at 8 a.m., followed by a service of thanksgiving at St Pauls' Church, an official lunch, another official supper and finally the evening reception at Government House. There, up to 1,200 guests wandered through the floodlit gardens, beneath the illuminated letters 'EIIR' suspended from the tower of Government House by the PWD, and listened to the music of the police band. For those senior officials obliged to squeeze themselves into ceremonial uniforms made for their younger, slimmer selves, the day presented a challenge. After reading the lesson in church one governor was forced to remain seated for prayers since, as he explained to his parents, 'I can't kneel in my tight trousers.'[24] Others felt that this was a small price to pay for the trappings of power. Despite enduring similar discomfort in his tight dress uniform Lloyd Phillips confessed that 'the pomp and circumstance of Empire appeal to me no end!'[25]

Apart from official displays of imperial power, social contact between Britons and Cypriots remained limited to such set pieces as the annual hockey match between the Secretariat and the Cypriot football team APOEL. The implications of this separation were particularly apparent to Lloyd Phillips, who had served in Palestine from 1938 to 1947. He attributed 'some of the bitterness which undoubtedly exists in Cyprus as far as the locals are concerned' to the fact that 'social relations between British and Cypriots are much more distant here than they were between ourselves and the Arabs and Jews in Palestine'.[26]

Even the career structure of the colonial service mitigated against direct contact with Cypriots. Although it might be 'much more fun being a commissioner'[27] out in the district, the centralised system of colonial administration meant that an individual's promotion depended on maintaining a visible and active presence back at base within the Secretariat.

Not surprisingly then, when Geoffrey Clifford spent four months on the island reviewing civil servants' salaries in 1946 he found the administration 'very much out of touch... Cypriots were very conscious that they were being treated like second-class citizens by an occupying power... one could sense the tension and the resentment'.[28] Clifford was appalled to learn that Cypriots, no matter how senior they might be in the administration, were still not allowed across the threshold of the Nicosia Club. In fact, the club was, very gradually, being forced to change – an unforeseen consequence of Winster's 10-year plan. Improvements to the island's infrastructure, in particular to its communications, and the consequent opening up of commercial opportunities resulted in an influx of businessmen keen to enter into commercial partnerships with Cypriots as equals. At the end of the war 'at least six of the officers serving at Wolseley Barracks took their release in Cyprus'[29] in order to establish businesses in the colony. Others, such as Battle of Britain pilot Gus Prattley, found work in Nicosia with an import/export company.

Expatriate society was no longer dominated by government officials and elderly administrators from other colonies who had come to the island to retire, and younger bloods at the Nicosia Club began pressing for change. By the early 1950s the Nicosia Club had reluctantly agreed to allow Cypriots through its doors. Expatriates and Cypriots also found some opportunity to socialise together in the 'Nicosia Excursionists Club', founded during the war to enable 'the town-dweller to enjoy the freedom of the countryside'.[30]

But the excursionists and the new entrance requirements at the Nicosia Club were still the exception. By and large such changes were painfully slow, and many Cypriots must have felt they had been condemned to occupy some historical backwater while the rest of the world moved into the modern age. The impression that an unforgiving administration was still exacting punishment for past slights was reinforced by the appointment of Andrew Wright as the new governor in 1949. Wright had served in the Storrs administration and in 1931 petrol from his upturned car had been used to ignite Government House. The Colonial Office, meanwhile, described the new governor in approving tones as being a 'fine Victorian type now almost extinct in the British colonial service'.[31]

The failure of the Winster constitution had prompted the Greek Orthodox Church to organise its own plebiscite on the question of *enosis*. In January 1950, registers were placed before the altar in churches across the island and congregants invited to add their names to a list of those calling for union with Greece. Some 95 per cent of Greek Cypriots responded, prompting the district commissioner of Nicosia to conclude that since 'the Greekness of Cyprus cannot be denied', it would be impossible to avoid 'making fairly substantial concessions in the reasonably near future'.[32] Turkish Cypriot leader Fazil Kutchuk voiced his concern, referring to the tolling of the 'bells of danger' and calling on the British administration to 'take the strictest measures'[33] to check it.

One of the church leaders who played a leading role in the organisation of the vote was Makarios, the young and recently elected Bishop of Kition. Makarios was only 37, a virtual infant by the standards of the gerontocratic Orthodox Church, and had just returned from a two-year scholarship to Boston Theological College in the United States. Clever, capable and charismatic, he had been born to a peasant family in the village of Pano Panaghia in the Paphos region, serving his novitiate at Kykkos Monastery where his abilities were encouraged by Bishop Chrysostomos.[34] He was elected Bishop of Kition in 1948 while in Boston. Two years later, after the death of the incumbent archbishop, he was elected Archbishop Makarios III. From this point on, his presence would dominate the Cyprus question but Makarios's role as ethnarch – a combined secular and spiritual leader whose claim to speak on behalf of Greek Cypriots arose primarily from his ecclesiastical position – was a concept that the British never felt comfortable with.

At some time during this period, possibly in July 1951, Makarios began discussions with Colonel George Grivas. Although the British would not be familiar with his name until several years later, he became synonymous with the problem of Cyprus and would, in British minds, be viewed as the archbishop's darker alter ego. Grivas came from the village of Trikomo on the eastern end of the Messaoria plain. He left Cyprus at 17 to enrol in the Athens Military Academy and spent the rest of his career in the Greek army, becoming a captain at 26. He was a fervent believer in the vision of a greater Greece and participated in the Asia Minor campaign of 1919–22 that was so disastrous for his adopted country. During the Nazi occupation of Greece and the civil war that followed, Grivas operated a shadowy far-right paramilitary organisation known as 'X'. Despite being over 50 when he returned to Cyprus he committed himself to the rigours of a guerilla campaign against the British that was to last for four years. Disciplined to the point of fanaticism, it was rumoured that before leaving Athens he had prepared for the deprivations ahead by limiting his diet to two pieces of fruit every hour, supplemented by meat every second day. The colonel's intellectual abilities certainly did not compare with those of Makarios and he conspicuously lacked the ethnarch's ability to deal with subtle and nuanced arguments. But his qualities of absolute ruthlessness and single-mindedness were to make him a formidable military leader.

These differences in character would be sufficient to account for much of the uneasiness that existed in the relationship between the two men. But they would also differ significantly in their tactical approaches to the campaign against British rule. Grivas advocated aggressive guerilla warfare, encompassing targeted assassinations of the British. He believed that if the British security services were provoked into violent reprisals against Cypriots then outraged international opinion would lead to the exertion of greater diplomatic pressure on Britain to withdraw. To that extent Grivas's campaign could be considered one of the first in which strategic military decisions were made on the basis of their impact on media coverage and public opinion. He also did not hesitate to order the execution of fellow Cypriots *pour encourager les autres,* or if he felt that an individual's actions risked jeopardising the cause. For his part, Makarios embraced more limited sabotage on a small scale.

The church plebiscite of 1950 effectively marked the start of the *enosis* campaign, but the British were slow to comprehend the emergence of a genuine mass movement – on a different scale to anything they had previously encountered in Cyprus. The next five years were characterised by long interludes of calm interspersed with periods of acute tension, during which an atmosphere of 'anxiety and mistrust of a peculiarly intense variety'[35] was generated.

From this point until the end of British rule, both Makarios and the British government in London sought to internationalise the question of the island's future, elevating it from the level of a domestic colonial dispute to one that had significant implications for the wider world. Makarios believed that, after decades of British intransigence, the only way Britain could be persuaded to revise its policy would be if other powerful nations, particularly America, exerted political pressure on Cyprus's behalf. From Britain's perspective, it was not only its regional strategic interests in the Middle East that were at stake, but also by extension the maintenance of a barrier against Soviet expansionism.

Rising Arab nationalism (especially in Egypt), the Suez crisis of 1956, and the 1958 revolution in Iraq were all to play a part in directing British policy in Cyprus during this period. As Robert Stephens lucidly explained, 'the long British retreat in the Middle East made a solution of the Cyprus problem more difficult'.[36] The disintegration of the Anglo-Egyptian treaty and Britain's consequent military withdrawal from Egypt reinforced a conviction, already widely held by imperial defence staff in London, that a military base in Cyprus could only be secured by retaining sovereignty over the entire island.

As Foreign Office Minister Selwyn Lloyd explained to the UN General Assembly in 1954, 'full administrative control is necessary because leases expire, treaties have a habit of being whittled away and Greek governments, like other governments, change'.[37] Greece had only recently emerged from two years of civil war and had seen no less than 24 elected governments fall between 1945 and 1951. Implicit in Selwyn Lloyd's allusion to the volatility of Greek politics was the message that to place strategically important military interests at the mercy of a similarly unpredictable, inexperienced Cypriot electorate was asking for trouble.

Strategic considerations apart, there was also a widespread belief within the ruling British Conservative party that too many concessions on Cyprus at a time of declining imperial influence in the Middle East would be viewed as signs of British weakness. At the same time, the prime minister, Anthony Eden, began to attach increasing significance to Turkish interests in Cyprus. This was largely due to Turkey's prominent position amongst the countries of the Baghdad Pact, an alliance engineered by Britain to link Turkey, Iran and Pakistan, that was intended both to counterbalance Soviet influence and to ensure that friendly governments remained in power in the oil-rich countries of the region. As Stephens explains: 'The desire not to offend Turkey merged imperceptibly into the more positive recognition that Turkey's objections to Greek control of Cyprus could be used to preserve the British position on the island'.[38]

From this point on virtually all decisions about Cyprus took place not in Nicosia, but in London, Athens, Ankara and New York, and the British civil servants of Cyprus, with their idiosyncratic, insular culture, had little influence on policy. Nevertheless, the administration's shortcomings, not least its singular, quixotic understanding of Cypriot identity, continued to play a role in shaping official attitudes towards the colony during the difficult years that followed. The incompetence of too many local officials, the romanticisation of Ancient Greece, the lack of social interaction between the colonised and the colonisers, the perception of Cypriots and their politics as infantile, and the consequent reluctance to believe that they were serious or united in their demands, all played some part in influencing events during the last years of British rule.

In February 1954, Robert Armitage, Wright's successor, was installed in Government House. Hesitant and indecisive, he has been described as 'the archetype of the failed Governor in the era of decolonization'.[39] Armitage was a convivial man who seems to have recognised early on that he stood little chance of grasping the subtleties of Cypriot politics, writing pathetically to his parents, 'the problem of *enosis* is like the velvety blackness of a nightmare, it clutches one everywhere and one strains to see a glimmer of light to guide one to safety and nowhere is there light'.[40]

There were other regional developments, well beyond Armitage's sphere of influence, that also impacted on his agenda. In June 1954, it was announced in London that Britain's Middle East Land and Air Headquarters would be transferred to Cyprus, the result of a new agreement with Egypt in which the Suez Canal Zone would be operated and administered by civilians in place of British troops. Up to 30,000 British troops would, as a result, be stationed in purpose-built military towns such as Episkopi which now stretched 'literally over hill and dale on the Southern Coast near Limassol'.[41] Cyprus was now more important than ever for the protection of British interests in the Middle East. A clumsily worded statement to this effect in the House of Commons spelt out that the island was one of those Commonwealth territories which, 'owing to their particular circumstances can never expect to be fully independent'.[42] The remarks incensed the Greek Cypriot community.

Armitage chose this moment, in 1954, to announce his intention to strengthen the administration's laws on sedition. Makarios responded to the challenge head on, preaching a succession of confrontational sermons. The governor, faced with the prospect of making the archbishop a political martyr by implementing his threat, backed down and the event marked a turning point in Anglo-Hellenic relations, which deteriorated from this point on. A subsequent abortive attempt by the Greek delegation to the United Nations to raise the question of Cyprus the following December resulted in a general strike, demonstrations by school children and the worst riots in Nicosia since 1931.

Armitage arrived in Cyprus at a time when the structure for an organised resistance to British rule was already established. Throughout the previous four years Grivas had built up a network of support amongst Greek Cypriot youth organisations and had made preparations to stockpile illicit weapons and munitions. The colonel's first arms cache arrived by boat a month after Armitage was sworn in. The administration's chaotic and disorganised intelligence services enabled at least two subsequent consignments to be safely unloaded and stored. Armitage, meanwhile, was fully occupied selecting designs for a new issue of notes and coins, explaining to his parents, 'we have to have one with the Queen's head'.[43]

It would, however, be unfair to place responsibility for all the administration's deficiencies at Armitage's door. He had inherited a fragmented, uncommunicative intelligence network that dissipated its efforts and wasted resources. The island's police commissioner, who had occupied the post for several years, was now well past his prime and strongly opposed to 'all innovations such as CID and special branches', or the use of radio communication. Sir John Prendergast, who later took over responsibility for intelligence, found that 'the prima donnas of the old organisation would not co-operate with the new arrivals. There was good intelligence available but frequently it remained locked in senior officers' "black books" '.[44]

It was against this background that on 25 January 1955, a fishing vessel, the *St George*, was intercepted as it brought Grivas's latest consignment of arms ashore at a quiet beach below the village of Khlorakas near Paphos. The caique, initially spotted from the air, was boarded by a British naval destroyer. Members of the crew and some villagers were arrested on the beach by security officers who had spent the previous five nights lying in wait.

It should have been clear to the British administration (despite the reluctance of some of its members to admit that the discovery of the arms consignment was anything more than the work of 'a few hotheads') that the struggle to cast off colonial rule and unite with Greece was entering a new and violent phase. A particularly complicated period was about to begin, one in which the tabling of successive initiatives, shifts in the international power balance and changing local allegiances, all at different times played a part. A succinct summary of the four years that followed can be found in Stephens' book *Cyprus a Place of Arms*.

It [the *enosis* campaign] was at its peak from October 1954 until the beginning of 1959 when the Zurich and London agreements on an independent

Cyprus were signed. During this period of about four and a half years, riot and rebellion, guerrilla warfare against the British and finally communal strife between Greek and Turkish Cypriots, alternated with intervals of truce, negotiation and an annual political agitation at the United Nations. There were five main bouts of negotiation or sets of proposals offered. They reflected to a large extent the British government's gradual advance from the position that its sovereignty over Cyprus would never be changed.[45]

The final bloody years of British rule were to cast a long shadow, one from which Cyprus has yet to fully emerge. Inevitably the material progress made on the island in the immediate post-war decade is obscured by our knowledge of the carnage that followed. But it is perhaps worth remembering that the death toll of the years of the EOKA struggle is dwarfed by the numbers of lives saved by the anti-malarial work of Mehmet Aziz.

Arguably the most damaging development of the 1955–58 period was the cleavage that developed between Greek and Turkish Cypriots, leading incrementally, over the decades that followed, to the partition that exists on the island today. This is why Aziz is entirely absent from contemporary Cypriot memory, why there are no statues, plaques or memorials to him and his mixed Greek and Turkish Cypriot team of 'front line fighters'. The militaristic culture that has left its stamp on Northern Cyprus has little space for memorials to civilians, while in the south, where the Turkish Cypriot experience has, until recently, been airbrushed out of classroom history, there is no knowledge of, let alone inclination to commemorate, the Cypriot who made the greatest single contribution to his country during the colonial period.

13

A Child's Game of Pretend
1955–58

The first explosions were heard just after midnight. Studios and transmitters at Cyprus Broadcasting Station, on a hill overlooking Nicosia, were destroyed. Other bombs exploded at the Secretariat and at Wolseley Barracks. The new Press and Information Officer, Lawrence Durrell, had stayed up for a farewell drink with his brother, the naturalist Gerald Durrell, who had just completed a field trip to the island. Suddenly 'parcels of steel plates began dropping from heaven on to paving stones, while pieces of solid air compressed themselves against the window frames making them jingle'.[1] Durrell drove to Paphos Gate Police Station. There he found the chief secretary with a blazer, trousers and a silk scarf thrown over his pyjamas composing a message to the secretary of state, as the police radio crackled with reports of bombs in Famagusta, Limassol and Larnaca.

This was the start of the armed struggle for union with Greece, fought by the National Union of Cypriot Fighters, *Ethniki Organosis Kyprion Agoniston* (EOKA), an organisation whose members were known to the British at the time as terrorists and have always been referred to by Greek Cypriots as freedom fighters. This dramatic opening salvo marked the start of a three-year campaign of violence and brutality which rapidly acquired a momentum and a warped logic of its own. It was a time when both EOKA and the British security services found themselves killing old men, pregnant women and young boys barely out of school. At a purely strategic level EOKA's achievement was remarkable. A small group of brave and committed activists succeeded in forcing the mighty British Empire into retreat and liberating their country from foreign rule for the first time in 800 years. But the price paid for doing so was

high. Not only did the men and women of EOKA succeed in killing many
more fellow Cypriots than Britons – but the fractures in Cypriot society that
emerged at this time, between Greek and Turkish Cypriots, and between Greek
Cypriots of the right and the left, are still evident today and form a major obstacle to co-existence on the island. One of the many ironies of the rebellion is
that while relations between Greek Cypriots and the British – the initial target
of EOKA's campaign of violence – have all but recovered (millions of British
tourists holiday on Cyprus every year, tens of thousands live permanently on
the island) the scars it left on Cypriot society have proved less easy to erase.[2]

As the synchronised bombs went off, leaflets were scattered about the major
towns, attributing the explosions to the work of 'Dighenis', a mythical Byzantine
warrior, applauded in mediaeval folk songs, who, according to legend, leapt
from Asia Minor to Cyprus where he grasped the Pentadactylos Mountain in
the Kyrenia range, leaving on it the imprint of his hand. The administration,
taken by surprise, and with only the most rudimentary intelligence support,
was unsure for some time whether 'Dighenis' was a man or a committee, and
whether the explosions were just isolated incidents or the start of a coordinated
campaign. It adopted a wait-and-see policy, while Armitage resolved to carry
on as usual so as not to 'create the impression that these subversive activities
have disrupted the normal life of the Government and people of Cyprus'.[3]

The explosions were followed by two months of relative calm with no further acts of violence, when, as Durrell described, it was easy to ignore the fact
that life in Cyprus had changed fundamentally:

> The morning, like some perfect deception, dawned fine, and nobody
> walking about the calm streets of the town, watching the shopkeepers
> taking down their shutters and sipping their morning coffee, could have
> told that some decisive and irrevocable action had taken place in the night;
> a piece of the land had broken away, had slid noiselessly into the sea. In
> a sense now there was no more thinking to be done. We had reached a
> frontier.[4]

But although the weeks that followed feature little in most histories of the
time, it is worth highlighting the events of 24 May 1955 since they illustrate a
salient characteristic of the uprising. It was one that confounded both civilian and military officials, making it difficult for them to respond effectively,
but which also contributed to the perpetuation of a profound misunderstanding
about the nature and appeal of the rebellion, and ultimately undermined the
nationalists' case.

Cyprus, unlike many other colonies, continued to celebrate Empire Day
on 24 May every year.[5] In 1955, the commemoration was marred when, as

the governor complained, Greek Cypriot schoolchildren created 'a thorough nuisance'.[6] Armitage's 'thorough nuisance' took the form of up to 500 teenagers stoning Government House. They were repelled only when troops were called in to restore order.

The involvement of schoolchildren in riots and demonstrations and, more seriously, in the movement of arms and the targeting of victims became a hallmark of the next three years. The recruitment of youngsters to the cause of the EOKA rebellion was a tactical masterstroke on the part of Colonel Grivas. It enabled him to utilise the existing structure of Makarios's national youth movement, the *Pankyprios Ethniki Organosis Neolaisas* (PEON),[7] for the recruitment of fighters to his armed units. But equally importantly, the participation of schoolchildren in high-profile acts of civil disobedience wrong-footed the British security services, making it almost impossible for them to respond without appearing thuggish and inappropriately heavy-handed. Media coverage of ham-fisted action taken by the authorities against children, along with the arrest and execution of gunmen, some of whom were barely out of their teens, discredited British rule in Cyprus and created a culture of martyrdom.

In his appeals to the youth of Cyprus, Grivas was pushing at a door which – largely thanks to British education policy on the island – was already wide open. As a result of the decision made by the secretary of state for the colonies in 1881 that Greek was to be the language of instruction in Greek Cypriot classrooms, successive generations of Greek Cypriot schoolchildren were taught from textbooks produced in Athens, which promoted a strong sense of Greek patriotism. Not surprisingly, they believed, more fervently than any other sector of society, that they were essentially Greek and that union with Greece 'meant something not unlike the mystic's Union with the Infinite'.[8] The standard text used in junior schools during this time, for example, contained a map of Greece entitled 'Our Motherland', along with pictures of the Greek flag captioned 'wherever you flutter, there flutters the soul of my country'. One new arrival in Cyprus commented that while such exhortations might be 'splendid stuff, and the best possible basis for bringing up Greek children to be Greek patriots', the textbook was 'a strange choice for those whose allegiance is claimed elsewhere'.[9]

The prominence accorded to schoolchildren and young people in the EOKA movement compounded the British administration's reluctance to take Cypriot political aspirations seriously. As the insurrection progressed and tensions within the classroom increased school closures became a regular occurrence. The frequent presence of thousands of schoolchildren on the streets of major towns, rioting, demonstrating and stoning soldiers, contributed to a general impression of unreality, a belief that the rebellion lacked either authenticity or the gravitas of a serious political movement. As a result, when photographer Guy Gravett was sent to Cyprus to cover the rebellion for *The Sunday Times*, his most enduring memory of the experience was being 'set upon by the girls of the Greek Cypriot gymnasium', who, as he subsequently recounted to Tony Willis, 'got him against a wall and pummelled him to the sound of enormous squeaks and giggles, and Guy said it was lovely!'[10]

Similarly, when British Labour MP Richard Crossman visited the colony in early 1955 he too gained the impression that both sides in the dispute were somehow posturing and that 'nothing is very serious, since no one on either side means what he says or does what he means'.[11] Even Red Cross worker Penelope Tremayne, who had more contact with Cypriots than most, felt there was an element of 'non-seriousness' about the EOKA campaign in the minds of ordinary Cypriots:

> It was not four-square to them: it was play-acting and a dream, turned suddenly, terrifyingly, real, but that might at any moment revert to unreality. And when more believable dangers threatened – forest fires, rumours of war – the child's game of pretend was put aside, until a more suitable time to go on with it.[12]

Paradoxically, although substantial sections of the administration now accepted that it was 'fundamentally inappropriate for Cyprus to continue to be under alien colonial rule',[13] any Cypriot expressions of resistance to such alien rule were somehow considered to be neither authentic nor sincere.[14]

Penelope Tremayne was one of six women who had been recruited by the Red Cross to provide elementary health care in remote parts of the island. The Red Cross fulfilled a particularly important role later in the conflict after Grivas insisted that village authorities suspend all cooperation with the British, thus denying poorer villagers access to, amongst other things, free medical attention. But there was also a political dimension to the work. A similar scheme providing basic medical aid had been adopted during the emergency in Malaya where it was believed to have led to an increase in public support for British rule. Tremayne, who had no nursing qualifications but spoke fluent Greek, was one of just a handful of Britons who continued to live and work amongst Cypriots throughout this period of violence and suspicion. Like her friend and mentor Durrell, whose house in Bellapaix she subsequently occupied after he left Cyprus, Tremayne was repelled by the insularity of the majority of permanent British residents on the island and by 'the all-pervading, unmistakable stamp of "British Made" that seems to mark every inch of roof or road, if not every leaf, where the Empire builders have been'.[15]

In June 1955, when two people were killed in an explosion at Nicosia Post Office and attacks were launched on police stations in Kyrenia, Nicosia and the mining village of Amiandos in the Troodos Mountains, it became clear that the

April explosions had been merely the opening shots in a co-ordinated rebellion. From this point on 'any attempt to sustain the appearance of normality ceased to be credible'.[16] In a ruling that went virtually unnoticed at the time, the colonists' annual summer migration to Troodos was cancelled, Armitage and his government were ordered by the colonial secretary to remain in Nicosia. The mountains, the colonists' refuge and retreat for the previous 80 years, had now become dangerous and sinister places. The administration had, symbolically at least, relinquished its claim to its spiritual summer home on Mount Troodos, to the guerilla fighters and *andartes* of the EOKA movement. Much of the romance with which the movement was associated in the popular Greek Cypriot imagination derived from its image as an elusive band of heroic mountain men, reminiscent of the fighters of the Greek Wars of Independence who occupied both the moral and topographical high ground.[17] The Olympian heights from which the British had once surveyed their colony now belonged to Colonel Grivas and his men. The departure of the British government from Troodos was arguably an appropriate symbol for what was to follow. A combination of weakness and duplicity meant that the imperial power's retreat from Cyprus would not be a magnanimous one.

Many of the large summer villas in Troodos were abandoned, while the mountain hotels that had once attracted tourists from Egypt and elsewhere were now commandeered by the British military. It is estimated that there were five EOKA guerilla groups based in the mountains around Kykko Monastery, which functioned as a main supply depot and communications hub.

In the summer of 1955, in an attempt to formulate a diplomatic response to the growing crisis, Harold Macmillan, the British foreign secretary, invited his Greek and Turkish counterparts to a tri-partite conference in London. But the news from Cyprus did not augur well for the talks. The night before it began a special branch police constable, Greek Cypriot Herodotus Poullis, was shot dead in Ledra Street. Macmillan had evolved a complicated and risky strategy for solving the problem, one which has been likened to 'standing next to a pile of explosive material with a burning brand'.[18] It hinged on encouraging Turkey's claim to a political and social stake in the future of Cyprus – one that rivalled Greek Cypriot claims for union with Greece. Britain, Macmillan believed, could then step into the breach between two quarrelsome vested interests and claim the role of an impartial arbiter. The foreign secretary hoped to secure agreement for a new constitution in which Britain retained sovereignty and Greece and Turkey assumed an advisory role. This arrangement, known as a 'tri-dominium', was seen by the Colonial Office as a recipe for disaster and was criticised by one anonymous official as being instead a formula for 'pandemonium', one that would see an end to any prospect of 'the Cypriots making up their own minds about their future in conditions of orderly progress'.[19] No Cypriot delegate was invited, leading Archbishop Makarios to denounce the meeting, with some justification, as 'a trap'.[20] Nevertheless the mood within the British expatriate community was one of optimism and relief that 'at last Cyprus was going to be submitted to the arbitration of the mind, and not allowed to rot slowly like a gangrened limb'.[21]

On 6 September, as the London conference drew to a close, reports spread that an explosion in a quiet residential street in Salonika in Greece had destroyed the house of the father of modern Turkey, Mustafa Kemal Attaturk. The reports, subsequently found to be erroneous, prompted serious anti-Greek riots in Turkey. In Istanbul, thousands of youths marched through the city carrying banners affirming that 'Cyprus is Turkish'. Greek and Armenian shops throughout the city were systematically attacked and looted by stick-wielding mobs which had been bussed in – allegedly by the government – for the purpose[22]; 72 Greek Orthodox churches were damaged. The months that followed saw what was arguably the biggest tragedy to result from the EOKA rebellion, when tens of thousand of Greeks packed up and left Istanbul forever, marking the beginning of the end of a substantial Greek presence in the city that had lasted for nearly 2,000 years.

Britain is often accused by Cypriots of having adopted a policy of divide and rule in the colony. But emphasising the differences between the two communities had, until September 1955, been a *consequence* of British efforts to govern the colony, rather than a policy in itself. With Macmillan's strategy this changed. Durrell observed that 'the fruitless conference had cut the frail cord which held us still attached, however tenuously, to reason and measure'.[23]

Just over a week later, on 17 September 1955, the British Institute in Nicosia was burned to the ground during three hours of anti-British rioting. The last person to lecture at the institute, which contained 'one of the finest British libraries in the Middle East', was the philhellenic wartime resistance hero Patrick Leigh Fermour. Soon afterwards Durrell began to carry a pistol, a precaution that he found to be both 'a consolation and an obscenity'.[24]

Soon after the burning of the British Institute 16 prisoners detained in Kyrenia Castle, all of them suspected EOKA members, escaped, knotting their bed sheets together and sliding down to 'the slab', a large flat rock immediately beneath the castle, where members of the exclusively British Harbour Club spent their afternoons sunbathing under armed guard. Several senior figures in the EOKA hierarchy were once again at large, but the event is most significant for the insight it gives into the complacency of British society at the time. As Tremayne recalls, 'the British ex-patriate people were lying there, sipping their mint juleps and they saw these chaps walking past right under their very noses, "Good afternoon," "Good afternoon," and off they went'.[25]

Events such as this served, in the minds of the newer, younger arrivals on the island, to underline the distance they felt existed between them and many of

The British Institute in Metaxas Square, Nicosia goes up in flames, 17 September 1955.

[© *The Collection of the Leventis Municipal Museum of Nicosia.*]

the established British residents. As former police officer Tony Willis recalled, 'one got the feeling, that they just weren't engaged, they did things like referring to Cypriots as "the Cyps" in front of them'.[26]

Public confidence in the administration in the aftermath of the Kyrenia Castle escape and the destruction of the British Institute reached an all-time low and the following month, in October 1955, Governor Armitage was recalled by the Colonial Office. The confusion that characterised his governorship was illustrated by an incident at a military parade to mark the Queen's Birthday, when Armitage omitted to call the correct number of cheers, prompting complaints in *The Times* that the governor had called for only 'two hips instead of three'.[27] Well meaning but hesitant and indecisive, Armitage had been hopelessly out of his depth. In fairness, at the time he arrived in Cyprus the future of the colony had been largely taken out of the hands of its governor. His tentative efforts to begin a dialogue with Makarios were blocked by the Colonial Office, while his attempts to meet all but a few closely vetted Cypriots were blocked by his own administration. Armitage wrote revealingly to his parents, 'everyone is most friendly and hospitable. That is those with whom we are on calling terms. There are the nationalists and the communists, those I never meet.'[28]

Even the ritual of village inspections was abandoned in case 'the youths might make demonstrations which would be embarrassing'.[29] The popular displays of 'Myrtle branches on the road, union jacks, triumphal arches', choreographed by villagers hoping for a new school or irrigation system and viewed by generations of administrators as genuine support for British rule, had at last come to an end.

The next governor was a serving soldier – the first to rule the colony since Robert Biddulph in 1879. Field Marshall Sir John Harding, who arrived on 3 October 1955, had been on the point of retiring as chief of the Imperial General Staff when he was asked by the prime minister to assume the governorship of Cyprus. Eden believed that the field marshal's experience suppressing anti-colonial insurrections in Malaya and Kenya could be usefully applied to the colony.

Harding's appointment marked a radical shift of gear in Britain's response to the crisis. His priority was to crack down hard on the insurrection, using military measures to restore order. At the same time he was instructed to initiate direct negotiations with Makarios, while also pursuing a 'hearts and minds' campaign to convince Cypriots of the merits of British rule. Neither the new governor nor the British prime minister appeared to see anything contradictory in a policy which involved threatening Cypriots while simultaneously attempting to convince them of Britain's goodwill. It was a paradox that reflected a fundamental failure to grasp the extent of EOKA's tacit support. The aim of union with Greece, if not the violent methods being employed to achieve it, had deep-rooted and widespread support. But in the colonial mind, the 'hotheads and trouble makers' responsible for the violence were an aberration, existing outside the parameters of 'normal' Cypriot society and unrepresentative of the silent majority.

Harding's greatest success as governor, from a British perspective, was his restructuring of the security and intelligence services. On arrival he found 'the government organisation totally inadequate' and was shocked to learn that the ciphers used for encoding official despatches to London were kept in a safe in the Government House lavatory.[30] He separated the administration of civil affairs, headed by the deputy governor, George Sinclair, from responsibility for security, which he placed in the hands of the chief of staff, Brigadier George Baker. Over the next two years he coordinated the operations of the police and armed forces, ensuring that they shared intelligence, and recruited police officers from other colonial and domestic forces.

The day after his arrival the new governor began face-to-face negotiations with Makarios, 'one of the most protracted and complex exchanges in the history of British decolonisation after the Second World War'.[31] The proposal that Harding placed before Makarios in the card room of the Ledra Palace Hotel essentially substituted the government's earlier statement that Cyprus could 'never' expect full independence, with one arguing that self-determination was not yet realistic. This was accompanied by an undertaking that the island's future could be reviewed once Cypriots had demonstrated their ability to govern themselves in a way that would safeguard 'the interests of all sections of the community'.[32] The semantics of the offer were argued over closely, obliging Harding to seek clarification from London, from where he was occasionally brought to heel for threatening to concede too much.

The two men appear, initially at least, to have liked one another and Makarios subsequently described Harding as the most intelligent and straightforward of governors. But the gulf between the career soldier and the Orthodox prelate was immense. Historian Robert Holland has articulated the differences between them succinctly. He described their attitudes to the proposals previously put forward by Macmillan at the London Conference, with 'Harding treating Macmillan's original text as if it possessed the admirable clarity of an Army field manual, and the Archbishop approaching it like some dubious production of an early schismatic, requiring careful and highly sceptical exegesis'.[33] Subsequent meetings took place in considerable discomfort at the home of the Anglican archdeacon in Nicosia, seated on straight-backed rush-bottomed chairs which tilted forward 'forcing you to sit more and more on the hard front edge of the seat and changing discomfort into torture'.[34]

Just weeks into his new post, while he was still adjusting to the unfamiliar new role of political negotiator, Harding was confronted with his first serious challenge to the maintenance of order. On 24 October 1955, the trial began of a 22-year-old civil servant from the government tax office, Michaelis Karaolis. He was accused of murdering Constable Herodotus Poullis, the policeman shot at point-blank range on the eve of the Tripartite Conference in London. The case against the defendant, who came from a respectable family and had been a prefect at the English School, hinged on the fact that the assassin had escaped on Karaolis's bicycle, later discarding it when he in turn was accosted by a passer-by. Karaolis had subsequently been detained carrying a compromising letter suggesting links to EOKA. After four days Karaolis was found guilty and sentenced to be hanged, the first EOKA gunman to face the death penalty. When his appeal to the Supreme Court failed riots broke out in Athens and Nicosia, where 'hundreds of school children ... were dispersed by troops using batons and tear gas, their task hampered by screaming girls'.[35]

For the colonists, this was the first time that the malign and shadowy forces threatening their lives and their world order had acquired a face. It was one that shocked the expatriate community, partly because of Karaolis's youth, but largely because of his otherwise blameless life. The administrative

Governor John Harding and Archbishop Makarios prepare to embark on their third round of negotiations at the home of the Anglican Archdeacon. The colony's Administrative Secretary, John Reddaway (with moustache), stands behind Harding, 1956.

[© *Cyprus Press and Information Office.*]

machinery that maintained British rule in Cyprus depended on thousands of respectable Cypriots like Karaolis playing their part. The prospect that other seemingly unremarkable civil servants could also be harbouring secret murderous thoughts against the British was profoundly disturbing. No corner of the administration could confidently be considered immune from possible infiltration. But for the British, by far the most alarming aspect of the Karaolis case was that the assassin had graduated not from Nicosia Gymnasium, or the Samuel School, or any of the other nationalist schools that supported union with Greece, but from the one institution intended to promote loyalty to empire and co-operation with the administration, the English School.

Since its foundation at the beginning of the century, the English School's intake had evolved from its original Levantine mix of pupils from eclectic ethnic backgrounds into a more homogeneous community of Greek and Turkish

Cypriots, with a few Armenians. During the final five years of British rule both staff and pupils occupied a unique and unenviable position, negotiating their way on a daily basis through the conflicted loyalties, compromises and individual acts of bravery and betrayal that characterised the period. The school's headmaster at this time, Paul Griffin, was, like Tremayne, one of a very small number of British people who lived alongside Cypriots during the rebellion. As headmaster of a boarding school, Griffin was in loco parentis to the 90 boys in his care and also acted as housemaster to 25 pupils whose boarding house was attached to the headmaster's own.

Griffin believed that the school's function was to 'educate the first generation of post-colonial administrators, statesmen and politicians to take over from us and carry things on without too much corruption'.[36] His account of living amongst idealistic teenagers caught up in a culture of violent patriotism beyond their control captures the schizophrenic atmosphere that pervaded the island during this time.

Today, Griffin looks back on both his staff and his 'lovely community of boys' with affection, adding 'we got on very well really'. The headmaster ate lunch with his pupils every day, he and his family slept in rooms adjoining their dormitories and relied on boarders from his house to baby-sit for his children in the evening. But Griffin's relationship with his 'boys' was complicated and functioned at several different levels. He and his English staff, while acting as surrogate parents, were also representatives of the hated colonial regime. Several pupils, active supporters of EOKA, sent death threats to the headmaster and certain members of staff, and two British teachers at the school were subsequently murdered. When one of them, a popular man called John Bray, who had been shot in the stomach in Ledra Street, appeared to be making a partial recovery, his pupils, 'anxious to know he would be all right', visited his bedside regularly. But the presence of so many teenage Cypriot boys in the hospital alarmed other British patients on the ward who complained about their visits. Home-made bombs sometimes appeared in classrooms, and there were numerous cases of arson. The most successful attack involved the ignition of petrol-filled bottles tied to the floor joists beneath the assembly hall. As a result, Griffin had to 'take assembly on the edge of a great black smoking pit with the smell of burnt stuff'.

For Griffin, the maintenance of a normal routine in itself became a part of the boys' education: 'After all, they were only boys, they were in my care and I had to show them how to behave'. Despite the fact that the school and its grounds were now surrounded by a mile of barbed wire, patrolled by armed guards, the governor continued to present the prizes at big sporting occasions and at football matches, both of which were considered 'far too serious for there to be disturbances'.[37]

But such events provided rare moments of light relief for the governor whose priority was responding to a growing number of 'disturbances'. On 26 November 1955 Harding declared a state of emergency. The government could now impose collective punishments on entire villages, deport senior clerics found guilty of sedition and even horse-whip offenders under 18, while convictions for carrying firearms, shooting and throwing bombs carried the death penalty, even if no loss of life ensued.

On the day that the new measures were announced, moments before Harding was due to arrive at the Ledra Palace Hotel for the annual Caledonian Society Ball, a bomb exploded in the ballroom. No one was killed and a few guests sustained only minor injuries, but the symbolic significance of the incident was immense: the rebels had brought violence and terror into the heart of polite British society. Like their predecessors 80 years before, the colonists believed that their public behaviour had an impact on the indigenous community and consequently placed great importance on setting an example. Conspicuously carrying on as normal became an important element in their 'coping strategies', both individually and at a broader societal level. The Caledonian Ball bomb represented not only a physical assault on those present in the Ledra Palace at the time, but also a psychological attack on some of the cultural assumptions that underpinned the colonial way of life.

Horse races at the Nicosia track might carry on as normal ('the only thing that was completely above politics, you felt perfectly safe'[38]), while the die-hard residents of Kyrenia continued to fly the Union flag among the eucalyptus trees, but the effort involved in maintaining a façade of normality against a backdrop of random, unpredictable violence produced 'a tension in the air that never wholly vanishes'.[39]

Admit it or not, Britons had to adapt their daily routines to cope with the changing atmosphere. Harding now travelled about the capital – to the Secretariat, fetes and school prize-givings – by helicopter, its whirring rotor blades providing a background sound to daily life in the capital. Other British residents were advised to vary their routes to and from work and avoid the bazaars. The summer ritual of evening drinks taken outside also had to be modified, it was 'against regulations to sit on verandahs with lights on',[40] so gin and tonics were now consumed in darkness.

For the 12,000 British servicemen stationed on the island,[41] off-duty recreation was particularly fraught. Soldiers and airmen had to remain armed and in full uniform at all times and could go out only in groups of four. As one of the few single British women working at RAF Nicosia, 19-year-old Sandra Oakey was in demand for dates and dances. These could be complicated occasions, involving 'four men in uniform with Sten guns. We were not allowed to sit with

Governor Harding, on one of his rare trips outside Nicosia, opens a new road at the village of Yerovassa, 1955.

[© *Cyprus Press and Information Office.*]

our backs to the windows or doors, and we had to sit with the wall behind us at all times to see the entrances'.

Oakey frequently went dancing at the Outspan Club, a favourite amongst service personnel. Dressed in 'big bouffant skirts with several stiff petticoats underneath and my pointy stilettos',[42] she regularly picked her way along Onasagoras Street, parallel to the notorious Ledra Street (or 'murder mile' as it became known to the British), accompanied by her four armed escorts.

But for many Britons, Ledra and Onasagoras Streets – if not the whole of the old city – were now effectively off limits. Will Harrap, whose father worked in the Land Survey Department, remembered the intense disappointment he felt as a child on learning that it was now too dangerous to visit Mavros, the capital's only toy shop, in Ledra Street. British children experienced the emergency differently from their parents. Matthew Parris and his younger brother

Roger developed 'a terror of tin cans', after being firmly told not to kick them in case they contained bombs. Seven-year-old Parris's feelings about bombs were mixed. Although they were frightening, 'they were also greatly looked forward to because they meant school would be closed. So we would listen to the radio, hoping desperately for bombs.'

Parris was a day pupil at Sessions School, a small establishment close to Nicosia Prison. When the headmistress, Margaret Sessions, began, like Griffin, to receive death threats, she was assigned a bodyguard, Major Walker Brash. The major came to school accompanied by his bloodhound and was employed on quiet days teaching current affairs to the older pupils. The headmistress, remembered as 'a great disciplinarian, rather stern, with arms that were very fat at the top', arrived each morning in a Morris Traveller, accompanied by her six miniature dachshunds dressed, according to the season, in winter and summer 'uniforms'. At the end of the school day the entourage would climb back into the tiny Morris Traveller, 'with Walker Brash and the bloodhound squeezed in next to her, his knees up around his ears and his shoulders squashed together so you could see the strap of his holster showing above the collar of his jacket, and they would set off'.[43]

For Parris and some of the expatriate boarders at Sessions School, holidays were often spent at 'The Children's Hotel' in the village of Myrtou, near Kyrenia. The 'hotel', which boasted an irrigation tank that doubled as a swimming pool for the children, and 'a windmill and a nice leafy garden', was run by a retired judge, George Griffith Williams, and his daughters. The majority of children had parents who worked in more distant colonies, too far away to be visited during the shorter school holidays. It was a short-lived venture – its fortunes linked to the empire which employed the parents of many of its young guests – but was remembered by those who stayed there as 'pure fun – it was always focussed entirely on children'.[44]

For the adults of Cyprus – Cypriots and British alike – the violence now began to have a significant impact on daily life. In early December 1955, a Greek Cypriot policeman and a Royal Marine were killed and seven soldiers injured in an ambush. Bombs exploded at the offices of Cyprus Airways and the district commissioner of Nicosia. In the village of Lefkoniko, Agricultural Department offices were destroyed and schoolchildren set fire to the village post office. Harding imposed the first collective punishment, adopting a pattern that was subsequently followed in villages across the island. A fine was imposed to meet the cost of making good the damage, and the villagers were placed under a blanket curfew until the penalty was paid.

Ten days later, 130 members of the communist party, AKEL, including the mayors of Limassol and Larnaca, were arrested and sent to the Pyla detention camp. AKEL and its youth wing, AON, had been proscribed under the emergency regulations, on the questionable grounds that they had been at the forefront of developing 'the whole paraphernalia of "struggle" against established authority – the mass demonstrations, political strikes, daubing of slogans, seditious propaganda and monster petitions'.[45]

The arrests constituted a tactical blunder on the part of the new governor, fresh from Malaya where communists had been the primary enemy and they represented a serious misreading of the complex Cypriot political landscape. The hostility of the left to the nationalists' policy of armed struggle had meant that although AKEL was also opposed to the perpetuation of colonial rule, areas of left-wing support had seen significantly less violence and unrest. As Holland points out, it is ironic that the first occupants of the hated British detention camps that featured so largely during the rebellion were men who were deeply opposed to EOKA.

Nonetheless, as long as Harding and Makarios kept talking, the colonists continued to believe the fear and violence would soon subside and that with some smart phrases and the flourish of a pen normal life would resume. On 26 February Colonial Secretary Alan Lennox-Boyd flew to Cyprus to participate in the discussions.

Several political and strategic factors played a part in the subsequent collapse of the Harding-Makarios dialogue, but underpinning them all was the incremental erosion of trust between the two parties. At the time he met Lennox-Boyd, Makarios had been on the point of provisionally accepting a draft text on self-determination, but the British contingent, presumably influenced by Harding, lacked confidence in the ethnarch and doubted his intentions. The archbishop's equivocal approach to negotiations, his technique of gradually chipping away at whatever was offered in an attempt to extract further concessions one by one, was the antithesis of Harding's direct military approach.

The tipping point came over the question of the paramilitaries. The British delegation, which erroneously believed that Makarios exerted direct and complete control over EOKA, requested that as a gesture of good faith, the archbishop should publicly denounce violence. A repudiation of EOKA would have been politically disastrous for Makarios, who was struggling to negotiate a path through a fractious and divided Greek Cypriot public opinion. At the same time, at the behest of Grivas, Makarios demanded an amnesty for all EOKA activists, including Karaolis. Harding's response was that of the conscientious soldier, with a duty to his men. He stated unequivocally that 'he could not continue to expose police and troops to ruthless attempts by dastardly terrorists who knew sooner or later they would escape [sic] for their crimes'.[46] At one level, despite the complicated constitutional formulae being discussed, the discussions broke down because of the responsibility felt by two officers towards their subordinates.

In Harding's view anything less than Makarios's full acceptance of the principles behind the terms on offer meant that further negotiations were no longer possible. This in turn meant that the archbishop was now perceived as an obstacle to a settlement. His hyperbolic public statements, while they may have been consistent with the rhetoric of public life in the Middle East, were, from a British perspective, considered to inflame public opinion and incite his supporters to violence. As a result, 10 days after the collapse of the Harding-Makarios talks the archbishop was deported and unceremoniously flown to the Seychelles by military transport plane. He was to remain there for the next 13 months.

The removal of Archbishop Makarios downgraded the search for a negotiated solution and triggered a new and more violent phase of the revolt. In one of the more bizarre coincidences of the rebellion, 9 March 1956, the date of the archbishop's departure, saw the appointment of Lawrence Durrell, that most iconoclastic and anti-establishment of British writers, as government censor.

The boys at the English School immediately responded to news of the deportation by refusing to sing hymns at morning assembly, prompting 'a stand-off with the headmaster that continued for several weeks'.[47] For its British teachers the school became a tense and anxious place. As Griffin recalled, 'sometimes the normal chatter and noise dropped and there was almost complete silence in the yard as sullen-faced boys waited for signals that somehow never came. As the bell rang each time, the boys moved reluctantly back to Maths and Geography, and [if I found that] no gunmen had invaded my office, my stomach would feel suddenly empty and my head swim with relief.'[48]

In fact, the decision to deport Archbishop Makarios had been influenced by developments elsewhere in the Middle East where British interests had taken a battering. The national government of President Nasser in Egypt had grown increasingly hostile to the concept of the Baghdad Pact, while in Jordan anti-British riots had culminated in the sudden expulsion of Glubb Pasha, the respected British head of the Arab Legion, the previous week. As a result, the prime minister came under increasing pressure from within the Conservative Party to demonstrate some muscle flexing that would repair British prestige. Eden hoped that the swift deportation of Makarios would both pacify the empire loyalists within his own party and increase his standing in the Middle East as a man of action.

For Eden and Macmillan, who both viewed Cyprus from the perspective of broader regional developments, the deportation had a certain logic to it. But from the point of view of negotiating an end to the violence in Cyprus it was disastrous. The removal of Makarios brought the process of negotiation to an end. There was no one else for Harding to talk to who could claim, with the same credibility, to represent the interests of the majority of Greek Cypriots. The assumption that by removing Makarios from Cyprus support for *enosis* would subside and the insurrection somehow run out of steam was based on the persistent and unshakable belief expressed by generations of colonial administrators on the island that most Cypriots remained basically content under British rule and were merely being lead astray by the political posturing of irresponsible and self-interested leaders.

The armed conflict intensified after the archbishop's departure. On 14 March an English police constable was murdered. A week later a bomb was discovered in Government House, hidden beneath Harding's bed. It had been placed there the previous afternoon by a manservant who had cycled to work with the explosives strapped to his stomach and concealed them under Harding's mattress, while he pretended to clean the floor of the governor's bedroom with a carpet sweeper. The temperature-sensitive mechanism had failed because of Harding's habit of sleeping with the window open.

The Greek Cypriot staff at Government House were all dismissed. The colonists' sense of being under siege increased, many recoiling from contact with Cypriots and retreating further into their secure armed compounds. Clare Harrap lived at number 48, 'Z' Compound, close to Government House. Surrounded by barbed wire and with a military checkpoint at the entrance, Harrap, like other residents, felt that 'once we were in the compound we were safe'. Her young sons, John and Will, had amassed a sizeable collection of cap badges from the soldiers at the gate, but, as Will remembered, once the emergency had been declared 'the mood changed, the soldiers didn't entertain colonial kids any more'.[49]

In practice it was impossible for the administration to seal itself off from contact with Cypriots. It was, numerically at least, a Cypriot organisation. By 1955 the British administration in Cyprus employed around 6,000 Cypriots and little more than 100 Britons.[50] Government buildings were dispersed at different sites around the capital, and EOKA infiltration of government departments as well as the security and the intelligence services was inevitable.

The few Britons who had previously attempted to maintain social contact with Cypriots now found this increasingly difficult. Cypriots who socialised with Britons exposed themselves to accusations of collaboration, a charge which placed them in considerable danger. Peter Twelvetrees, stationed at Kyrenia Castle, remembers that 'the people were frightened to talk to us so the feeling was a bit uneasy, you couldn't get friendly with anybody'.[51] Nonetheless a few servicemen adopted the dangerous strategy of attempting to date Cypriot girls – but with an ulterior motive. Sandra Oakey remembers 'any boy who went out with a Cypriot girl would be interviewed by an officer, but if he refused to stop seeing her he would be posted elsewhere. So I knew of some boys who took up with Cypriot girls deliberately, just to get away from Cyprus'.[52] The British visitor returning to Cyprus hoping to look up old friends, meanwhile, was advised that 'if they are Greek-Cypriots it is kinder not to do so, for he would be putting them in a difficult position'.[53] Paul Griffin described a climate in which 'a friend you had known in better days could suddenly turn his back, either in fear of having the acquaintance known, or in a real conviction of treachery and betrayal. In any relationship between Greek and British, only half the mind trusted'.[54] The new crudely polarised society that emerged after Makarios's deportation left little room for subtlety or nuances. All Britons were now regarded, however reluctantly, as synonymous with the exertion of colonial power.

The violence continued. In April 1956, 10 Greek Cypriot civilians and two Greek Cypriot policemen were killed, along with three British soldiers and the first British civilian. On 14 April Karaolis's appeal against his death sentence was rejected by the Privy Council. The final decision on whether or not to grant clemency now passed to Harding, a strong advocate of the principle of capital punishment. The British government was inundated with appeals to commute the sentence. Hanging Karaolis, the British ambassador to Athens feared, would inflict even greater damage on Anglo-Greek relations than the deportation of Makarios.

The next morning, when Paul Griffin led prayers for the governor and his difficult decision at the English School's morning assembly, his Greek Cypriot pupils threatened to walk out. 'The Greek boys took it that I was praying for the hanging to go ahead', he said, 'when in fact I was terrified of them hanging him'.[55] As the date fixed for the execution came closer the atmosphere grew tense. The Royal Navy was placed on standby in the Mediterranean, ready to evacuate British nationals in Greece. Violent demonstrations in Athens resulted in nine deaths and the United States consulate in Salonika was burned down. In Nicosia, telephone lines were cut off by the government and vehicular traffic banned. Outside the prison Greek Cypriots mounted a vigil. At night the 20 or so British families who lived in the gated compound adjacent to the prison lay awake, listening to the continuous chants of 'e-e-enosis' accompanied by the sound of prisoners banging their tin mugs on the wall.

Michaelis Karaolis was eventually hanged on the morning of 10 May 1956. Executed with him was Andreas Demetriou who had killed no one but had been convicted of carrying and discharging a firearm just two days after the Emergency Regulations came into effect. Today, the statue of Karaolis which stands opposite the English School's main entrance is a tangible reminder of the importance accorded to his death in the public narrative of Cypriot independence. The deaths of Cook and Bray, the two British men who taught at the school and also died as a result of the EOKA rebellion, are not commemorated.

The May 1956 hangings, like the deportation of Makarios, marked another milestone in Anglo-Cypriot relations, one at which, as Holland points out, 'the iron of ill usage' entered the soul of many Greek Cypriots. Grivas retaliated by executing two British soldiers that EOKA had taken as hostages. Six more British soldiers were killed during May 1956, together with three Greek Cypriots and one British civilian. After a bomb was thrown at security forces near Phaneromeni Church, a bastion of nationalism in the centre of the old city, Greek Cypriot restaurants and cinemas were closed for a week and all vehicular traffic banned in the city after darkness. Collective punishments, curfews and unnecessarily destructive searches alienated the previously moderate and apolitical and boosted support for the nationalists. Corporal I.W.G. Martin, a Greek interpreter attached to the Royal Ulster Rifles (RUR), watched men from his regiment searching a bookshop in Famagusta and 'smashing up every single thing in the place: books, cups and plates, chair, tables, furniture, mirrors etc... with everyone except me thoroughly enjoying themselves, especially the RUR officers of course'.[56]

The Gordon Highlanders also had a reputation for handling civilians roughly during house-to-house searches. The destructiveness of one such search in the old city of Nicosia was tempered only when soldiers caught sight of a calendar sent by family friends in Edinburgh which depicted kilted folk dancers besides Loch Lomond. Early attempts to impose the other hated mass punishment – the curfew – on the capital were more hit and miss. At one point the government announced that when an air-raid siren sounded everyone within the city walls should stand still. When this policy failed it was replaced with a directive that the siren should be the cue for everyone to return home immediately, with the result that 'everyone who owned a car in Nicosia went and jumped in it and drove somewhere else', so that the centre of the Mediaeval walled city became 'like the roads round Twickenham after an international'.[57]

By May 1956, with his reforms of the police and security services complete, Harding was at last ready to launch the first of a series of co-ordinated military offensives against Grivas. At this stage in the conflict the EOKA leader was estimated to have seven groups of fighters in the mountains, 47 urban cells and 75 part-time village bands armed with shotguns, but no more than 200 active fighting men. The first action, 'Operation Pepperpot' in the mountain range above Kyrenia, led to the capture of several senior EOKA fighters after six men were found concealed beneath the floor of a farm house. It was soon followed by 'Operation Lucky Alphonse', which targeted the Troodos Mountains where Grivas was thought to have his headquarters.

As the second of these operations began Harding travelled to England for discussions on a new constitution for the island being formulated by the law lord, Lord Radcliffe, one in which self government would be placed 'under consideration' by NATO after a period of 10 violence-free years. As yet another 'partisan and ill-informed'[58] House of Commons debate on Cyprus started (they occurred during 1956 almost on a monthly basis), Harding waited anxiously for news that Alphonse had indeed got lucky and that his men had bagged the colonel.

The mountain operations, backed by helicopters, severely disrupted the guerilla cells and hampered their operational efficiency. British troops captured 17 EOKA fighters and seized large quantities of ammunition. The campaign had forced Grivas out of the field – driving him into hiding in a basement in Limassol, from where he would be forced to control his rebellion at arms length. But it did not succeed in catching him.

During the course of 'Operation Lucky Alphonse' British forces suffered their largest single loss of life of the entire campaign; 20 men of the Gordon Highlanders died in a single day in June 1956, not as a result of bombs or bullets, but because of a vast forest fire, its impact compounded by the paralysing suspicion and misunderstanding which now permeated virtually all Anglo-Cypriot relationships.

The experiences of the thousands of British troops garrisoned in Cyprus during this period merit a study of their own. The way the rebellion is remembered by both British and Cypriot veterans of the conflict is complex and even today remains emotionally charged. For British troops in Cyprus, many of them young national servicemen just out of school, life could be frightening and dangerous. They faced determined EOKA fighters, who had resolved to end British rule on the island by whatever means necessary, and several saw their friends killed or maimed. In the context of a book which attempts merely a broad sweep across 82 years of British colonial rule, it is not possible to do justice to their stories,[59] but some incidents, such as the 'Alphonse' fire, have been highlighted because of the broader light they shed on Anglo-Cypriot relationships during this period.

The causes of the fire of June 1956 are still fiercely contested. EOKA supporters claim it was started by British troops in a desperate attempt to force Grivas from his hiding place. British military sources alleged it was caused by guerillas attempting to divert attention from their leader's headquarters. Most likely it was an accident, for it would have taken little more than a discarded cigarette to ignite the tinder-dry undergrowth of the Troodos Forest in the height of summer.

When the fire began soldiers declined offers of local Cypriot help, fearing they might be lured into a trap. The delay allowed the fire to grow and gain ground. The majority of casualties occurred when a convoy of Bedford trucks, jammed on a single-track mountain road by an oncoming reconnaissance vehicle, exploded as the flames reached their petrol tanks. Strong winds then propelled the fire uphill so fast that it was impossible to outrun it. Instead, Cypriot forest guards, experienced in fire-fighting and familiar with the terrain, tried to convince survivors of the blast that their best chance lay in running through occasional gaps in the flames onto burned ground left in the fire's wake. The soldiers, mistrustful of the foresters' motives, refused, despite the fact that 'the foresters urged and pleaded, and even laid hold of some of them and tried to drag them through; but it was no good'.[60] In desperation one well-built forestry officer resorted to picking a young soldier up and physically carrying him through the flames to safety.

Ten days later Penelope Tremayne was at the scene of a second forest fire in the same region and witnessed the reactions of villagers after a requested British military contingent failed to materialise. 'Such concentrated bitterness against the English I had never felt before,' she wrote, 'nor ever did again … It seemed to them all that the British were not taking action because they wanted the Cypriots to burn, or else because of the fearful casualties they had had in the fire 10 days ago, they were afraid to try their hands again.'[61] The gulf separating Britons from Cypriots – even when confronting a common adversary together – had now become virtually unbridgeable.

Wreaths for the funerals of the Gordon Highlanders and other Britons killed during this time were made up by Eirwen Harbottle, at her flower farm in the Kyrenia Pass. Her family's floral export business had declined since the emergency when the packing around the flowers began to be routinely ripped open during security checks. Instead, as Harbottle remembers, 'a lot of business now came from making wreaths for dead British soldiers and that absolutely crucified me. Sometimes we had to make up to 20 wreaths, and we would be up most of the night making them and you knew it was going to be a hot day and the flowers would be dead a few hours later. It all just seemed so pointless.'[62]

While the British hunted the guerillas in the mountains the random urban killings of civilians continued. A Maltese shopkeeper was shot in Ledra Street on his way to meet his fiancée, soon after a British customs official and his pregnant wife were gunned down while on a picnic near Kyrenia. In the climate of fear and constant anxiety induced by these arbitrary murders many Britons came to believe that particular Greek Cypriots were instrumental in protecting them. How many of these convictions were based on fact, at a time when targeting was often haphazard and identity frequently mistaken, would be impossible to ascertain, but when relationships between Britons and Cypriots had become profoundly distorted, the notion of a 'guardian Cypriot', interceding on behalf of a particular family, provided a degree of reassurance that enabled many Britons to continue with their lives.

Thus Eirwen Harbottle remembers that her husband's position as a judge at Nicosia's races meant 'we were protected by Nicos Sampson, and I was vouched for by someone at Cyprus Broadcasting'. In the same way, Jean Meikle was convinced that her family was protected by a member of the Gabrielides family, a man she knew only as 'Gabs', one of the first Cypriots to be admitted to the elite Nicosia Club, who was subsequently believed to have sheltered Grivas: 'I swear that the person who kept my father alive, my brother and my husband was old

Gabs'. Paul Griffin, who 'could have been shot at any time', also believed that 'something was protecting me a bit. Some of the staff perhaps were responsible'. Such strategies were a way of retaining faith in relationships that would otherwise have been eroded by the environment of suspicion and the new unpredictable order of things in which giggling schoolchildren placed bombs in quiet suburban streets, patients feigned sickness in order to assassinate their doctors, and any civilian could turn out to be a gunman or a grenade thrower.

While the violence drove a wedge between the British and Greek Cypriots, the uprising also resulted in significant changes in the balance of power between the colonists and their Turkish Cypriot subjects. Grivas had, at the outset of the campaign, explicitly forbidden the targeting of Turkish Cypriots. But as increasing numbers were recruited into the police, to fill the gap left by their intimidated Greek Cypriot colleagues, they inevitably bore the brunt of attacks on the civilian security services. The antipathy this generated in turn fuelled further – specifically inter-communal – violence. Many Turkish Cypriots believed that the British authorities were incapable of providing adequate protection against attacks by EOKA and established their own paramilitary organisation, *Volkan*. A succession of inter-communal killings in the spring of 1956 led to the erection of the first barrier – a barbed wire fence with a series of gates that could be closed whenever trouble broke out – between the Greek and Turkish Cypriot sectors of Nicosia.

As nerves remained on edge throughout the long hot summer of 1956, six more EOKA men were hanged for terrorist offences in August and September. Grivas responded by ordering the killing of 9 civilians and 10 members of the security forces. In response, a total curfew was imposed on the Greek areas of the old city, affecting an estimated 12,000 people. Short respites intended for people to find food led to more violence as residents struggled frantically to find bread. The curfew lasted eight days, by the end many residents, unable to work, had run out of money and British soldiers were obliged to distribute food to the needy.

EOKA's attacks on Cypriot 'traitors' intensified: people were assassinated in coffee houses, barbers' shops and, in one case, at a wedding – public places where the message of the killings would have maximum impact. One incident involving British troops which generated particular outrage occurred at the village of Lefkoniko. On 23 October two British soldiers were disembowelled and four seriously wounded as they drank from a booby-trapped water fountain after a football match. The signal to trigger the explosion had been given by two village girls waving their handkerchiefs towards accomplices nearby. Enraged soldiers rampaged through the village. Claims for damages and complaints of military brutality by the villagers were subsequently found by a government inquiry to be unsubstantiated.

Despite atrocities such as these, Harding's efforts to restructure the security services gradually began to bear fruit. The mountain sweeps continued and several EOKA cells were effectively disabled. Then, to Harding's intense frustration, just as he believed his troops were on the point of flushing out Grivas, they were 'whisked away'[63] and placed on standby for action in Egypt.

The previous July Nasser had shocked the world by suddenly announcing the nationalisation of the Anglo-French Suez Canal Company. In response, Britain and France conspired with Israel to concoct a scheme that would give the British a pretext to launch an attack in Egypt to protect the canal. On 31 October, bombers took off from RAF Akrotiri to attack Egyptian airfields near Cairo and former British bases in the Canal Zone.

Even at this late stage in colonial rule British policy on Cyprus was, as ever, subordinated to the accommodation of imperial interests elsewhere. It was Britain's defeat at Suez that prompted the Conservative government to slowly start reassessing whether the retention of full sovereignty over the island best met its changing military needs. But it was not a straightforward process. The Suez crisis fundamentally affected the balance of power not only in the Middle East, but equally importantly within Britain's governing Conservative party as well. The loss of prestige that followed left the government increasingly sensitive to accusations from its own right wing that it was merely presiding over the slow decline of the Empire. In the short term these internal pressures made the government disinclined to make concessions over Cyprus and less capable of responding to the situation imaginatively. The experience of Suez had also led Eden to reassess Turkey's strategic importance. Turkey was now the only power in the region unaffected by pan-Arab nationalism, any interest it declared in Cyprus could not, therefore, be ignored. All these factors played a part in determining the particular course that Cyprus was to follow towards independence.

The Suez debacle also provided EOKA with an unexpected bonus in the form of access to increased supplies of arms that now passed through the island. A few changed hands for money, but many more were acquired by theft or carelessness. One good source was the Dome Hotel in Kyrenia, used for stopovers by air crews flying troop carriers to the island. Several crews would stay there at a time, 'all with weapons and they would all go down to dinner forgetting them and they would disappear. EOKA snaffled them'.[64] Regular soldiers who lost their weapons were court-martialled, a fate that some sought to avoid by discretely paying a Turkish Cypriot 'entrepreneur' who could provide replacements.[65]

Meanwhile, Lord Radcliffe's constitution, laboriously drafted over the summer, was about to be released. Although the proposals allowed for a directly elected legislature in which the Greek Cypriots were guaranteed a majority,

Britain would retain control of defence, internal security and foreign affairs and consider self-government only after an interim period of 10 years. It was too little too late, an inadequate response both to the political currents that were buffeting the island and the highly charged emotional climate. 'Not fit for Zulus' was the disdainful Greek Cypriot response.

It was in the context of presenting the proposals, unremarkable in themselves, that the spectre of the island's partition was conjured up for the first time in official discourse, primarily as a tactical manoeuvre to frighten Greek Cypriots and compel them 'to reconsider the merits of the status quo'.[66] It was a prospect that was to be seized and clung to tenaciously by the Turkish government. When the colonial secretary, Alan Lennox-Boyd, met Adnan Menderes, the Turkish prime minister, he was advised to jettison the constitution altogether and press ahead with immediate partition. The Turkish leader added cheerily 'we have done this sort of thing before and you will see that it is not as bad as all that'.[67]

The Radcliffe Report was also delivered, in great secrecy, to Makarios in the Seychelles, its couriers travelling incognito to save the British government the embarrassment of being seen to consult the archbishop. Despite these elaborate charades the folly of exiling the one man capable of coaxing the vast bulk of Greek Cypriot public opinion towards a compromise was becoming increasingly evident. The problem was how to bring Makarios back without loss of face.

While the cabinet pondered over how to end Makarios's exile, January 1957 witnessed separate bursts of inter-communal rioting in Nicosia and Famagusta, which in turn prompted further assaults on property and the imposition of curfews. In the same month, Markos Drakos, one of EOKA's most experienced fighters, was shot dead in the Troodos Mountains in an unsuccessful attack on a military patrol. In March, soldiers of the Duke of Wellington's regiment surrounded the mountain hideout of Grigoris Afxentiou, Grivas's right-hand-man. Afxentiou fought bravely and was killed only after a protracted stand-off that lasted many hours.

Nine days later, 18-year-old Evagoras Pallikarides was executed after being found guilty of carrying firearms, an offence for which the death sentence was now mandatory. The execution of a teenage boy for carrying a gun provoked substantial international protest. Hours after the execution Grivas, who had been expected to authorise immediate reprisals, surprised the governor and his security advisers by declaring a truce. The announcement was probably made because the colonel needed time to regroup. EOKA had taken some strong blows as a result of Harding's security operation, the mountain gangs were decimated and several leading members of the movement in Nicosia had been arrested. But Grivas nevertheless managed to seize the political initiative, announcing that the truce was intended to create conditions for the return of Makarios to Cyprus.

Finally, in the face of strong opposition from the right of the party, Macmillan, who had replaced Eden as prime minister after Suez, decided to release Makarios at the end of March. The news reached Cyprus in the evening of 28 March 1957, when Metaxas Square and the area in front of the Archbishopric in Nicosia filled with an ecstatic crowd. Church bells rang out continuously, blue and white flags were draped over balconies as people celebrated what they believed to be the end of hostilities. Soldiers on foot patrols 'were stopped and kissed. People began dancing at traffic intersections, and paper streamers and balloons began appearing'.[68] But not everyone believed the celebrations to be benign. That night Paul Griffin and his family went to bed to chants of 'Ma-ka-rios' from the old city, 'the noise swelled and throbbed from the city with a frightening, jeering quality that caused us to shut our windows and wonder what lay ahead'.[69]

The release of the archbishop immediately resulted in improvements in daily life. Soldiers no longer carried guns, and restrictions on movement and newspaper censorship was eased. Penelope Tremayne recalled Britons and Cypriots mingling 'with a good-will that seemed, if anything, enhanced by the two years separation'.[70] When three weeks later, on 17 April Makarios arrived in Athens tens of thousands turned out to greet him as he rode, standing in the back of an open-top white Cadillac, his black robes billowing in the wind, from Hellenikon Airport to the Grande Bretagne Hotel. The hotel was to be his home for the next year. Despite the rapturous welcome in Greece, Makarios was still not allowed to return to Cyprus.

The first six months of 1957, while Grivas's ceasefire held, saw important positional shifts on the part of both Britain and Turkey. Crucially, Harding's assessment of the island's value had changed. The field marshal had always been convinced it would be impossible to retain control of Cyprus indefinitely in the face of co-ordinated local opposition. From now on, he concluded, Britain's military interests would have to be served by the retention of two or three military bases. His main concern was to 'disengage with honour'.[71]

In April 1957, a defence White Paper was published which outlined, in the aftermath of Suez, a significant reduction in overseas military commitments. Shortly afterwards the defence minister, Duncan Sandys, visited the island, ostensibly to discuss with the governor how the garrison could be streamlined according to the plans outlined in the White Paper. But Sandys also took the opportunity to assess the viability of retaining military bases on the island in the event of loss of sovereignty.

But if certain British articles of faith no longer seemed inviolable, Turkey's position became more entrenched as Prime Minister Menderes repeated his conviction that only partition could solve the problem of Cyprus. One consequence of Turkey's increasing belligerence was that Turkish Cypriots were encouraged to become more militant and to match the levels of violence perpetrated by EOKA. Inter-communal violence in Cyprus, Ankara's logic went, would prove that the two communities could not live alongside each other and thus hasten the implementation of partition. From the British perspective the necessity of maintaining Turkey's goodwill, specifically its active participation in the Baghdad Pact, buttressing the West against Communism, increased dramatically during the summer of 1957 when Syria, Turkey's southern neighbour, came under Soviet influence.

Fear of communism also shaped the character of the conflict in Cyprus at another, more individual, level. In August 1957 Grivas's obsessive, highly personal crusade against the left prompted him to abandon his ceasefire and begin a series of vicious attacks against followers of AKEL. Easier targets than either the British or the more militant Turkish Cypriots, AKEL members consequently fell victim to some of the most barbaric of EOKA's atrocities.

Harding's men were, for the moment at least, no longer the primary target of EOKA's armed attacks. But the field marshal was confronted by an entirely new situation, one that he found far harder to respond to. His newly structured security service had been long handicapped by a shortage of reliable intelligence, with the result, as one insider explained, that 'almost everything is dependent on interrogation'.[72]

At a dramatic press conference in Athens in July 1957 Archbishop Makarios provided graphic accounts, submitted by no less than 317 Greek Cypriots, of atrocities suffered at British hands. The archbishop highlighted what he claimed was casual brutality inflicted during army searches. Although his precise accusations cannot be proved, there is evidence that troops used violent methods. One young British soldier, on national service in Cyprus, Private I.W.G. Martin, provided his parents in England with his own graphic account of an arrest and detention operation in one village in which the men were rounded up and placed in barbed wire enclosures:

> [they] have to make people sit with legs spread out touching their toes etc. which the old men simply can't do: they get yelled at incessantly by thick [soldiers] who can't or won't grasp the simple fact that they don't understand English: resulting in such amusing incidents as when one old man who dared to stand up from his place in the cage and motion that he wanted to be sick was forcibly pushed back and punched in the stomach and beaten on the head with a baton while actually being sick.[73]

Martin observed a culture of brutality towards individuals or communities suspected of having EOKA sympathies, one that was tacitly condoned by the military hierarchy. He described accompanying his regiment to a village near Famagusta where his company began a search of the village by 'throwing chairs at people in order to get them into the coffee shops. When people refused to take down slogans they got bashed around with batons until they did, even then the majority still refused'. He added that following a complaint by the village priest, a senior British police officer came to investigate:

> Not that he is really concerned about it. The Company Commander swears that no ill-treatment took place, or if so he never saw any: he asks his officers if there was, and they in turn ask their NCOs, all of whom blandly say that they never saw anything, which is the usual form out here.

The soldier added grimly, 'you can ... get away with anything in this country as long as you don't leave any bruises, but just "poke people around a bit", while the 'farcical pretence' that Cypriots were not ill treated could only be sustained because 'everyone in authority has perjured themselves again and again'.[74]

It is clear that, on some occasions at least, soldiers used excessive force against Cypriot civilians. But other allegations were also directed at the security services, namely that detainees held at interrogation centres in Platres and Ormophita were systematically tortured by intelligence officers. The allegations highlighted the cases of two Greek Cypriots, Andreas Panaghiotou and Nikos Georghiou, who both died in the course of interrogation in police custody in Platres.

There was, beyond question, a culture amongst sections of the British security services which tacitly – or even actively – endorsed the use of torture. In April 1956, two army officers stationed on the island, Captains O'Driscoll and Linzee of the Gordon Highlanders, had been court-martialled and found guilty of assault causing actual bodily harm and conspiracy to pervert the course of justice in an attempt to conceal evidence of abuse. Makarios's allegations were taken seriously in Britain and questions were asked in the House of Commons.

Harding, intensely loyal to his staff, immediately accused EOKA of 'a campaign of denigration' designed to foster hatred. The governor was first and foremost a soldier, whose personal moral code demanded that he stood by his men and, where necessary, took the flak for them. His loyalty clouded his judgement and, crucially, he resisted an independent inquiry. In doing so he did untold damage to Britain's standing in Cyprus. The consequences of his decision are evident today: references to the 'the widespread use of torture by the police' and 'the establishment of concentration camps'[75] occur commonly in

Greek Cypriot public discourse about the period. Riding alongside Harding's sense of moral obligation were more pragmatic concerns over the potential damage that would be inflicted on the morale and effectiveness of his security forces if any aspect of the allegations were found to be true. Today, such an issue would be viewed primarily through the prism of human rights, but, like Harding, Makarios also saw it from a political perspective. As a result, a file on the alleged atrocities that had been lodged with the United Nations Secretariat was subsequently withdrawn by the Greek delegation as a gesture of goodwill towards Britain, while five allegations of torture due to be heard by the Council of Europe's Human Rights Commission were quietly dropped after the signing of the Zurich Agreement in 1960.

In October 1957, as he approached the end of his two-year appointment, Harding resigned. He had achieved considerable success in his primary objective, the restoration of law and order, although his achievements would have been greater had British resources on the island not been diverted by Suez. But politically he believed he had been abandoned. Harding's failure to negotiate a solution to the crisis has been attributed to his political inexperience, but his efforts had also been frustrated by Whitehall. The Conservative government had alternated between tackling the issue as though it were part of the 'great game' of high Victorian diplomacy, one in which a few deft manoeuvres would see all the cards fall correctly into place, and being forced into a policy of rigid inflexibility by the imperial nostalgia of its own right wing. Neither perspective had constituted an adequate response to the complexities confronting their man on the ground and Harding bitterly accused the prime minister of treating Cyprus 'like a spare time matter'.[76]

The frightened British expatriate community believed that Harding's departure clearly marked the end of Britain's commitment to the colony. For the first time, Paul Griffin recalled, 'one became aware of people looking over their shoulders and preparing escape routes from the island'.[77]

14

Wheel on the Idealist
1958–60

It is early morning on Ledra Street in Nicosia on 3 April 2008. An important event is about to take place in this divided city. The Greek Cypriot National Guard post and the Turkish army post that used to face each other and keep the street blocked have been removed. Now, hundreds of apprehensive Greek and Turkish Cypriots are hoping to be amongst the first for half a century to cross this narrow 80 metre stretch of United Nations-controlled no-man's land. The war-damaged sandstone buildings on either side of the walkway where pedestrians will soon be able to cross are partially concealed behind brightly coloured tarpaulins. Impatient onlookers, bored with waiting, attempt to tweak the corners and take a look at the buildings behind but are ushered away by UN peacekeepers. Finally, after speeches from local and international political figures, 50 multi-coloured balloons are released into the air and the two sections of Ledra Street, once the busiest shopping thoroughfare in Cyprus, are reconnected.

Ledra Street runs from north to south through the centre of Nicosia. When violence broke out between the two communities in 1958, British troops erected a barbed-wire barricade three quarters of the way along the street. It was subsequently reinforced, before being made permanent in 1974 after the Turkish invasion. Today, Cypriots from both sides can walk across, provided they are prepared to show passports or identity cards to the Turkish Cypriot authorities. Unrestricted movement throughout the island still appears some way off. The physical and psychological scars from the era of inter-communal violence and the Turkish invasion have not yet faded.

The events that led directly to the creation of a dividing line across the island took place in the 1960s and 70s. What is sometimes overlooked is the degree to which the roots of the inter-communal crisis go back to the last years of British rule, coinciding with the governorship of Harding's successor, Hugh Foot.

Foot had served as colonial secretary in Cyprus for the last two years of the Second World War and had been popular with both Cypriots and expatriates. But that had been an entirely different climate and the British, bereft of their field marshal, were now 'doubtful' about 'this rather left-wing chap, from a left-wing family'.[1] Foot was a more adroit manipulator of public image than his predecessor and announced his arrival by walking unarmed along the length of Ledra Street, talking to Cypriots as he went. In his first weeks on the island he released 100 Greek Cypriot detainees and lifted restrictions on 600 villagers who had been confined to their homes under curfew. He travelled widely, often riding through villages on an impressive black stallion, the Duke of Kermia. He inspected the controversial detention centres and even urged British troops to adopt a policy of friendship with Cypriots. For the islanders themselves the reduction in tension that accompanied his arrival was manifest in countless small and seemingly insignificant ways. Children who had been restricted to playing indoors during the Harding era, for instance, now found that their parents allowed them out into the street again. Foot was a 'hearts and minds' governor, whose conciliatory policy was mocked in a *Daily Express* cartoon which showed British soldiers in the colony defending themselves with chocolates, mints and olive branches. But although *Express* readers may have objected to his approach, the governor's skills at bridge building were the very qualities that had convinced the Colonial Office that he was the man for the job. To this extent Grivas's crudely expressed fears that Foot would 'try to make use of old friends and acquaintances and worm his way into their confidence'[2] were well founded.

Yet despite Foot's liberalism (Macmillan noted his arrival at cabinet meetings by announcing disparagingly, 'wheel on the idealist'[3]) and his subsequent role in effecting the transition to independence, his reputation amongst Cypriots today is tarnished. It was, as Holland has observed, 'the unfortunate fate of Sir Hugh Foot and his "colonial idealism" to be caught up in the unpretty death-throes of a failing regime'.[4] During Foot's governorship, what had hitherto been a straightforward 'up and down' colonial insurrection (however violent) fragmented along internecine and ideological lines, degenerating into violence between Greek and Turkish Cypriots, and between Greek Cypriots of the right and the left. In the process the Cyprus problem, which had essentially been a dispute between the island's inhabitants and their rulers, became progressively internationalised and ultimately moved beyond the control of either party. In the course of this dynamic the foundations of the de facto partition which exists today were first established. Foot's attempts to gain the confidence of the Greek Cypriot community simultaneously alienated Turkish Cypriots, while his relationship

Governor Hugh Foot and officials visiting villages in the Kyrenia District on horseback, 1958.

[© *Cyprus Press and Information Office.*]

with the Turkish government of Adnan Menderes was hampered from the outset by the Foot family's association with liberalism. It seems perverse to believe that Menderes had a particular antipathy towards this serious-minded family of non-conformists from the English west country, but Ankara was convinced that Foot's hereditary liberalism marked him out as Philhellenic, partisan and intrinsically anti-Turk. These suspicions accounted in part for the speed with which Foot's first proposals for a solution were rejected out of hand.

The gulf between Foot and Harding had not just been a matter of style. By the end of his term Harding had concluded that any interim political solution would also need to address the controversial issue of the island's ultimate sovereignty. Foot's plan, by contrast, envisaged a limited seven-year period of self-government, which could then be followed by discussions over the island's final status. This, the Turkish foreign minister, Fatin Zorlu, feared was merely a ruse to bring about *enosis* through the back door. Turkish anxieties that Britain was about to agree to *enosis* were manifested on the streets of Nicosia through the formation of a separatist paramilitary organisation *Turk Mudya Teskilat* (TMT). More militant than its predecessor, *Volkan*, it was 'permeated with the fanaticism which was associated with EOKA' and rallied supporters with the cry 'partition or death'.[5] Most significantly it was directed by the Turkish government in Ankara. Over the next year the threats posed by TMT's activities were to form a crucial element in the diplomatic calculations being made in Whitehall.

Penelope Tremayne arrived at the aftermath of one TMT assassination as she drove alone from Nicosia to Famagusta across the empty Messaoria plain. She came across two men who had been shot at point-blank range in the cabin of their lorry. One, whose face had been blown away, died in her arms. Tremayne later learnt that the dying men had been EOKA activists and that her efforts to help them had – inadvertently – won her the gratitude of Grivas. The colonel later sent a messenger to her hotel to pass on his thanks.

November 1957 marked the start of nine months of inter-communal violence. Two days after Foot's arrival in Cyprus, on 5 December 1957, the dismembered bodies of three Turks who had been hacked to death were discovered in a village close to Paphos; 48 hours later, on the eve of yet anther UN debate about Cyprus, serious riots broke out in Nicosia. Disturbances began when pupils at the Pancyprian Gymnasium attacked security forces with bottles and stones. The clashes precipitated a violent response from a larger crowd of Turkish Cypriots which rampaged through the Greek Cypriot sector, smashing shops and burning buildings. British security forces rushed to close the barbed-wire boundary that separated the two sectors of the city.

This was the point at which a 'straightforward' struggle to oust the British became 'a colonial conflict with a potentially vicious communal struggle wrapped up inside it'.[6] It was a struggle, moreover, that would have less and less to do with modalities of government, or what either Foot, Archbishop Makarios, or even Grivas wanted for Cyprus, and would become increasingly determined by external geopolitical interests, the balances of power within NATO and between the West and the Soviet bloc. To that extent there is much about the dying days of British Cyprus that is beyond the scope of this study. But some of the characteristics that had defined British rule on the island, in particular a reluctance to take Cypriot political demands seriously and a willingness to put Cyprus aside when more important issues presented themselves, can still be traced in the final two years of colonial rule.

Despite Turkish objections to Foot's plan for Cyprus, the governor nonetheless accompanied the foreign secretary, Selwyn Lloyd, to Ankara in January

1958. It was a humiliating trip during which both men were browbeaten and bullied. Foot was conspicuously ignored by Zorlu (whom he described as 'the rudest man I ever met'[7]) and marginalised by other senior officials. But as Foot kicked his heels on the sidelines in Ankara, Nicosia was once again on the point of anarchy. TMT-backed protesters clashed with the security forces, sparking off three days of rioting. Seven people were killed, two of them by a British army truck driving at speed through an angry crowd, and hundreds were injured. It was explained to the British delegation in Ankara that the riots had been arranged at Turkey's behest and that if Britain rejected partition it would 'have to face the joint resistance of the Turkish Cypriot and the Turkish Government'.[8] Confronted with the 'brutal intransigence'[9] of the Turkish foreign minister, Selwyn Lloyd promised that no decision on the island's future would be made without Turkish agreement. Foot returned to Cyprus with no 'positive political policy'[10] to replace the one rejected by Menderes, to find that both sectors of the mixed Cypriot community were attacking one another – whilst each conducting separate rebellions against the British.

In the spring of 1958, while the administration was still on the back foot in terms of a Cyprus policy, Grivas announced a campaign of passive resistance and an immediate boycott of Commonwealth products. The list of banned goods ranged from 'tractors to Kleenex'[11] and their prohibition complicated life for many Cypriots. Numerous British products, aided by the policy of Imperial Preference, had successfully penetrated the Cypriot market and as a result 'the smart young Cypriot wore a tweed jacket, and among his friends drank whisky if he could afford it, or beer if he could not'.[12] While the majority maintained the appearance of complying with the boycott, many middle-class Greek Cypriot women in Nicosia continued to wear imported British underwear 'just because the local stuff was so dreadful'.[13] A few, such as photographer George Lanitis, who had recently returned from study in England and was attached to his British-bought wardrobe, risked the threats – or worse – of his compatriots because 'you only had to wash Cypriot-made clothes once and they became ridiculous'. Lanitis had bought his clothes in England, 'so no one could say I was unpatriotic. I just couldn't bring myself to throw my Hush Puppies away'.[14] The boycott created more serious economic problems for Cypriot importers who found themselves with warehouses full of stocks they had already paid for. TMT meanwhile responded by applying its own boycott, attacking Turkish Cypriots who used Greek Cypriot shops.

As even the act of getting dressed in the morning became, for many Cypriots, a political statement, the number of bombings steadily increased. There were over 50 in April 1958 alone. Foot's liberalism had frequently placed him at odds with his military advisers and as the bombings began again he came under increasing pressure to revive Harding's emergency regulations.

His chief of operations, General Douglas Kendrew, was sufficiently concerned at the governor's practice of releasing detainees that he forwarded his own assessment of the policy's security risks directly to Whitehall. In May, when two British soldiers and a senior intelligence officer were killed by EOKA gunmen the governor capitulated to Kendrew's demands: extensive army searches were resumed and the death penalty was reintroduced for carrying arms. But the threat posed by EOKA was, for the British, now overshadowed by that of TMT, and the fear that their paramilitaries had potential access to extensive supplies of weapons through contacts in the Turkish Cypriot-staffed police force.

The spring and summer of 1958 represented the bloodiest and most divisive period of the rebellion. Over 100 Cypriots were killed and twice that number seriously wounded in inter-communal and politically motivated killings. The murders became increasingly barbaric and Cyprus lurched incrementally towards civil war. When EOKA launched a series of particularly vicious attacks on left-wing activists in May, TMT followed suit, assassinating Turkish Cypriot members of AKEL because of their co-operation with Greek Cypriot trade unionists. Relations between Greece and Turkey also deteriorated sharply, forcing NATO to confront the possibility that two of its members might be sucked into armed conflict with one another. On the night of 7 June 1958, Foot stood on the balcony of Government House watching 'what looked like the whole of Nicosia aflame' as gangs of youngsters took to the streets and the city was convulsed with inter-communal riots. The days that followed brought 'what we had always most feared, civil war between the Greek and Turkish communities in the island'.[15] Five days later eight Greek Cypriots were killed by Turkish Cypriots near the village of Guenyeli outside Nicosia. This incident, perhaps more than any other, reinforced Greek Cypriot suspicions that the British were collaborating with Turkish Cypriots in order to oppress them and is still remembered with bitterness today. Thirty-two Greek Cypriot men, armed with home-made weapons, had been arrested by a British patrol on the outskirts of the mixed village of Skylloura on the Messaoria Plain. As they were being taken to Nicosia Police Station, news reached the patrol of a separate local disturbance at the station and the soldiers were given instructions en route to release the men. Controversially, the officer in charge of the convoy released the men on the outskirts of the Turkish Cypriot village of Guenyeli where they were ambushed and eight were hacked to death. This atrocity damaged both Anglo-Greek relations and Foot's personal prestige, which never recovered.

As rumour spread and terror of the other community increased, Cypriots themselves took the first steps towards the physical partition of their island when 600 frightened Greek Cypriots abandoned their homes. Turkish Cypriot

villagers from Aghoursos in the Paphos district followed suit, moving wholesale to a mixed village on the Messaoria Plain, taking livestock, agricultural
machinery and implements with them. When news reached the Greek Cypriot
suburb of Varosha outside Famagusta that the inhabitants were about to be
attacked by Turkish Cypriots, large numbers abandoned their homes. Jean
Somerville, whose husband Ronald was stationed at the British garrison in the
city, recorded in her diary the sight of 'lorry loads of household goods [going]
down [the] road, escorted by police'. When a Greek Cypriot friend asked for
help in protecting his home Somerville attempted to reassure him that 'there are
plenty of troops about. [But] Paris looks disbelieving. I say "do you not trust
the troops?" He says "No! Look at Guenyeli!" '[16]

Remarkably, the ethnically mixed English School managed to remain open
until July, although the staff, as Griffin recalled, 'lived on a knife edge. Every
time I saw a boy congratulate another of a different community on the sports
field I thanked God for our tradition'.[17] Finally, after a frightened boy confided
in Griffin that another youngster had drawn a knife on him, the school closed
two weeks early for the summer holidays.

By this stage, virtually every possible permutation for governing the colony
had been tried and rejected by one or all of the parties involved. Devoid of new
ideas, Whitehall attempted to revive Macmillan's three-year-old 'tridominium',
now re-hashed as the Foot-Macmillan Plan. The crucial difference was that this
time, in the absence of the agreement of the prime minister of Greece or Turkey
or of Archbishop Makarios, Britain would unilaterally impose its own constitution. This included two separate assemblies for each community, Greek and
Turkish 'partners', and provision to review the island's status in 15 years' time.

All three parties rejected the plan out of hand and Macmillan shuttled
between Nicosia, Athens and Ankara seeking agreement, tweaking and fudg-
ing details as he did so. The British prime minister finally succeeded in convincing Menderes to accept the deal, in part because the provision of two
separate assemblies and the absence of a central legislature was seen – from the
Turkish perspective – as a positive move towards incremental partition. While
Menderes stuck doggedly to the prospect of geographical partition, Macmillan
equivocated, referring with deliberate vagueness to the administrative and
even the 'metaphysical' partition of the island.[18]

The following month the Turkish foreign ministry revealed to Labour MP
Barbara Castle – then on a visit to Ankara – that Britain had, in fact, already
signed a secret document guaranteeing to honour its promise to partition the
island. As Holland observes, by this stage in the rebellion 'British credentials
were very far from being in perfect order'.[19] For his part, Foot gained some
comfort from the knowledge that his government did at least now have a plan –
albeit one that relied on a dangerous and desperate strategy.

In Cyprus, the carnage continued: a pregnant woman and a farmer were mown down by accidental fire from a British military vehicle and two British soldiers were killed by EOKA in revenge. Four Greek Cypriots were killed by their Turkish Cypriot compatriots in a Nicosia suburb, precipitating the ambush of a bus by EOKA on which five Turkish Cypriot workers were shot. Zorlu, the obstreperous Turkish foreign minister, meanwhile, told the British ambassador in Ankara that if Britain did not take steps to halt the violence then 'a small Turkish force'[20] would be capable of doing the job for it.

On 17 July 1958, Foot ordered an island-wide standstill. Civilian movement and communication were totally restricted and over the next three days nearly 2,000 Greek Cypriots were arrested and detained. The operation's primary value was to demonstrate the security services' capacity for decisive action and 'to bring in certain suspected people who live openly in the villages'. To do this, one British soldier observed, 'they have to round up the whole male population of each village, continually mess them about and keep them in the boiling sun for hours'. It is questionable how many EOKA leaders were picked up in this indiscriminate sweep, but the 'systematic viciousness'[21] with which it was conducted inevitably boosted support for the fight against the British.

EOKA's ability to spread fear by surprise attacks remained undiminished. During the first week in August the organisation killed a British colonel at his home in Limassol and shot dead an army sergeant as he walked through the market in the Nicosia suburb of Ayios Dhometios hand-in-hand with his two-year-old son. Privately, Foot was in despair, believing that 'there seemed no hope at all'.[22] On 4 August 1958, possibly for tactical reasons, to give his men time to re-group, Grivas abruptly announced a ceasefire. Hostilities against both the British and Turkish Cypriots would end. The TMT followed suit. There was no more inter-communal violence during British rule in Cyprus.

The administration was now focussed on the imminent deadline of 1 October, the date when the Foot–Macmillan plan was to be unilaterally implemented. Foot gave security chiefs in Whitehall a chilling assessment of the risks the plan involved. In going ahead, he explained, the government was 'going to precipitate a crisis. The result of this crisis may be unpredictable: it may be civil war, or war between Greece and Turkey, or it may be possible to come through the storm into calmer waters on the other side'.[23]

As tension began to rise again Penelope Tremayne was invited to a tea dance at a smart Limassol hotel to meet a man she knew only as Papadimas. There, amongst 'over-tailored men dancing with rather large ladies', she was presented with a bouquet of yellow gladioli, 'a gift from General Grivas'. As Tremayne and Papadimas danced, it was politely explained that Grivas wished the governor to understand that ' "if young men have guns they can only be persuaded to keep their fingers off the trigger for so long, but not indefinitely." I said that I quite understood and wondered if he might have any idea how long Colonel Grivas had in mind. He said probably about one week'.[24] By the time Tremayne got back to Nicosia it was 2 a.m. Foot saw her immediately and she passed the message on. Five days later, on 13 September 1958 the ceasefire was broken when a British soldier was killed in an ambush in the Paphos district. The death led to more accusations of military brutality, when troops from the victim's battalion rushed out to neighbouring villages to take revenge. Buildings were damaged, several villagers were badly beaten, and two British soldiers were stabbed by angry Greek Cypriots in the village of Kathikas. Shortly afterwards, General Kendrew narrowly escaped death in a bomb attack on his car.

That September, when the academic year began, none of the Greek Cypriot pupils at the English School returned to classes. They had received letters from EOKA instructing them to stay away. For Griffin, an honourable imperialist doing an impossible job, this represented a personal failure because 'we at the English School had been given the task of holding the young of the two main Cypriot communities together, and we had failed to do so'.[25]

Duplicitous and high-handed though it undoubtedly was as a strategy, Macmillan's brinkmanship had succeeded. Makarios was by now seriously concerned about the possibility of partition. If the Foot-Macmillan plan contained the seeds of administrative partition, the recent inter-communal killings had created the right environment for their gestation and maturity into geographical separation. In September, using Barbara Castle as an intermediary, Makarios announced a radical change of position. The archbishop was no longer determined to achieve 'enosis and only enosis' and was now prepared to consider independence after an interim period of self-government.

This was a significant development with profound implications. Up to this point the two stated positions had seemed immovable: Makarios's insistence that nothing short of enosis would do, and Britain's corresponding insistence that only retention of the entire island could safeguard its military interests. Now there was room for movement. Cypriot independence, with provision for British military bases, became an acceptable bottom line for both parties. The component parts of a political settlement were on the table, they only needed to be nudged into place. Curiously, it took some time for this momentous shift in position to be translated into a new diplomatic initiative, and at the level of day-to-day life in Cyprus, the mood showed no obvious sign of change. British representatives in NATO dismissed the archbishop's announcement as 'nothing new'.[26] The Foot-Macmillan plan had by now acquired its own momentum and officials were suspicious of any new developments that might delay its implementation.

Then, on the afternoon of 3 October, an event took place that risked blowing the entire process apart. Catherine Cutliffe, the wife of a British army captain, was shot and killed at point-blank range while shopping in Famagusta. Mrs Cutliffe, who had been accompanied by her daughter Margaret and friend Elfreide Robinson (who was seriously injured), had been looking for items for her daughter's wedding.

Foot and Kendrew, fearing 'it would be impossible to hold our troops', flew immediately by helicopter to Famagusta. But 'already the troops had gone wild'.[27] A curfew had been imposed on the city and all Greek Cypriot men between the ages of 14 and 26 were being rounded up and held in large wire cages for questioning. At least two people died in the process and hundreds more received head injuries at the hands of irate troops. In some cases soldiers continued to beat the detainees inside the cages. An officer who drove through the centre of Famagusta shortly afterwards noted that 'there was not an intact window in sight, cars were overturned and the roads were full of broken glass, it just looked like the whole city had been trashed'.[28]

The anger that swept through the British community in Famagusta that night is captured in the comments that Jean Somerville made in her diary. Somerville, who believed the troops were 'justified in being a bit rough considering what happened', became furious when she tuned into Cyprus Broadcasting and heard the 'bloody mayor of Famagusta protest about action of troops and not ONE WORD of sympathy, let alone any other mention of cowardly shootings'.[29] The hours that followed the Cutliffe murder were certainly brutal, but the precise sequence of events is unclear. One report from an anonymous British witness spoke of 'wholesale rape and lootings and murder' and listed a series of alleged atrocities, none of which can now be independently corroborated. The night after the Cutliffe murder the same witness 'sat in the garden in the commissioner's house and tried to escape from the mess in town but even from there I could hear the screaming in the police station in Varosha'.[30]

The intensity of the hatred felt on both sides was unprecedented. After visiting Cutliffe's three bereaved children at their home Somerville wrote chillingly in her diary: 'Today's funny story. Royal Military Police (RMP) searching house of Greek doctor inform him two British women shot. "Good show" says doctor. "Say that again" say RMPs, he does – is taken to own clinic with fractured jaw and no teeth!'[31] As Foot and Kendrew made their way back to Nicosia the governor 'could see nothing but hatred and violence ahead'.[32] Catherine Cutliffe was buried in Wayne's Keep Cemetery in what is now the buffer zone, alongside other Britons killed during the emergency. Her daughter Margaret, who, having confronted her mother's killer, was advised to conceal her identity, attended the funeral 'completely covered by a black satin shawl.'[33] Catherine Cutliffe's killer was never found. Grivas, who had not hesitated to assume responsibility for the deaths of other British women, consistently denied any EOKA involvement in the murder. That month, a further 45 people were killed and 370 injured. Foot's gloomy prediction that the plan bearing his name might trigger a civil war on the island looked like being depressingly accurate.

Then, suddenly, with no obvious warning, and no intervention by either the British or the Cypriots, the issue moved, decisively, into its final phase. On 4 December 1959, at the UN General Assembly in New York, after another inconclusive debate on Cyprus, the Turkish foreign minister, Fatin Zorlu, approached his Greek counterpart, Evangelos Averoff, in a corridor, and casually suggested a meeting. With this almost nonchalant, seemingly spontaneous gesture, the end of British rule in Cyprus began.

Zorlu was not the brightest foreign minister of his day. Macmillan credited him with little intellectual ability other than 'a low cunning'. What had convinced his government suddenly to seek accommodation with Greece over Cyprus? The answer seems to lie in Turkey's geopolitical perspective on the region at that time. The previous summer a military coup in Iraq had ousted the pro-British monarchy, replacing it with a regime that was potentially antagonistic to Turkey. Menderes already had one Soviet-backed country – Syria – on his southern border. Moscow was ratcheting up tension over Berlin and it seemed that a crisis between the West and Turkey's historic adversary was imminent. Holland suggests that Turkey's high-risk strategy in Cyprus, one that could easily lead to war with Greece, had become too dangerous to pursue, now that Turkish interests in the east were also potentially under threat. Ismet Inonu, the Turkish opposition leader (who, as Attaturk's successor, had inherited the unwavering support of the army), began to voice strong criticism of Menderes for engaging in precisely the sort of 'foreign adventurism' that the father of the modern Turkish state had condemned.

Initial contacts between the two foreign ministers went well and another meeting was scheduled for a NATO summit in Paris later that month. London responded – as it had done to the news of Makarios's change of policy – as if nothing had happened. Suggestions that security operations might be scaled down as a gesture of goodwill were dismissed. General Kenneth Darling, who had succeeded General Kendrew the previous month as chief of security in the colony, was, as a result of a new intelligence-driven approach, tantalisingly close to seizing Grivas. He was consequently reluctant to agree to anything that might deny his men their long-awaited strike.

At this point a dramatic complication occurred – one with all the suspense of a Hollywood movie – that risked scuppering the embryonic Greco-Turkish dialogue and presented Foot with a personal crisis. Two EOKA activists convicted of murdering a Greek Cypriot as he slept were scheduled to be hanged in the early hours of 18 December 1958. During his time in office Harding had authorised the execution of nine EOKA activists, but despite the violence of the previous 12 months, the slowness of the appeals process meant that Foot had not yet been presented with a death warrant to sign. After hearing the advice of his attorney general and the Executive Council that the evidence against the killers was conclusive, Foot realised 'with a heavy sense of foreboding' that 'there was not the slightest justification for a reprieve'. By this stage the governor's relationship with his security chiefs had reached such a low ebb that a refusal to proceed would have cost him their confidence. At the same time, authorising the executions would place a permanent political solution out of his reach and mark 'the end of any contribution that I could make' to solving the problem.

Foot reluctantly signed the warrants, and plans for the executions went ahead. A hangman was flown out from England and security around the prison was tightened. As midnight on 17 December approached Foot sat up in his office waiting for news that the executions had been carried out, knowing 'that night or very soon afterwards British soldiers, policemen or civilians would be killed by EOKA in reprisal'. At 11.40 p.m. the phone in the governor's private quarters rang. It was Lennox-Boyd calling from Paris, where the Greek and Turkish foreign ministers had been talking at the NATO summit. He was calling to ask Foot to 'reconsider' his decision in the light of a new development. In a joint approach to the British foreign secretary, Zorlu and Averoff had asked for clemency for the killers on the grounds that their fragile entente would be irrevocably damaged if the executions went ahead. To ignore the appeal would fatally undermine Britain's dwindling moral and political case for retaining any control of the situation in Cyprus.

A last-minute pardon by the governor had to be delivered in person. But with only 15 minutes to go before the executions were carried out Foot could not hope to reach the prison in time. He telephoned the director of prisons to ask for a delay. The director initially failed to understand what the governor wanted and asked him to ring back in half an hour by which time 'it would all be over'. Foot, in desperation, was forced to shout down the telephone; 'You don't understand, I'm coming down to stop it.' The governor arrived at the prison as the two men, Constantinides and Athanassiou, were receiving the last rites from an Orthodox priest. They are remembered today as a minor historical footnote, but had their executions gone ahead their deaths might have tipped their country into civil war.

The reasons for the governor's last-minute 'change of heart' could not be revealed without jeopardising the delicate negotiations that were continuing in Paris. Foot was, therefore, accused of indecision and 'contemptible play acting'. His relationship with his security forces suffered as predicted, with the police and troops 'confused and angered by my apparent vacillation'.[34] Harding, retired and living in Dorset, had on previous occasions expressed regret at his successor's policies in indignant contributions to the *Daily Express* and now had to be restrained from firing off another furious letter by the personal intervention of the colonial secretary.

But there were two more deaths, the last service casualties of the Cyprus Emergency. Grivas, anticipating that Constantindes and Athanasiou would hang, had ordered a reprisal killing. His order was never rescinded and on 20 December 1958, as two young RAF men made a routine trip from their radio station in the Karpas Peninsula to collect their rations, they were blown apart by a land mine.

Neither Cypriot nor British residents of Cyprus had anything to do with the next stage in the colony's history, which unfolded elsewhere. On 11 February 1959 Averoff and Zorlu, meeting in Zurich, reached an agreement on the island's future. It was to be determined by three documents – the Basic Structure of the Republic of Cyprus, a Treaty of Guarantee and a Treaty of Alliance – none of which was drafted by either the colonisers or the colonised. The two foreign ministers then travelled to London to explain to the British prime minister their plans for his colony, while the Greek prime minister, Konstantinos Karamanlis, visited Makarios in Athens to inform the archbishop what would happen to his homeland.

The Zurich Agreement was presented – to Makarios, and to a lesser extent to the British – as a fait accompli. The two foreign ministers stressed that speed was essential and that London and Nicosia would only be able to negotiate details relating to the British bases on the island. Ultimately it was neither Foot's willingness to listen to the views of Cypriots nor General Darling's ability to crush Grivas's insurrection that secured the existence of the new state, but 'the coincidental dynamics of Greek and Turkish policy'.[35]

After receiving a written assurance from Makarios that he broadly accepted the terms of the Zurich Agreement, Macmillan hastily issued invitations to a conference at Lancaster House in London on 17 February 1959 to finalise the details. There was little left to discuss – the event was to be a display of grand political theatre, carefully stage-managed to prevent Makarios from seeking further concessions. The days that followed were certainly theatrical, although not in the sense that Macmillan might have wished.

On the afternoon of 17 February the plane carrying the Turkish prime minister crashed in fog close to Gatwick Airport, south of London, bursting into flames as it hit the ground. Menderes – along with 10 of the 22 passengers – survived, but his injuries prevented him from participating in the conference which opened without him. That evening, as the formal dinner marking the start of the conference began, Macmillan received a message that General Darling's new approach to crushing EOKA was about to come good. Grivas had been traced to a house in Nicosia, which was at that moment surrounded by surveillance officers. Darling sought permission to storm the building. By this stage the prime minister's principal concern was to ensure that nothing jeopardised the establishment of secure British military bases on the island. After enquiring obliquely of Averoff what impact Grivas's arrest might have on the outcome of the conference, Macmillan instructed Darling not to proceed.

Makarios, who had brought a 41-strong delegation with him to Lancaster House, then forced the extension of the conference by 24 hours after a demonstration of brinkmanship which left delegates guessing over his intentions. There has been much speculation over what finally convinced the archbishop to accept the agreement during the night of 18 February, and whether he was blackmailed by MI5 allegations about his sexuality. It seems far more likely that Makarios – who knew that Greek support for *enosis* would be withdrawn if he rejected the agreement – had every intention all along of signing up to the text. His summons to London – to sign the document which would determine the future of his country, his people and his own political career, one that had been deliberately drafted without his involvement – followed years of exile and political marginalisation by the British. Under such circumstances even the most saintly of politicians would have relished keeping three prime ministers on tenterhooks for 24 hours.

The next day, with Makarios's consent finally in the bag, the prime ministers of Greece and the United Kingdom, bearing 'an appropriately grand silver ink pot',[36] travelled to the London Clinic in Harley Street where the Turkish prime minister was recovering from his injuries. The new Republic of Cyprus thus came into being in a hospital.

Britain's marginalisation at such a critical stage in the process of decolonisation was exceptional. Retaining control over the mechanics of the transition was crucial to Britain's understanding of her own imperial role, one in which the Empire was graciously relinquished, as much from a sense of moral duty as through economic – or even military – pressures. The usual parting gifts – democracy and a railway – were both denied to the new republic. The new constitution was not drawn up by British legal experts steeped in their country's traditions of justice and impartiality but was based on 'an international treaty recognising the existence of the new Cypriot state'.[37] As for the unprofitable railway, that had been torn up long before.

Makarios returned to Cyprus on Sunday 1 March 1959, courtesy of a plane provided by the shipping magnate Aristotle Onassis. He was greeted, as protocol demanded, by the governor, the district commissioner of Nicosia and the Anglican archdeacon – before being enveloped in the ecstatic communal embrace of 200,000 of his compatriots, little short of the island's entire adult Greek Cypriot population.[38] Just over two weeks later Nicosia Airport witnessed the departure of Grivas. After being within a hair's breadth of arresting the man whose fanaticism and ruthlessness had cost so many lives, General Darling could not bring himself to 'take part in the charade, which now necessarily had to be played' and left the island. The military official carefully selected in Darling's absence to replace him at the official farewell was Lieutenant Colonel Bill Gore-Langton of the Coldstream Guards. At six foot four he towered above the diminutive guerilla leader and could 'gaze down may be with disdain, on Givas from a considerable height'.[39] Crucially, Gore-Langton had lost his right arm in the war, a disability which consequently made it impossible for him to salute.

The next 18 months were a kind of breathing space. The fear and tension over, both sides grasped the chance to return to something like normality. For the British this involved receptions at Government House to meet Makarios, a resumption of amateur theatricals and 'a good many parties and picnics, since many officials were beginning to drift away to fresh postings and needed a good send off'.[40] No one knew how many would remain on the island once independence had been declared, and there was considerable relief when the Anglican archdeacon of St Paul's received assurances from Makarios that 'English people would be welcome'.[41]

Eirwen Harbottle remembered a party at Cyprus Broadcasting Service during this time at which 'everyone gathered and it was all, "You see Michalakis over there? He had the screw that was going to detonate the bomb", and Stavros, he was going to do something else and it was all ho-ho-ho and terribly funny. But it wasn't really funny, it was just that there were no hard feelings, I suppose, which was nice in a way. It was hard to believe it had ever really happened.'

For Foot, the year that followed was one of 'sheer happiness'. The return of peace was accompanied by the resurrection of that enduring conviction that had sustained generations of liberal colonials, that they were making the world a better place. His administration was employed in 'constructive work'[42] making new ministries, organising the island's first elections with full adult suffrage, and reducing the size of the British garrison on the island. At last 'the idealist' had the chance to make a difference and go some way to salvaging the tattered reputation of Her Majesty's Government. Foot assumed responsibility for protecting the interests of Cyprus's three minority communities, Armenians, Maronites and Latins, on the grounds that 'the United Kingdom has a special responsibility to see that the interests of the minor communities are safeguarded; if we don't, no one else will'.[43] He proved tenacious in the face of strong Turkish Cypriot opposition, securing for each minority recognition as a distinct religious group, along with the right to elect its own member to the newly formed Cypriot Parliament, the House of Representatives.

Foot was less successful in attempting to uphold a series of risible demands by the island's 2,000-strong British community, a large proportion of whom now lived in Kyrenia. Under the constitution of the new republic, all Britons born in Cyprus after November 1914 would automatically acquire dual British and

Cypriot nationality. The British community demanded the right to renounce Cypriot nationality, retaining only British citizenship, on the grounds that dual status would afford no British Consular protection in Cyprus. This was, in itself, not unreasonable, but at the same time, the British also lobbied for their own member in the House of Representatives, on the grounds that like the Armenians, Maronites and Latins they would constitute a minority within the new republic. It was an indefensible argument which may have sounded acceptable to the more insular members of the Kyrenia Harbour Club, but one which Foot wisely abandoned. Securing representation for the island's minorities was Britain's only significant input into the constitution, which was drawn up in Nicosia by representatives from Greece and Turkey, along with an academic lawyer from Switzerland.

Negotiations over the precise acreage of the British bases, meanwhile, became protracted. The sole issue over which the archbishop retained negotiating power was never going to be resolved rapidly. Macmillan had appointed his son-in-law, the staunch imperialist Julian Amery, to be Makrios's sparring partner in the negotiations. As a result, independence was delayed by several months, until in July 1960 agreement was eventually reached that the area of the British Sovereign Bases would span 99 square miles of territory, encompassing the two bases of Akrotiri and Dhekalia and other smaller immovable installations elsewhere on the island.

One of the final ironies of the British occupation was the generosity of the terms offered to departing officials. After decades of poor and unattractive salaries resulting in under-paid and generally under-performing bureaucrats, the last generation of British administrators in Cyprus received terms that were 'more generous than those of any other colonial administration in the period of decolonisation'.[44] Thanks to Harding's intervention, short-term staff recruited during the emergency and even 'ordinary British residents' also received compensation. George Meikle, who had been the colony's deputy chief police officer, received £10,000, which was, as his wife Jean remembered, 'a lot of money in those days'.

At midnight on 16 August 1960, during one of the hottest summers the island had seen, a simple ceremony took place at Government House and 82 years of British rule in Cyprus came to an end. The next day Foot saluted the Royal Horse Guards and the Black Watch and set sail with his family to the sound of a salute of guns fired from 'the ancient walls of Famagusta'.[45]

So, how can the legacy of British rule in Cyprus best be summarised? Thanks to budget airlines and cheap construction techniques which have made the retirement home in the sun an affordable dream for many ordinary Britons, there are now many more British residents on the island (an estimated 60,000) than at any time during the colonial period. Many superficial reminders of the

Foot and his family leave St Paul's Nicosia for the last time, August 1960.
[© *Cyprus Press and Information Office.*]

island's colonial past remain, such as driving on the left and early closing on Wednesdays, along with a legal system modelled on the British one and the widespread use of English.

As in other new, post-colonial nations, the urban landscape of Cyprus has changed out of all recognition. In the rush towards modernity and economic prosperity nearly all the old colonial buildings have been torn down and the skyline of southern Nicosia is characterised by tall new office blocks and high rises, whose ground floors are filled by big international chains. After generations of acute poverty Cypriots have embraced consumerism with relish and the country boasts the fifth highest per capita rate of car ownership in the world.

For many this process of coming of age was completed when their country gained membership of the European Union. Throughout the British occupation Cyprus was habitually referred to as part of the geographically closer Middle East. Today, any such connections with a region which, for many Cypriots, has

connotations of backwardness are generally downplayed. On 1 May 2004, the
Republic of Cyprus was at last recognised as a fully–fledged European nation,
able to sit side by side with the former colonial power, an equal member of the
same exclusive club.

But in practice, only part of the island has joined. Although EU citizenship extends to individual Turkish Cypriots, the institutions of the unrecognised Turkish Republic of Northern Cyprus remain outside EU boundaries.
Negotiations on the accession of northern Cyprus can begin only if agreement
is reached on reuniting the island. In fact, any consideration of the colonial
legacy is inextricably bound up with the knowledge of the inter-communal violence and partition that followed.

It is often said in Cyprus that the island's division owes much to a British
colonial policy of divide and rule. In fact, (apart from Macmillan's attempts at
high-level international political manoeuvring in 1956) such divisions evolved
from attempts to respond to the situation on the ground, rather than from a
deliberate plan to drive a wedge between the two communities. It is possible
that if Cyprus had been staffed by a better paid, more capable class of civil servants some of these situations may have been handled better. But probably far
more damaging to Cypriots' chances of establishing a post-independence tradition of bi-communal consensus politics was their exclusion from democratic
political participation in the decades that followed the burning of Government
House in 1931. It was a policy that deprived subsequent generations of political
leaders of the experience they so desperately needed if they were to have any
chance of making the complicated 1960 constitution work.

But there is another equally important but less tangible post-colonial legacy. It is a pervading lack of belief in anything Cypriot. Without an indigenous
aristocracy to share (however nominally) the business of colonial government,
Cypriots seldom saw their own culture recognised or validated by the British,
resulting in a lack of national self-belief that persists amongst educated Cypriots
even today. Despite the presence of doctors and surgeons comparable with the
best in northern Europe or America, many affluent Cypriots still choose to
go abroad if they need surgery or medical care. In the same way, concerts by
the Cyprus State Orchestra attract a far less glamorous crowd than those by
international performers organised by the Pharos Trust. Controversial plans by
the architect Zaha Hadid for the development of Eleftheria Square have been
applauded primarily because of Hadid's international reputation and prestige
– and the hope that some of it will rub off on Cyprus – rather than on their
intrinsic architectural merit. Even the colonists' uncertainty about Cypriot
identity has trickled down to Cypriots themselves. Few islanders today would
refer to themselves as Cypriots without feeling obliged to prefix it with the
term 'Greek' or 'Turkish'. It is unusual to see the flag of either the Republic of

Cyprus or its counterpart in the unrecognised Turkish republic of Northern Cyprus flying without the flag of either Greece or Turkey next to it. The elusive concept of 'Cypriotness', of confidence in what it means to be from and of the island, will need to be more deeply rooted if there is to be any hope of creating an integrated Cypriot community.

When considered in the context of the Cyprus problem, this insecurity contributes to the widely held belief that the issue will ultimately be resolved by outside intervention. It reinforces the prevailing conviction that the international community will, at a stroke, solve the problem (created by foreign powers in the first place) and find a solution that is acceptable to both sides. The morning after EU accession a sign appeared in Eleftheria Square in Nicosia that read 'Thank you Europe'. Its message implied that, rather than acceding to the union through its own efforts, by conforming to successive chapters of the *acquis communautaire*, Cyprus had been graciously allowed to join, thanks to the generosity and goodwill of the European community.

Perhaps, given the complexities of the island's colonial past, it is not surprising that the relationship between Cyprus and Britain remains ambivalent. Today, a substantial part of the Cypriot construction and development sector relies on selling coastal properties to retirees from the United Kingdom, while the economy of the southern part of the island depends on the regular arrival of over 1 million British tourists each year. Cypriots meanwhile strive to send their children to British universities.

Yet at times of stress – such as the 2004 referendum on reunification, or when Queen Elizabeth attended the Commonwealth Heads of Government meeting in 1993 – anti-British feeling is not hard to re-ignite. Latent resentment at the presence of British military bases on the island periodically flares up. In 2005, before he became president, Demetris Christofias described Britain as the island's 'long-time nemesis'.[46]

Britain and Cyprus have too much common history and share too many memories – sweet as well as bitter – to shut the door on the past. Removing British street names, pulling down colonial buildings and installing a Cypriot president in what was Government House have done much to reinforce the island's independent identity. But Cyprus cannot erase the experience – for better or worse – of 82 years of colonial rule that began when Sir Garnet Wolseley's troops stepped nervously ashore at Larnaca on a stifling August Sunday in 1878.

Notes

1 Where Are the Forests? 1878–82

1. Cavendish, Anne, ed. *Cyprus 1878 The Journal of Sir Garnet Wolseley* (Cyprus Popular Bank Cultural Centre, Nicosia, 1991), p. 18.
2. A subsequent visitor to the island claimed that the redundant coal boxes, filled with water, were placed around Government House for use as fire extinguishers. Baker, Samuel, *Cyprus as I Saw It in 1879*, Chapter 9, p. 194 printed at 12 point, single spacing (Project Gutenberg Etext no. 3656, release date 1 January 2003).
3. Scott-Stevenson, Esme, *Our Home in Cyprus* (London 1880), p. 38.
4. Cavendish, *The Journal of Sir Garnet Wolseley*, p. 21.
5. Ibid., p. 6.
6. Letter from the Marquis of Salisbury to Austen Layard, British Ambassador to Istanbul, 30 May 1878. Quoted in Orr, C.W.J., *Cyprus under British Rule* (Zeno Publishers, London, 1972), p. 185.
7. Cavendish, *The Journal of Sir Garnet Wolseley*, p. 5.
8. Ciftlik is the Turkish word for farm or plantation. The name roughly translates as Lord's Farm.
9. Scott-Stevenson, *Our Home in Cyprus*, p. 38.
10. Cavendish, *The Journal of Sir Garnet Wolseley*, p. 21.
11. Ibid.
12. Ibid., p. 22.
13. Kitchener, Horatio Herbert, 'Notes from Cyprus', *Blackwood's Edinburgh Magazine* no. 126, 1879. Cited in ΒΙΚΤΩΡΙΑΝΑ ΚΕΙΜΕΝΑ ΓΙΑ ΤΗΝ ΚΥΠΡΟ 1878–1891 ed. Κυριάχος Ν. Δημητρίου (Κέντρο Μελετών Ιεράς Μονίς Κύκκου, Nicosia, 2000), p. 211.
14. Scott-Stevenson, *Our Home in Cyprus*, p. 25.
15. Ibid., p. 23.
16. Cavendish, *The Journal of Sir Garnet Wolseley*, p. 56.
17. Poole, Reginald Stewart, 'Cyprus: Its Present and Future'. *Contemporary Review*, no. 33. 1878, cited in ΒΙΚΤΩΡΙΑΝΑ ΚΕΙΜΕΝΑ ΓΙΑ ΤΗΝ ΚΥΠΡΟ 1878–1891 ed. Κυριάχος Ν. Δημητρίου (Κέντρο Μελετών Ιεράς Μονίς Κύκκου, Nicosia, 2000), p. 125.
18. *Cyprus: A Weekly Journal of Agriculture and Commerce*, 29 August 1878, Larnaca Municipal Museum.

19. Ibid., 24 October 1878.
20. *Cyprus Herald* 7 July 1883, Larnaca Municipal Museum.
21. Poole, 'Cyprus: Its Present and Future', p. 120.
22. Donne, Donisthorpe, *Records of the Ottoman Conquest of Cyprus and Cyprus Guide and Directory* (Laiki Group Cultural Centre, Nicosia, 2000), p. 119.
23. Burke, U.R., 'What Have We Done for Cyprus?' *National Review* no. 11 1888 cited in ΒΙΚΤΩΡΙΑΝΑ ΚΕΙΜΕΝΑ ΓΙΑ ΤΗΝ ΚΥπΡΟ 1878–1891, p. 250.
24. *Cyprus Herald* 9 November 1881.
25. High Commissioner's Annual Report, 1881, cited in *The Handbook of Cyprus, 1931*, Storrs Ronald, ed. (London 1930), p. 179.
26. *Cyprus Herald* 3 May 1882.
27. *Cyprus Herald* 14 December 1882.
28. His farms were near the village of Dali, between Nicosia and Laranca and close to the village of Kouklia in the district of Famagusta.
29. Luke, Harry, ed. *The Handbook of Cyprus 1913*.
30. Donne, Donisthorpe, *Records of the Ottoman Conquest of Cyprus*, p. 142.
31. *Cyprus Herald* 19 March 1883.
32. *Cyprus: A Weekly Journal of Agriculture and Commerce*, 29 August 1878.
33. Scott-Stevenson, *Our Home in Cyprus*, p. 201.
34. Cavendish, *The Journal of Sir Garnet Wolseley*, p. 10.
35. Poole, 'Cyprus: Its Present and Future', p. 115.
36. Lang, R.H., 'Cyprus II', *Macmillan's Magazine*, no. 38, 1878 cited in ΒΙΚΤΩΡΙΑΝΑ ΚΕΙΜΕΝΑ ΓΙΑ ΤΗΝ ΚΥπΡΟ 1878–1891, p. 60.
37. Ibid., p. 78.
38. Poole, 'Cyprus: Its Present and Future', p. 124
39. Cavendish, *The Journal of Sir Garnet Wolseley*, p. 163.
40. Ibid., p. 160.
41. Letter from Lady Wolseley to her husband, quoted in Taylor, Lou, 'Lady Brassey, 1870–1886: Traveler, Writer, Collector, Educator, Woman of Means, and the Fate of Her Cypriot Artifacts', in V. Tatton-Brown (ed) *Cyprus in the 19th Century AD: Fact, Fancy and Fiction. Papers of the 22nd British Museum Classical Colloquium December 1998* (David Brown Book Co., Connecticut, August 2001), p. 245.
42. Cannadine, David, *Ornamentalism: How the British Saw Their Empire* (Penguin, London, 2001), p. 12.
43. Cavendish, *The Journal of Sir Garnet Wolseley*, p. 154.
44. Brown, Samuel, *Three Months in Cyprus during the Winter of 1878–9* (Edward Stanford, London, 1879), quoted in Schaar, Kenneth W., Given, Michael and Theocharous, George, *Under the Clock* (Bank of Cyprus, 1995), p. 12.
45. The building, on Byron Avenue, still serves as government offices, housing the Cyprus Interior Ministry.
46. *Cyprus Herald* 5 April 1882.
47. Ibid., 11 January 1882.
48. Ibid.

49. Cavendish, *The Journal of Sir Garnet Wolseley*, p. 40. McGaw's grave, a striking
white marble sarcophagus, can still be seen in the British cemetery in Kyrenia.
According to the art historian Dr Rita Severis the original British cemetery
described by Scott-Stevenson was higher up the hill.
50. Scott-Stevenson, *Our Home in Cyprus*, p. 45.
51. *Cyprus Herald* 19 February 1883. In fact the heavily padded and quilted Cypriot
saddle had evolved to accommodate the weakness of the forelegs of Cypriot mules.
The saddle enabled the rider to sit relatively far back on the animal's stronger
hindquarters.
52. Lang, R.H., 'Cyprus II', p. 89.
53. Poole, 'Cyprus: Its Present and Future', p. 115.
54. For an interesting discussion of the ambiguous position of the Christian inhabitants of Malta in nineteenth-century systems of racial classification and of the
relationship between the Christian church and the colonial administration see
Goodwin, Stefan, *Malta, Mediterranean Bridge* (Praeger, Santa Barbara, CA,
2002), pp. 84–86.
55. Scott-Stevenson, *Our Home in Cyprus*, p. 23.
56. *Cyprus Herald* 10 May 1882.
57. Ibid., 19 February 1883.
58. Cavendish, *The Journal of Sir Garnet Wolseley*, p. 95.
59. Ibid., p. 116.
60. Ibid., p. 145.
61. Taylor, Lou, 'Lady Brassey, 1870–1886', p. 245.
62. Roussou-Sinclair, Mary, *Victorian Travellers in Cyprus: A Garden of Their Own*
(Cyprus Research Centre, Texts and Studies of the History of Cyprus, Nicosia,
2002), p. 102.
63. Cavendish, *The Journal of Sir Garnet Wolseley*, p. 164.
64. Scott-Stevenson, *Our Home in Cyprus*, p. 23.
65. *Cyprus: A Weekly Journal of Agriculture and Commerce*, 24 October 1878.
66. Ibid.
67. Scott-Stevenson, *Our Home in Cyprus*, p. 296.
68. Letter from Garnet Wolseley. Foreign Office Correspondence C.O. 67 Volume 4.
N.A. Kew, quoted in Thirgood, J.V., *Cyprus: A Chronicle of Its Forests, Land and
People*, p. 91.
69. *Cyprus Herald* 19 March 1883.
70. Ibid., 2 November 1881.
71. Scott-Stevenson, *Our Home in Cyprus*, p. 9.
72. *Cyprus Herald* 14 November 1882.
73. Ibid.

2 The Whitest of White Elephants. 1882–90

1. *The Times of Cyprus* 1 April 1893.
2. The reasons for the collapse would not become clear until archaeological excavations in the early twenty-first century revealed the foundations had been laid

262 SWEET AND BITTER ISLAND

above the remains of the ancient city of Ledra. The church had been built above stone pits containing devotional terracotta figures of the seventh century BC.

3. Letter to *The Times*. 21 October 1894.
4. Knapland, Paul, *Gladstone's Foreign Policy* (Frank Cass and Co., London, 1935), p. 6.
5. Quoted in Alastos, Doros, *Cyprus in History* (Zeno Publishers, London, 1976), p. 307.
6. Forbes, Archibald, 'The 'Fiasco' of Cyprus', *Nineteenth-Century Magazine* no. 4 (1878).
7. Cavendish, *The Journal of Sir Garnet Wolseley*, p. 50.
8. Ibid., p. 158.
9. *The Times of Cyprus* 3 October 1883.
10. Letter from Gladstone to the Duke of Westminster, 13 March 1896. Quoted in Reddaway, John, *Burdened with Cyprus: The British Connection* (Weidenfeld & Nicholson, London, 1986), p. 10.
11. Reddaway, John, *Burdened with Cyprus: The British Connection*, p. 12.
12. Storrs, Ronald, *Orientations* (Readers Union, London, 1939), p. 482.
13. *The Times of Cyprus* 25 July 1894.
14. *Cyprus Herald* 17 November 1884.
15. *The Times of Cyprus* 25 July 1894.
16. Georghallides, G.S. 'Churchill's 1907 Visit to Cyprus. A Political Analysis'. *Journal of the Cyprus Research Centre* Volume III, 1970, pp. 167–220 (Cyprus Research Centre, Nicosia, 1970).
17. *The Times of Cyprus* 14 August 1894.
18. RHO: Papers of Charles Woolley. Mss. Brit Emp s 515 Box 4/5 Amery, Leo, Tribute Memorandum to the British Cabinet, 1924. Quoted in confidential letter from Charles Woolley to Sir George Gater, permanent under-secretary at the Colonial Office, February 1943.
19. *The Times of Cyprus* 22 June 1894.
20. Ibid., 3 November 1894.
21. Ibid., 28 November 1894.
22. Ibid., 5 December 1894.
23. The development of palatable, ultimately exportable, wine depended on the development of a road network. In remote areas where wine had to be transported by mule, it was carried in goat skins, sealed with tar which, while practical, gave the wine an 'abominable flavour'. See Green, Colonel A.O., *Cyprus: A Short Account of Its History and Present State* (M. Graham Coltart, Scotland, 1914), p. 44.
24. Interview with Dr Akis Petris, former Government Vet, 10 November 2005. Dr Petris's grandfather had the contract for transporting senior government officials to Troodos using horses that had been trained in this way.
25. SA1/4065/1902.
26. *Illustrated London News* 18 October 1879.
27. Interview with Jane D'arcy, daughter of Governor Battershill. April 2005.
28. Schaar, Given and Theocharous, *Under the Clock*, p. 53.

29. Prinsep, Val, quoted in Morris, Jan, *Pax Brittanica* (Faber & Faber, London, 1968), p. 263.
30. RHO: Correspondence and papers of Sir William Denis Battershill GB 162 MSS. Brit. Emp. s. 467, unpublished autobiography, p. 10.
31. The chief secretary, who ran the offices of the Secretariat in Nicosia.
32. *The Times* 12 October 1932.
33. Biddulph, Robert, Lecture to the Royal Geographical Society, London, November 1889.
34. *Illustrated London News* 18 October 1879.
35. RHO: Papers of William Battershill, unpublished autobiography, p. 10.
36. RHO: Papers of Robert Hepburn Wright GB162 MSS Brit Emp 515, 10 July 1943.
37. RHO: Papers of William Battershill, 24 July 1940.
38. Peto, Gladys, *Malta and Cyprus* (Outward Bound Library, J.M. Dent & Sons, London, 1927), p. 169.
39. Interview with Jane D'Arcy, daughter of Governor William Battershill, April 2005.
40. Luke, Harry, writing of his time as ADC to Governor Hamilton Goold-Adams, 1911–1915. *The Cyprus Review* February 1955.
41. Peto, *Malta and Cyprus*, p. 182.
42. *Cyprus Herald* 6 October 1883.

3 A High Degree of Mental Culture. 1900

1. A comparison originally made in Schaar, Given and Theocharous, *Under the Clock*, p. 72.
2. The English School was originally situated on Victoria St, inside what is now the northern part of the old walled city. It moved to purpose built accommodation (now the Nicosia Law courts to the south of the Green Line) in 1912, moving again after that building was requisitioned by the military in 1932. The present building was built mainly in 1938.
3. *Cyprus Herald* 9 November 1881.
4. Report of the English School annual concert and prize giving *Anglo-Cypriot* 11 March 1908.
5. English School Mark Book, 1905. Contained in Newham's trunk. Office of the Secretary of the Board of Governors, Nicosia English School.
6. The first recorded games of football and hockey on the island in 1900 were played by boys at the English School.
7. Speech delivered by the colony's senior judge Anton Bertram, on Victoria Day, 1908. Reported in *Anglo-Cypriot* 3 June 1908.
8. Interview with Eirwen Harbottle, November 2006.
9. *Anglo-Cypriot* 11 March 1908 Robert Biddulph spoke frequently at such events during the first decade of the school's existence. Although his post as high commissioner had ended in 1886, his daughter Constance had married his private secretary, Charles King-Harman, who subsequently served as High Commissioner

of Cyprus from 1904 to 1911. Biddulph and his wife appear to have been regular visitors to Government House during this period. Lady Biddulph died while staying with her daughter and son-in-law in April 1903 and is buried in Nicosia Cemetery.

10. In particular those of Weir, W.W. *Education in Cyprus* (Cosmos Press, Nicosia, 1952) and of Persianis, Panayiotis, K., *Church and State in Cyprus Education* (Nicosia, 1978), G. S. Gheorghallides' definitive volume *A Political and Administrative History of Cyprus 1918–1926* (Cyprus Research Centre, Nicosia, 1979) also covers the subject extensively, pp. 47–64.

11. Baker, Samuel, *Cyprus as I Saw It in 1879*. Chapter XVII, p. 299 (Project Gutenberg Etext no. 3656).

12. Despatch from Biddulph, 22 July 1880. Included in Parliamentary Paper C.2930. Quoted in Orr, C.W.J., *Cyprus under British Rule*, p. 122

13. Ibid., p. 123.

14. Despatch from Lord Kimberley to Biddulph 10 June 1881, Included in Parliamentary Paper C2930, Quoted in Persianis, Panayiotis, K., *Church and State in Cyprus Education* (Nicosia, 1978), p. 24

15. Bowen, James, 'Education, Ideology and the Ruling Class: Hellenism and the English Public Schools in the Nineteenth Century'. *Rediscovering Hellenism. The Hellenic Inheritance and the English Imagination* (Cambridge University Press, Cambridge, 1989), p. 176.

16. Interview with Paul Griffin, English School headmaster, 1956–1960. November 2006.

17. Arnold, Thomas, *Miscellaneous Works*, p. 351 quoted in Clarke, M.L., *Classical Education in Britain 1500–1900* (Cambridge University Press, Cambridge, 1959), p. 80.

18. Interview with Paul Griffin, November 2006.

19. James, 'Education, Ideology and the Ruling Class', p. 176.

20. Not all governors and high commissioners were university educated however. Garnet Wolseley, Robert Biddulph, Hamilton Goold-Adams and John Harding all attended military academies, while the Labour peer, Rex Winster was educated at the Royal Naval College.

21. Storrs, *Orientations*, p. 487.

22. Stanley, A.P. *The Life of Thomas Arnold* (1844) Volume I, p. 129 Quoted in Jenkyns Richard, *The Victorians and Ancient Greece* (Basil Blackwell, Oxford, 1980), p. 62.

23. Letter to *The Times* 29 July 1889 from Sidney Colvin, Chairman of the Cyprus Exploration Fund.

24. It is interesting that in 1955, when George Grivas, the leader of the armed uprising against British rule assumed a *nom de guerre*, he chose to distance himself from the heroes of ancient Athens and Sparta, whose names had already been assimilated into imperial culture. His chosen name 'Dighenis' was taken instead from that of an eighth-century folk hero, Dighenis Akritas, who defended the frontiers of the Byzantine Empire against the Saracens.

25. Bernal, Martin, 'The Image of Ancient Greece as a Tool for Colonialism and Cultural Hegemony'. In *Social Construction of the Past. Representation as Power*, ed. Bond, George C. and Gilliam, Angela (Routledge, London, 1994), p. 126

26. Storrs, *Orientations*, p. 507.

27. Luke, Harry, *Cyprus* (George G. Harrap & Co., London, 1965), p. 173

28. Herzfeld, Michael, *Ours Once More: Folklore, Ideology and the Making of Modern Greece* (Pella Publishing, New York, 1986), p. 15.

29. Storrs, *Orientations*, p. 494.

30. Peto, *Cyprus and Malta*, p. 193.

31. Letter to the Greek language newspaper *Eleftheria*, 9 October 1909. Quoted in Weir, *Education in Cyprus*, p. 108.

32. *Eleftheria* 13 November 1909. Ibid.

33. Persianis, *Church and State in Cyprus Education*, p. 61.

34. Bernal, 'The Image of Ancient Greece', p. 127.

35. Lord Kimberley Parliamentary Paper C2930. Quoted in Orr, *Cyprus under British Rule*, p. 123.

36. Ibid., p. 186.

37. C.O. 67/127 5 March 1901 Quoted in Persianis, *Church and State in Cyprus Education*, p. 160.

38. Michael Attalides *Cyprus: Nationalism and Internal Politics* (Q. Press, Edinburgh, 1979), p. 26.

39. Ibid, p. 114.

40. Orr, *Cyprus under British Rule*, p. 130.

41. Weir, *Education in Cyprus*, p. 115.

42. Storrs, *Orientations*, p. 485.

43. Ibid., p. 485.

44. Hill, Sir George Francis *A History of Cyprus. Volume 4: The Ottoman Province, the British Colony, 1571–1948* (Cambridge University Press, Cambridge, 1952), p. 492.

45. Buettner, Elizabeth, *Empire Families Britons and Late Imperial India* (Oxford University Press, London, 2004), p. 40.

46. Interview with Jane D'Arcy, April 2005.

47. RHO: Papers of William Battershill, 24 October 1939.

48. RHO: Papers of Ivan Lloyd Phillips, *GB 162* MSS. Brit. Emp. s. 499 18 9 April 1951.

49. Interview with Matthew Parris, November 2006.

50. Peto, *Malta and Cyprus*, p. 170.

51. One of the few colonial street names to have been retained after independence in 1960.

52. Interview with Clare Harrap, November 2006.

53. Interview with Donald Waterer, November 2006.

54. Buettner, *Empire Families*, p. 64.

55. Interview with Eirwen Harbottle, November 2006.

56. Buettner, *Empire Families*, p. 144.

57. Peto, *Cyprus and Malta*, p. 169.

4   Softening our Rough Peasantry. 1900–14

1. Donne, *Records of the Ottoman Conquest of Cyprus*, p. 44.
2. Quoted in Turner, B.S., *The Story of the Cyprus Government Railway* (Mechanical Engineering Publications, London, 1979), p. 11.
3. Abbott, George C., 'A Re-examination of the Colonial Development Act'. *The Economic History Review*, New Series, Volume 24, no. 1 (February 1971), pp. 68–81.
4. *The Times of Cyprus* 3 March 1894 and 13 May 1894.
5. SA1/C679/1902 Confidential memo from Charles Bellamy. 24 July 1902.
6. Pusey, G.B., 'Servitude Preferred', an unpublished memoir quoted in Georghallides, G.S., *Journal of the Cyprus Research Centre, Volume XI 1981–2* pp. 275–334.
7. Orr, C.W.J., *Cyprus under British Rule*, p. 155.
8. Pusey, 'Servitude Preferred', pp. 275–334.
9. IWM: Documents Collection: Towers C.L. PP/MCR/227 7 April 1945.
10. Ibid.
11. In the private collection of Dr Rita Severis.
12. C.O. 883/7, No. 69. Quoted in Georghallides, G.S., 'Churchill's 1907 visit to Cyprus', *Journal of the Cyprus Research Centre Volume III 1969–70*, pp. 167–220.
13. Ibid.
14. Ibid.
15. *Anglo-Cypriot* 22 April 1908.
16. *Cyprus News* 14 January 1931.
17. Orr, C.W.J., *Cyprus under British Rule*, p. 81.
18. Baker, *Cyprus as I Saw It in 1879*, Chapter V.
19. Ibid., Chapter III.
20. Ibid., Chapter V.
21. Medlicott, J.H. *The Handbook of Cyprus, 1901*, p. 8.
22. Concrete, British-built water troughs can still be seen in most villages on the island. Functional and unadorned, they were built in the 1950s and stamped PWD, their no- nonsense utilitarian design reflecting the priorities of a colony where every penny counted.
23. Geddes, Mr and Mrs Patrick, 'Cyprus and Its Power to Help the East'. *The Report of the International Conference on Armenian Aid*. May 1897.
24. Baker, *Cyprus as I Saw It in 1879*, Chapter XIV.
25. Today, the mud brick buildings of Athalassa Farm, with their foundation stones bearing the names of two of the island's governors, are derelict, in danger of being swallowed up by a new Nicosia by-pass.
26. When the writer Rider Haggard, author of *King Solomon's Mines*, visited Cyprus in 1900 he was appalled by what he described as the 'filthy farm buildings' surrounding the keep, suggesting that if they were 'swept away' and 'suitable additions' made to Kolossi Castle it could be transformed into 'a delightful country house'.

27. *Cyprus Journal* 6 February 1906.

28. Home, Gordon, *Cyprus Then and Now* (J.M. Dent & Sons, London, 1959), p. 180.

29. Baker, *Cyprus as I Saw It in 1879*, Chapter II

30. RHO: Papers of Sir Robert Armitage. *GB 162* MSS. Afr. s. 2204 Letter to Maurice Howarth 5 November 1954 The wooden plough was still in use as late as 1954, when Governor Robert Armitage noticed 'amusing contrasts such as a donkey and a cow harnessed together and pulling a wooden plough and next door a Massey Harris combine harvester or tractor roaring across the fields'.

31. Baker, *Cyprus as I Saw It in 1879*, Chapter II.

32. Ibid., Chapter III.

33. Given, Michael, *The Archaeology of the Colonised* (Routledge, London, 2004), p. 3.

34. Interview with Donald Waterer, November 2006.

35. *Cyprus Review* July 1948.

36. RHO: Papers of David Athelstane Percival MSS. Brit. Emp. s. 364. Letter to Alicia, 21 March 1940.

37. Luke, Harry, *Cities and Men, An Autobiography. Volume Two* (Geoffrey Bles, London, 1953), p. 35.

38. *Anglo-Cypriot* 18 July 1908.

39. Ibid.

40. Green, *Cyprus: A Short Account of Its History*, p. 76. Green's guide for his tour of the island was Alfred Bovill, the genial Chief Forestry Officer, but progress was delayed by Bovill's insistence on frequent stops to brew up tea in his new 'tiffin basket' a recent gift from the acting high commissioner, with which the forestry officer was 'as pleased as a child with a new toy', Green, *Cyprus: A Short Account of Its History*, p. 104.

41. *The Times of Cyprus* 28 May 1894.

42. Baker, *Cyprus as I Saw It in 1879*, Chapter XI.

43. Rider Haggard's *A Winter Pilgrimage: Being an Account of Travels through Palestine, Italy, and the Island of Cyprus, Accomplished in the Year 1900* (Longmans, Green & Co., London, 1901), p. 136.

44. It is estimated that 20–30 thousand Armenians died in a succession of massacres that took place across Turkey between 1894 and 1896.

45. Geddes, 'Cyprus and Its Power to Help the East'.

46. 'Cotton Picking Notes', *The Cyprus Journal: A Quarterly Review of the Agriculture and Industries of Cyprus*, July 1906.

47. 'Society for the Prevention of Cruelty to Animals', ibid.

48. 'Letters from the Districts', *The Cyprus Journal*, April 1906.

49. *The Cyprus Journal*, July 1906.

50. *Anglo-Cypriot* 8 April 1908.

51. Ibid., 11 March 1908.

52. RHO: Papers of Sir Robert Armitage. Letter to his parents. 27 February 1954.

53. Haggard, *A Winter Pilgrimage*, p. 132.

54. Scott-Stevenson, *Our Home in Cyprus*, Introduction, p. VIII.

55. Peto, *Cyprus and Malta*, p. 131.
56. An opera about an Italian bandit by the French composer, Auber.
57. Green, *Cyprus: A Short Account of Its History*, p. 59.
58. Peto, *Cyprus and Malta*, p. 161.
59. Green, *Cyprus: A Short Account of Its History*, p. 47.
60. Said, W. Edward, *Orientalism* (Routledge & Keegan Paul, London, 1978), p. 58.
61. Peto, *Cyprus and Malta*, p. 160

5   Clauson Will Do the Best He Can. 1914–18

1. *Cyprus Herald* 26 January 1882.
2. Luke, Harry. See: http://janus.lib.cam.ac.uk/db/node.xsp?id=EAD%2FGBR%2F0115%2FCobham
3. *Anglo-Cypriot* 6 May 1908.
4. Racing at Larnaca, was a more casual affair than in the capital, and took place close to the beach, on the site of what is today Larnaca Airport.
5. It was renamed the Governor's cup during the 1930s after the then governor, Richmond Palmer.
6. Interview with Akis Petris, November 2005
7. Luke, Harry, *Cities and Men Volume One* (Geoffrey Bles, London, 1953), p. 212.
8. Quoted from the memoirs of John Davidson, who visited Cyprus in 1913, in Rhodes James, Robert, *Memoirs of a Conservative, J.C.C. Davidson's Memoirs and Papers* (Wieidenfeld and Nicholson, London, 1969), p. 13.
9. Interview with Akis Petris, November 2005.
10. NA CO 67/173, p. 227. Discussion of Goold-Adams amendments to quarantine regulations on the island.
11. NA CO 67/173. 28 August 1914, p. 28.
12. Ibid., 14 August 1914.
13. Rhodes James, *Memoirs of a Conservative*, p. 17.
14. NA CO67/174. 3 October 1914.
15. NA CO67/182. 11 December 1916.
16. Barnett, Corelli, *The Great War* (Penguin Classic Military History, London, 1979).
17. NA CO 67 173. 31 August 1914.
18. Ibid.
19. NA CO 67/174. 3 October 1914.
20. Rhodes James, *Memoirs of a Conservative*, p. 13.
21. NA CO 67/174. 4 November 1914.
22. Ibid.
23. NA CO 67 175. 11 November 1914.
24. NA CO 67 174, p. 147. 20 November 1914
25. Luke, *Cities and Men Volume Two*, p. 3.
26. NA CO 167/179. 7 July 1915.
27. NA CO 67/189. 19 December 1918.
28. Luke, *Cities and Men Volume Two*, p. 4.

29. Luke subsequently served under Goold-Adams' successor in Cyprus.
30. Faiz, Suha, *Recollections and Reflections of an Unknown Cyprus Turk* (Avon Books, London, 1998), p. 8.
31. Luke, *Cities and Men Volume One*, p. 223.
32. Luke, *Cities and Men Volume Two*, p. 3.
33. NA CO 323/638/84. 18 November 1914.
34. NA CO 67/174. 20 November 1914.
35. NA CO 67 175. 29 December 1914.
36. NA CO 67/182. 9 September 1915.
37. NA CO 67/180.
38. SA1/3741/1902. 12 November 1902.
39. *The Times of Cyprus* 3 June 1894.
40. Keshishian, Kevork, K. *Nicosia, Capitol of Cyprus Then and Now* (Moufflon Bookshop, Nicosia, 1960), p. 81. Keshishian refers to the 'Jirit parade ground', the moat between Roccas and Mula bastions, east of Ledra Palace Hotel.
41. Keegan, John, *The Price of Admiralty* (Hutchinson, London, 1988), p. 103.
42. NA CO 67 173. 21 September 1914.
43. NA CO 67/174. 2 November 1914.
44. Faiz, *Recollections and Reflections*, p. 36.
45. Quoted in McHenry, James, A. *The Uneasy Partnership on Cyprus, 1919–1939* (Garland Publishing, New York, 1987), p. 118.
46. Malcolm Stevenson to the Duke of Devonshire, quoted in McHenry, *The Uneasy Partnership*, p. 133.
47. McHenry, *The Uneasy Partnership*, p. 125.
48. NA CO 70/10. *Cyprus Gazette* 5 January 1916.
49. NA CO 56/174 24 October–2 November 1914.
50. NA CO 67/180.
51. NA CO 167/179. 8 July 1915.
52. NA CO 67/178. *The Near East Magazine* 23 July 1915.
53. MECA: *Bible Lands*, Volume 5 April 1916.
54. Cyprus: Notes from a Correspondent. *The Near East Magazine* 23 July 1915
55. NA CO 67/178. 27 August 1915.
56. NA CO 67/180.
57. NA CO 67/178. 22 October 1915.
58. NA CO 67/186. 13 October 1917.
59. NA CO 67/173. 25 August 1914.
60. NA AIR 2/1465.
61. Luke, *Cities and Men* Volume Two, p. 43.
62. *Cyprus Gazette* 21 February 1916.
63. NA CO 67/189. 27 October 1915.
64. NA CO 67/188. 4 January 1918.
65. NA CO 67/173. 14 August 1914.
66. *Cyprus Gazette* 7 April 1916.
67. NA CO 67/179. 21 August 1915.

68. NA CO 67 176. 19 April 1915.
69. NA CO 67/186. 4 December 1917.
70. NA CO 167/179. August 7 1915.
71. *Cyprus Gazette* 7 April 1916.
72. NA CO 67/173. 11 September 1914.
73. NA CO 67/189. 4 November 1918.
74. NA CO 67 176. 25 March 1915.
75. NA CO 67/190. 21 August 1918.
76. NA CO 67/176. 8 March 1915.
77. Mackenzie, Compton, *Greece in My Life* (Chatto & Windus, London, 1960), p. 25.
78. NA CO 67/176. 3 April 1915.
79. Ibid., 10 May 1915.
80. A Cypriot pound consisted of 180 piastres; 9 piastres made a shilling, 20 shillings made a pound.
81. NA CO 67/180.
82. NA CO 67/190. 16 April 1918.

6   Showing Benevolent Neutrality. 1916–19

1. Mackenzie, Compton, *First Athenian Memories* (Cassel & Co., London, 1931), p. 341. Mackenzie identifies Samson merely as 'V'.
2. Ibid., p. 75.
3. NA CO 67/182. 11 December 1916, Clauson to secretary of state for the colonies. Summary of naval and military action in Cyprus 1914–16.
4. Mackenzie, *First Athenian Memories*, p. 110.
5. NA CO 67/180. 6 March 1916.
6. NA KV1/18 Imperial Overseas Intelligence 1918: Cyprus Section and Appendices.
7. Ibid.
8. NA CO 67/182 Despatches. October–December 1916, p. 23.
9. Ibid.
10. NA KV1/18.
11. Ibid.
12. Ibid., p. 43.
13. It was actually torpedoed on 12 August 1917.
14. NA KV1/18, p. 43.
15. Ibid., p. 5.
16. Ibid., p. 32.
17. Mackenzie, *First Athenian Memories*, p. 256.
18. NA KV1/18.
19. NA KV1/18 Sometimes the French patrol vessels got things badly wrong. The caique Evangelistra was sunk off Paphos after it was erroneously believed to be supplying petrol to German submarines. The ship's captain was imprisoned in Egypt and only narrowly escaped execution. He was subsequently absolved and awarded compensation. I'm grateful to Rita Severis for drawing the incident to

my attention. For a detailed account see Κελέσης, Αντρέας, *Ναυτικά Κιάλια (ΕΚΔΟΣΕΙΣ ΓΕΡΜΑΝΟΣ).*

20. NA CO 67/190. 22 July 1918. The War Office expected Cyprus to pay for the installation costs, a total of £1,200, commenting snidely that '... when most other members of the Empire are contributing both men and money to the common cause, Cyprus might wish to take this suitable opportunity of making a contribution towards the cost of the war'.
21. NA CO67/184. 8 April 1917.
22. Ibid.
23. NA CO 67/184. 13 August 1917.
24. NA KV1/18.
25. NA CO 323/819. 14 January 1919.

7 Gentle Somnambulance. 1918–26

1. Pusey, G.B., 'Servitude Preferred' an unpublished memoir quoted in Georghallides, G.S., *Journal of the Cyprus Research Centre, Volume XI 1981–2*, pp. 275–334.
2. Letter to *The Times* 4 February 1919.
3. MECA: Jerusalem and the East Mission Bible Lands Volume 7 January 1920.
4. NA AIR 2/1465 Importance of Retention of Cyprus as an air base.
5. Georghallides, G.S. *A Political and Administrative History of Cyprus 1918–1926* (Cyprus Research Centre, Nicosia, 1979), p. 231.
6. McHenry, *The Uneasy Partnership*, p. 161.
7. Ibid., p. 411.
8. SA1 696/1886 Harry Thompson, Commissioner of Paphos, 18 May 1886 Quoted in Katsiaounis, Rolandos, *Labour, Society and Politics in Cyprus during the Second Half of the Nineteenth Century* (Cyprus Research Centre, Nicosia, 1996.), p. 33.
9. NA CO 67/188. 13 May 1918 Handwritten note attached to file.
10. Ibid., 3 June 1918.
11. Georghallides, *A Political and Administrative History of Cyprus 1918–1926*, p. 321
12. Ibid., p. 285.
13. Ibid., p. 378.
14. Comments made by A.J. Dawe, a junior Colonial Office official who visited Cyprus in 1926. Quoted in Georghallides, *A Political and Administrative History of Cyprus 1918–1926*, p. 406.
15. Peto, *Malta and Cyprus*, p. 171.
16. *On Crown Service: A History of HM Colonial and Overseas Civil Services 1837–1997*, Kirk-Greene, Anthony (I.B.Tauris, London, 1999), p. 21.
17. G.S. Georghallides, *A Political and Administrative History of Cyprus 1918–1926*, p. 406.
18. Interview with Eirwen Harbottle, November 2006.
19. Pusey, G.B., 'Servitude Preferred', an unpublished memoir quoted in Georghallides, G.S., *Journal of the Cyprus Research Centre, Volume XI 1981–2*, pp. 275–334.

20. RHO: Papers of Clive Watts MSS. Brit. Emp. s. 291.

21. Storrs, *Orientations,* p. 499.

22. Harding, Gilbert, *Along My Line* (Popular Book Club, London, 1955), p. 118.

23. RHO: Papers of Vivian Hart-Davis MSS. Brit. Emp. s. 346, unpublished memoir, Personal Reminiscences. Gold Coast, Fiji and Cyprus.

24. Peto, *Cyprus and Malta,* p. 207.

25. RHO: Papers of Vivian Hart-Davis. Gold Coast, Fiji and Cyprus.

26. Peto, *Cyprus and Malta,* p. 207.

27. Known today as Saray Square.

28. Schaar, Given and Theocharous, *Under the Clock,* p. 061.

29. Letter to *The Times* 28 September 1929.

30. RHO: Papers of William Battershill, unpublished memoir 'Reflections After Nine Years Absence'.

31. A standard Ottoman land measurement quantified as being forty paces in breadth and width, it corresponded to 9,895 square feet.

32. Evelyn Newman, unpublished memoir 1962.

33. Today the single-storey stone farmhouse is occupied by a Chinese restaurant, and its garden opens on to a busy main road that links Karavas with other Kyrenian suburbs.

34. Interview with Eirwen Harbottle, November 2006.

35. Ibid.

36. Thirgood, J.V. *Cyprus, A Chronicle of Its Forests, Land and People* (University of British Colombia Press, Vancouver, 1987). Footnote to, p. 137.

37. Chapman, Geoff, unpublished memoir, Chapter Three.

38. Storrs *Orientations,* p. 505.

39. Thirgood, *Cyprus, A Chronicle of Its Forests, Land and People.* Footnote to p. 139.

40. Chapman, unpublished memoir, Chapter Three.

41. Neither did Unwin's extensive understanding of forestry management extend to the control of his departmental budget, and after a series of errors, the colonial administration was forced to appoint an accountant with sole responsibility for Forestry Department finances.

42. If Unwin seemed intimidating to his departmental colleagues he was a terrifying figure to many colonial children, largely due to his insistence that if his own children did not finish their food it should be served up repeatedly, however mildewed, until it was eaten. Eirwen Harbottle, a contemporary of Unwin's son George remembers a dread of visiting George at home 'because all these disgusting things would be served up with bits of green fur on them'.

43. Chapman, unpublished memoir, Chapter Three.

44. Interview with Donald Waterer, November 2006.

45. Chapman, unpublished memoir, Chapter Four.

46. Thirgood, *Cyprus, A Chronicle of Its Forests, Land and People,* p. 145.

47. Luke, *Cities and Men Volume One,* p. 36.

48. Storrs, *Orientations,* p. 505.

49. Cavendish, Anne, ed. *The Journal of Sir Garnet Wolseley,* p. 22.

50. Poole, Reginald Stuart, 'Cyprus: Its Present and Future', *Contemporary Review* no. 33, 1878.

51. Baker, Samuel, *Cyprus as I Saw It in 1879* Chapter XIII, p. 245 (Project Gutenberg Etext no. 3656).

52. Proceedings of the Royal Geographical Society. New Series. Volume 11 1889., p. 705.

53. Under the 1913 Goat Law goats could be excluded from village land if the majority of villagers voted for them to be removed.

54. Thirgood, *Cyprus, A Chronicle of Its Forests, Land and People*, p. 146.

55. Georghallides in *A Political and Administrative History of Cyprus 1918–1926*, p. 318 refers to the villagers of Mitsero, who were asked to pay 24 shillings a year for permission to graze animals worth only 10 shillings.

56. The Sales family ran a large plant and seed nursery in Wokingham.

57. RHO: Papers of Gilbert Noel Sale. GB 162 MSS. Medit. s. 23, diary entry 26 June 1922.

58. Interview with Donald Waterer, November 2006.

59. Ibid.

60. RHO: Papers of Gilbert Noel Sale. 6 August 1924, p. 145.

8   No More Mixed Tea Parties. 1926–38

1. The tiny bell tower at the western end of the church reveals that the original roof was made of red tiles.

2. Morgan, Tabitha, ' "An unpretentious but vigorous character," or, "a distinct spirit of complacency"? The Anglican community in Cyprus 1878–1960', in A. Varnava, N. Coureas and M. Elia (eds) *The Minorities of Cyprus: Development Patterns and the Identity of the Internal-Exclusion* (Cambridge Scholars Publishing, Newcastle, 2008).

3. It was called Latomia.

4. MECA: Papers of the Anglican Church Jerusalem and the East Mission GB 165/0161 Box 88/1 4 June 1931.

5. Georghallides, G.S. *Cyprus and the Governorship of Sir Ronald Storrs* (Cyprus Research Centre, Nicosia, 1985), p. 3.

6. Ibid.

7. SA1: Papers of Ronald Storrs, Reel 11 Box IV Folder I Correspondence with A.T. Wilson, February 1927.

8. Storrs, *Orientations*, p. 507.

9. Georghallides, *Cyprus and the Governorship of Sir Ronald Storrs*, p. 11.

10. 'Meeting of the Social Hygiene Council', *Cyprus News* 28 February 1931.

11. SA1: Papers of Ronald Storrs, Reel 11 Box IV Folder I, 30 March 1927.

12. Georghallides, *Cyprus and the Governorship of Sir Ronald Storrs*, p. 40.

13. The Leo Amery Diaries , Volume I 1826–1929 J. Barnes and D. Nicholson (eds) (Brandon Hutchinson, London 1980), pp. 515–17 quoted in Georghallides, *Cyprus and the Governorship of Sir Ronald Storrs*, p. 51.

14. Ibid., pp. 367–68 quoted in Georghallides, *Cyprus and the Governorship of Sir Ronald Storrs*, p. 51.
15. SA1: Papers of Ronald Storrs, Reel 11 Box IV Folder I Letter from King-Harman to Storrs, 15 October 1927.
16. Kirk-Greene, Anthony, *On Crown Service A History of HM Colonial and Overseas Civil Services, 1837–1997* (I.B.Tauris, London, 1999), pp. 21–28.
17. Interview with Donald Waterer, November 2006. All subsequent quotes attributed to Donald Waterer derive from this interview.
18. Storrs, *Orientations*, p. 508.
19. *The Times* 12 July 1928.
20. Minutes of the Legislative Council 1928, quoted in Georghallides, *Cyprus and the Governorship of Sir Ronald Storrs*, p. 75.
21. NA CO 67/223/39093. Quoted in Georghallides, *Cyprus and the Governorship of Sir Ronald Storrs*, p. 77.
22. *The Times* 5 May 1928.
23. Storrs, *Orientations*, p. 509.
24. Ibid., p. 509.
25. *The Times* 12 July 1928.
26. Georghallides, *Cyprus and the Governorship of Sir Ronald Storrs*, p. 89.
27. Ibid., p. 93.
28. Storrs, *Orientations*, p. 352.
29. Meinertzhagen, Richard, *Middle East Diary, 1917–1956* (London, 1959), p. 187 Quoted in Miller, Rory, 'Sir Ronald Storrs and Zion: The Dream that Turned into a Nightmare', in Middle Eastern Studies, Volume 36, no. 3, July 2000, pp. 114–44.
30. *Cyprus News* 25 April 1931.
31. Storrs, *Orientations*, p. 502.
32. Ibid., p. 503.
33. Government Blue Book, 1938.
34. Batten, Jean, My Life (George G. Harrap & Co., London, 1938), p. 43.
35. MECA: Jerusalem and the East Mission GB 165/ 0161 Box 86/Misc. *Cyprus the Garden of the Near East* (Office of the Commissioner, Queen Anne's Chambers, London, 1927).
36. Storrs, *Orientations*, p. 507.
37. Such as the Aqueduct, which claimed to be the only hotel in the city under English management. *Cyprus News* 24 December 1930.
38. SA1: Papers of Ronald Storrs, Reel 11 Box IV Folder I, 17 February 1927
39. *Bible Lands* Volume 7 (July 1924).
40. Storrs, *Orientations*, p. 519
41. Archdeacon Potter, 'Cyprus Today', *Bible Lands* Volume 7 January 1926
42. Storrs to Lord Passfield, 27 March1930 CO 67/238/41174/31 quoted in McHenry, *The Uneasy Partnership*, p. 137.
43. Colonial Office file on Mehmet Munir July 1932 CO 67/247/98679 Quoted in McHenry, *The Uneasy Partnership*, p. 138.
44. *Cyprus News* 10 January 1931.

45. Keshishian, Kevork K., *Nicosia, Capital of Cyprus Then and Now*, p. 292.
46. Lyautey, Marshall, 'Problems of Empire. Why the English are Great Colonisers. Where Democracy Fails', *Cyprus News* 14 January 1931.
47. Peto, *Malta and Cyprus*, p. 173.
48. Schaar, Given and Theocharous, *Under the Clock*, p. 54.
49. RHO: Papers of Vivian Hart Davis: Gold Coast, Fiji and Cyprus.
50. Interview with Eirwen Harbottle, November 2006. All subsequent quotes attributed to Eirwen Harbottle derive from this interview.
51. Ibid.
52. RHO: Papers of Vivian Hart-Davis, unpublished memoir, Personal Reminiscences. Gold Coast, Fiji and Cyprus.
53. Peto, *Malta and Cyprus*, p. 173.
54. Ibid., p. 184.
55. RHO: Papers of Vivian Hart-Davis, unpublished memoir, Personal Reminiscences. Gold Coast, Fiji and Cyprus
56. Peto, *Malta and Cyprus*, p. 184.
57. A home-spun fabric, very soft, it was used mainly for bed sheets and men's shirts.
58. Interview with Jean Meikle, November 2006. All subsequent quotes attributed to Jean Meikle derive from this interview. Jean's father George Ridgeway was the agile Shell agent who had refuelled Jean Batten's plane by balancing on the wing.
59. Interview with Donald Waterer, November 2006.
60. RHO: Papers of Vivian Hart-Davis, unpublished memoir, Personal Reminiscences. Gold Coast, Fiji and Cyprus
61. Interview with Donald Waterer, November 2006.
62. Peto, *Malta and Cyprus*, p. 183
63. Ibid., p. 187
64. RHO: Papers of Vivian Hart-Davis, unpublished memoir, Personal Reminiscences. Gold Coast, Fiji and Cyprus
65. Interview with Jean Meikle, November 2006
66. Interview with Donald Waterer, November 2006.
67. Peto, *Malta and Cyprus*, p. 193.
68. Ibid., p. 203.
69. Interview with Eirwen Harbottle, November 2006.
70. Ibid.
71. RHO: Papers of William Battershill, diary entry 25 June 1936.
72. Peto, *Malta and Cyprus*, p. 180.
73. Haggard, *A Winter Pilgrimage*, p. 183.
74. Interview with Eirwen Harbottle, November 2006.
75. Storrs, *Orientations*, p. 537.
76. Faiz, Suha, *Reflections and Recollections of an Unknown Cypriot Turk* (Avon Books, London, 1998), pp. 35–38.
77. RHO: Papers of Vivian Hart-Davis, unpublished memoir, Personal Reminiscences. Gold Coast, Fiji and Cyprus.

78. Faiz, Suha, *Reflections and Recollections of an Unknown Cypriot Turk*, p. 64

79. *Cyprus News* 24 December 1930. The King's speech on empire trade at the Guildhall broadcast on the BBC on 16 December 1930 was heard by listeners in Famagusta, but the BBC's Empire Service proper did not begin until December 1932.

80. *Cyprus News* 10 January 1931

81. Georghallides, G.S., *Cyprus and the Governorship of Sir Ronald Storrs*, p. 701

82. Surridge, B.J., *A Survey of Rural Life in Cyprus* (Cyprus Government Printing Office, Nicosia, Cyprus, 1930), p. 35 By contrast, farm workers in the United Kingdom at this time were paid £1.11s.8d.

83. Georghallides, G.S., *Cyprus and the Governorship of Sir Ronald Storrs*, p. 50. Since 1878 The Tribute had been allocated for the payment of interest on the Ottoman loan of 1855. Each year, after the interest had been paid, there had been a surplus of 11,000. The Legislative Council hoped that with the abolition of the Tribute the accumulated surplus would be returned to Cyprus as a lump sum. It was not.

84. Despatch from the governor of Cyprus to the secretary of state for the colonies. 11 February 1932. Reproduced in full in (*Journal of Cyprus Studies*), January 2006

85. Storrs, *Orientations*, p. 529

86. Despatch from the governor of Cyprus to the secretary of state for the colonies. 11 February 1932.

87. Storrs, *Orientations*, p. 530

88. Despatch from the governor of Cyprus to the secretary of state for the colonies. 11 February 1932.

89. Storrs, *Orientations*, p. 530

90. Faiz, Suha, *Reflections and Recollections of an Unknown Cypriot Turk*, p. 31

91. Chapman, Geoff, unpublished memoir, Chapter Three

92. Attalides, *Cyprus: Nationalism and Internal Politics*, p. 29

93. Even this is disputed. Greek Cypriot sources claim the number was closer to fifteen.

94. Storrs, *Orientations*, p. 537

95. Ibid., p. 538

96. Richter, Heinz, A. 'Benevolent Autocracy 1931–1945', in H. Faustman and N. Peristianis (eds), *Britain in Cyprus: Colonialism and Post-Colonialism 1878–2006*, p. 138.

97. Despatch from the governor of Cyprus to the secretary of state for the colonies. 11 February 1932.

98. Alastos, Doros, *Cyprus in History*, p. 359.

99. Palmer, Richmond, Forward to Newman, Phillip, *A Short History of Cyprus* (Longman, Green and Co., London) 1940. Palmer's forward was omitted from later editions.

100. Harding, Gilbert, *Along My Line*, p. 116.

101. Ibid., p. 114.

102. Richter, 'Benevolent Autocracy 1931–1945', p. 141.

103. 'Servitude Preferred', Excerpts by G.B. Pusey. Georghallides, G.S., *Journal of the Cyprus Research Centre, Volume XI 1981–2*, pp. 275–334.

104. Palmer, Richmond, 'Cyprus' (*Journal of the Royal Central Asian Society*, Volume 26 [1939]). Quoted in Richter, 'Benevolent Autocracy 1931–1945', p. 141.

105. RHO: Papers of William Battershill, diary entry 25 July 1936.

106. Palmer to J.H. Thomas, CO 67/265/9055 quoted in McHenry, *The Uneasy Partnership*, p. 201.

107. Interview with Jane D'Arcy, April 2005.

108. MECA: Jerusalem and the East Mission GB 165/0161 Box 1 Folder 2 1933–47, 24 August 1934.

109. Ibid. Report by Archdeacon Maxwell. October 1937–31 March 1938.

110. *The Times* 21 April 1934.

111. RHO: Papers of Sir Charles Campbell Woolley. Box 5 File 3 Administrative Memorandum no. 5 Produced by Governor Richmond Palmer, 5 June 1938: Official Calls on H.M. Ships.

112. RHO: Papers of Sir William Battershill, diary entry 25 June 1936.

113. Harding, Gilbert, *Along My Line*, p. 122.

114. RHO: Papers of Sir William Battershill, diary entry 25 June 1936.

115. MECA: Papers of the Anglican Church Jerusalem and the East Mission GB 165/0161 Box 1 Folder 2 1933–47.

116. RHO: Papers of William Battershill, diary entry 25 June 1936.

117. MECA: Jerusalem and the East Mission GB 165/0161 Box 86 Folder 2 1933–47 Account of the Work of the Church in Cyprus by Ven. Archdeacon Malcolm Maxwell 6 June 1939.

118. Interview with Eirwen Harbottle, November 2006.

119. Storrs, *Orientations*, p. 494.

120. Interview with Donald Waterer, November 2006.

121. Ibid.

9 Bread Stuffed with Raisins. 1939–41

1. RHO: Papers of Sir William Battershill, Letter to his mother. 6 September 1939.

2. NA CO 67/300/1.

3. MECA: Jerusalem and the East Mission GB 165/ 0161 Letter from Archdeacon Maxwell to his Bishop in Jerusalem, February 1939.

4. RHO: Papers of David Percival, Letter to his mother. 25 August 1939.

5. SA1 1415 1938.

6. SA1 1415 1938 Letter from the governor to the chief secretary 10 July 1940.

7. Interview with Jane D'Arcy, April 2005.

8. SA1 1415 1938. 26 April 1940 Memo from Group Captain, Commanding no 259 Wing, RAF. H.W. Mermagen.

9. Ibid. Memo from Battershill to Commander in Chief R.A.F. M.E. 15 May 1940.

10. RHO: Percival, Letter to his mother. 6 October 1939.

11. RHO: Percival, Letter to 'Darling'. 16 December 1939.

12. RHO: Battershill, Letter to his mother. 17 April 1940.

13. *The Times* 22 November 1881.
14. Percy Arnold *Cyprus Challenge A Colonial Island and Its Aspirations: Reminiscences of a Former Editor of the 'Cyprus Post'* (Hogarth Press, London, 1956), p. 142.
15. Ibid., p. 84.
16. WO 201 145 1942 Plans .for enemy attack on Cyprus
17. NA CO 820/58/10 Cyprus Volunteer Force and Cyprus Regiment 1943. In the spring of 1940, after the 700 Cypriot muleteers in France were evacuated to Melton Mowbray. Richard Wayne, the Commissioner of the Cyprus Office in London attempted to show his government's appreciation of their efforts by organising a guided tour of London zoo.
18. NA CO 323 1787. Transcript of Greek broadcast from Breslau, February 1940.
19. *The Times* 18 February 1940. It is a stark indication of the low levels of health and nutrition amongst Cypriots, that less than half of all applicants were considered sufficiently physically sound to be accepted for military service.
20. NA CO 852 3157.
21. NA HS 3/120 SOE Much of the silk was spun at the Lanitis family factory in Yermasogia.
22. The standard daily rate for a man with dependents was eighteen piastres. This was two piastres less than the government's own assessment of the minimum wage needed to support a family of five made nine years earlier.
23. Quoted in Lewis, Bernard, *The Emergence of Modern Turkey* (Oxford University Press, London, 1968), p. 296.
24. Thirgood, J.V. *Cyprus: A Chronicle of Its Forests, Lands and Peoples*, p. 191.
25. NA CO 323/1787/38.
26. Interview with George Lanitis, April 2004.
27. NA CO 323 1651 11 Broadcasting. BBC Empire Service. Use of Foreign Languages 1939.
28. NA CO 323 1787 8 BBC Empire Broadcast Service Foreign Languages 1940.
29. Ibid.
30. NA CO 323 1651 12 Broadcasting in Foreign Languages 1939.
31. NA CO 323 1787 8 BBC Empire Broadcast Service Foreign Languages 1940.
32. An office staffed by a Cyprus government commissioner whose primary responsibility was the promotion of Cypriot products and the development of exports to Britain. During the war its function changed substantially.
33. NA CO 875 3 4 Broadcasting use of Foreign languages to Cyprus.
34. Subsequently President of Cyprus from 1993–2003.
35. In fact most homes, unlike Government House, had shutters with adjustable louvers which provided an adequate barrier, and made black-out drapes unnecessary.
36. Gilbert, Martin, *The Second World War: A Complete History* (Henry Holt & Co., New York, 1989), p. 80.
37. *The Times* 12 June 1940.
38. RHO: Battershill, Letter to his mother. 14 June 1940.

39. NA SOE Cyprus no. 5, The Angellic Scheme Report by O. Wideson. 28 April 1944.
40. NA CO 852/493/17.
41. RHO: Papers of Sir Charles Campbell Woolley Box 5 File 3:
42. NA HS 3/120SOE.
43. RHO: Battershill, Letter to his mother. 19 September 1940.
44. RHO: Percival, Letter to his mother. 22 November 1940.
45. RHO: Battershill, Letter to his mother. 30 November 1940.
46. NA CO926/1/10 Cyprus Reactions on Entry of Greece into the war 1940.
47. Quoted in Catselli, Rina, *Kyrenia: A Historical Study* (Kyrenia Flower Show Edition, Nicosia, 1979).
48. RHO: Battershill, Letter to his mother. 18 November 1940.
49. CO 323 1737 1 Broadcasting. Use of Foreign Languages BBC Broadcasts to Cyprus.
50. Ibid.
51. Ibid.
52. RHO: Battershill, Letter to his mother. 26 March 1941.
53. NA CO 323/1864/7 Greek and Yugoslav Governments: Their Possible Establishment in Cyprus and Palestine 1941.
54. Ibid.
55. Gilbert, *A Complete History of the Second World War*, p. 174.
56. NA HS 3/120.
57. NA CO 323/1864/7 Greek and Yugoslav Governments: Their Possible Establishment in Cyprus and Palestine 1941.

10   Stripped for War. 1941–42

1. RHO: Papers of Sir William Dennis Battershill, Letter to his mother. 24 May 1941.
2. Ibid., 30 May 1941.
3. *The Times* Nicosia, 5 June 1941.
4. Ibid.
5. IWM: Sound Archive: Interview with Boyagis, George Lawrence 8706/11. Tape 10.
6. Geoff Chapman, unpublished memoir, Chapter Six.
7. NA: CO 968/6/9 Defence of Cyprus and the Question of Evacuation of Civil Government.
8. They were to be deployed in the first wave of the invasion of Syria.
9. NA: CO 968/6/9 Defence of Cyprus and the Question of Evacuation of Civil Government.
10. Interview with Eirwen Harbottle, November 2006.
11. *The Times* 18 June 1941.
12. NA: CO 968 67 Evacuation of Polish Refugees, Jews, and Certain British Subjects 1941. The list included Munir Bey and Sir Panayiotis Cacoyannis, whose son read

the nightly news bulletins from Bush House on the newly established Greek language Cyprus news network.

13. *The Times* 18 June 1941.
14. Jennifer Griffiths Williams' temporary nanny was an Austrian Jewish refugee and Potts, the army chaplain, employed a married Jewish couple as domestic servants.
15. *The Times* 5 June 1941.
16. NA HS 3/ 120 (SOE).
17. *The Times* 8 June 1941.
18. Ibid., 18 June 1941.
19. Chapman, Geoff, unpublished memoir, Chapter Six.
20. RHO: Papers of Sir William Dennis Battershill, Letter to his mother. 17 June 1941.
21. NA: CO 67 316 19 Financial Assistance to Government Officials whose families have been evacuated.
22. Chapman, unpublished memoir, Chapter Seven.
23. RHO: Papers of Robert Hepburn Wright. Letters Home from Cyprus 1942–64.
24. I.W.M. Documents Collection: Captain CWK Potts MC Con Shelf and 92/28/1. 14 May 1941.
25. Chapman, unpublished memoir, Chapter Seven.
26. RHO: Papers of Sir William Dennis Battershill 25 July 1941.
27. The vast Chanteclair Building now occupies the site of the cabaret and open air restaurant. Admission was two and a half shillings including your first drink.
28. Chapman, unpublished memoir, Chapter Six.
29. Arnold, Percy, *Cyprus Challenge: A Colonial Island and Its Aspirations: Reminiscences of a Former Editor of the 'Cyprus Post'* (Hogarth Press, London, 1956), p. 68.
30. NA: WO 169 249 25.
31. I.W.M. Sound Archive: Interview with Boyagis, George Lawrence 8706/11. Tape 11.
32. NA: HS 7/85 SOE Activities in Arab Countries, Persia, Egypt and Cyprus 1941–43.
33. NA: AIR 23 60 96 Plan 'Arcadia' Cyprus Stages X, Y & Z Most Secret. RAF April 1942.
34. Chapman, unpublished memoir, Chapter Six.
35. Reardon, Tim, forthcoming history of Cyprus during World War Two.
36. I.W.M. Sound Archive Collection: Interview with Burdon-Taylor, Major Charles, 10613/21. Tape 7.
37. Ibid.
38. I.W.M. Sound Archive Collection: Interview with Iceton, George, 119 38/54. Tapes 19–20.
39. I.W.M. Sound Archive Collection: Chambers, George Pearson 104 15/4. Tape 2.
40. I.W.M. Documents Collection: Edward Charles Stirling 99/22/1.
41. I.W.M. Sound Archive Collection: Rogers, John Crawford 11202/5.
42. I.W.M. Sound Archive Collection: Eric Neville Hooper 11208/12.

43. IWM: Sound Archive Collection: John Crawford Rogers 11202/5.

44. NA: CO 820 515 Cyprus Volunteer Force.

45. Interview with George Lanitis, April 2004.

46. NA: WO 201 145.

47. Stark, Freya, *Dust in the Lions Paw* (John Murray, London, 1962), p. 136.

48. Chapman, unpublished memoir, Chapter Six.

49. IWM: Sound Archive Collection: Sinclair Edward Nelson 11954/23.

50. Chapman, unpublished memoir, Chapter Seven.

51. NA: CO 67/315/13 Unemployment Relief 1940.

52. Richter, Heinz, A., 'Benevolent Autocracy 1931–1945' in Faustman and Peristianis (eds), *Britain in Cyprus: Colonialism and Post-Colonialism 1878–2006* (Bibliopolis, Mannheim & Mohnesee, Germany, 2006).

53. Kelling, George Horton, *Countdown to Rebellion: British Policy in Cyprus 1939–55* (Greenwood Press, New York, 1990).

54. NA: CO 67/315/6 Strikes and Governor's Powers.

55. Chapman, unpublished memoir, Chapter Six.

56. NA: CO 67/315/6.

57. RHO: Battershill Papers: Letter to Joanie 25 July 1941.

58. RHO: Battershill Papers: Letter to mother 27 August 1941.

59. Rankin, Nicholas *Churchill's Wizards The British Genius for Deception 1914–1945* (Faber & Faber, London, 2008), p. 177.

60. NA: WO 169 249 25.

61. Ibid.

62. The deceptions appear to have been successful. On the night of the 26th of June 1942 an Italian reconnaissance plane developed engine trouble as it flew over the western end of the island. The crew baled out and after interrogation revealed that they had been photographing the Polis coast, where previous photographs had indicated extensive military activity works.

63. NA: WO 201 146.

64. I.W.M. Sound Archive: de Martin, Peter Lawrence 12669/5. Tape 2.

65. IWM: Sound Archive: Hooper, Eric Neville 11208/12. Tape 5.

66. I.W.M: Sound Archive: Chambers, George Pearson 104 15/4. Tape 2.

67. I.W.M: Sound Archive: Iceton, George11938/54. Tape s 19–20.

68. IWM: Sound Archive: Self, George 10413/21. Tape 9.

69. IWM: Documents Collection: Edward Charles Stirling 99/22/1.

70. I.W.M. Sound Archive: George Self 10413/21. Tape 9.

71. IWM: Sound Archive: Hooper, Eric Neville 11208/12. Tape 5.

72. NA: WO 222 335 Quarterly Medical Report.

73. MECA: Papers of the Anglican Church Jerusalem and the East Mission GB 165/0161 Box 86 Folder 1933–47 The Bishop of Jerusalem noted that cases of sexually contagious diseases were 'abnormally high'.

74. NA: CO 67 316 21 Social Hygiene: Enquiry by Mr Pickthorn.

75. I.W.M: Documents Collection. Captain CWK Potts MC Con Shelf and 92/28/1 1 August 1941.

76. MECA: Papers of the Anglican Church Jerusalem and the East Mission GB 165/0161 Box 86 Folder 2 1933–47.

77. Lees, Robert, 'Venereal Disease in the Armed Forces Overseas', in *British Journal of Venereal Diseases* Volume 22, no. 4 (1946): 155. Quoted in Levine, Philippa, *Prostitution, Race and Politics: Policing Venereal Disease in the British Empire* (Routledge, London, 2003).

78. MECA: Papers of the Anglican Church Jerusalem and the East Mission GB 165/0161 Box 86 Folder 2 1933–47.

79. I.W.M: Sound Archive Iceton George, 11938/54. Tapes 19–20.

80. NA: WO 222 335 Quarterly Medical Report. Cyprus Medical Services.

81. NA CO 67 316 21 Social Hygiene.

82. I.W.M: Sound Archive Interview with Iceton George, 11938/54. Tapes 19–20.

83. IWM: Potts.

84. IWM: Documents Collection: Lever, R. 97/3/1.

85. *The Times* 31 March 1942.

86. Lavender, David, *The Story of the Cyprus Mines Corporation* (Huntington Library, California, 1962), p. 338.

87. *The Times* 19 August 1942.

88. Gilbert, Martin, *The Second World War: A Complete History* (Henry Holt & Co., New York, 1989), p. 277.

89. *The Times* 5 October 1942.

90. NA: HS 3/120.

91. NA: WO 201 147 November 1942.

92. Ibid.

93. Chapman, unpublished memoir, Chapter Seven.

94. Including Electra Megaw, whose husband Peter was head of the Cyprus Antiquities Department.

95. Interview with Eirwen Harbottle, 1 November 2006.

11   The Levant Fishing Patrol and the Angelic Scheme. 1942–45

1. Chapman, Geoff, unpublished memoir, Chapter Seven.

2. NA: HS 3/120 SOE Cyprus no. 6 Directive for SOE Field Commander Cyprus, Caiques, the Maritime scheme, Cyprus and the War.

3. NA: HS 3/120 SOE.

4. Ibid.

5. Chapman, Geoff, unpublished memoir, Chapter Seven.

6. IWM: Documents Collection. Papers of Lieutenant Colonel A.C. Simonds, 08/46/1, unpublished memoir, *Pieces of War*.

7. Ibid.

8. Interview with Eirwen Harbottle, November 2006.

9. NA: HS 3/120 SOE.

10. Ibid.

11. Chapman, Geoff, unpublished memoir, Chapter Seven.

12. Interview with Donald Waterer, November 2006.

13. IWM: Simonds, A.C., unpublished memoir, *Pieces of War.*

14. Holland, Jeffrey, *The Aegean Mission: Allied Operations in the Dodecanese, 1943* (Greenwood Press, New York, 1988), p. 3.

15. Interview with Donald Waterer, November 2006.

16. NA: HS 3/120 SOE.

17. IWM: Simonds, A.C., unpublished memoir, *Pieces of War.*

18. Chapman, Geoff, unpublished memoir, Chapter Eight.

19. NA: HS 3/120 SOE.

20. NA: HS3 119.

21. Wideson was killed by EOKA in 1956 because of his pro-British sympathies.

22. NA: HS3 119.

23. Ibid.

24. NA HS3 120.

25. NA: HS3/117.

26. IWM: Sound Archive William Herbert Jalland 11944/14.

12 The Great Liberator. 1945–55

1. Interview with Donald Waterer, November 2006.

2. SA1 V13 Heidenstam Dr F.C: Fevers of Cyprus.

3. *Cyprus Review* June 1948.

4. Ibid., February 1950.

5. Stephens, Robert, *Cyprus, A Place of Arms* (Pall Mall Press, London, 1966), p. 128.

6. Ibid., p. 124.

7. Aburish, Said, Nasser, The Last Arab (Duckworth, UK, 2004), p. 21.

8. Holland, Robert, *Britain and the Revolt in Cyprus 1954–59* (Oxford University Press, London, 1998), p. 15.

9. Crawshaw, Nancy, *The Cyprus Revolt, An Account of the Struggle for Union with Greece* (George Allen & Unwin, London, Boston, Sydney, 1978), p. 34.

10. Interview with Donald Waterer, November 2006.

11. Holland, *Britain and the Revolt in Cyprus 1954–59*, p. 16.

12. *Cyprus Review* February 1949.

13. The former premises of the Public Information Office today house the Cypriot Parliament, the House of Representatives.

14. *Cyprus Review* July 1948.

15. RHO: Papers of Ivan Lloyd Phillips, March 1950.

16. MECA: Papers of the Anglican Church Jerusalem and the East Mission GB 165/0161 Castle, Reverend W.T.F. *Bible Lands* April 1949.

17. MECA: Bible Lands Volume 12, p. 474 'Cyprus since 1945'.

18. *Cyprus Review* January 1949.

19. Ibid.

20. RHO: Papers of Ivan Lloyd Phillips Letters home. 19 January 1950, 18 March 1950.

21. *Cyprus Review* January 1947.

22. RHO: Papers of Ivan Lloyd Phillips. 18 October 1949.

23. MECA: Papers of the Anglican Church Jerusalem and the East Mission. Castle, Reverend W.T.F.: *Bible Lands* April 1949.

24. RHO: Papers of Armitage, Letter to his parents. 12 June 1954.

25. RHO: Papers of Ivan Lloyd Phillips. 4 December 1949.

26. Ibid., 26 November 1949.

27. Ibid., 13 June 1949.

28. RHO: Papers of Sir Geoffrey Miles Clifford, *GB 162* MSS. Brit. Emp. s. 517.

29. IWM: Sound Archive: William Herbert Jalland 11944/14. Tape 13.

30. *Cyprus Review* November 1945.

31. Quoted in Holland, *Britain and the Revolt in Cyprus 1954–59*, p. 16.

32. RHO: Papers of Ivan Lloyd Phillips, 19 January 1950.

33. Crawshaw, *The Cyprus Revolt*, p. 48.

34. The same Bishop Chysostomos who had previously played a significant role in eradicating goats from Paphos Forest.

35. Holland, *Britain and the Revolt in Cyprus 1954–59*, p. 19.

36. Stephens, *Cyprus, A Place of Arms*, p. 131.

37. Quoted in Stephens, *Cyprus, A Place of Arms*, p. 137.

38. Stephens, *Cyprus, A Place of Arms*, p. 139.

39. Holland, *Britain and the Revolt in Cyprus 1954–59*, p. 33.

40. RHO: Papers of Sir Robert Armitage, 29 May 1954.

41. Home, Gordon, *Cyprus Then and Now* (J.M. Dent & Sons, London, 1959), p. 193

42. Parliamentary Debates (Commons), 1953–4, Volume 531, 28 July 1954, cols: 504–7 Quoted in Holland, *Britain and the Revolt in Cyprus 1954–59*, p. 38.

43. RHO: Papers of Sir Robert Armitage, 29 May 1954.

44. RHO: Papers of General Sir Kenneth Darling, unpublished memoir, 'Cyprus, the Final Round', quoting from Sir John Prendergast, chief of intelligence, p. 21.

45. Stephens, *Cyprus, A Place of Arms*, p. 132.

13 A Child's Game of Pretend. 1955–58

1. Durrell, Lawrence, *Bitter Lemons of Cyprus* (Faber & Faber, London, 1982), p. 180.

2. The last five years of British rule stand apart from the preceding six decades and have already been comprehensively documented by historians and military and constitutional experts. The definitive account is Robert Holland's 'Britain and the Revolt in Cyprus: 1954–59'. Other works that provide useful, if sometimes partisan, insights are Nancy Crawshaw's 'The Cyprus Revolt' and John Reddaway's Burdened with Cyprus.

3. Quoted in Holland, *Britain and the Revolt in Cyprus 1954–59*, p. 55.

4. Durrell, *Bitter Lemons of Cyprus*, p. 183.

5. Most other colonies had by now replaced this official celebration of imperial power with other, less controversial events.

6. RHO: Papers of Sir Robert Armitage. Letter to his Parents. 28 May 1955.

7. Established in 1951, the organization was proscribed by the British in 1953 after its alleged involvement in riots in Paphos, in protest at the coronation of Queen Elizabeth. It continued to function clandestinely.
8. Durrell, *Bitter Lemons of Cyprus*, p. 128.
9. Tremayne, Penelope, *Below the Tide* (Hutchinson, London, 1958), p. 106.
10. Interview with Tony Willis, August 2006.
11. Holland, *Britain and the Revolt in Cyprus 1954–59*, p. 23
12. Tremayne, *Below the Tide*, p. 111.
13. RHO: Papers of John Reddaway. Mss. Medit.s. 25, unpublished memoir, 'Reflections on an Unnecessary Conflict'.
14. How substantial the level of Greek Cypriot support for the armed struggle was during this period is beyond the scope of this study. But the degree of intimidation practised would suggest that it was not universal.
15. Tremayne, *Below the Tide* p14.
16. Holland, *Britain and the Revolt in Cyprus 1954–59*, p. 61.
17. In practice EOKA was at its most effective in creating a climate of terror in urban areas, where its assassins could strike and escape rapidly and its assassinations were highly visible.
18. Holland, *Britain and the Revolt in Cyprus 1954–59*, p. 70.
19. Ibid., p. 65.
20. Panteli, Stavros *The Making of Modern Cyprus* (Interworld Publications, New Barnet, Herts, 1990), p. 166.
21. Durrell, *Bitter Lemons of Cyprus*, p. 191.
22. Pope, Nicole and Pope, Hugh *Turkey Unveiled* (Overlook Press, 2000), p. 90.
23. Durrell, *Bitter Lemons of Cyprus*, p. 204.
24. Ibid., p. 207.
25. Interview with Penelope Tremayne, August 2006.
26. Interview with Tony Willis, August 2006.
27. RHO: Papers of Sir Robert Armitage, Letter to his parents. 12 June 1954.
28. RHO: Papers of Sir Robert Armitage, Letter to Maurice Howarth. 11 May 1954.
29. Ibid., 27 November 1954.
30. Carver, Michael *Harding of Petherton* (Weidenfeld & Nicholson, London, 1978), p. 203.
31. Holland, *Britain and the Revolt in Cyprus 1954–59*, p. 85.
32. The Cyprus Question, Negotiations 4 October 1955 to 5 March 1956, the Royal Ministry for Foreign Affairs, Athens 1956. Quoted in Reddaway, John, Burdened with Cyprus The British Connection , p. 88.
33. Holland, *Britain and the Revolt in Cyprus 1954–59*, p. 86.
34. Reddaway, John, *Odi et Amo, Vignettes of an Affair with Cyprus* (K. Rustem & Brother, London, 1990), p. 56.
35. Crawshaw, *The Cyprus Revolt*, p. 145.
36. Interview with Paul Griffin, November 2006.
37. Ibid.

38. Ibid.

39. Home, Gordon, *Cyprus Then and Now* (J.M. Dent & Sons, London, 1959), p. 196.

40. Tremayne, *Below the Tide*, p. 31.

41. In response to requests from Harding the First Battalion Gordon Highlanders and the First Battalion of the Royal Norfolk Regiment were hastily flown to Cyprus in October and November1956.

42. Interview with Sandra Oakey, March 2005.

43. Interview with Ruth Keshishian, October 2004.

44. Interview with Matthew Parris, November 2006.

45. Crawshaw, *The Cyprus Revolt*, p. 150.

46. Harding, telegram to Lennox-Boyd CO926/261 Quoted in Holland, Britain and the revolt in Cyprus, p. 111.

47. Interview with Paul Griffin, November 2006.

48. Griffin, Paul, unpublished memoir, 'Sounds and Sweet Airs'. Section 15.

49. Interview with Will Harrap, November 2006

50. RHO: Papers of John Reddaway. Unpublished Memoir. 'Reflections on an unnecessary conflict'.

51. Interview with Peter Twelvetrees, November 2006.

52. Interview with Sandra Oakey, September 2006.

53. Home, *Cyprus Then and Now*, p. 192.

54. Griffin, unpublished memoir, 'Sounds and Sweet Airs'. Section 34.

55. Interview with Paul Griffin, November 2006.

56. IWM: Documents Collection: Papers of IWG Martin. Auto ID: 501598.

57. Griffin, unpublished memoir, 'Sounds and Sweet Airs'. Section 34.

58. Crawshaw, *The Cyprus Revolt*, p. 197.

59. For personal accounts of the fire see: http://www.britains-smallwars.com/cyprus/Davidcarter/fire/PaphosFire.html

60. Tremayne, *Below the Tide*, p. 56.

61. Ibid., p. 35.

62. Interview with Eirwen Harbottle, November 2006.

63. Carver, Michael, *Harding of Petherton* (Weidenfeld & Nicholson, London, 1978), p. 217.

64. Interview with Tony Willis, August 2006

65. Redgrave, Roy, Balkan Blue, Family and Military Memoirs (Leo Cooper, UK, 2000), p. 157.

66. Holland, *Britain and the Revolt in Cyprus 1954–59*, p. 163.

67. Ibid., p. 166.

68. Tremayne, *Below the Tide*, p. 158.

69. Griffin, unpublished memoir, 'Sounds and Sweet Airs'. Section 38.

70. Tremayne, *Below the Tide*, p. 163.

71. Holland, *Britain and the Revolt in Cyprus 1954–59*, p. 198.

72. Ibid., p. 134.

73. IWM: Papers of I.W. Martin Auto ID: 501598.

74. Ibid.

75. Efthyvoulou, Alex, and Vryonidou-Yiangou, Marina, *Cyprus 100 Years* (Laiki Bank, Nicosia), p. 184.

76. Holland, *Britain and the Revolt in Cyprus 1954–59*, p. 209.

77. Griffin, unpublished memoir, 'Sounds and Sweet Airs'. Section 43.

14   Wheel on the Idealist. 1958–60

1. Interview with Paul Griffin, November 2006.

2. *Memoirs of General Grivas*, ed. Foley, Charles (Longmans, Longmans, 1964), p. 129.

3. Holland, Robert, *Britain and the Revolt in Cyprus 1954–59* (Oxford University Press, Oxford, 1998), p. 212.

4. Foot, Hugh, *A Start in Freedom* (Harper & Row, New York, 1964), p. 232.

5. Crawshaw, Nancy, *The Cyprus Revolt, An Account of the Struggle for Union with Greece*, (George Allen & Unwin, London, Boston, Sydney, 1978), p. 287.

6. Holland, *Britain and the Revolt in Cyprus 1954–59*, p. 220.

7. Foot, *A Start in Freedom*, p. 150.

8. Holland, *Britain and the Revolt in Cyprus 1954–59*, p. 230. Quoting FO371/136330, RGC10344/52.

9. Holland, *Britain and the Revolt in Cyprus 1954–59*, p. 229.

10. RHO: Papers of General Sir Kenneth Darling GB 162 Mss Medit. s. 30 Unpublished memoir 'Cyprus the Final Round', p. 6.

11. Crawshaw, *The Cyprus Revolt*, p. 131.

12. Tremayne, Penelope, *Below the Tide* (Hutchinson, London, 1958), p. 122.

13. Interview with Ruth Keshishian, October 2004.

14. Interview with George Lanitis, November 2004.

15. Foot, *A Start in Freedom*, p. 169.

16. IWM: Documents Collection. Papers of Jean Somerville, Auto ID: 50183,

17. Griffin, unpublished memoir, 'Sounds and Sweet Airs'. Section 48.

18. Holland, *Britain and the Revolt in Cyprus 1954–59*, p. 285.

19. Ibid., p. 253.

20. Ibid., p. 266. Quoting FO 371/136339, RGC10344/236.

21. IWM: Documents Collection. Papers of I.W.G. Martin. Auto ID: 501598.

22. Foot, *A Start in Freedom*, p. 170.

23. Quoted in Holland, *Britain and the Revolt in Cyprus 1954–59*, p. 281.

24. Interview with Penelope Tremayne, August 2006

25. Griffin, unpublished memoir, 'Sounds and Sweet Airs'. Section 51.

26. Holland, *Britain and the Revolt in Cyprus 1954–59*, p. 284.

27. Foot, *A Start in Freedom*, p. 175.

28. Interview with Wing Commander Jim Beveridge, June 2006.

29. IWM: Documents Collection. Papers of Jean Somerville

30. IWM. Papers of I.W.G. Martin Auto ID: 501598.

31. IWM: Documents Collection. Papers of Jean Somerville

32. Foot, *A Start in Freedom*, p. 175.

33. Foot, Sylvia, *Emergency Exit* (Chatto & Windus, London, 1960), p. 89.

34. Foot, *A Start in Freedom*, p. 178.

35. Holland, *Britain and the Revolt in Cyprus 1954–59*, p. 311.

36. Ibid., p. 317.

37. Ibid., p. 308.

38. The Greek Cypriot electorate was 238,000.

39. RHO: Papers of General Sir Kenneth Darling Unpublished memoir 'Cyprus the Final Round', p. 27.

40. Griffin, Paul, unpublished memoir, 'Sounds and Sweet Airs'. Section 56.

41. MECA: Jerusalem and the East Mission, GB 165/0161 Box 88, Letter from Archdeacon Goldie.

42. Foot, *A Start in Freedom*, p. 181.

43. CAB 134/1595 Quoted in Faustman, Hubert, 'Ethnic and Religious Minorities during the Transitional Period 1959–1960. The Struggle for Recognition and Political Rights'. Presented at the IV International Cypriological Congress of The Society of Cypriot Studies, Nicosia, 29 April–3 May 2008.

44. Holland, *Britain and the Revolt in Cyprus 1954–59*, p. 332.

45. Foot, *A Start in Freedom*, p. 185.

46. *Cyprus Mail* 8 February 2005.

Bibliography

Abbott, George C., 'A Re-examination of the Colonial Development Act'. *The Economic History Review*, New Series, Vol. 24, no. 1 (Feb 1971)

Aburish, Said, Nasser, *The Last Arab* (Duckworth, U.K., 2004)

Alastos, Doros, *Cyprus in History* (Zeno, London, 1976)

Allen, Charles, *Plain Tales from the Raj* (Abacus, London, 2001)

Anderson, Benedict, *Imagined Communities: Reflections on the Origin and Spread of Nationalism* (Verso, London, 2006)

Arnold, Percy, *Cyprus Challenge: A Colonial Island and Its Aspirations: Reminiscences of a Former Editor of the 'Cyprus Post'* (Hogarth Press, London, 1956)

Attalides, Michael, *Cyprus: Nationalism and Internal Politics* (Q. Press, Edinburgh, 1979)

Baker, Samuel, *Cyprus as I Saw It in 1879* (Project Gutenburg Etext no. 3656 Release date January 1, 2003)

Balakian, Peter, *The Burning Tigris: The Armenian Genocide* (Heineman, London, 2003)

Barnett, Corelli, *The Great War* (Penguin Classic Military History, London, 1979)

Batten, Jean, *My Life* (George G. Harrap & Co., London, 1938)

Beever, Antony, *Crete, the Battle and the Resistance* (Penguin, London, 1992)

Bond, George C. and Gilliam, Angela (eds), *Social Construction of the Past; Representation as Power* (Routledge, London, 1994)

Bowker, Gordon, *Through the Dark Labyrinth, A Biography of Lawrence Durrell* (Sinclair Stevenson, London, 1996)

Brassey, Lady Anne, *Sunshine & Storm in the East* (Longmans, London, 1881)

Brown, Samuel, *Three Months in Cyprus during the Winter of 1878–9* (Edward Stanford, London, 1879)

Buettner, Elizabeth, *Empire Families: Britons and Late Imperial India* (Oxford University Press, London, 2004)

Byford-Jones, W., *Grivas and the Story of EOKA* (Robert Hale Limited, London, 1959)

Calotychos, V. (ed) *Cyprus and Its People: Nation, Identity, and Experience in an Unimaginable Community (1995–1997)* (Westview Press, Boulder, CO, 1998)

Cannadine, David, *Ornamentalism: How the British Saw Their Empire* (Penguin, London, 2001)

Carlton, David, *Anthony Eden. A Biography* (Allen Lane, London, 1981)

Carver, Michael, *Harding of Petherton* (Weidenfeld and Nicholson, London, 1978)

Castle, Wilfred, T. F., *Cyprus: Its Postal History and Postage Stamps* (Robson Lowe, London, 1952)

Catselli, Rina, *Kyrenia: A Historical Study* (Avghi, Nicosia, 1979)

Cavendish, Anne (ed), *Cyprus 1878: The Journal of Sir Garnet Wolseley* (Cyprus Popular Bank Cultural Centre, Nicosia, 1991)

Chacalli, George, *Cyprus Under British Rule* (Phoni Tis Kyprou, Nicosia, 1902)

Chapman, Olive Murray, *Across Cyprus* (Travel Book Club, London, 1945)

Clark, G.W. (ed), *Rediscovering Hellenism: The Hellenistic Inheritance and the English Imagination* (Cambridge University Press, Cambridge, 1989)

Clarke, M.L., *Classical Education in Britain 1500–1900* (Cambridge University Press, Cambridge, 1959)

Clogg, Richard, *A Concise History of Greece*. Second Edition (Cambridge University Press, Cambridge, 2002)

Clogg, Richard (ed), *Greece 1940–1949 Occupation, Resistance, Civil War, A Documentary History* (Palgrave Macmillan, New York, 2002)

Crawshaw, Nancy, *The Cyprus Revolt, An Account of the Struggle for Union with Greece* (George Allen & Unwin, London, 1978)

Δημητρίου, Κυριάχος N. (ed), *ΒΙΚΤΩΡΙΑΝΑ ΚΕΙΜΕΝΑ ΓΙΑ ΤΗΝ ΚΥΠΡΟ 1878–1891* (Κέντρο Μελετών Ιεράς Μονής Κύκκου, Nicosia, 2000)

Donne, Donisthorpe, *Records of the Ottoman Conquest of Cyprus and Cyprus Guide and Directory* (Laiki Group Cultural Centre, Nicosia, 2000)

Durrell, Lawrence, *Bitter Lemons of Cyprus* (Faber & Faber, London, 1982)

Faiz, Suha, *Recollections and Reflections of an Unknown Cyprus Turk* (Avon Books, London, 1998)

Faulkner, Peter, *Against the Age: An Introduction to William Morris* (George Allen & Unwin, London, 1980)

Faustman, H., and Peristianis, N. (eds), *Britain in Cyprus. Colonialism and Post Colonialism 1878–2006* (Bibliopolis Mannheim und Mohnesee, Wamel, Mohnesee, 2006)

Foley, Charles, *Island in Revolt* (Longmans, London, 1962)

Foley, Charles (ed), *Memoirs of General Grivas* (Longmans, London, 1964)

Foot, Hugh, *A Start in Freedom* (Hodder & Stoughton, London, 1964)

Foot, Sylvia, *Emergency Exit* (Chatto & Windus, London, 1960)

Fromkin, David, *The Peace to End all Peace: Creating the Modern Middle East 1914–1922* (Andre Deutsche, London, 1989)

Geddes, Mr & Mrs Patrick, 'Cyprus and Its Power to Help the East'. *The Report of the International Conference on Armenian Aid*. May 1897

Georghallides, G.S., 'Churchill's 1907 Visit to Cyprus. A Political Analysis'. *Journal of the Cyprus Research Centre* Volume III, pp. 167–220 (Cyprus Research Centre, Nicosia, 1970)

Georghallides, G.S., *A Political and Administrative History of Cyprus 1918–1926* (Cyprus Research Centre, Nicosia, 1979)

Georghallides, G.S., *Cyprus and the Governorship of Sir Ronald Storrs: The Causes of the 1931 Crisis* (Cyprus Research Centre Nicosia, 1985)

Georgiou, Christakis, 'The English School', in Klaus Detlev Grothusen, Winifried Steffani, Peter Zervakis (eds) *Sudosteuropa-Handbuch* [Handbook of South Eastern Europe], Vol. VIII Zypern (Vandenhoeck and Ruprecht, Gottingen, 1988)

Gilbert, Martin, *The Second World War, A Complete History* (Henry Holt & Co., New York, 1989)

Given, Michael, 'Father of His Landscape: Lawrence Durrell's Creation of Landscape and Character in Cyprus'. in *Deus Loci: The Lawrence Durrell Journal* 5, 1997

Given, Michael, 'Star of the Parthenon, Cypriot mélange: Education and Representation in Colonial Cyprus'. in *Journal of Mediterranean Studies* 7:59–82.1997

Given, Michael, *The Archaeology of the Colonised* (Routledge, London, 2004)

Glover, T. R., *Greek Byways* (Cambridge University Press, Cambridge, 1932)

Green, Colonel A.O., *Cyprus: A Short Account of its History and Present State* (M. Graham Coltart, Scotland, 1914)

Grivas, Dighenis, George, *The Memoirs of General Grivas*, ed. Charles Foley (Longmans, London, 1964)

Gunnis, Rupert, *Historic Cyprus* (Methuen and Co., London, 1936)

Haggard, Rider, *A Winter's Pilgrimage in Palestine, Italy and Cyprus* (Longmans, Green and Co., London, New York, Bombay, 1901)

Hall, Catherine, *Cultures of Empire. A Reader* (Manchester University Press, Manchester, 2000)

Harding, Gilbert, *Along My Line* (Popular Book Club, London, 1955)

Herzfeld, Michael, *Ours Once More: Folklore, Ideology and the Making of Modern Greece* (Pella Publishing, New York, 1986)

Hill, Sir George Francis, *A History of Cyprus. Volume 4: The Ottoman Province, the British Colony, 1571–1948* (Cambridge University Press, Cambridge, 1952)

Holland, Jeffrey, *The Aegean Mission: Allied Operations in the Dodecanese, 1943* (Greenwood Press, New York, 1988)

Holland, Robert, *Britain and the Revolt in Cyprus 1954–59* (Oxford University Press, London, 1998)

Holland, Robert and Markides, Diana, *The British and the Hellenes: Struggles for Mastery in the Eastern Mediterranean 1850–1960* (Oxford University Press, London, 2006)

Home, Gordon, *Cyprus Then and Now* (J.M. Dent & Sons, London, 1959)

Hunt, Sir David (ed), *Footprints in Cyprus: An Illustrated History* (Trigraph, London, 1982)

Hutchinson, Sir T.H. and Claude Delaval Cobham, *A Handbook of Cyprus* (Edward Stanford, London, 1907)

Izzard, Molly, *Freya Stark: A Biography* (Hodder & Stoughton, London, 1993)

Jenkyns Richard, *The Victorians and Ancient Greece* (Basil Blackwell, Oxford, 1980)

Katsiaounis, Rolandos, *Labour, Society and Politics in Cyprus during the Second Half of the 19th Century* (Cyprus Research Centre, Nicosia, 1996)

Keegan, John, *The Price of Admiralty* (Hutchinson, London, 1988)

Kelling, George Horton, *Countdown to Rebellion: British Policy in Cyprus 1939–55* (Greenwood Press, New York, 1990)

Keshashian, Kevork K., *Nicosia, Capitol of Cyprus Then and Now* (Moufflon Bookshop, Cyprus, 1990)

Kinross, Patrick, *Attaturk: The Rebirth of a Nation* (Phoenix Giant, London, 1993)

Kirk-Greene, Anthony, *On Crown Service: A History of HM Colonial and Overseas Civil Services 1837–1997* (I.B.Tauris, London, 1999)

Knapland, Paul, *Gladstone's Foreign Policy* (Frank Cass & Co., London, 1935)

Lang, R. Hamilton, *Cyprus: Its History, Its Present Resources and Future Prospects* (Macmillan and Co., London, 1879)

Lavender, David, *The Story of the Cyprus Mines Corporation* (Huntington Library, California, 1962)

Leask, Nigel, *British Romantic Writers and the East: Anxieties of Empire* (Cambridge University Press, Cambridge, 1992)

Lee, Laurie, and Keane, Ralph, *We Made a Film in Cyprus* (Longmans Greene and Co., London, 1947)

Levine, Philippa, *Prostitution, Race and Politics: Policing Venereal Disease in the British Empire* (Routledge, London, 2003)

Lewis, Bernard, *The Emergence of Modern Turkey* (Oxford University Press, London, 1968)

Luke, Harry, *Cities and Men. An Autobiography. Volumes 1–3* (Geoffrey Bles, London, 1953)

Luke, Harry, *Cyprus: A Portrait and An Appreciation* (George G. Harrap & Co., London, 1965)

Mackenzie, Compton, *Greece in My Life* (Chatto & Windus, London, 1960)

Mackenzie, Compton, *First Athenian Memories* (Cassel & Co., London, 1931)

MacNiven, Ian, *Lawrence Durrell, A Biography* (Faber & Faber, London, 1998)

Mango, Andrew, *Attaturk* (John Murray, London, 1999)

Marangou, A.G., *Nicosia, A Special Capital* (Cyprus Research Centre, Nicosia, 1995)

McCarthy, Justin, *The Ottoman Peoples and the End of Empire* (Arnold, London, 2003)

McHenry, James, A., *The Uneasy Partnership on Cyprus, 1919–1939* (Garland Publishing Inc, New York, 1987)

Medlicott, J.H., *The Handbook of Cyprus, 1901* (Government Printing Office, Nicosia, 1901)

Miller, Rory, 'Sir Ronald Storrs and Zion: The Dream That Turned into a Nightmare'. *Middle Eastern Studies*, Vol. 36, no. 3, July 2000. pp. 114–44

Ministry of Information, *The Campaign in Greece and Crete* (HMSO, 1942)

Moorhead, Alan, *Mediterranean Front* (Hamish Hamilton, London, 1942)

Morris, Jan, *Pax Brittanica: The Climax of an Empire* (Faber & Faber, London, 1968)

Morris, Jan, *Heaven's Command: An Imperial Progress* (Harcourt Brace & Co., San Diego, New York, London, 1973)

Morris, Jan, *Farewell the Trumpets: An Imperial Retreat* (Faber & Faber, London, 1978)

Morrow, John, Jr, *The Great War, An Imperial History* (Routledge, London, 2004)

Murphy, Lady Emily Alice, *ABC of Flower Gardening in Cyprus* (The Times of Cyprus, 1956)

Newman, Philip, *A Short History of Cyprus* (Longmans Greene and Co., London, New York, Toronto, 1940)

Orr, Charles William James, *Cyprus under British Rule* (Reprinted: Zeno, London, 1972)

Palmer, Alan, *The Gardeners of Salonkia* (Simon & Schuster, New York, 1965)

Panteli, Stavros, *The Making of Modern Cyprus* (Interworld Publications Limited, New Barnet, Hertfordshire, England, 1990)

Parris, Matthew, *Chance Witness: An Outsider's Life in Politics* (Penguin, London, 2002)

Persianis, Panayiotis, K., *Church and State in Cyprus Education* (Violaris, Nicosia, 1978)

Peto, Gladys, *Malta and Cyprus* (Outward Bound Library, J.M. Dent & Sons, London and Toronto, 1927)

Pope, Nicole and Hugh, *Turkey Unveiled* (Overlook Press, 2000)

Poulton, Hugh, *Top Hat, Grey Wolf and Crescent: Turkish Nationalism and the Turkish Republic.* (Hurst and Company, London, 1997)

Purcell, H.D., *Cyprus* (London, 1969)

Rankin, Nicholas, *Churchill's Wizards: The British Genius for Deception 1914–1945* (Faber & Faber, London, 2008)

Reddaway, John, *Burdened with Cyprus: The British Connection* (Weidenfeld and Nicholson, London, 1986)

Redgrave, Roy, *Balkan Blue, Family and Military Memoirs* (Leo Cooper, U.K., 2000)

Rhodes James, Robert, *Memoirs of a Conservative, J.C.C. Davidson's Memoirs and Papers* (Wieidenfeld and Nicholson, London, 1969)

Roessel, David, 'Something to Stand the Government in Good Stead': Lawrence Durrell and the Cyprus Review in *Deus Loci, the Lawrence Durrell Journal*, Vol. 3 1994

Roessel, David, *In Byron's Shadow: Modern Greece in the English and American Imagination* (Oxford University Press, London, 2002)

Roussou-Sinclair, Mary, *Victorian Travellers in Cyprus: A Garden of Their Own. Texts and Studies of the History of Cyprus* (Cyprus Research Centre, Nicosia, 2002)

Said, W. Edward, *Orientalism* (Routledge & Keegan Paul, London, 1978)

Said, W. Edward, *Culture and Imperialism* (Vintage Books, London, 1993)

Schaar, Kenneth W., Given, Michael, and Theocharous, George, *Under the Clock* (Bank of Cyprus Cultural Foundation, Nicosia, 1999)

Scott-Stevenson, Esme. Our Home in Cyprus *(Chapman & Hall, London, 1880)*

Serephim-Loizou, Elenitsa, *The Cyprus Liberation Struggle, 1955–59 through the Eyes of a Woman EOKA Area Commander* (Epiphaniou Publications)

Severis, Rita C., *Travelling Artists in Cyprus 1700–1960* (Phillip Wilson, London, 2000)

Shipman, Pat, *To the Heart of the Nile: Lady Florence Baker and the Exploration of Central Africa* (Perennial, New York, 2004)

Shirley, Rodney, *Kitchener's Survey of Cyprus 1878–1883* (Bank of Cyprus Cultural Foundation, Nicosia, 2001)

Spencer, T.J.B., *Fair Greece, Sad Relic: Literary Philhellenism from Shakespeare to Byron* (Weidenfeld and Nicholson, London, 1954)

Stanley, Robert, *King George's Keys* (Johnson Publications, London, 1975)

Stark, Freya, *Dust in the Lions Paw* (John Murray, London, 1962)

Stephens, Robert, *Cyprus, A Place of Arms* (Pall Mall Press, London, 1966)

Stewart, Basil, *My Experiences of Cyprus.* 1st ed revised (George Routledge, London, 1908)

Storrs, Ronald, *Orientations* (Readers Union, London, 1939)

Storrs, Ronald and B.J. O'Brien, *The Handbook of Cyprus* (Christophers, London, 1930)

Strachan, Huw, *The First World War* (Simon & Schuster, New York, 2003)

Surridge, Brewster Joseph, *A Survey of Rural Life in Cyprus* (Crown Agent for the Colonies, London, 1935)

Tatton-Brown, Veronica (ed), *Cyprus in the 19th Century AD: Fact, Fancy and Fiction. Papers of the 22nd British Museum Classical Colloquium December 1998* (Oxbow Books, Oxford, August 2001),

Thirgood, J.V., *Cyprus A Chronicle of Its Forests, Land and People* (University of British Colombia Press, Vancouver, 1987)

Thomson, John, *Through Cyprus with a Camera, in the Autumn of 1878* (Trigraph, London, 1985)

Tremayne, Penelope, *Below the Tide* (Hutchinson, London, 1958)

Tugwell, Maurice (ed), *The Unquiet Peace: Stories from the Post-war Army* (Allan Wingate, London, 1957)

Turner, B.S., *The Story of the Cyprus Government Railway* (Mechanical Engineering Publications Limited, London, 1979)

Wallace, Paul W. (ed), *Sources for the History of Cyprus: Visitors, Immigrants, and Invaders in Cyprus* (Greece and Cyprus Research Centre, University at Albany, State University of New York, 1995)

Wallace, Paul, W. and Orphanides, Andreas, G., *Sources for the History of Cyprus Volume IX The Final Days of British Rule in Cyprus: Dispatches and Diaries of Consul General Taylor Belcher and Edith Belcher,* Selected and edited by Martin, David, W. and Wallace, Paul, W. (Greece and Cyprus Research Centre, University at Albany, State University of New York, 2000)

Weir, W.W., *Education in Cyprus: Some Theories and Practices in Education in the Island of Cyprus since 1878* (Cosmos Press, Nicosia, 1952)

Wilson T.M. and Donman H., *The Mukhtar's Handbook* (Government Printing Office, Nicosia, 1929)

Wodehouse, C.M., *Modern Greece: A Short History* (Faber & Faber, London, 1998)

Index

Strategic importance of Cyprus, 199, 200, 207
  uncertainty over, 2, 3, 18, 20, 21, 22
  WWI, 69, 70
  WWII, 97, 161–2, 168
Suez Canal, 21, 161, 199, 208
Syria
  WWI, 70, 76, 88–90
  WWII, 153, 162, 163, 168, 182, 183

Taylor, Mary, 176
Thessalonika, *see* Salonika
T.M.T. (*Turk Mudya Teskilat*), 242, 243, 244, 246
Tourism, 1, 5, 8, 16, 30, 116, 117, 203
Tremayne, Penelope, 214, 216, 221, 231, 235, 242, 246, 247
Tribute, *see* Ottoman legacy in Cyprus
Troodos Forest, 140, 142, 230
Troodos Mountains, 87, 111, 130, 229, 230
  summer seat of government, 25–32, 69, 70, 142, 146, 215
  WWI, 77, 78, 79
  WWII, 148, 162, 167, 172, 182, 183, 187
Tsolakoglu, Georgios, 180
Turkey, 96, 98, 104, 135, 208
  EOKA period, 207–8, 215–16, 233, 235–6, 243–6, 249, 254, 257
  WWI, 70, 71, 75, 76
  WWII, 141, 148, 157, 158, 160, 190
Turkish army, 83, 123
Twelvetrees, Peter, 227

Unwin, George, 105, 114, 139, 186
  goat wars, 107–9, 140

Venizelos, Eleftherious, 92, 96, 97
Volkan, 232, 242

Warren, Colonel Falk, 7, 20
Water, *see* Irrigation
Waterer, Brenda, 48

Waterer, Donald, 47, 48, 105, 116, 121, 140
  airport, 116, 130
  corruption, 124
  goats, 108
  malaria, 197
  villagers, 59
Waterer, Nora, 105, 121
Waterer, Ronald, 105, 113, 121, 184
  relations with Cypriots, 139–40
  SOE work, 184–6, 189–90, 192, 195
Watts, Clive, 101
Wavell, General Archibald, 149, 157–8, 162, 163
Wayne, Richard, 151
Wellington, Duke of, 2
White, Colonel, 17
Wideson, Odysseus/"Constant," 193–4
Willis, Tony, 214, 217
Wilson, General Maitland, 157
Winster, Lord, 60, 200–2, 205
Wolseley Barracks, *see* Nicosia
Wolseley, Louisa, 9
Wolseley, Sir Garnet, 4, 21, 22, 33, 128, 176, 257
  arrival, 2
  doubts over occupation of Cyprus, 2–3, 4, 6, 20–2
  Esme Scott Stevenson, 5, 15, 16
  eucalyptus trees, 17
  Government House, 9, 33, 128
  Nicosia camp, 5
  reputation, 2, 16
Wooley, Charles, 180, 181
Wright, Andrew, 128, 143, 146, 205
Wroclaw, *see* Breslau
Wynne-James, Jane, 165, 176

Zaptiehs, 12, 74, 75
Zorlu, Fatin, 242, 243, 246, 249, 250, 251
Zurich Agreement, 238, 251